£19.99

Oxford
Philosop

Oxford Studies in Philosophy of Law

Volume 2

EDITED BY

LESLIE GREEN
University of Oxford

BRIAN LEITER
University of Chicago

OXFORD
UNIVERSITY PRESS

OXFORD
UNIVERSITY PRESS

Great Clarendon Street, Oxford, OX2 6DP,
United Kingdom

Oxford University Press is a department of the University of Oxford.
It furthers the University's objective of excellence in research, scholarship,
and education by publishing worldwide. Oxford is a registered trade mark of
Oxford University Press in the UK and in certain other countries

© the several contributors 2013

The moral rights of the authors have been asserted

First Edition published in 2013
Impression: 1

Published in the United States of America by Oxford University Press
198 Madison Avenue, New York, NY 10016, United States of America

British Library Cataloguing in Publication Data
Data available

ISBN 978–0–19–967982–9 (Hbk.)
978–0–19–967983–6 (Pbk.)

Printed and bound in Great Britain by
CPI Group (UK) Ltd, Croydon, CR0 4YY

Links to third party websites are provided by Oxford in good faith and
for information only. Oxford disclaims any responsibility for the materials
contained in any third party website referenced in this work.

Contents

List of Contributors

Bruno Celano is Professor of Legal Philosophy at the University of Palermo.

Luís Duarte d'Almeida is Chancellor's Fellow in Law, School of Law, University of Edinburgh, Scotland.

R. A. Duff is Professor of Law at the University of Minnesota and Professor of Philosophy at the University of Stirling, Scotland.

Michael Giudice is Associate Professor of Philosophy at York University, Toronto.

Matthew H. Kramer is Professor of Legal and Political Philosophy at Cambridge University.

Barbara Baum Levenbook is Associate Professor of Philosophy, North Carolina State University.

Stephen Perry is John J. O'Brien Professor of Law and Professor of Philosophy at the University of Pennsylvania.

Hanoch Sheinman is Professor of Law and Philosophy, Bar-Ilan University, Ramat Gan, Israel.

C. L. Ten is Professor of Philosophy at the National University of Singapore.

I

Political Authority and Political Obligation[1]

STEPHEN PERRY

I. INTRODUCTION

Legitimate political authority, it is agreed by many, involves a right to rule. One very widespread and powerful understanding of what this means is that a political regime has a right to rule only if, among other things, it has a fairly extensive Hohfeldian power to change its subjects' normative situation by, for example, imposing obligations or conferring rights on them.[2] No doubt a right to rule involves much more than this.[3] Perhaps it involves not just a power to impose obligations but also a claim-right to compel compliance with those obligations by means of force or the threat of force.[4] For present purposes, however, it will be

---

[1] I have benefitted from discussion when earlier versions of this chapter were presented at the annual Analytic Legal Philosophy Conference (2009), as a lecture to the Bryn Mawr philosophy department, and at conferences or workshops at the following law schools: Cardozo, Graz, King's College London, McGill, Penn, Tel Aviv, Toronto, UCLA, University College London, USC, and Yale. I am particularly indebted to the following persons for their comments: Matthew Adler, Anita Allen (who was my commentator at Penn), Jules Coleman, Kory DeClark, Bill Edmundson, David Enoch, Les Green, Mark Greenberg, Matthew Kramer, Dennis Klimchuk, Brian Leiter, George Letsas, Andrei Marmor, Helen McCabe (who was my commentator at Graz), Joseph Raz, Arthur Ripstein, Seana Shiffrin, Nicos Stavropoulos (who was my commentator at UCL), Jeremy Waldron, Douglas Weck, Ernest Weinrib, and Lorenzo Zucca.

[2] Joesph Raz, *The Morality of Freedom* (Oxford: Clarendon Press, 1986), 24: "The obligation to obey a person which is commonly regarded as entailed by the assertion that he has legitimate authority is nothing but the imputation to him of a power to bind."

[3] See infra note 49 and accompanying text.

[4] Theories of legitimate political authority tend to fall into one or the other of two categories: (1) those that focus initially on the justification of a normative power on the part of the state to change persons' normative situation; and (2) those that focus initially on the justification of the state's right to use coercion against its subjects. For the most part, the difference between these two types of theory concerns the justificatory relationship between the state's

sufficient to focus on the point that legitimate political authority requires possession of extensive normative powers. Joseph Raz calls political regimes which have effective control over a population and which also claim legitimate authority for themselves, meaning they claim extensive powers to change the normative situation of their subjects, de facto authorities. Raz argues, in my view rightly, that a political regime can only have law and a legal system if it is a de facto authority in this sense. For present purposes it will be convenient to focus on the case of de facto authorities, which we can think of loosely as the governments of states with legal systems. Because such governments can, in the exercise of the extensive authority that they claim for themselves,[5] affect their

---

normative power and its right (which is presumably a claim-right) to use coercion. Theories of the first kind typically look for a justification of the state's power to change its subjects' norma-tive situation that is independent of the right to use coercion, and then attempt to justify the right to coerce by reference to, inter alia, the normative power. Theories of the second type reverse this order of justification: They first offer a justification of the state's right legitimately to use force under certain circumstances, and then offer a justification of the state's general powers to change its subjects' normative situation that makes essential reference to this prior right. For a distinguished version of this second type of theory, see Arthur Ripstein, "Authority and Coercion," *Philosophy and Public Affairs*, 32 (2004), 2. The theories of political authority that I discuss in this chapter are all of the first type, but since theories of the second type do not typically deny that states have the normative power to change their subjects' normative situation, I believe that one of the article's most important conclusions—that it is implausi-ble to think that such a normative power can be justified by reference to an aggregation of the state's normative relations to its citizens considered one by one—generally applies to this cat-egory of theory as well. The key to Ripstein's Kantian theory, for example, is the idea that "rights [of individuals against one another] are understood as reciprocal limits on the freedom of everyone, which means that, if people are to have rights, all must be subject to the same limits." Ibid. 26. The idea of reciprocal limits on the freedom of all would seem to count, in the admittedly loose sense of the term that I employ in section VI below, as part of a non-aggregative justification of political authority. It is perhaps worth mentioning that there are some theories of the second type which claim to justify a Hohfeldian liberty or "justification-right" on the part of states to use coercion which does not involve a corresponding obligation on the part of citizens to obey. See, for example, Robert Ladenson, "In Defense of a Hobbesian Conception of the Law," *Philosophy and Public Affairs* 9 (1980), 139. (The term "justification-right" is Ladenson's.) For a convincing critique of Ladenson's view, see Raz, *The Morality of Freedom*, supra note 2, at 24–8.

   [5] Raz argues that because legal systems, unlike other normative systems such as commercial companies and sports organizations, acknowledge no limitations on the spheres of behavior which they have the power to regulate, their claim of authority is "comprehensive." Joseph Raz, *The Authority of Law* (Oxford: Clarendon Press, 1979), 116–17. Elsewhere he makes a similar point by observing that even in states in which the power of the legislature to legislate is con-stitutionally limited, "the law" nonetheless claims unlimited authority for itself "because the law provides ways of changing the law and of adopting any law whatsoever." Raz, *The Morality of Freedom*, supra note 2, at 76–7. I have some doubts as to whether all legal systems really do make claims of unlimited authority of the kind Raz has in mind. In some countries some

subjects' lives in very significant ways and often against their will, the authority they claim to possess is moral in nature.[6] Although legal systems claim to be able to change the normative situation of their subjects in almost any conceivable way—for example, by granting permissions, conferring claim-rights, or creating immunities or new powers[7]—I will focus on the most fundamental power that legal systems claim for themselves, which is the power to impose obligations.[8] Let me refer to the product of the exercise of a claimed power to impose obligations as a directive. If a directive was issued by an organ of a government which not only claims but also possesses legitimate authority, then those persons who fall within the scope of the directive have an obligation to obey it. Because legitimate authority is moral authority, this obligation is a moral obligation.

In section II, I observe that many who have written on the nature of legitimate political authority approach this issue by arguing for or against the existence of a general obligation to obey the law. I consider the general conditions that must be met before a general obligation to obey the law can be said to exist, and, borrowing from the work of Leslie Green and Joseph Raz, I set out five conditions that seem to be very plausible requirements for this purpose. I note that most existing theories of political obligation fail to satisfy one of the conditions— universality of application—but I further note that this fact is more of practical than of theoretical interest. Nonetheless, almost every extant theory of political obligation fails to satisfy at least one, and sometimes more than one, of the other four conditions. Of greater interest for present purposes, however, is the fact that to argue for legitimate political

constitutional provisions may, according to the local constitution itself, be immune to amendment, as I understand may be the case with India. However, the point is not a significant one for present purposes. I do agree with Raz that (almost) all legal systems claim *supreme* authority, in the sense that wherever a subject matter is liable to regulation by law, the law is entitled to have the final say on the matter.

[6] See, e.g., Joseph Raz, "Hart on Moral Rights and Legal Duties," *Oxford Journal of Legal Studies* 4 (1984), 123.

[7] Cf. Stephen Perry, "Law and Obligation," *The American Journal of Jurisprudence* 50 (2005), 263 at 267. Given the point stated in the text, the properly generalized version of a general obligation to obey the law is a claim that every legal norm has the normative effect that it purports to have. If the norm purports to impose an obligation, then it succeeds in creating an obligation; if it purports to create a claim-right, then it succeeds in creating a claim-right; and so on. See further ibid. 271–2.

[8] In this chapter, I use the terms "obligation" and "duty" interchangeably.

authority by means of an intermediate conclusion that there exists a general obligation to obey the law is a very problematic strategy. This is because, although it is true that legitimate political authority (in the sense of a moral power) entails the existence of a general obligation to obey the law, the existence of a general obligation to obey the law does not, in and of itself, entail legitimate political authority. I call this "the reverse entailment problem," which I illustrate with several examples.

In section III, I ask why Green's five conditions for the existence of an obligation to obey the law seem to be plausible ones, and reply that it is because they intuitively reflect the fact that an obligation to obey the law must flow from the exercise of a moral power to change someone else's normative situation. This suggests that the conditions can be reformulated, and in some cases reformulated more precisely, by casting them in terms of authority (power) rather than in terms of obligation. This suggests in turn that we should begin our analysis of the related problems of political authority and political obligation by focusing *directly* on the existence conditions for the appropriate kind of moral power, rather than on conditions that will justify the supposedly mediating conclusion that there exists a (general) moral obligation to obey the law. I begin to undertake this task by offering a conception of a moral power that seems plausible for this purpose. Relatedly, I argue that the idea, accepted implicitly or explicitly by many writers, that the normative correlative of "a right to rule" is an obligation, is mistaken. For one thing, treating the right to rule and an obligation to obey as correlatives tends to lead to reverse entailment problems. But secondly and more importantly, since the right to rule must be understood as a Hohfeldian power rather than, say, as a claim-right, the appropriate normative correlative is, in Hohfeldian terms, not an obligation but a *liability*. I further argue that this latter point is not merely a technicality but an important conceptual characteristic of legitimate political authority that places certain limits on what can count as an argument in favor of the moral legitimacy of the state.

Drawing on the conception of a moral power (and the associated conception of a liability) that I give, I describe two novel and surprisingly strong conditions, which I call the value-of-intentionality condition and the prospectivity condition, which bear directly on the existence or otherwise of legitimate political authority. The essence of the value-of-intentionality condition is, very roughly, that the conceptual and moral core of legitimate political authority (and probably of most forms of legitimate practical authority) is the ability of one person intentionally to change the normative situation of another, where it is sufficiently valuable or desirable that the first person possess such an ability with respect to the second. I call the resulting characterization of authority the "value-based" conception. The idea that the general concept of legitimate political authority should be analyzed by reference to the value-based conception is one of the fundamental claims of this chapter. The value-of-intentionality condition itself demands that any substantive theory which is meant to establish, in whole or in part, the moral legitimacy of the state must be consistent with the value-based conception. The second of the two conditions I mentioned, namely, the prospectivity condition, holds that any such substantive theory must also be consistent with the fact that a legal directive which is issued by a legitimate political authority takes on obligatory force, in the usual case, at the exact moment that it is enacted or signed into law, and not at some later point in time. I then show how some of the standard criticisms of existing theories of political authority and political obligation can be reformulated by reference to these two conditions, and how the two conditions give rise to powerful new objections to these theories.

I should make clear that in this chapter I do not argue that the term "political legitimacy" (and related expressions) must necessarily be understood in terms of a Hohfeldian power and a Hohfeldian power only. These terms have been accorded many meanings in the literature. There are, for example, those theories, mainly of Kantian inspiration, that take the starting-point for determining political legitimacy to be the justification of coercion by the state.[9] There are also theories that argue that political legitimacy is founded on or supported by one or more of the following types of considerations: justice, equality, democracy, popular support, or hypothetical consent.[10] I *do* argue, however, that a Hohfeldian power—the ability of a state intentionally to change the normative status of its subjects—is, both morally and conceptually, the core understanding of political legitimacy. Obviously more needs to be said in support of this proposition, and I offer arguments in its defense in

---

[9] See supra note 4.

[10] John Rawls, for example, says of his own theory of justice as fairness that "its principle of legitimacy [has] the same basis as the substantive principles of justice." John Rawls, *Political Liberalism* (New York: Columbia University Press, 1993) at 225.

section III. For present purposes, I will simply make the following three brief observations. First, one dimension of the "Hohfeldian power" tradition is that it asks a question that is both clear and of great theoretical and moral significance: When the state, under color of its own claimed authority, tells us to do something, under what circumstances do we in fact have an obligation to do it as it says? Some of the theories that link legitimacy to democracy, say, or to popular support, do not ask such a crisp and important question, nor do they always make clear exactly what they take to be at stake, morally speaking, in characterizing a state as "legitimate."[11] Second, different conceptions of "political legitimacy" are not necessarily in conflict with one another, so long as we understand that the term is being used in different ways. Third, although I do not think that a state must be, say, democratic in character to be politically legitimate, the link that many discern between political legitimacy and democracy can, as we shall see in section VI, be taken into account *within* the "Hohfeldian powers" approach, when it is appropriate to do so.

In section IV of the chapter, I identify two distinct but related problems of political authority. In the literature these are not always clearly distinguished, as they must be if we are to understand the concept of political authority as precisely as possible. The first problem, which I call the problem of justification, is one of the main topics of the chapter: When, and under what circumstances, do states ever hold the legitimate moral authority that they claim for themselves? The second problem,

---

[11] A. John Simmons has gone some ways towards clarifying what is morally at stake in such theories by distinguishing between "legitimacy" and "justification." He defines legitimacy more or less as I have done here, namely, as a Hohfeldian power to impose obligations. (I will have more to say on Simmons' understanding of legitimacy in section III below.) He defines "justification" as "showing that some realizable *kind* of state is on balance morally permissible (or ideal) and that it is rationally preferable to all feasible nonstate alternatives" (emphasis added). A. John Simmons, *Justification and Legitimacy: Essays on Rights and Obligations* (Cambridge: Cambridge University Press, 2001), 125–6. While this distinction is important and helpful, it should be pointed out that Simmons' definition of 'justification' is stipulative and idiosyncratic; most writers on political philosophy tend to use the terms "legitimate" and "justified" as more or less synonymous, or at least as systematically related. Rawls, for example, writes that "[t]he basic structure and its public policies are to be *justifiable* to all citizens, as the principle of political *legitimacy* requires" (emphasis added). Rawls, *Political Liberalism*, supra note 10, at 224. See also Thomas Nagel, *Equality and Partiality* (New York: Oxford University Press, 1991), 330: "[T]he task of discovering the conditions of *legitimacy* is traditionally conceived as that of finding a way to *justify* a political system to everyone who is required to live under it" (emphasis added). I would prefer to say that Simmons has identified two different ways in which the term "political legitimacy" (and related terms) are used in the literature.

which I call the subjection problem, is this: When are individuals ever justified in submitting their will to that of another person? The most important version of the subjection problem in the political context asks a mandatory rather than a permissive question: When are individuals ever *obligated* to subject their will to that of another person? The justification problem and the mandatory form of the subjection problem clearly overlap, but they are not, as some authors sometimes seem at least implicitly to assume, either identical or co-extensive.

The main topic of sections V and VI of the chapter is Joseph Raz's famous service conception of authority. In section V, I offer arguments intended to show that, even though Raz correctly diagnoses the problem of legitimate authority as a question about the existence and justification of a moral power claimed by the state, and even though he offers his theory as one that is intended directly to establish that states have the capacity to possess the full legitimate authority that they claim for themselves—a point, it should be noted, that is consistent with their never, as a matter of empirical fact, ever fully achieving this capacity— his theory of legitimate authority nevertheless falls victim to a number of problems. These include, but are not limited to, failing to meet both the value-of-intentionality condition and the prospectivity condition. I suggest that Raz's theory is best regarded as a response to the subjection problem rather than the justification problem.

In section VI, in the course of further discussion of Raz's theory, I suggest consideration of an alternative substantive account of legitimate political authority, which is that the most important answer to the question of whether or not states ever possess such authority should be assessed by reference to the following idea: The most important function of the state is to accomplish particularly important moral goals that states are uniquely suited, or at least particularly well suited, to achieve on behalf of their subjects by means of the normative instrument of a capacity to impose obligations. Following Leslie Green, I call this the "task-efficacy" theory of authority. It is exemplified in the work of, among others, Elizabeth Anscombe and John Finnis. It should be emphasized that the task-efficacy view is a *substantive* theory of political authority, which is offered within the conceptual framework of the value-based conception described above. At times Raz seems to understand his service conception of authority mainly as a piece of conceptual analysis. At other times he clearly regards it as a substantive theory which is addressed to the justification problem, and which therefore contains within itself the resources for determining whether, and to what extent, particular states are morally legitimate. I argue that the value-based conception of authority provides a superior conceptual analysis to that of the service conception, and that the task-efficacy view offers a superior substantive theory.

In the course of the discussion in section VI, I observe that many important theories of political authority—including Raz's theory and all forms of so-called "voluntaristic" theories, including consent theories and the theory based on the principle of fair play—regard political authority in what I call an *aggregative* fashion. By "aggregative" I mean that the extent of legitimate authority of any given state—where such authority is regarded, obviously, as a matter of degree—is taken to be a function of (1) the total number of individuals over whom, considered one by one, the state can be said to hold legitimate authority and (2) the extent of legitimate authority held over each individual. Raz expresses this general idea when he writes that his particular theory of authority "concentrate[s] exclusively on a one-to-one relation between an authority and a single person subject to it," adding that "[i]t is an advantage of [this] analysis that it is capable of accounting for authority over a group on the basis of authority relations between individuals."[12] Raz goes on to conclude that the service conception "invites a piecemeal approach to the question of authority of governments, which yields the conclusion that the extent of governmental authority varies from individual to individual, and is more limited than the authority governments claim for themselves in the case of most people."[13] In the course of the discussion in section VI, I suggest that an aggregative approach to political authority is generally mistaken, and that the task-efficacy theory that I sketch should be understood in non-aggregative terms.

II. THE NATURE OF A GENERAL OBLIGATION TO OBEY THE LAW

In an article surveying the state of the art in philosophical work on the issue of whether or not there exists a general duty to obey the law, William Edmundson expresses a widely held view when he writes that

---

[12] Raz, *The Morality of Freedom*, supra note 2, at 71.
[13] Ibid. 80.

"The question: Is there a duty to obey the law? seems particularly urgent insofar as a No answer calls into question the very legitimacy of the state."[14] Raz can be understood as making a similar point in an indirect and somewhat less dramatic fashion when he writes:

> If there is no general obligation to obey, then the law does not have general authority, for to have authority is to have a right to rule those who are subject to it. And a right to rule entails a duty to obey.[15]

As was noted in the preceding section, Raz accepts that the right to rule which political authority involves must be understood as a moral power to issue obligation- or duty-imposing directives. If all the directives that have been issued by the state do in fact succeed in imposing or creating obligations, then of course anyone who falls within the scope of a given directive is bound by the obligation that, by hypothesis, the directive creates. Raz is thus correct to say, in the quote displayed above, that "a right to rule entails a duty to obey," where I take him to mean that a right to rule entails a *general* duty to obey. If the state's legitimate power to issue obligation-imposing directives has in all cases been exercised correctly, then every directive it has issued not only purports to impose an obligation but does in fact impose an obligation, from which it follows that we have, at the very least, a pro tanto obligation to obey each and every such directive; in that sense, we have a general obligation to obey the law. If, however, the state has issued at least some directives that, for whatever reason, fail to impose obligations, then it is false that we have a general obligation to obey the law; there are at least some directives that we do not have even a pro tanto obligation to obey. It readily follows by modus tollens that the state does not possess the right to rule. If a state lacks the right to rule, then it lacks legitimacy in the sense defined at the beginning of this article. It is of course true that Raz, like many other theorists, allows for the possibility that the right to rule, and the associated conception of legitimacy, can be matters of degree. For present purposes, however, the important point to note is simply that, according to premises accepted by Edmundson, Raz, and many other writers, there is a clear sense in

---

[14] William A. Edmundson, "State of the Art: *The Duty to Obey the Law*," *Legal Theory* 10 (2004), 215, at 215.

[15] Joseph Raz, *Ethics in the Public Domain* (Oxford: Clarendon Press, 1994), 325.

which the absence of a general obligation to obey the law calls into question the law's legitimacy.

I believe that Edmundson and Raz are clearly correct that there is a general connection between the existence of a general obligation to obey the law and the moral legitimacy of the state. As Raz says, "a right to rule entails a [general] duty to obey;" if there is no duty to obey then there is no right to rule, in the sense of a general power on the part of the state to impose obligations; if there is no such power, there is at least one important sense in which the state lacks (full) legitimate authority. Of course, the proposition that a right to rule entails a general duty to obey does not itself entail, certainly as a matter of logic, that a general duty to obey entails a right to rule. Moreover, we can easily imagine circumstances in which there is a general obligation to obey the law, at least in the sense that there is an obligation to conform one's conduct with each and every legal directive, but we nonetheless remain, at best, uncertain as to whether or not the state has a right to rule. Let me call this the "reverse-entailment" problem. Its essence is that the existence of legitimate authority logically entails an obligation to obey, but an obligation to obey does not logically entail the existence of legitimate authority. Note that this problem does not depend on the understanding of legitimate authority as a Hohfeldian power. It can arise even if legitimate authority—the right to rule—is understood as, say, a claim-right. The difficulty is that the general obligation to obey might not be the right *kind* of obligation to support the existence of legitimate authority, however the latter concept is understood.

Imagine, for example, that there is a duty to conform one's conduct with each and every directive of a given state because, as it happens, each and every directive reproduces an independent moral obligation. Thus there is an obligation to conform one's conduct to a directive prohibiting unjustified killing because there is an independent moral obligation not to commit acts of unjustified killing; there is an obligation to conform one's conduct to a directive prohibiting theft, because there is an independent moral obligation not to commit acts of theft; and so on. Even if there were, in a given state, a general obligation to "obey" each and every directive in the sense just characterized, we would still be justified in withholding judgment on the question of whether or not the state had the legitimate authority—the moral power—to enact these directives. All we could say for sure is that the state had, as it happened, enacted directives with good moral content.

Referring to the situation described in the previous paragraph, it could perhaps be argued that if people are motivated to do as the law requires, not because the law requires it, but rather because they are conforming with independent obligations of morality, they are not really obeying the *law* at all. On the other hand, it seems very odd to say, if one refrains from taking another's book for the sole reason that it would be morally wrong to do so, that one has somehow failed to obey the law of theft. These puzzles indicate that if we are truly to understand the relationship between legitimate political authority and a general obligation to obey the law, we must state much more clearly just what a general obligation to obey the law is. As we shall see in section III, some writers have come very close to maintaining that a general obligation to obey the law entails the existence of a right to rule. At the very least, they appear implicitly to presuppose the truth of some version of this proposition, since they offer arguments that are clearly intended to bear on the existence of a right to rule, but which are formulated entirely by reference to the question of whether or not there is a general obligation to obey. What, then, does it mean to say that there is a general obligation to obey the law?

Leslie Green has very helpfully set out five conditions that an argument (or set of arguments) must meet in order to establish the existence of a general obligation to obey the law,[16] and his formulation provides an excellent starting-point for discussion.[17] To justify the conclusion that there is, within a given legal system, a general obligation to obey the law, the supporting argument or arguments must, according to Green, show that this obligation is (i) a moral reason for action; (ii) a content-independent reason for action, meaning a reason to do as the state directs because the state directs it and not because its directives have a certain content; (iii) a binding or mandatory reason for action, as opposed to a reason which simply happens to outweigh other relevant reasons; (iv) a particular reason for action, meaning a reason that arises only for the directives of a citizen's (or subject's) own state, and not for the directives of other states; and, finally, (v) a universal reason for action, in the double sense that it binds all of a state's citizens to all of

---

[16] Leslie Green, *The Authority of the* State (Oxford: Clarendon Press, 1990), 224–9.

[17] I should note that Green clearly does not make the mistake of assuming that a general obligation to obey the law necessarily entails the existence of a right to rule.

that state's laws. Green argues, along with Raz, A. John Simmons, and others, that no argument (or combination of arguments) for a general obligation to obey the law that has so far been advanced succeeds in meeting all five conditions. The most pervasive difficulty, according to Green, is a failure to meet condition (v), the universality condition. As an empirical matter, argue Green and many others, it is never true that, for any given legal system, each and every legal directive gives rise to a moral obligation to obey that directive which holds for each and every person who falls within the directive's scope. This is a very plausible claim. Since, however, our current interest is in the theoretical connection between political legitimacy and a (general or partial) obligation to obey the law, and not in the empirical fact, if it is indeed a fact, that no general obligation to obey ever actually exists, we can for present purposes set condition (v) aside. In any event, as has already been noted, many writers accept that, even if there is no general obligation to obey because condition (v) has not been met, the existence of even a partial obligation to obey is relevant to the legitimacy of the state, because legitimacy is not an all-or-nothing matter; it is, they argue, a matter of degree.

Condition (i), which states that a general obligation must be a moral reason for action, is clearly of a piece with Raz's idea that the law claims for itself not just authority, but moral authority; if the claim is justified, then there exists, not just an obligation, but a moral obligation, to obey the law. Condition (iii) is, in a sense, simply a restatement of the requirement that an obligation to obey the law must be an *obligation*. There are various interpretations of what the mandatoriness of an obligation consists in—Raz's theory of exclusionary reasons is a prominent example—but this is not an issue that must be settled for present purposes. Condition (iv) states that if a legal system gives rise to a general (or partial) obligation to obey the law, then it binds only those citizens (or subjects) who are, in some appropriate sense, subject to that legal system. This is a rather vaguely stated requirement, but it has often been cited to rule out arguments for an obligation to obey the law which are based on John Rawls' thesis that there is a "fundamental natural duty of justice" which "requires us to comport and comply with just institutions that exist and apply to us."[18] Although interesting attempts have been made to give

---

[18] John Rawls, *A Theory of Justice*, rev. edn (Cambridge, Mass.: Harvard University Press, 1999) 99.

content to Rawls' idea that the natural duty of justice only arises in cases of just institutions that "apply to us,"[19] these are controversial. The prevalent view is probably that of Ronald Dworkin, who argues that Rawls' natural duty to comport and comply with just institutions is tied insufficiently tightly to the institutions of one's own state, as opposed to just institutions wherever they may be found in the world.[20] Beyond that, it is in any event not entirely clear how a natural duty to "comport and comply with" just *institutions* translates into a general obligation to obey the *law*.

Green labels condition (ii) of his five conditions for the existence of a general obligation to obey the law "Content-Independence." He writes that "the core idea [of content-independence] is the fact that some action is legally required must itself count in the practical reasoning of the citizens, independently of the nature and merits of that action."[21] Notice that this formulation in fact expresses two sub-conditions, or, as I shall call them, constraints. One is negative in character, and the other positive. The negative constraint is that the "nature and merits" of a legally required action must not count in the practical reasoning of citizens as they decide whether or not they are obligated by the relevant legal directive. It is this negative constraint which is properly labeled one of "content-independence," or, better, "merit-independence."[22] The second, positive constraint requires "that the fact that some action is legally required must itself count in the practical reasoning of the citizens." Robert Paul Wolff states an often-cited and influential version of a very similar requirement when he writes that "[o]bedience is not a matter of doing what someone tells you to do. It is a matter of doing what he tells you to do *because he tells you to do it*."[23] The point that Wolff and Green are making is sometimes put by saying that obedience requires not just

---

[19] For a distinguished example, see Jeremy Waldron, "Special Ties and Natural Duties," *Philosophy and Public Affairs* 22 (1993), 3.

[20] Ronald Dworkin, *Law's Empire* (Cambridge, Mass.: Harvard University Press, 1986), 193.

[21] Green, *The Authority of the State*, supra note 16, at 225.

[22] The term "content-independence" was originally introduced by Hart. As John Gardner has pointed out, the essential idea is that legal reasons derive their status as *legal* reasons independently of their merit, not independently of their content as such. John Gardner, "Legal Positivism: 5 ½ Myths," *American Journal of Jurisprudence* 46 (2005), 199, at 208–9.

[23] Robert Paul Wolff, *In Defense of Anarchism* (New York: Harper & Row, 1970), 9 (emphasis in original).

conformity with a directive, where conformity means simply doing what the directive requires. Obedience, it is said, also demands *compliance*, which means that the directive must actually figure in the practical reasoning which leads an individual to do as the directive requires.[24] While it may well be true that, in some contexts, "obedience" does require compliance in addition to conformity, as a general matter this is simply not true when we are speaking of obligations to obey the law, and this is so whether we are speaking of a general obligation to obey (i.e. an obligation on the part of all subjects to obey all laws), or simply of obligations to obey specific legal directives on specific occasions. This is clearly true as a matter of general usage, and it is usually true as a matter of legal usage as well. This latter point is true because the law, for the most part, does not care why we do what it requires, so long as we do it.[25] Furthermore, most theoretical discussions of the obligation to obey the law also assume, at least implicitly if not always explicitly, that conformity is generally sufficient to count as obedience.

The difficulty with Green's formulation of his condition (ii) is that both the negative and the positive constraints are formulated in terms of the actual practical reasoning that is supposedly required of persons to ensure that what they are doing counts as obeying the law. The preferable formulation, I suggest, should simply look to what is required for the existence of the obligation. Thus the negative constraint—the one con-

---

[24] Raz discusses the distinction between conformity and compliance in *Practical Reason and Norms*, rev. edn (Princeton: Princeton University Press, 1990), 178–9. Edmundson draws a similar distinction using slightly different terminology: See Edmundson, supra note 14, at 217. In more recent work Green states explicitly the view I am attributing to him in the text when he writes that "to obey is not merely to comply with the law; it is to be *guided* by it" (emphasis in original). Les Green, "Legal Obligation and Authority," Stanford Encyclopedia of Philosophy, <http:/plato.stanford.edu/entires/legal-obligation> at 5. (Green here uses the term "comply" in the sense that I am using the term "conform," but I believe this is just a matter of different terminology.)

[25] Sometimes the law requires that one must not just conform with a specific legal directive but also comply with it, but, at least so far as ordinary citizens are concerned, such cases are exceptional. Scott Shapiro has emphasized that it is a crucial aspect of H. L. A. Hart's theory of law that officials, as opposed to ordinary persons, must, when acting in their official capacity, comply with the law and not just conform with it. (I have expressed the point using my terminology, not Hart or Shapiro's.) This is the key to understanding Hart's notion of the internal point of view. For ordinary persons, according to Hart, it is sufficient for what they do to count as obeying the law if they conform with it. See Scott J. Shapiro, "On Hart's Way Out," *Legal Theory* 4 (1998), 469, discussing H. L. A. Hart, *The Concept of Law*, 2nd edn (Oxford: Oxford University Press, 1994, P. Bulloch and J. Raz eds.), 113–17, 203.

cerning content-independence—should be that the (moral) merits of the directive, considered apart from its status as law, should not figure in the argument demonstrating that the directive gives rise to an obligation. Content-independence is thus understood as a constraint on the type of argument that can be offered to demonstrate that a directive is obligatory, and this is of course a very different matter from a constraint on the practical reasoning of persons who are supposedly bound by the directive.

How, then, are we to understand the positive constraint of Green's condition (ii), if not in terms of the distinction between conformity and compliance (and thus not by reference to the actual practical reasoning of individuals)? The better understanding of the positive constraint is, I believe, captured by Raz when he writes that "[t]he obligation to obey the law implies that the reason to do that which is required by the law is the very fact that it is so required. At the very least this should be part of the reason to obey."[26] Notice that this formulation makes no mention of the practical reasoning of individuals who obey (or disobey) the law, but speaks, rather, of the "reason to do that which is required by the law." I take this to mean that the argument for the existence of the obligation to obey the directive must make essential reference to the existence of the directive, in a sense of existence to be spelled out either by reference to the fact of the directive's individual enactment by a de facto authority or to its status as one enacted directive in a system of such directives. A different way to formulate the positive constraint would be to say that the existence of the legal directive must be the ground, or at least part of the ground, of any moral duty to obey the directive which arises by virtue of its status *as* a legal directive.[27] Putting the positive and negative constraints together, we arrive at something like the following: In the case of any legal directive which attempts to impose a requirement on someone to do X, any argument demonstrating that there is a

---

[26] Raz, *The Authority of Law*, supra note 5, at 234.

[27] It is worth mentioning that this way of reading Green's condition (ii) has the incidental benefit of explaining how there can ever be a moral duty that flows from the law to do that which we already have an independent duty to do. For example, even though we already have an independent moral duty not to kill others without justification, a legal directive that specifies that we are prohibited from killing others without justification is, in principle, capable of giving us a new ground for the same moral duty, at least so long as a moral argument can be given that, inter alia, meets condition (ii). There is of course no reason in principle why a given moral duty cannot have more than one ground.

moral duty to obey the directive which arises by virtue of the directive's status as law must take the existence of the directive as the ground or part of the ground of the duty, but must not make essential reference to the independent merits of doing X. This reworking of Green's condition (ii) formulates its positive and negative sub-conditions not as constraints on anyone's actual practical reasoning, but rather as constraints on what can count as an argument that is capable of establishing that there is a (moral) obligation to obey a legal directive, such that the obligation can be said to arise by virtue of the directive's status as law. Since our main purpose in formulating conditions for the existence of a general obligation to obey the law is precisely to discover whether or not there is or can be a systematic moral duty to obey legal directives which arises from the status of such directives as law, condition (ii), as reformulated, has a very strong claim to be regarded as the theoretically most significant of Green's five conditions. I will sometimes refer to the reformulated condition (ii) as the "directive-as-ground" condition—DAG for short— where this condition is to be understood as including both the positive and negative constraints as I have discussed them. From now on, I will assume that Raz's version of the positive constraint, quoted earlier, should be understood in terms of the DAG condition as I have just formulated it. I believe this is reasonable, because even though Raz does not specifically mention the negative constraint—content-independence—he appears to assume it.

The formulation of the DAG condition that I offered in the preceding paragraph is clearly a first approximation only, and would undoubtedly require much refinement to ensure that it applies only to the arguments that, intuitively, we think it should apply to. As Raz points out, in connection with what I have been calling the positive constraint, "[i]t is easy to find examples where the fact that the law requires an act is a reason to perform it."[28] Many such examples will arise from odd circumstances that, intuitively, we would not think capable of being generalized so as to support a general obligation to obey the law. Raz gives the example of a person who has a reason not to break the law because his or her doing so will aggrieve a loved one.[29] Raz says that

---

[28] Ibid. 234.

[29] Notice that the loved one might be aggrieved only by the breaking of laws which have a certain content, for example those which regulate sexual morality. In that case we would appear to have an example of an argument to obey (certain) laws that meets the positive,

such considerations "do not even tend to show that there is an obligation to obey the law," because "[t]he obligation to obey the law is a
general obligation applying to all the law's subjects and to all the laws
on all the occasions to which they apply."[30] Ideally, then, it would obviously be desirable to have a much more refined and discriminating
version of both the DAG condition in general and of its positive constraint in particular, but it is difficult to see how to go about making
the necessary refinements, and Raz does not make the attempt. All he
says is that, while the grounds of obedience need not be the same for
everyone or for every occasion, they should be of sufficient generality
so that a few sets of such considerations "will apply on all occasions."
He continues:

> The search for a [general] obligation to obey the law of a certain country is
> an inquiry into whether there is a set of true premises which entail that
> everyone... ought always to do as those laws require and which include the
> fact that those actions are required by law as a non-redundant premiss.[31]

Although Raz does not offer a more precise version of the DAG condition, he does give several examples of argument-types which he apparently thinks meet the requirement of sufficient generality as stated in the
passage displayed above. The first is the argument that at least some
persons have a reason, on at least some occasions, to obey the law so
as not to set a bad example for others. The second type of argument is
based on promises or other types of commitments that individuals
sometimes give to obey the law. The third type of argument is based on
estoppel and various kinds of semi-estoppel.[32] Thus, for example, if
I knowingly induce another person to obey the law by acting in a way
that leads him or her to believe that I will obey the law myself, I should,
all other things being equal, obey the law, at least if disobeying it would
adversely affect the person whom I have induced to rely. I believe that all
three argument-types can be shown to meet the DAG condition. Raz

---

directive-as-ground constraint, but that does not meet the negative constraint of content-
independence. If correct, I believe this goes some way towards showing that the two constraints
are independent of one another.

[30] Ibid. Notice that the reason Raz gives as to why these considerations are insufficient
to establish a general obligation to obey the law amounts to a failure to meet Green's condition (v), which is the universality condition.

[31] Ibid.

[32] Ibid. 238–9.

states, correctly, that all three types of argument are important, and capable of establishing that individuals at least sometimes have obligations to obey the law on at least some occasions. But he also states, very plausibly, that as an empirical matter these arguments are not capable, either individually or jointly, of establishing a *general* obligation to obey the law. Putting the point in terms of Green's conditions, there is a massive failure, on the part of all three arguments, to meet condition (v), the universality condition.

For purposes of considering a concrete example, let me focus on the argument that one should obey the law because failing to do so will set a bad example for others. This argument clearly meets the directive-as-ground requirement, since the existence of an enacted directive requiring one to do X is at least one necessary element of the argument that one should indeed do X; it is only because there exists a legal directive requiring that X should be done that failing to do X could set a bad example. Raz is clearly correct that this argument will, for empirical reasons, invariably fall short of establishing a general obligation to obey the law. But since the failure is due to empirical considerations, we can easily perform the following thought experiment. However implausible this may seem, imagine that circumstances are such that, for a given legal system, any instance of law-breaking whatsoever will inevitably take place under conditions that will set a bad example for others, and that for that reason every subject of the legal system has at least a pro tanto obligation to obey each and every law. Perhaps new technologies make it virtually impossible to conceal acts of law-breaking, and perhaps the moral sensibilities of each and every person subject to the law are such that the breaking of any law, whatever its specific content (good or bad) or however trivial its subject matter, will have the effect of encouraging more law-breaking. It should be noted that, so long as this latter assumption is true, then the good that will come from setting a good example by obeying the law will not depend on the content of the particular law obeyed, from which it follows that the resulting argument for a general obligation to obey the law will meet the negative as well as the positive constraint of the DAG condition.[33]

---

[33] To keep the example simple, assume that every act of obeying a law has a general and indiscriminate tendency to encourage all other persons to obey all laws, and that every act of disobeying a law has a general and indiscriminate tendency to encourage all other persons to

I believe it is clear that the argument from not setting a bad example would, under the conditions described in the preceding paragraph, meet all five of Green's conditions for the existence of a general obligation to obey the law, where condition (ii) is understood by reference to the reformulated DAG condition. But I think it is equally clear that, intuitively, the fact that there is a general obligation to obey all the directives of a legal system which is based on the undesirability of setting a bad example is insufficient to establish that the relevant de facto authority had the legitimate moral authority—the moral power—to enact those directives. Putting the point more strongly, the argument from setting a bad example does not even appear to be an argument of the right type. The very idea of setting a bad example seems to assume either that the content of at least some laws has independent moral merit or—perhaps more to the point—that there is some good to be derived, at least potentially, from some persons having the moral power to subject other persons to obligations. It is arguments that are capable of establishing the latter conclusion that we are interested in, but, far from being such an argument itself, the argument from not setting a bad example presupposes either that such a power already exists and has been exercised in beneficial ways, or that at least some laws have independent moral merit.[34] Here, then, we have a very clear example of a reverse entailment problem.

break all laws. To make the example work, we do not need to assume that every law is a good or a just one, because we are supposing that the breaking of *any* law, whether good or bad in content, will lead to the breaking of further laws, and that the breaking of further laws, whether these are good or bad in content, is on balance a bad thing. These assumptions make most sense if at least some laws—we do not need to know which ones—have good or just content, but consider another possibility. Suppose that *every* law in a given system has bad or unjust content, but we have no way of knowing this. Since, by hypothesis, all law-breaking encourages more law-breaking, a plausible result of an epidemic of law-breaking might be utter social chaos. On one set of moral and empirical assumptions, such chaos would be a morally worse situation than the original set of unjust laws. (However, it should be noted that because this conclusion would partly depend on both moral and empirical premises, it is also conceivable that a set of unjust laws is so evil that social chaos would be the morally preferable alternative.)

[34] Perhaps it might be suggested that, because the argument from not setting a bad example presupposes that at least some laws have moral merit—whether because of their independent content or because they were enacted by a legitimate authority—the argument does not meet the content-independence constraint. In response, note first that, as was suggested in the preceding footnote, a version of the argument can be constructed even on the assumption that no law has any moral merit whatsoever. But set that possibility aside, and assume that at least some laws have moral merit. The argument that one should obey *this* particular directive would not be grounded

Green's five conditions for the existence of a general obligation to obey the law—with condition (ii) reformulated as the DAG condition—are as plausible a set of conditions for the existence of such an obligation as I can at present imagine. But even so, I think the example of the argument from not setting a bad example shows that satisfaction of those conditions is insufficient to establish that the state that enacted the laws had the legitimate moral authority to do so. Nor is there any reason to think that this failure is peculiar to the argument from not setting a bad example. The argument as I formulated it only met condition (v)—the universality condition—because of the very artificial empirical circumstances that I stipulated. Under actually existing conditions, the argument ordinarily fails the universality test. Most of the arguments that have been offered in the literature as candidates for establishing the existence of a general obligation to obey the law likewise fail to meet the universality condition. In addition, most also fail to meet at least one of the other four conditions, so they do not even get as far as my admittedly very artificial version of the argument from not setting a bad example. Usually this is enough to demonstrate, perhaps intuitively but nonetheless quite powerfully, that the argument is incapable of establishing the moral legitimacy of the relevant de facto authority. Let us consider a few examples.

I have already mentioned that, without more, Rawls' view that there is a "fundamental natural duty of justice" which "requires us to comport and comply with just institutions that exist and apply to us" fails Green's condition (iv).[35] Condition (iv) is the requirement that a general obligation to obey the law must be a particular reason for action, meaning a

in the merits of doing what this particular directive happens to require, but rather in the fact that there is reason to think that, as a general matter, *some* laws—where, let us suppose, we cannot specify which ones—have meritorious content. I am not sure whether this feature of the argument would meet a properly reformulated constraint of content-independence or not. All I can think to suggest here is that if someone thinks this, then he or she should explicitly set out the properly reformulated content-independence constraint so that it can be assessed in its own terms.

[35] It might be argued that the requirement that the institutions be "just" means that the argument fails the constraint of content-independence. This is not strictly true, since the argument does not purport to make the obligation to obey this particular directive depend on the fact that this directive is a just one. On the contrary, the whole idea is to make the obligation to obey particular laws depend on a more systemic requirement of justice, which could well entail that one has an obligation to obey laws that, considered on their own, are unjust. As an empirical matter, it is almost certain that any legal system appropriately characterizable as "just" will contain at least some laws that are unjust. Even so, it is possible that the argument from a natural duty of justice fails a reformulated and more general requirement of content-independence. See further the discussion in the preceding note.

reason that arises only for the directives of a citizen's (or subject's) own state, and not for the directives of other states. It is possible that arguments such as Jeremy Waldron's, which are intended to make more precise the idea that given institutions "apply to us," are capable of rectifying the failure to meet condition (iv).[36] I cannot undertake the task of assessing that claim here. For present purposes, it will have to suffice to point out that overcoming the failure to meet condition (iv) will not just make Rawls' argument more precise, but will in all likelihood fundamentally transform it. On its face, the failure to tie the purported obligation to obey the law to the laws of a person's own state makes it impossible to justify the fact that de facto authorities do not simply make a general or unlimited claim of authority over everyone in the world, but rather make more specific claims of authority over members of a particular group.[37] The details of how membership is or should be specified are usually conceived at least in part by reference to citizenship—a moral notion that itself requires explanation—or residency, either permanent or temporary, within a particular territory. Any argument that hopes to justify the claim of this particular state to hold legitimate authority over this particular group of persons, and only this particular group of persons, will have to specify some such notion of membership.

Consider next the argument that, under certain conditions, and more particularly the condition that there is a plausible interpretation of the state's laws, considered as a whole, such that those laws can be said to treat citizens with equal respect and concern, there arises a general obligation to obey the law which is analogous to the so-called associative obligations that arise within families and among friends. Ronald Dworkin's argument for the existence of a general obligation to obey the laws of one's own state if those laws meet his test of overall integrity is the best-known contemporary version of such a theory.[38] This type of argument faces many obstacles, one of which is that, while the argument

---

[36] See Waldron, *supra* note 19.

[37] The *content* of the state's claim of authority over the members of the group is said by Raz to be unlimited, in the sense that it acknowledges no limits on the spheres of behavior which the state has the power to regulate. In my view it is not obvious that the state's claim of authority is always unlimited, but the point is a minor one for present purposes. See further *supra* note 5.

[38] Dworkin, *Law's Empire*, *supra* note 20, at 176–224.

maintains that citizens stand in a relation to one another that is—like the relations among friends and family—appropriately particularistic, it simply does not make good on the claim that citizenship is sufficiently similar to the intimate and very personal relationships of friendship and family to sustain the argument based on analogy.[39] This objection amounts, in effect, to a claim that the argument from integrity does not, superficial appearances to the contrary notwithstanding, meet Green's condition (iv) (the requirement of particularlity).

Another, even more formidable obstacle faced by arguments like Dworkin's is the objection that associative obligations are not, for the most part, thought to include obligations to *obey*, but rather to be limited to obligations to assist, trust, and respect the views of one's friends and the members of one's immediate family.[40] If this objection is correct, then we do not even reach the stage of asking whether any obligations the argument might be capable of justifying meet Green's five conditions, because those conditions only apply to obligations of *obedience*. A *fortiori*, the argument would seem incapable of justifying a *power* to enact directives that impose obligations of obedience.

Consider next the argument from fair play. This argument, in the important formulation offered by A. John Simmons,[41] claims something like the following: When persons are engaged in a certain kind of cooperative enterprise, which is, let us assume, governed by rules, those who have accepted the benefits of the enterprise, in an appropriate sense of "accepted," have a duty "to do their fair share" by submitting to the rules when the rules require it.[42] I believe that this argument is capable, in

---

[39] Jules Coleman, for example, makes this argument. See Jules Coleman, "Beyond the Separability Thesis: Moral Semantics and the Methodology of Jurisprudence," *Oxford Journal of Legal Studies* 27 (2007), 581 at 591.

[40] See Denise Réaume, "Is Integrity a Virtue? Dworkin's Theory of Legal Obligation," *University of Toronto Law Journal* 39 (1989), 380; Green, "Associative Obligations and the State," in Justine Burley, ed., *Dworkin and His Critics* (Oxford: Blackwell Publishing, 2004), 267. Elsewhere I have attempted to offer an interpretation of Dworkin's argument that would meet this objection. See Stephen Perry, "Associative Obligations and the Obligation to Obey the Law," in Scott Hershovitz, ed., *Exploring Law's Empire: The Jurisprudence of Ronald Dworkin* (Oxford: Oxford University Press, 2006), 183. Dworkin has, however, rejected this interpretation. See Ronald Dworkin, "Response," in Hershovitz, *Exploring Law's Empire*, 291 at 304–5.

[41] A. John Simmons, "The Principle of Fair Play," *Philosophy & Public Affairs* 8 (1979), 307.

[42] Simmons does not in fact insist that the enterprise be governed by rules. See ibid. 310.

appropriate circumstances, of justifying a duty "to do one's fair share," and that this duty may include a duty to submit to the rules of an enterprise, in an appropriate sense of "submit." In the political context, the duty that arises will almost always, as an empirical matter, fail Green's condition (v) (the universality condition); the existence of the duty is conditioned on a voluntary act, namely, the acceptance of benefits, and most people, most of the time, cannot be said to have engaged in such an act. But of course, for present purposes, our interest is in whether or not the duty that arises meets the other four conditions. There is much to be said about this question, which cannot be considered in detail here. But one powerful argument that the duty which is sometimes generated by the argument from fair play fails, in effect, to meet our reformulated condition (ii)—the duty-as-ground condition—is offered by Jules Coleman: "If there is a duty of fair play to comply with the law, it is not grounded in law, but is instead contingent upon the compliance of others with the law. It is not a duty whose ground is the law, but a duty we owe others not to take advantage of their compliance with the law."[43] It is difficult to see how the argument from fair play can be reformulated so as to meet this point, and thereby be brought into compliance with the DAG condition.

Consider, finally, the argument from consent. This argument comes in many varieties, but one of the most powerful contemporary versions is advanced by Green himself.[44] Green of course recognizes that any obligations generated by consent will usually fail to meet condition (v) (the universality condition). But he maintains, plausibly, that an obligation based on consent will usually meet his other four conditions. Is this sufficient to establish that consent, to the extent that it has been given, justifies the power to enact the laws that, by hypothesis, there is an obligation to obey? Green argues that it is sufficient. This argument is a plausible one, because it is plausible to think that consent is, in essence, a promise to be bound by exercises of the very power to bind that is claimed by the state. Despite the plausibility of this argument, I nonetheless believe that it fails. Showing this is a complicated matter,

---

[43] Coleman, supra note 39, at 591.

[44] Green, *The Authority of the State*, supra note 16, at 158–87, 220–47. Green, like Simmons, conceives of consent as given voluntarily, one by one, by citizens or (or subjects) of existing states. His view is thus to be distinguished sharply from the social contract tradition, which I do not consider at all here.

and the details are accordingly left to another occasion. But the basic argument, which if correct applies to all "voluntaristic" arguments for a general obligation to obey the law, including the argument from fair play, is this. Any argument that offers to justify the state's claimed moral power to impose obligations cannot be conditioned on such contingencies as whether or not citizens (or, more generally, subjects of the law) have engaged in a particular kind of act—for example, the acceptance of benefits, or the making of a promise. This is so because any obligations that arise from the exercise of the power will be categorical, and as such cannot be conditioned on this kind of contingency. Of course, it is plausible to think that the existence of a legitimate authority must be conditioned on the existence of *some* empirically contingent factors, the most important of which is likely to be the effectiveness of the state's de facto authority. But, for reasons which have to do with the fact that the law's claim to authority is not only conceptually necessarily categorical but also morally necessarily categorical, neither the law's legitimate authority (where it exists) nor the obligations that result from its exercise can be conditioned on contingencies that involve voluntary acts by citizens.[45]

III. AUTHORITY, POWER, LIABILITY, AND OBLIGATION

Why do we find Green's five conditions for the existence of an obligation to obey the law—more precisely, the first four, theoretical, conditions—intuitively appealing? I think the correct answer is that these conditions seem implicitly to characterize obligations that can plausibly be regarded as flowing from the exercise of a moral power, and the existence of a moral power is the conceptual and normative core of

---

[45] The argument from consent is different from the other arguments for a general obligation to obey the law we have been considering, in that it really is capable of giving rise to such an obligation. As noted in the text, Green's first four conditions are met, and the fifth condition, the universality condition, can at least in principle be met if, as an empirical matter, all subjects of the legal system just happen to give their consent. My argument is that a general obligation to obey that arose in this way still does not entail legitimate authority, for the reasons sketched in the text. As Arthur Ripstein put the point to me, the fact that the state had a moral power over every individual in the state because each one had promised to obey it would, under these circumstances, be a mere accident that had nothing to do with the univocal and categorical authority that the state claims over its citizens as a group. However, even if I am wrong about this, that does not call into question the understanding of legitimate authority that I develop in section VI. It would simply mean that legitimate authority can sometimes be justified in more than one way.

legitimate political authority. I will elaborate more fully on this point shortly. For the moment, I will simply observe that, despite this intuitive appeal of the first four conditions, the discussion of the preceding section shows that even an argument that establishes the existence of a general obligation to obey the laws of a given state—i.e. an argument that meets all five of Green's conditions, including the universality condition—does not necessarily establish that that state has the moral authority to enact those laws. In other words, a reverse entailment problem can arise even when the argument purporting to establish the existence of a general obligation to obey the law has impeccable conceptual credentials. This was the upshot of the hypothetical based on the argument that breaking the law may set a bad example. This suggests that, if we wish to determine whether or not the state's claimed moral power to impose obligations is justified, *we must look to arguments which attempt to establish that conclusion directly*, and not by way of an intermediate conclusion to the effect that there is a (general) obligation to obey the law.

To begin, we need a more precise understanding of what a moral power is. One very plausible view takes something like the following form: One person *A* has a power to effect a certain kind of change in the normative situation of another person *B* if there is reason for regarding actions which *A* takes with the intention of effecting a change of the relevant kind as in fact effecting such a change, where the justification for so regarding *A*'s actions is the sufficiency of the value or desirability of enabling *A* to make this kind of normative change by means of this kind of act.[46] If this understanding of a power is along the right lines,

---

[46] Raz offers a characterization of a moral power that is roughly along these general lines. See Raz, *The Authority of* Law, supra note 5, at 18. I do not claim that this is the only possible characterization of a power. Matthew H. Kramer offers the following, quite different characterization in "Rights Without Trimmings," in M. Kramer, N. E. Simmonds, and H. Steiner, eds., *A Debate Over Rights* (Oxford: Clarendon Press, 1998), 7 at 20: "Someone who holds a *power* can expand or reduce or otherwise modify, in particular ways, his own entitlements or those held by some other person(s)." This definition of a power does not explicitly incorporate the value-of-intentionality condition, and Kramer's exposition makes clear that he does not wish to incorporate any such condition. (Indeed, if I read him correctly, he may not even mean to incorporate a condition of intentionality.) Now there are obviously situations where person *A* can, either intentionally or unintentionally, change person *B*'s normative situation by means that do not possess value; perhaps, in some contexts, such an ability should even be recognized as a species of Hohfeldian power. For example, assuming a universal natural duty of mutual assistance, *A* can place *B* (along with himself, it might be noted) under a duty that is both onerous and unnecessary by tossing non-swimmer *C* into a river that is in close proximity to all three of them. (For purposes of the example, I am assuming that there is no general or

notice first that any argument intended to justify the claim that *A* possesses a normative power over *B* must make essential reference to the value or desirability of *A*'s being able *intentionally* to change *B*'s normative situation by means of the specified kind of action.[47] Let me refer to this requirement as the "value-of-intentionality" condition, and to this conception of a legitimate moral power, and the associated conception of legitimate political authority, as the "value-based" conception. The general idea is simple but powerful: Legitimate moral authority can only exist if there is something sufficiently good or valuable about one person being able intentionally[48] to change the normative situation of another person. This is one of the core claims of this chapter.

systemic value in *A*'s possession of such a "power," although one can readily imagine particular situations in which there would be value in the *result* that *B* is placed under this new duty. For present purposes, we can ignore such complications.) But even if there is sometimes something to be said for characterizing *A*'s ability to change *B*'s normative situation in these kind of cases as a "power," such a conception of a power clearly has no place in a discussion of political authority. This is for the reason that, whatever else we might want to say about political authority, surely its ultimate point is precisely to allow one person intentionally to change the normative situation of another, where it is *valuable* that the former person have such a capacity with respect to the latter person. H. L. A. Hart clearly had a similar idea in mind when he wrote that "rules of change" and "rules of adjudication"—two types of power-conferring rules that, on Hart's view, figure prominently in the law—respectively allow for the intentional correction of the *defects* of unchangeability and inefficiency in what Hart called pre-legal systems of primary rules. Hart, *The Concept of Law*, supra note 25, at 92–6. Hart was clearly assuming, very plausibly, that the power intentionally to correct such defects in a normative system is a valuable thing. Note also that either type of correction will involve a change in the normative situation of at least some persons, even if this change consists only in the creation or removal of a liability.

[47] There are further conditions which must be met if a moral power is to be translated into legitimate authority. Some of these conditions are helpfully discussed by David Enoch in his account of "robust reason-giving." See David Enoch, "Authority and Reason-Giving," forthcoming in *Philosophy and Phenomenological Research*. One of the conditions Enoch formulates is that in order to exercise a moral power to impose an obligation on *B*, *A* must not only intend to impose an obligation on *B*, but must also *communicate* this intention to *B*. Such a condition makes most sense in the case of face-to-face authority, such as that involved in the parent–child relationship. In the case of political authority, which is the subject of this chapter, the matter is more complicated, since it is a practical impossibility to ensure that a given law is actually communicated to each and every individual among the millions of individuals who are subject to the law. The condition becomes something like: The state must make an intense and good-faith effort to ensure that every law is communicated to every person affected by that law. Such a condition is clearly tightly bound up with the general publicity condition that is associated with the rule of law. These are complicated issues, and cannot be further considered here.

[48] What should we say about the situation where a lawmaker goes through the motions, as it were, of legislating, but does not actually have the appropriate intention? It seems to me that the right thing to say is analogous to the private law solution to such problems, which is that we attribute intentions based on objective manifestations of behavior. So the lawmaker has in fact made law, despite not possessing the appropriate intention. Still, the paradigm case, upon

Before we proceed, there is an important point that should be emphasized. While the "Hohfeldian power" account of political legitimacy
that I am developing obviously places the value-based conception of a
moral power at the center of the account, the existence of a power is not
all there is to the matter. To borrow a metaphor from property theorists,
political legitimacy consists of a "bundle" of Hohfeldian relationships,
the most fundamental of which is precisely the power of the state intentionally to change its subjects' normative status. There may not be complete agreement among theorists about the other elements in the bundle,
but various plausible suggestions have been made.[49] The upshot of this
point is that the "Hohfeldian power" account of political legitimacy is
much more subtle and nuanced than might appear if we focused on the
moral power alone.

which such examples are parasitic, is that in which the appropriate intention *is* present. David
Enoch correctly states that the case where the intention is present enjoys explanatory priority.
Enoch, ibid. It is worth noticing that, since in the paradigmatic case it is a necessary condition
of *A*'s exercising a power over *B* that *A* must actually intend to change *B*'s normative situation,
A must presumably believe that she *can* change *B*'s normative situation in the relevant way. Of
course her belief might well not be formulated under that description, using the terminology
employed here. But *A* must have *some* belief along these general lines. If this is so then as a
general matter one cannot possess a normative power without believing (under some appropriate description) that one possesses it, and this suggests in turn that, at least for someone who
accepts the very plausible thought that the concept of law is closely bound up with the concept
of a normative power, Raz is correct in his view that law by its very nature claims for itself
moral authority, meaning a moral power to impose obligations.

[49] For example, David Copp argues that "the legitimacy of a state would consist in its having [the following] cluster of Hohfeldian rights": "First, a legitimate state would have a sphere
of privilege within which to enact and enforce laws applying to the residents of its territory.
Second, a legitimate state would have the power to put its residents under a *pro tanto* duty to
do something by enacting a law that requires its residents to do that thing, provided that
the law falls within its sphere of privilege and is otherwise morally innocent. Third, a legitimate
state would have the privilege to control access to its territory.... Fourth, a legitimate state
would have a [claim-right] against other states that they not interfere with its governing its
territory. Fifth, a legitimate state would have an immunity to having any of these rights extin-
guished by any action of any other state or by any other person." David Copp, "The Idea of a
Legitimate State" *Philosophy and Public Affairs* 28 (1999), 3 at 44–5. I am not sure that Copp's
analysis is correct in its entirety, but, generally speaking, I think he is on the right track. An
interesting question that arises, but that cannot be properly dealt with here, concerns to whom
a duty that is created by the exercise of the relevant power is owed. Some writers think it is
owed to the state itself, or to the legislature or lawmaker, but David Enoch argues persuasively
that the duty is owed to one's fellow citizens (which, incidentally, is Dworkin's position on legal
obligation). See Enoch, "Authority and Reason-Giving," supra note 47. Elsewhere I have
argued that the obligation is owed to the community as a whole, which I think comes to much
the same thing. See Perry, "Law and Obligation," supra note 7, at 282 n.36.

I will have more to say about the value-based conception throughout the remainder of the chapter. Here I simply wish to make the following two important points. First, the value-based conception is a *conception* in the sense that it is meant to render both as explicit and as precise as possible the content of the concept of a legitimate moral power (and, therefore, to do the same for the concept of legitimate political authority). It is *not* meant to be a substantive theory which establishes, say, that under such and such conditions, a state or government possesses moral legitimacy. It does not even presuppose that such a theory exists. Second, the idea of "sufficient value" which is associated with the value-based conception is, strictly speaking, concerned with the value of the possession by the power-holder of the capacity to intentionally change the normative situation of others, and not with, say, the value of states of affairs that might result from the exercise of that capacity. Of course, one would expect that instrumentally-oriented substantive theories of legitimate political authority would discern a systematic link between the one kind of value and the other, and the substantive theory I will sketch in section VI will be of this kind. But, as we shall see, substantive theories which do not depend on such a link are at least conceivable.[50]

The value-based conception of a moral power, together with the value-of-intentionality requirement that it incorporates, helps to explain the intuitive appeal of Green's first four conditions for the existence of an obligation to obey the law. The point is obvious in the

---

[50] The example of promising should help to make this point clear. A special case of the value-based conception of a moral power as I characterized it in the text concerns the circumstance where *A* and *B* are the same person, i.e. the case of moral powers to change one's own normative situation. The most important example is the power to obligate oneself by making a promise. The value-based conception of a power directs us to ask why there is or might be value in a person's having the capacity intentionally to change his own normative situation in this way. Not all theories of promising can be understood as answers to this question, but Raz's theory provides an insightful and nuanced direct response. See Raz, *The Morality of Freedom*, supra note 2, 86–8. Raz argues that there are two types of value associated with the capacity, as he puts it, to impose moral demands on oneself. One is the instrumental value "of forming and pursuing projects that give shape and content to one's life." But the other type of value is concerned with the fact that the very capacity to obligate oneself to another is partially constitutive of the value of certain kinds of human relationships. Raz does not use this term, but I take the point to be that the capacity to impose moral demands on oneself can have intrinsic moral value. As we shall see in section VI, it is possible to make arguments—by no means directly analogous to Raz's argument about promising—that the capacity intentionally to impose obligations on others can also have intrinsic value.

case of condition (i), the morality condition, and condition (iii), the bindingness condition, since the result of exercising a legitimate moral power to impose obligations must be a morally binding obligation. Condition (ii), the content-independence or DAG condition, holds, it will be recalled, that a moral obligation to obey a legal directive which arises by virtue of the directive's status as law must take the existence of the directive as the ground or part of the ground of the obligation, but must not make essential reference to the independent merits of doing X. This condition becomes both intelligible and more precise when it is realized that a morally binding directive only comes into existence as the result of the intentional action of another person, where by hypothesis there is value in that person's being able intentionally to change the normative situation of someone else by issuing such directives; what matters, morally speaking, is the will of the power-holder, and not the content (meaning the independent merits) of the directive he or she issues. Condition (iv) is the particularity condition, which states that an obligation to obey the law must arise only for the directives of a citizen's (or subject's) own state, and not for the directives of other states. Stated simply in terms of obligation, this condition is, as we saw in section II, rather amorphous, and it is difficult to determine how one would go about establishing that the obligation is restricted in the stated manner. But once we bring the idea of a moral power into the picture, the general character of the particularity condition comes into focus. A moral power is a normative relationship between the power-holder and those persons over whom the power is held, and, as a conceptual matter, at least, there is no reason why the latter cannot be a limited group, such as the citizens of a given state. It is relevant here that states generally only *claim* authority over their own citizens (and other persons who happen to be within their territory). Of course a moral argument is required to establish both the existence of the power and its restriction to a particular group, but the general character of the particularity condition is nonetheless relatively clear.

Most of the standard theories that are discussed as possible candidates for justifying or helping to justify the existence of a general obligation to obey the law cannot be said, even when understood as an intermediate conclusion on the way to establishing the existence of legitimate moral authority, to meet the value-of-intentionality

condition.[51] The natural duty to support and comply with just institutions fails on its face to meet the condition simply because it is
framed in terms of a *natural* duty, i.e. a duty that holds among all
human beings, and not in terms of a restricted moral power. The
argument from fair play fails to meet the condition because it is not
the fact that the relevant directives were issued in accordance with a
legitimate moral power that matters, but rather the fact that other
people have obeyed the directives (however they came into existence)
and one has, under certain circumstances, a duty to reciprocate.[52]
Dworkin's argument fails to meet the condition if only because the
normative status within his theory of enacted directives, i.e. the normative status of directives issued one by one by a de facto authority,
is quite unclear.[53] Although the argument from consent raises, as was

---

[51] John Finnis's argument for the conditions under which authority is legitimate is, it is
worth mentioning, one of the few contemporary theories which explicitly attempts to meet the
"value of intentionality" condition. Finnis's argument—more accurately, the *type* of argument
which Finnis offers—will be considered in section VI below.

[52] It is worth pointing out that Simmons, the leading interpreter and exponent of the argument from fair play, does not think that the argument even requires rules, let alone authoritatively enacted rules, to have effect. See supra note 42.

[53] Dworkin explicitly characterizes "the classical problem of the legitimacy of coercive
power" as essentially equivalent to the problem of whether "citizens have genuine moral
obligations just in virtue of law" (where he is clearly using the term "coercive power" not in
the sense of a moral power, but rather in the sense of the coercive use of force). Dworkin,
Law's Empire, supra note 20, at 91. He then adds that "[a] state is legitimate if its constitutional structure and its practices are such that its citizens have a general obligation to obey
political decisions that purport to impose duties on them." Ibid. This all sounds quite traditional, and indeed Dworkin proceeds to argue for the superiority of his theory of a general
obligation to obey the law over the natural duty theory, the fair play theory, and so on.
However, the traditional ring of this aspect of his account is very much in tension with his
account as a whole, which has very little to say about the theoretical nature of those "political
decisions"—are they the result of the exercise of a moral power, for example—but rather
finds law, and the general obligation to obey the law, in a holistic interpretation of legal and
political institutions as a whole, where individual "political decisions" do not directly give
rise to particular obligations but are simply one element of the social practices that are to be
interpreted holistically. His theory is thus ultimately of a quite different character from, say,
the principle of fair play, which, in the hands of Simmons, its leading exponent, is meant to
demonstrate that if the principle of fair play can establish a general (or partial) obligation on
the part of a government's subjects to obey its laws, then the government has over those
subjects a correspondingly general (or partial) authority, in the sense of a legitimate moral
power, where there is supposed to be a direct correlation between each exercise of the power
and the moral obligatoriness of the particular directive that is thereby produced. For Dworkin, to establish a general obligation to obey the law, in accordance with his theory of law as
integrity, *simply is*, subject to minor qualifications not relevant here, to establish the legitimacy of the state. For Simmons, on the other hand, to establish a general obligation to obey

earlier noted, complex issues that cannot be fully dealt with here, one can nonetheless make the initial observation that what seems primarily to matter for consent theories is the intention of the person giving consent rather than the intention of the holder of a moral power.

Let me turn at this point to another feature of moral powers. I will approach the point I wish to make indirectly, by initially speaking of the terms "right to rule" and "legitimacy" which are so commonly employed, often interchangeably, in discussions of political authority and political obligation. Many writers have suggested that the right to rule and the duty to obey are correlates of some kind, and this is a line of thought that might well be regarded as pointing to the conclusion which, in section II, we saw to be potentially problematic, namely, that not only does the right to rule entail a general duty to obey, but a general duty to obey entails a right to rule. The concern, in other words, is with the "reverse entailment" problem. Simmons, for example, has written that "legitimacy is...the logical correlate of the (defeasible) individual obligation to comply with the lawfully imposed duties that flow from the legitimate institution's processes."[54] One might think that Simmons can avoid the reverse entailment problem by arguing that he has limited the "obligation" that is the "logical correlate" of legitimacy to a matter of compliance "with the lawfully imposed duties that flow from the legitimate institution's processes." But this manoeuvre does not help him escape the reverse entailment problem, at least if his theory is to avoid being completely vacuous.

Note that, in his formulation, Simmons speaks of an "*obligation* to comply with...lawfully imposed *duties*."[55] Legitimacy, for Simmons, is clearly a moral concept that has moral force, and one would therefore expect that legitimacy's correlate, obligation, would likewise be a moral concept with moral force. But this only makes sense if the phrase "the...duties that flow from the legitimate institution's processes" is

---

the law, in accordance with his voluntaristic political theory, is an intermediate step on the way to establishing the legitimacy of the state in the sense of a moral power. (Whether Simmons' view lives up to its claims is another issue, of course, which I will discuss in a moment.)

[54] Simmons, *Justification and Legitimacy*, supra note 11, at 155 (emphasis added).

[55] Recall that, in this chapter, I am using the terms "duty" and "obligation" synonymously. See supra note 8. Simmons, in the passage under discussion in the text, is clearly assigning the terms different meanings.

being used *descriptively*, in a sense more or less synonymous with the way I have been using the term "directive" throughout this chapter.[56] The important moral question for Simmons then becomes: When does a duty in his sense—i.e. a morally inert directive—take on morally obligatory force? Simmons has an answer to this question, which is that a duty/directive becomes obligatory for individuals when they perform certain voluntaristic acts such as consent, or acceptance of benefits under the principle of fair play. But the moral principles of consent and fair play *have nothing to do with* the processes that generate directives, and therefore cannot reasonably be regarded as the moral basis of legitimacy (the right to rule). Thus Simmons' formulation does in fact give rise to a version of the reverse entailment problem. For his theory to work, not only must legitimacy entail an obligation to obey, but an obligation to obey, generated by the voluntaristic processes that he permits, must entail legitimacy, i.e. legitimate authority. What else could it mean to say that legitimacy and the obligation to obey are "logical correlates"? But this latter entailment cannot be true if the reasons for regarding a directive as obligatory are completely independent of whether or not there is a legitimate moral power that was exercised so as to produce that directive.

It might yet be argued on Simmons' behalf that he does not conceive of legitimacy as a moral power, but rather as a claim-right, so that the claim-right to rule which constitutes legitimacy would be a Hohfehldian correlate of a moral obligation to obey. This proposition seems completely empty and uninformative about the nature of political authority, but in any event, as I noted in section II, the reverse entailment problem can arise even when legitimate authority is understood as a claim-right. However, I believe that the best interpretation of what Simmons has in mind when he speaks of legitimacy is in fact a Hohfeldian power,[57] and

---

[56] At the beginning of section I, I defined a "directive" as "the product of the exercise of a *claimed* power to impose obligations." A claimed power is not necessarily morally legitimate, and hence the definition is descriptive, not normative or moral, in character.

[57] As far as I can tell, Simmons does not use the common phrase "right to rule," but instead speaks always of "legitimacy." He defines "legitimacy" as "the exclusive moral right to impose on some group of persons binding moral duties, to be obeyed by those persons, and to enforce those duties coercively." Simmons, *Justification and Legitimacy*, supra note 11, at 155. This definition in fact refers to three different rights, and Simmons simply does not say in what Hohfeldian sense he understands any of them. It seems to me that the first right, "the exclusive right to impose on [others] binding moral duties," is dynamic in the way that only a power can

I will assume as much from now on. That a right to rule should be understood as a Hohfeldian power is the explicit view of Raz and Green, who both nonetheless agree with Simmons that there is a correlation of some special kind between a legitimate power to obligate and the genuine moral obligations that result from such a power's exercise. Raz states that "[t]he obligation to obey a person which is commonly regarded as entailed by the assertion that he has legitimate authority is nothing but the imputation to him of a power to bind."[58] Green rightly recognizes that the true Hohfeldian correlate of a power is a liability, not an obligation,[59] but dismisses this as "a somewhat technical point," going on to write that "the correlation between a right to rule [meaning a legitimate moral power] and a duty to obey is distinctive only of the case of political power."

Whatever Simmons and Raz might have had in mind when they wrote that legitimacy (or a right to rule), meaning legitimate political authority understood as a moral power, is in some sense the correlate of lawfully imposed genuine obligations or duties, they are simply mistaken if they took this to be a correlation in Hohfeld's sense. As we have just seen, the true Hohfeldian correlate of a power to impose duties is not a duty but, rather, a *liability*, meaning in this context a liability to be subjected to duties. Focusing, as most writers in this area tend to do, on a power to impose duties, as opposed to a power to change the normative situation of others in almost any conceivable way[60]—by creating

be; it is no more and no less than a power to change other persons' normative situation in a certain specified way. We should not be misled by the fact that the specified way involves imposing an obligation and that the Hohfeldian correlate of an obligation is a claim-right, since, as I have emphasized several times, in the political context legitimate authority consists of a legitimate power to change the normative situation of others in any of a myriad number of ways, for example, by creating rights, immunities, liabilities, new powers, etc. In Perry, "Law and Obligation," supra note 7, at 284–6, I argue that a complex power of this kind cannot be reduced to a simple power to impose obligations.

[58] See, Raz, *The Morality of Freedom*, supra note 2, at 24. Raz continues the passage quoted in the text as follows: "For the obligation to obey is an obligation to obey if and when the authority commands, and this is the same as a power or capacity in the authority to issue valid or binding directives." This is a rather odd way to characterize the correlation or special relationship between a power to obligate and the resulting obligation, since it asserts an identity relation of some kind between the two. This seems implausible.

[59] Green, *The Authority of the State*, supra note 16, at 235. See also Perry, *Law and Obligation*, supra note 7, at 272–5.

[60] See supra note 57.

a claim-right, say, or a permission, or a new power, or an immunity—
perhaps tends to obscure this point, since the result of properly
exercising a power to impose duties is of course a duty. That the
duty comes into existence by reason of the fact that one is under a
genuine liability to be subjected to duties might at first seem to
have no implications for substantive political philosophy, but I shall
argue that that is not so. At the very least, the fact that the Hohfeldian correlate of a power is not a duty but rather a liability should
heighten our suspicion that a general obligation to obey the law
does not, in and of itself, entail political legitimacy; it should, in
other words, heighten our awareness that reverse entailment problems may be lurking.

Why is the fact that the true Hohfeldian correlate of a moral power
to impose duties is not itself a duty, but rather a liability to be subjected
to duties, not simply a technical point that has no substantive implications? If the correlate of a power to impose duties were in fact a duty, it
would make sense to think that the power only exists if the correlative
duty exists, which could only be the case if the power had in fact been
exercised. But once we recognize that the Hohfeldian correlate of a
power to impose duties is a liability, not a duty, it is easy to see that, in
principle, the power can exist without ever having been exercised: The
normative status of the person over whom the power is held is that he
or she is liable to be subjected to a duty, not that he or she is in fact
under an existing duty. In fact we can make a stronger point still, which
is that the existence of the power is, in the sense just described, *necessarily* a prospective matter. It is of course true that a lawmaker can,
either explicitly or implicitly, postpone the time at which a law comes
into effect, or else condition its taking effect on the occurrence of some
future event. But, leaving aside the possibility of such qualifications,
what should the default rule be concerning the time that a given directive comes to have normative force? Given that both the power to
impose the obligation, and, necessarily, the correlative liability to be
subject to the obligation, must exist at the time that the directive is
enacted, what other nonarbitrary default rule could there be except that
the directive takes effect at the very moment it is enacted or signed into
law? From now on I will assume that any argument attempting directly
to justify a moral power to impose obligations must not violate this
understanding of the default rule concerning prospectivity, and I will

refer to this constraint on such arguments as "the prospectivity condition."[61]

The prospectivity condition has very significant implications that may not be immediately apparent. It does not, for example, simply apply when a state first comes into being, at a point in time when the nascent state has not yet issued any directives. The condition applies, barring any qualification imposed by the lawmaker of the kind discussed in the preceding paragraph, *to each and every directive issued by the state.* The normal state of affairs is that the pre-existing moral liability to be subjected to obligations is triggered at the moment that the moral power is exercised, i.e. at the moment when the relevant directive is enacted or signed into law. Thus any argument for the conclusion that a given state possesses legitimate moral authority which depends on facts that only come into being at a time subsequent to the enactment of laws must be treated as suspect. This is true whether the argument is framed directly in terms of legitimate authority, or in terms of an intermediate conclusion that there is a general obligation to obey the law. For example, Dworkin's argument for a general obligation to obey the law is based on the condition that the existing laws of a state can be interpreted, as a whole, to meet the test of integrity. But the prospectivity condition insists that the existence of legitimate authority cannot be subject to an after-the-fact assessment of the success of many different laws, passed at many different times, in meeting a certain content-based restriction, particularly when that assessment is, as in the case of Dworkin's theory, a holistic one that applies to *all* of the state's laws simultaneously. Or consider the argument from fair play. The argument depends on the acceptance of benefits associated with a certain state of affairs, namely, the compliance of other persons with the rules, that normally can only come into existence, where it does come into existence at all, at a time

---

[61] It is worth mentioning that we generally think it is possible for legal directives, if suitably qualified, to have retrospective as well as prospective effect. Of course we also think that, generally speaking, retrospective lawmaking is a very bad thing, because of rule of law considerations, and that laws made in this way are in some important sense defective. Is it truly possible for a law to be retroactive, in the sense that it can actually change the past normative status of persons? I am not sure, but I doubt it. Either way, I do not think the possibility of a law's having retrospective effect can affect anything I have said in the text about the prospectivity condition, which is, after all, a matter of default. It only takes effect when the lawmaker has not made clear that his or her intention is, say, to pass a law with retrospective effect.

after the rules have been enacted. Because this is so, the argument cannot plausibly be regarded as justifying the existence of a moral power to issue morally binding rules in the first place. This is, stated at the most fundamental level, the reason why Simmons' proposition about legitimacy and the obligation to obey the law being "logical correlates" gives rise, at least for his particular substantive theory, to a version of the reverse entailment problem.

It might be argued that the prospectivity condition is itself suspect because it is almost universally agreed that one necessary condition of a state's possessing legitimate political authority is that the state must be a de facto authority, which means, among other things, that it is *effective*, which means in turn that persons will generally obey its directives. Effectiveness, the argument would continue, can only be established retrospectively, by examining whether or not people do, in fact, generally obey the state's directives. One way or another, the argument would conclude, a justification for the existence of a state's claimed power *must* therefore be establishable retrospectively, by reference to a condition that can only possibly come into existence at a point in time after at least some exercises of the state's claimed moral power have taken place. In response to this objection, let me say first that it is true, on any plausible view, that effectiveness will indeed be one condition that a state must meet if it is actually to possess the moral power to impose obligations that it claims for itself. However, effectiveness is not properly understood by reference to future acquiescence as such, but rather by reference to an expectation of future acquiescence. More specifically, what effectiveness requires is that at the moment in time that a claimed moral power to impose obligations is purportedly exercised, there must exist a *general and generally justified expectation* that the exercise of the power will be followed by widespread future acquiescence, i.e. by general obedience. It is true that evidentiary concerns might well generally lead us, as a practical matter, to assess a state's effectiveness by examining its actual track record. The strongest evidence that a state's directives will be obeyed in the future might well be the fact that, generally speaking, its directives have been obeyed in the past. But it is crucial to recognize that this backward-looking consideration is just a matter of practical evidentiary concern, and as such does not tell us anything significant about the true theoretical character of the effectiveness requirement.

By way of illustrating the argument of the preceding paragraph, consider the following statement by John Finnis: "[T]he sheer fact that virtually everybody *will* acquiesce in somebody's say-so is the presumptively necessary and defeasibly sufficient condition for the normative judgment that that person has (i.e. is justified in exercising) authority in that community."[62] I believe that a fair reading of Finnis's general discussion of this statement makes clear that he understands effectiveness not as a matter of future acquiescence as such, but rather as a matter of present expectation of future acquiescence.[63] It is worth mentioning here two further points about Finnis's theory of legitimate political authority. First, as I believe the quoted passage makes clear, Finnis is offering an argument which claims *directly* to justify the conclusion that de facto authorities possess legitimate moral authority; it is not an argument based on a mediating conclusion that there is a general moral obligation to obey the law. To be sure, Finnis accepts that central cases of legal systems do give rise to a prima facie general moral obligation to obey the law, but this is a consequence of, not the basis for, his view about the nature of legitimate political authority. Second, as I believe the quoted passage also makes clear, for Finnis, effectiveness is not just a condition that a state must meet in order to possess legitimate authority; it is the very core of the argument for possession of legitimate authority. That is why effectiveness is said to be not only a (presumptively) necessary condition for the possession of legitimate political authority, but a (defeasibly) sufficient condition as well. It is an interesting question whether effectiveness is in effect a third condition, in addition to the value-of-intentionality and prospectivity conditions, which partly defines the very nature of legitimate authority. I take it that Finnis regards effectiveness as a—indeed, *the*—defining feature of legitimate political authority, whereas Raz believes that it is an extrinsic factor which, as a practical and empirical matter, will almost inevitably figure in most substantive theories of political authority, but that it is not an element of the very concept of such authority. Needless to say this is a moral and not a purely conceptual question, but not one that can be taken up here.

---

[62] John Finnis, *Natural Law and Natural Rights*, 2nd edn (Oxford: Oxford University Press, 2011), 250 (emphasis in original).

[63] See, e.g., ibid. at 249: "[T]he required state of facts is this: that in the circumstances the say-so of this person or body or configuration of persons *probably* will be, by and large, complied with and acted upon" (emphasis added).

Perhaps it might be argued that one or more of the standard arguments for an obligation to obey the law can be understood in terms similar to those in which I discussed effectiveness. Thus it might be suggested that the reasonable prospect that most people will comply with the law in the future creates, according to the terms of the fair play argument, an obligation for me now, at the time when the law is enacted. This is an intelligible suggestion, but as a matter of first-order moral theory it is very implausible. The core of the fair play argument is the idea that I have an obligation because I have accepted benefits which, in the case of law, depend on other persons' obeying the law. But it is difficult to see how I can accept benefits which have not yet come into existence. I believe that similar objections will befall all of the standard arguments for the existence of a general obligation to obey the law.

IV. TWO PROBLEMS OF POLITICAL AUTHORITY[64]

In sections V and VI below, I discuss Joseph Raz's influential service conception of authority, and suggest that it falls victim to a number of the theoretical pitfalls that were discussed in sections II and III above. Before getting to the details of Raz's theory, however, it will first be helpful to distinguish between two different problems of political authority, both of which have figured prominently in Raz's work. The first problem is the fundamental question of whether or not and under what circumstances states ever in fact possess the extensive normative powers which they claim for themselves to be able to change the normative situation of their subjects. The concern, in other words, is with the question of whether or not and to what extent the claim of de facto authorities to possess legitimate authority is justified. Let me call this the problem of justification.[65] Since the claim that states make to possess legitimate political authority is moral in nature, the problem of justification is a

---

[64] In this and the following two sections I draw on, and greatly expand, arguments that I first offered in Stephen Perry, "Two Problems of Political Authority," *American Philosophical Association Newsletter on Philosophy of Law*, 6(2) (2007), 31.

[65] Note that I am not using the term "justification" in the same sense as Simmons when he distinguishes between "justification" and "legitimacy." See supra note 11 on Simmons' distinction. I argue there that while the distinction itself is helpful, Simmons' definition of the term "justification" is idiosyncratic. In contemporary usage, "justified" authority and "legitimate" authority seem to be treated as virtually synonymous terms. Or, if not exactly synonymous, they are treated as terms which are systematically related. See further note 11.

moral problem, and attempts to address it must have recourse to substantive moral argument. The upshot of the discussion in section II is that this problem must be addressed directly, and not via the mediating conclusion that the theory does, or would under certain circumstances, give rise to a general obligation to obey the law. The upshot of section III is that proposed solutions to the justification problem must meet the prospectivity and value-of-intentionality conditions.

The second problem of political authority concerns the question of whether or not an individual can ever be justified in subjecting his or her will to that of another person. Let me call this the subjection problem. This too is a moral problem, at least insofar as the issue is taken to be one of maintaining moral autonomy or making important decisions in one's life in accordance with one's own independent judgment.[66]

The two problems of political authority that I have identified are clearly related, since a response to the justification problem which purports to show that political authority can under some circumstances be legitimate must show that, at least under those circumstances, it is justified to subject one's will to that of another. But the two problems are nonetheless distinct. A demonstration that one is justified, in appropriate circumstances, in subjecting one's will to that of another is a necessary condition of the legitimacy of political authority, but there is no reason to think that it is a sufficient condition. Beyond that, the problem of subjection arises in many contexts besides that of political authority. According to one understanding, the problem arises whenever one is faced with a directive, a command, or some similar intentional attempt to change one's normative situation, whether this occurs in a political or a nonpolitical context. According to another, broader understanding, the problem arises in the circumstances just described, but also whenever one is faced with a demand or request by another person that one behave in a certain way. Demands are not generally intended to be exercises of a normative power, and requests never are. According to another,

---

[66] See, particularly Wolff, *In Defense of Anarchism*, supra note 23, at 3–19. Scott Shapiro offers a very illuminating discussion of issues raised by both of these problems of authority in Scott J. Shapiro, "Authority," in J. Coleman and S. Shapiro, eds., *The Oxford Handbook of Jurisprudence and Philosophy of Law* (2002), 382. Shapiro does not use my term "subjection problem," but writes, rather, of the "paradoxes of authority." But the issues raised by what he calls the paradoxes of authority overlap extensively with the issues raised by what I am calling the subjection problem.

still broader understanding of the subjection problem, it arises whenever one is faced with the possibility of relinquishing control over some aspect of one's life by acting according to someone else's view about what one ought to do, rather than according to one's own view. On this—the broadest—understanding, the subjection problem arises, for example, for a person who more or less automatically relies on the advice of a friend, or on the general recommendations of a self-help book, about what to do in a particular kind of situation, rather than on his or her own judgment. In other words, the subjection problem understood in this third sense can arise even when there is no intentional attempt, of the kind involved in commands, directives, demands, and requests, to motivate one to act in a certain way; it is enough to trigger the problem that one blindly follows another's advice or even another's impersonally expressed views about how persons ought in general to behave in some specified type of circumstance.

The best known and most influential discussion of what I have been calling the subjection problem is, at least in the political context, that of Robert Paul Wolff.[67] Wolff maintains, following Kant, that "moral autonomy is a combination of freedom and responsibility," and that the autonomous person, "insofar as he is autonomous, is not subject to the will of another."[68] Wolff further writes that autonomy involves both "a submission to laws one has made for oneself" and "the duty of attempting to ascertain what is right."[69] The autonomous person will not necessarily refuse to do what others either command or advise, but he will deliberate about the matter first. "He may listen to the advice of others, but he makes it his own by determining for himself whether it is good advice."[70] Similarly, the autonomous person will not necessarily refuse to do as the law requires, "but he will deny that he that he has a duty to obey the laws of the state *simply because they are the laws.*"[71] Using the terminology I adopted in section II, the autonomous person ought to conform his behavior with the law when he determines that, all things considered, this is the right thing to do, but he is never justified

---

[67] Wolff, *In Defense of Anarchism*, supra note 23. The term "subjection problem" is mine, not Wolff's.

[68] Ibid. 14.

[69] Ibid. 14, 13.

[70] Ibid. 13.

[71] Ibid. 18 (emphasis in original).

in *complying* with the law. Wolff views political authority essentially as Raz does, namely, as "the right to command, and, correlatively, the right to be obeyed."[72] While he does not use the term "power" in the sense that I have been using it in this chapter, he clearly regards the "right to command" as involving a power to impose obligations. Wolff's ultimate conclusion, not surprisingly, is that "there can be no resolution of the conflict between the autonomy of the individual and the putative authority of the state."[73] The state's claim to legitimate authority is, quite simply, impossible to justify.

I earlier phrased the subjection problem as the question of whether or not an individual can ever be justified in subjecting his or her will to that of another person. To put this question in Hohfeldian terms, the question is whether or not the individual is ever permitted, or at liberty, to subject his or her will to that of another person.[74] Wolff thinks that one is never permitted to subject one's will to another, but he also clearly thinks—this would be true *a fortiori*—that one never has a duty to subject one's will to that of another. But if one did not take as strong a line on autonomy as Wolff does, and hence thought that it is at least sometimes justified, or permitted, to subject one's will to that of another, one might also ask, is one ever under a *duty* to subject one's will to that of another? This is still a version of the subjection problem, but it is a version of the problem that is formulated in mandatory rather than permissive terms. As we shall see, this appears to be the version of the subjection problem with which Raz is most concerned.

V. RAZ'S SERVICE CONCEPTION OF AUTHORITY

Raz's deservedly famous service conception of authority appears to have been offered, at least in its early formulations, as a response to both the justification problem and the subjection problem. In this section, I will

---

[72] Ibid. 4.

[73] Ibid. 18.

[74] Hohfeldian terminology might not seem completely appropriate here, because the Hohfeldian correlate of a permission is a no-right. If Wolff is correct that one is *not* ever permitted to subject one's will to another, this is not because anyone else has a *right*. Similarly, when Wolff writes that everyone always has a duty to deliberate and, after deliberating, to do what he or she thinks is the best thing to do overall, this is not a duty which is owed to anyone else. If the duty is owed to anyone, it is owed to oneself.

argue that while the service conception does indeed offer an important insight about when one is either permitted or under a duty to subject one's will to that of another (the subjection problem), and to that extent addresses an important dimension of the justification problem, it nonetheless does not succeed as a comprehensive response to the justification problem, meaning it does not offer a comprehensive account of the conditions that a de facto political authority must meet in order to possess the legitimate moral authority that it claims for itself. The difficulty, in brief, is that even if the service conception correctly identifies many of the situations where one is justified in subjecting one's will to that of another, and even if it gives rise, in many situations, to an obligation to obey the other person, it does so in a way that does not depend on whether or not the other has exercised or purported to exercise a moral power to impose a binding obligation. But the possession of a moral power to change the normative situation of another is, by Raz's own lights, the heart of legitimate authority. If the service conception does not directly address the question of whether or not the possession of such a power is justified, then it has not truly come to grips with the problem of justifying political authority. The upshot is that the service conception both suffers from a version of the reverse entailment problem and also fails to meet the value-of-intentionality condition.

It is a further question whether or not any obligations to which the service conception might give rise in the political context are capable of meeting the five conditions for the existence of a general obligation to obey the law that were discussed in section II above. This issue will be briefly discussed later.

The heart of the service conception is the normal justification thesis (the NJT), which in Raz's early formulations asserted that "the normal way to establish that one person has authority over another person," and hence the normal way to show that the latter "should acknowledge the authoritative force of [the former's] directives," is to show that the second person will in general do better in complying with the reasons that apply to him "if he accepts [the first person's] directives as authoritatively binding and tries to follow them, rather than trying to follow the reasons that apply to him directly."[75] At this stage, three points should

---

[75] Raz, *The Morality of Freedom*, supra note 2, at 53. As Scott Hershovitz has pointed out, the terminology Raz uses here is confusingly different from the terminology which he uses in *Practical Reason and Norms*, and which I adopted in section II above. See Scott Hershovitz, "Legitimacy, Democracy, and Razian Authority," *Legal Theory* 9 (2003), 201, at 206–7. To put

be noted about the NJT. First, it is explicitly offered as a full-fledged response to the justification problem: To "establish" that one person has authority over another person can only mean to offer a substantive justification for the conclusion—explicitly acknowledged by Raz to be moral in nature—that the one has legitimate authority over the other.[76] Second, Raz also offers the NJT as a response to the subjection problem.[77] Roughly speaking, the general idea is that, if one will better comply with right reason in a specified set of circumstances by allowing oneself to be guided by the judgment of another rather than by trying to act according to one's own judgment about what ought to be done, then one is justified in subjecting one's will to that of the other. This is the core of his response to Wolff's reason-based anarchist challenge. In effect, Raz fights reason with reason. Third, the NJT is clearly intended by Raz to be understood as a necessary and core element of the very concept of practical (and therefore of political) authority, much as a I argued in section III for a similar conclusion regarding the value-based conception of a moral power.[78] Since we have competing conceptions of the core element of the concept of legitimate authority, I will refer to this issue as "the conceptual problem." This is, in effect, a third problem of political authority, in addition to the justification and subjection problems. Needless to say, the arguments required to resolve the conceptual problem will not be purely conceptual; they will in no small part be moral,[79] as we shall see in discussions below of the debate concerning whether

the NJT in the terminology of section II, we should say that one person has a duty to *comply* with another's directives when by doing so the former will better *conform* with reasons that apply to her than if she tries to act on her own judgment. Notice that this seems to demand more of individuals than the law does, since, as was discussed in section II, it is ordinarily sufficient to obey the law that one's conduct merely conform with the law, as opposed to comply with it. Having pointed out this terminological issue, in the remainder of this section I will for the most part follow Raz's usage in *The Morality of Freedom*.

   [76] See *The Morality of Freedom*, supra note 2, at 63: "The service conception is a normative doctrine about the conditions under which authority is legitimate and the manner in which authorities should conduct themselves."

   [77] See ibid. 38–42, where Raz discusses the problem of "surrendering one's judgment."

   [78] See ibid. 64, where Raz states that he is developing "a normative-explanatory account of the core notion of authority."

   [79] This is in keeping with Raz's idea that his own theory is "a normative-explanatory account of the core notion of authority." See preceding note. As Raz states, in this area of inquiry "there is an interdependence between normative and conceptual argument." Ibid. 63. In my view, "normative" here can only mean "moral."

the value-based conception or the NJT best captures the most fundamental aspects of the concept of legitimate political authority.

Given the three points enumerated in the preceding paragraph, Raz is
clearly asking a great deal of the NJT. For the moment, my concern is
with the NJT understood as a full-fledged response to the justification
problem. The difficulty that the NJT faces in justifying legitimate
authority can be brought out by considering one of the two main types
of case to which Raz says that it has application, namely, cases in which
the person issuing the directive has greater expertise than the person to
whom the directive is issued. (The other type of case, which involves
situations where the person issuing directives is in a position to achieve
valuable coordination among the activities of several people, will be discussed in section VI.) To avoid unnecessary complications, I will focus
on a case where the "background reasons" that apply to the person to
whom directives have been issued both are moral in character and constitute categorical reasons, where a categorical reason is one that applies
to the person independently of his or her particular goals and aspira-
tions.[80] Suppose, for example, that the issue is how safely to transport a
certain dangerous substance, where transporting the substance poses
potentially serious risks of harm to other persons. The relevant background reasons that apply to transporters of the substance are reasons to
avoid creating such risks for others, and are therefore categorical in
nature. Suppose that a given governmental agency in fact knows much
more about the transportation of this substance than I do, and that I
will therefore do much better in complying with the background reasons of safety that apply to me if I obey the agency's directives than if I
try to decide for myself how the substance ought to be transported. The
general idea of the NJT is that this fact gives me reason to comply with
the directives the agency has issued, and that since it would be "double-
counting" if I were also to try to take account of the background reasons
directly, I should treat the directives as "preempting" those background
reasons.[81] The fact that the background reasons are preempted is sup-

---

[80] On categorical reasons see John Gardner and Timothy Macklem, "Reasons," in *The
Oxford Handbook of Jurisprudence and Philosophy of Law*, supra note 66 440, at 465.

[81] Raz, *The Morality of Freedom*, supra note 2, at 41–2, 57–9. It is worth noting that, in Raz's
early formulations of the service conception, binding directives were apparently supposed to
exclude acting on *all* the background reasons (or dependent reasons, as Raz sometimes calls
them), because that would be double-counting. See, e.g., ibid. 42: "[R]easons that could have

posed to explain the mandatory nature of my reason to follow the directives.[82] Furthermore, by preempting the background reasons, the
directives are supposed to replace those reasons for me. Since the background reasons are categorical in nature, it is very plausible to think that
a reason that replaces them is likewise categorical. If whenever I engage
in the activity of transporting the dangerous substance I have a reason to
follow the agency's directives that is both mandatory and categorical,
that would appear to be sufficient to establish that I have a moral *obligation* to follow the directives.[83] If I have a moral obligation to comply
with the directives, that would appear to be sufficient to establish that
the agency has the legitimate authority to issue the directives, which is
simply to say that it possesses the normative power that it claims for
itself and that it purports to be exercising in issuing the directives.

Let me call the argument of the preceding paragraph the normal justificatory argument. The difficulty with the argument comes in the last
step, where Raz moves from the interim conclusion that I have a moral

been relied upon to justify [an arbitrator's] decision before his decision cannot be relied upon
once the decision is given." However, in a recent article, Raz appears to have weakened the
double-counting prohibition to some extent. Binding authoritative directives are now said to
exclude acting only on those background reasons which the lawmaker was meant to consider
and which conflict with the directive. Raz observes, quite sensibly, that the preemptive or
exclusionary nature of a binding directive does not exclude relying on reasons for behaving in
the same way as the directive requires, but only those reasons "on the losing side of the argument." Joseph Raz, "The Problem of Authority: Revisiting the Service Conception," *Minnesota
Law Review*, 90 (2006), 1003 at 1022. Sensible as this is, it clearly permits double-counting,
since there is nothing to prevent me from acting on both the directive *and* the winning background reasons. Furthermore, since it is difficult to see how I can act on the winning reasons
without knowing and taking account of the fact that they outweigh the losing ones, it seems
to follow that, even though I cannot act on the losing reasons *alone*, I can nonetheless act on
the *totality* or *balance* of background reasons, and indeed I must do so whenever I act on the
basis of the winning reasons. In light of these considerations, it is no longer clear exactly what,
on Raz's general account of practical reasoning, a preemptive or exclusionary reason is supposed to exclude. Notice that this is relevant to the issue, mentioned in note 74 above, of
whether Raz's theory demands compliance with the law or merely conformity.

   [82] Raz, *The Morality of Freedom*, supra note 2, at 60.
   [83] I wish to emphasize that, in reconstructing Raz's argument, I am trying to be as sympathetic as possible to its claims, and, in particular, I am granting that there are at least some
circumstances where the NJT does in fact give rise to a moral obligation. For that reason,
I have chosen a case where the background reasons are both moral and categorical, as this
seems to be the set of circumstances where the claim that the NJT produces a moral obligation
is strongest. Other critics have argued that, in cases where the background reasons are not
moral, or are not categorical but rather reasons that bear more or less weight—first-order reasons, in Raz's terminology—the NJT faces difficulties in producing a moral obligation as out-
put. The issue is complicated, but it is not my concern here.

obligation to obey the agency's directives to his final conclusion, which
is that the agency has the legitimate authority to issue the directives that
it claims to have.[84] Suppose that everything about the example remains
the same, with the sole exception that the governmental agency issues
advisory recommendations about how the dangerous substance ought
to be transported, rather than directives that are meant to be obligatory.
In other words, the agency does not purport to exercise a power to
impose an obligation on me; it simply offers me advice, and then leaves
it up to me to make a decision about what precautions to take if I decide
to transport the substance in question. To ensure that no other aspect of
the hypothetical is modified, we have to assume that the background
reasons of safety, at least insofar as they apply to me, are not affected by
the possibility that fewer persons overall will comply with the agency's
views about how to transport the substance if those views are issued not
as obligatory directives but simply as advisory recommendations. Let
me therefore assume that the case is one in which my reason to follow
the agency's directives depends *solely* on its expertise.[85] The assumption,
then, is that I will do better in complying with the safety reasons that
apply to me in transporting the dangerous substance if I follow the
agency's views about what ought to be done, regardless of how many
other people do likewise. On that assumption, the normal justificatory
argument appears to go through, right up to the second-last step (the
existence of the obligation). Given that the background reasons are categorical, and given that I will do better in complying with those reasons
if I treat the agency's recommendations as preemptive and hence as
mandatory, it is difficult to see how to avoid the conclusion that I have
a moral obligation to follow the agency's views even though they are
only issued as recommendations and not as directives. In other words,
I have a moral obligation regardless of whether the agency purported to

---

[84] Cf. Perry, "Law and Obligation," supra note 7, at 280–1.

[85] This means, among other things, that we are not dealing with a certain kind of case that
Raz has discussed elsewhere, in which it would be futile for me to follow a given standard of
conduct unless many other people also follow it. See Raz, *The Authority of Law*, supra note 5,
247–8. Raz gives the following example. If a sufficiently large number of people refrain from
polluting a river, then the river will be clean. Any given person has a reason not to pollute only
if a sufficiently large number of others do likewise, since otherwise the action of a single individual in refraining from polluting will be futile. Notice that this is a case where any given
individual's reasons are affected by the existence or non-existence of a general social practice,
but where the practice does not amount to a Lewis-style solution to a coordination problem.

exercise a normative power to impose an obligation on me. But if I have the obligation regardless of whether or not the agency claimed to possess and purported to exercise a power to obligate me, it is difficult to see how the *last* step of the normal justificatory argument, which is the conclusion that the agency possesses such a power, can be justified.

Perhaps it might be suggested that, even though I have the obligation in both cases, that is not a reason to deny that, if the agency does happen to claim and to purport to exercise a power to impose obligations, the normal justificatory argument is sufficient to justify the conclusion that it possesses this power it claims for itself. But this suggestion would lead to some strange results. Suppose that no governmental agency exists to regulate the transportation of dangerous substances, but that I have a friend who has exactly the same level of expertise that we have been attributing to the agency. My friend gives me advice about how to transport the substance that is identical in content to the directives or recommendations that we were supposing would have been issued by the governmental agency. So long as I have reason to know that I will do better in conforming with the background categorical reasons that apply to me by following my friend's advice than if I were to try to follow my own judgment, it is once again difficult to avoid the conclusion that the normal justificatory argument establishes that I have a moral obligation to follow my friend's advice. But now suppose that, instead of simply advising me, my friend claims to exercise a power to obligate me to do as she says. In accordance with this claimed power she does not simply advise me but *commands* me, or issues a *directive* to me, to do such-and-such if and when I transport the dangerous substance. Does the normal justificatory argument establish that she does, in fact, possess the moral power to obligate me that she claims for herself? It seems very odd that the mere possession of a certain kind of expertise, coupled with nothing more than a claim that one possesses a normative power to obligate others, should be sufficient to establish that one does, in fact, possess such a power. Raz himself draws attention to the similarity, from the point of view of the NJT, between obligatory directives and advice when he writes that, in pure expertise cases, "the law is like a knowledgeable friend."[86] But this similarity, far from lending support to the normal justificatory argument, actually undermines it. If, in cases of pure

---

[86] Joseph Raz, *Ethics in the Public Domain*, supra note 15, at 332.

expertise, the normal justificatory argument is sufficient to justify the existence of a moral obligation to follow the views of another person about what to do, it does so whether the other person simply offers advice or claims to issue binding directives. And if the suggestion is made that whenever the normal justificatory argument justifies an obligation on the part of *B* to do as *A* says then it also justifies any claim that *A* might happen to make to have the *power* to obligate *B*, then we will be led to find normative powers in some rather odd places.

More generally, the fact that the NJT is capable on its own of giving rise to obligations that do not flow from the exercise of a moral power, and indeed does not even presuppose the existence of a moral power, makes clear that the normal justificatory argument faces a massive reverse entailment problem. Raz in effect concludes that a successful application of the NJT in establishing an obligation entails the existence of a moral power, and hence the existence of legitimate authority. But, as the considerations in the preceding discussion make clear, this entailment is false, and that is the essence of a reverse entailment problem.

To come at the difficulty from a slightly different direction, consider again what it means to say that one person possesses a normative power over another. I said in section III that the most plausible view, which I called the value-based conception, takes something like the following form: One person *A* has a power to effect a certain kind of change in the normative situation of another person *B* if there is reason for regarding actions which *A* takes with the intention of effecting a change of the relevant kind as in fact effecting such a change, where the justification for so regarding *A*'s actions is the sufficiency of the value or desirability of enabling *A* to make this kind of normative change by means of this kind of act.[87] One way to formulate the difficulty that I am arguing the normal justificatory argument faces is to point out that, in trying to justify the conclusion that one person possesses authority over another, the argument makes no essential reference to the value or desirability of the first person being able *intentionally* to change the normative situation of the other. It fails, in other words, to meet the value-of-intentionality condition. The NJT looks out at the world, so to speak, from the perspective of an individual who is seeking assistance wherever he can find it in helping him to conform to right reason. From this

---

[87] Raz, *The Authority of Law*, supra note 5, at 18.

point of view, leaving aside for the moment problems of coordinating activity, there is no particular reason to distinguish advice from directives claiming to be authoritative. For that matter, it does not particularly matter whether the "advice" comes from a person or from a black box which, for all I know, might not even be subject to the control of another person. So long as I know or can readily come to know, on whatever basis, that if I follow the "recommendations" that appear on the screen of the black box then I will do better in complying with the background reasons that apply to me, the normal justificatory argument seems to go through right up to the point of establishing an obligation to do as the black box recommends.

Notice that it is not sufficient to distinguish advisory recommendations from obligatory directives to say that, in the former case, the recommendations give me reasons for belief but not reasons for action, or that the advisor is a mere theoretical authority for me but not a practical authority. In the case of the governmental agency, for example, the normal justificatory argument appears to go through whether the agency issues advisory recommendations or obligatory directives. Furthermore, in the case of both recommendations and directives, the argument only goes through if I have a basis for knowing, *as a general matter*, that I will do better by complying with the agency's views than if I try to act on my own judgment.[88] It may or may not be true that, on any particular occasion when I transport the dangerous substance, that I have a reason to believe that I will do better on that occasion by following the agency's views, and this so whether those views take the form of advisory recommendations or authoritative directives. What matters in both cases is, to repeat, that I must have good reason to believe that I will *in general*

---

[88] Raz explicitly acknowledges the epistemic basis of his account of legitimate authority when he writes that "[i]f one cannot have trustworthy beliefs that a certain body meets the conditions of legitimacy [i.e. the NJT and an "independence condition" which holds that it more important, in the relevant type of case, to conform to reason than to decide for oneself], then one's belief in its authority is haphazard and cannot... be trusted. Therefore, to fulfill its function, the legitimacy of an authority must be knowable to its subjects." Raz, "The Problem of Authority: Revisiting the Service Conception," supra note 81, at 1025. It is worth noting in this regard that Raz further acknowledges that, in the case of both authority and advice, it is ultimately up to each individual to decide for himself whether or not the conditions of legitimacy are met: "[I]n following authority, just as in following advice,... one's ultimate self-reliance is preserved, for it is one's own judgment which directs one to recognize the authority of another, just as it directs one to keep one's promises [and] follow advice." Ibid. 1018.

better comply with the reasons of safety that apply to me if I follow the views of the agency.

Understood as a full-fledged response to the justification problem, the NJT appears to fail not just the value-of-intentionality condition that was identified in section III, but also the prospectivity condition. This is because the fact that I will do better in complying with reasons that apply to me by obeying a given directive might only arise at a point in time later than the time at which the state issued its directive. Even if the NJT is correct that I come under an obligation to obey the directive at that later point in time, this is insufficient to show that the state had the legitimate (as opposed to the claimed) power to issue a directive that was binding at the very moment that it is was issued. As we saw in section III, the prospectivity condition holds that the default position as to when an exercise of a power has binding effect is the moment the power is exercised.

In light of the above considerations, it is noteworthy that, in his most recent work on authority, it is no longer clear that Raz means to offer the service conception as a full-fledged response to what I have been calling the justification problem, i.e. the problem of how to substantively justify legitimate political authority in particular cases. In a recent article, Raz states that the service conception is driven by a theoretical problem and by a moral problem.[89] The theoretical problem concerns the issue of "how to understand the [normative] standing of an authoritative directive." The moral problem is, "how can it ever be that one has a duty to subject one's will and judgment to those of another?" The moral problem is clearly just a version of the subjection problem that has been phrased in mandatory rather than in permissive terms. The theoretical problem, however, is *not* the same as the justification problem. In response to the theoretical problem, Raz observes that "[a] person can have authority over another only if there are sufficient reasons for the latter to be subject to duties at the say-so of the former." He adds that this observation does not tell us when anyone has authority over another or even that anyone ever can have such authority. It only states what has to be the case for one person to have authority over another, and "[t]hat is all that one can ask of a general account of authority." The theoretical

---

[89] Ibid. 1012–13.

problem thus apparently raises no more than a bare conceptual issue, which is answered, in essence, by pointing out that one person can have authority over another only if there are sufficient reasons to justify the possession by the former of a normative power to impose obligations on the latter. (Raz does not use the term "power" here, but that nonetheless appears to be what is at issue.) Not only is the service conception not explicitly advanced as a general response to the justification problem, but the justification problem is not even formulated as a distinct problem in its own right. The task of determining who has authority over whom and with regard to what "is a matter of evaluating individual cases."

Raz's response to the theoretical problem—"[a] person can have authority over another only if there are sufficient reasons for the latter to be subject to duties at the say-so of the former"—sounds rather like a less refined version of the value-based conception of a moral power that I introduced in section III. Notice that Raz's formulation makes no mention of the NJT. It will be recalled that the third of the three initial observations that I offered about the NJT at the beginning of the present section was that, at least in his early writings on the subject, Raz clearly regarded the NJT as a foundational element of the very concept of practical (and therefore of political) authority. I said that the value-based conception of legitimate authority provided a competing conception of authority in this regard, and referred to the need to resolve this disagreement as the "conceptual problem." At this stage, I would like to make two points: First, what Raz now calls the theoretical problem and what I am calling the conceptual problem appear to be one and the same. Both offer an analysis of the concept of legitimate authority, and neither is intended to serve as a substantive response to the justification problem. Rather, each provides a conceptual framework within which substantive justifications can be offered in specific cases. Second, Raz's response to "the theoretical problem," insofar as it makes no mention of the NJT and bears a certain resemblance to the value-based conception of a moral power, might indicate that Raz is possibly moving away from his earlier conceptual analysis of legitimate authority, which made the NJT central, and moving tentatively in the direction of the value-based conception. Such a move, I wish to suggest, would be warranted. I will return to a discussion of the conceptual problem in section VI.

Raz goes on, in the same article, to offer the service conception of
authority as a specific response to the *moral* problem, which, as I have
already noted, appears to be a mandatory version of the subjection problem. It is worth quoting Raz's restatement of the service conception in
full:

> The suggestion of the service conception is that the moral question is
> answered when two conditions are met, and regarding matters with respect
> to which they are met: First, that the subject would better conform to rea-
> sons that apply to him anyway (that is, to reasons other than the directives
> of the authority) if he intends to be guided by the authority's directives than
> if he does not (I will refer to it as the normal justification thesis or condi-
> tion). Second, that the matters regarding which the first condition is met
> are such that with respect to them it is better to conform to reason than to
> decide for oneself, unaided by authority (I will refer to it as the independ-
> ence condition).[90]

Raz anticipates the objection that the two conditions do not solve
the moral problem because the second condition merely restates it.
He responds that the independence condition "merely frames the
question," and that part of the answer to the moral problem is to be
found in the first condition, namely the NJT.[91] Raz argues that "the
key to the justification of authority" is that, far from hindering our
rational capacity, i.e. our capacity to guide our conduct in accordance with reason, authority actually facilitates this capacity. We value
our rational capacity not just because we value the freedom to use it,
but also because "its purpose, ... by its very nature, [is] to secure
conformity with right reason." When the conditions of the NJT are
met, we are better able to achieve this purpose by acting in accordance with the relevant authority's directives than if we try to exercise
our rational capacity directly. In such cases, Raz argues, the importance of conforming our actions to right reason outweighs the
importance of self-reliance and acting on our own independent judgment. He goes on to point out that, because we are hardwired to
respond instinctively to certain dangers, sometimes we do better in
achieving the purpose of our rational capacity by acting on our emotions. More generally, authority is just one technique among others

---

[90] Ibid. 1014.
[91] Ibid. 1017–18.

that is capable of helping us to achieve this purpose: The primary value of our general ability to act by our own rational judgment can also be met, according to Raz, by "making vows, taking advice, binding oneself to others long before the time for action with a promise to act in certain ways, or relying on technical devices to 'take decisions for us,' as when setting alarm clocks, speed limiters, etc." To understand authority properly we must therefore see it "not [as] a denial of people's capacity for rational action, but rather [as] simply one device, one method, through the use of which people can achieve the goal (*telos*) of their capacity for rational action, albeit not through its direct use."

This discussion of our rational capacity is illuminating and insightful. It shows that the two conditions of the service conception, namely the NJT and the independence condition, together offer a response to a very broad understanding of the subjection problem. In doing so it makes clear why we are justified, in appropriate circumstances, in subjecting our will not just to certain demands or requests by other persons that we behave in a certain way, but also to advice that others give us and even to mechanical devices such as speed limiters. (Recall the earlier discussion of a black box which dispenses "advice" but which may not be under the control of, or even have ever been programmed by, a human being.) However, in drawing attention to the fact that authority is just one device or technique among others that can enable us better to comply with right reason, this response to the subjection problem simply underscores my earlier point that the NJT makes no essential reference to the claim of de facto authorities to be exercising a moral power to impose obligations when they issue their directives. As I noted earlier, the NJT looks out at the world from the perspective of an individual who is seeking assistance wherever he can find it in helping him to conform to right reason. So long as I have reason to know that I will in general do better in complying with the reasons that apply to me in a given type of case by following the views of another person rather than by acting on my own judgment, it does not matter whether those views are offered in the form of advice or in the form of directives. No doubt it is a necessary condition of one person's possessing legitimate authority over another person that the subjection problem must have been solved, and the service conception is one means—perhaps among others—to solve it.[92] But this does not mean that the service conception can be understood as a full-fledged response to the problem of justifying legitimate authority. The perspective of the service conception is that of an individual looking for practical guidance, not that of either a putative power-holder or a putative subject of a power. For these reasons, the service conception is not in the end best viewed as a conception of practical or political authority at all, but rather as a general response to a very broad understanding of the subjection problem. As such, it provides a robust and convincing answer to Wolff's anarchist challenge, which, as we saw in the preceding section, is primarily grounded not in the justification problem but in the subjection problem, and a very broad understanding of the subjection problem at that.

For purposes of the discussion in this section, I have been assuming that the service conception is, in fact, capable of generating obligations when the condition of the NJT is satisfied.[93] So long as I know, or can readily come to know, on whatever basis, that if I do as another person advises or directs then I will do better in conforming with the background reasons that apply to me, the normal justificatory argument appears to succeed in establishing an obligation. Thus the argument at least sometimes will support the conclusion that I have a duty not just to obey the law—i.e. to conform my conduct to what the law requires—but to comply with it. As was noted in section II, this appears to be more than the law itself demands; ordinarily, we think that conformity with the law is sufficient to count as obedience. Even so, we can still ask whether the obligation that the NJT generates satisfies the five conditions set out in section II for the existence of a general obligation to obey

---

[92] One is tempted to say that whenever one person has an obligation to do as another person directs then the subjection problem, one way or another, must have been resolved. Otherwise, how could it be the case that one has an *obligation*? Since it is hardly obvious that, whenever one has an obligation to do as another person directs, one will do better in conforming to the reasons that apply to one by fulfilling one's obligation, this suggests that there must be other ways to solve the subjection problem than by satisfying the NJT. I find this suggestion plausible, but will not pursue it further here.

[93] See supra note 83. A natural question to ask is, to whom are such obligations owed? The discussion of the NJT in the text suggests that they are owed only to oneself, or, perhaps, to no one. But this is in conflict with a natural intuition that legitimate obligations to obey the law are owed to one's fellow citizens, or to one's community as a whole. See further supra note 49.

the law. Raz himself thinks that the NJT is capable in principle of establishing a general obligation to obey the law, but that as a practical matter it never does. To put the difficulty in terms of the five conditions, condition (v)—the universality condition—will not in practice ever be met. Sometimes particular directives will bind only some persons and not others, and sometimes they will bind no one at all. But what about the other four conditions?

As I will argue in the following section, the NJT appears to require that, if I will do better in conforming to the reasons that apply to me by following the law of California rather than the law of Pennsylvania, and if I know or can readily come to know this, then I have an obligation to follow the law of California and not the law of Pennsylvania, and this is true whether Pennsylvania sees the matter this way or not. If it is correct that the NJT has this implication, then the obligations that it generates appear not to meet Green's condition (iv). Condition (iv), it will be recalled, holds that an obligation to obey the law must be a particular reason for action, meaning a reason only for a citizen's own state and not for the laws of other states. If is true that, according to the NJT, I am obligated by the law of California and not by the law of Pennsylvania, and that this is true even though Pennsylvania regards me as subject to its jurisdiction and California does not, then even though the NJT is correct that I have an obligation, the particularity condition has not been met.[94]

VI. COLLECTIVE POLITICAL GOALS

In the preceding section I argued, with respect to one of the two main types of case to which Raz says the NJT has application, namely, expertise cases, that the NJT fails as a substantive theory of political authority, i.e. a theory which is intended to address the justification problem. In this section I begin by arguing that the NJT also fails as a substantive

---

[94] I believe this is, in essence, the problem identified by Jeremy Waldron in Waldron, "Authority for Officials," in L. H. Meyer, S. L. Paulson, and T. W. Pogge, eds., *Rights, Culture, and the Law: Themes from the Legal and Political Philosophy of Joseph Raz* (Oxford: Oxford University Press, 2003), 45 at 64. For the most part Waldron discusses the problem as one that holds for authority relations among officials, but, as he recognizes, the problem is in fact a pervasive one for the NJT.

theory with respect to the other main type of case that Raz discusses, namely, coordination problems. Towards the end of the section, I discuss the conceptual problem of political authority that was briefly mentioned in the preceding section.

In his recent restatement of the service conception, Raz writes that "[t]he function of authorities is to improve our conformity with ... background reasons by making us try to follow their instructions rather than the background reasons."[95] It is not entirely clear what Raz means by "function" here, but the two most likely possibilities are that he intends this statement to address either the justification problem or the conceptual problem. For the time being, I will take it as addressing the justification problem.

If we are to conceive of the function of political authority in terms of the justification problem, consider the following substantive account as an alternative to the NJT. The function of governments is not to improve our conformity with right reason for its own sake, but rather to accomplish important moral goals or tasks that governments are uniquely situated, or at least particularly well situated, to achieve on behalf of their subjects by means of the normative instrument of a power to impose obligations. Let me call this account, following Leslie Green, the "task-efficacy theory."[96] The relevant moral goals will generally be, in some

[95] Raz, "The Problem of Authority: The Service Conception Revisited," supra note 81, at 1019.

[96] In what follows, my aim is simply to sketch, for purposes of illustration, a type of substantive theory of authority which is to be offered as a response to the justification problem, i.e. the problem of justifying legitimate political authority. Accounts of the kind I have in mind are relatively common in the literature, particularly in the natural law tradition. Taking the views of Elizabeth Anscombe and John Finnis as examples, Leslie Green calls such theories "task-efficacy" justifications of legitimate authority. Leslie Green, "The Duty to Govern," *Legal Theory* 13 (2007), 165. The basic idea, as Green describes it, is that "[necessary tasks in life] fall to those who can as a matter of fact effectively settle problems of coordination and the common good." Ibid. at 173. Even though Green is talking not about a single theory but rather a family of theories, it will, for present purposes, be convenient to refer in the text to *the* task-efficacy theory. See further Elizabeth Anscombe, "On the Source of the Authority of the State," *Ratio* 20 (1978) 1, at 6; Finnis, *Natural Law and Natural Rights*, supra note [62], at 246. I believe that David Copp's substantive account of legitimate authority should also be regarded as falling into this family of views. See Copp, supra note 49. The same is true of the account offered by George Klosko; Klosko's stated reliance on a fairness principle is a misdescription of his own theory. See Klosko, "Presumptive Benefit, Fairness, and Political Obligation," *Philosophy and Public Affairs* 16 (1987), 241. Green interestingly characterizes Finnis as holding that "some [persons] have a nonvoluntary duty to govern, grounded in their effectivenesss at a morally necessary task," and that it is this duty—this *responsibility*—that ultimately grounds these

loose sense that I do not for the moment attempt to define, collective in nature. Consider, by way of example, the idea that some instances of governmental power are justified by reference to the ability of governments to achieve large-scale coordination among the activities of many persons. Raz has always regarded appeal to the ability of governments to achieve such coordination, understood in a broad sense and not just as a solution to a narrowly conceived, Lewis-style coordination problem, as one of the two main ways that the service conception can justify political authority.[97] Although any response to the justification problem which is based in whole or in part on securing coordination must contend with a number of difficult questions,[98] it nonetheless seems clear that, one way or another, the ability of governments to coordinate complex activity will inevitably play a prominent role in the justification of most political authorities, to the extent that they can be justified at all. It also seems clear that any justification of political authority which rests on the ability of governments to coordinate activity must at some point appeal to an interest which people generally have in the successful achievement of coordination. There is no harm in saying that, because people have such an interest, they have a background reason "to wish for a convention,"[99] as Raz has put it, or something along those lines.

We nonetheless overlook an important dimension of what is valuable about coordination if we limit ourselves to saying that the power to issue coordination-securing directives is justified because the possession and exercise of this power will enable people *to better conform their own actions* with the requirements of right reason. Often a "a reason to wish for" coordination is indeed best understood as a background reason for action, meaning a reason to act in such a way that one's particular activities are coordinated with those of others. But it is important to recognize that persons also have a background *interest* in the existence of general social coordination, meaning coordination in many different aspects of public life, which goes far beyond ensuring that *their* actions are coordinated with the actions of others. I will benefit, for example, in countless

persons' legitimate authority over others. Green, "The Duty to Govern," supra, at 167. Although it is not a point that can be discussed here, Green has highlighted a very significant feature of Finnis's theory of authority.

[97] See, e.g., Raz, *The Morality of Freedom*, supra note 2, at 49–50.
[98] Cf. Leslie Green, *The Authority of the State*, supra note 16, at 89–121.
[99] Raz, *The Morality of Freedom*, supra note 2, at 50.

different ways because other people's activities have successfully been coordinated so as to ensure that the transportation of goods on the highways is fast and safe, and that the air traffic control system operates efficiently and with a high degree of security. For example, such coordination of the activities of others ensures that there is food for me to buy at local stores, and that planes do not regularly fall out of the sky and injure me. The achievement of coordination is a valuable moral goal in its own right, quite apart from the extent to which particular individuals might in their own actions better conform with reasons that apply to them. The fact that many people will benefit from a set of directives which successfully coordinates the air traffic control system will surely figure in any plausible argument for the conclusion that the government is justified in issuing these directives, and this is so even though the directives do not directly engage the background reasons for action of many (and perhaps most) of the people who benefit in this way. Persons who benefit in this "passive" way may well have a "reason to wish for" a convention or, more generally, for coordination or cooperation among others, but in this context a "reason to wish for" is best understood as an interest of a certain kind, and not as a reason for action. As we shall see below, the task-efficacy view, understood as operating within the conceptual framework of the value-based conception of legitimate authority, has no difficulty handling this type of case.

As Raz has observed, his general view of authority entails the substantive moral thesis that all political reasons are subordinated to ordinary individual morality.[100] Let me refer to this as the "political subordination thesis." Even if this thesis is true, which is not a self-evident matter, it is important to make clear that the relevant background reasons of individual morality are often very general and only indirectly related to the actions the government is empowered to take. As Raz says, the fact that everyone has reason to improve their own economic situation does not mean that everyone has a reason to raise taxes: "[T]hose helping us may have good grounds for pursuing the goals set by reasons that apply to us in ways that are not open to us," and indeed "they may be assigned the task of helping us precisely because of that."[101] While this is certainly

---

[100] Ibid. 72.
[101] Raz, "The Problem of Authority: Revisiting the Service Conception," supra note 81, at 1030.

correct, it nonetheless seems strained to say that the government's role in such a case is to help every individual to act in ways which better conform with the reason they have to improve their own economic situation, as opposed to saying that the government's role is, quite simply, to achieve the moral goal of improving everyone's economic situation. This latter formulation is what the task-efficacy view would have to say on the matter.

To see the general point more clearly, consider the following example. Suppose that a society has good reasons of security to have a standing army of a certain size, but that it would be wasteful of resources to have an army of any larger size. Assume that the government is justified in achieving this goal by conscripting the required number of soldiers from the pool of citizens who are generally fit to serve in the army, and that it is also justified in determining who is to be drafted by instituting a fair lottery. It is no doubt true, in such a case, that each citizen has a background moral duty to contribute in appropriate ways to maintaining the security of the society, so that it is true of each citizen who is drafted that she is complying with a background reason that applies to her. But does it follow that she is *better* complying with that reason by obeying the directive to serve in the army? After all, she only has the duty to serve because her name happened to come up in the lottery. Similarly, is it sensible to say that the *function* the government is fulfilling in instituting the draft-by-lottery is to enable each citizen who has been drafted to conform better with a background reason that applies to her? If that were the government's function, why is it only helping Susan by drafting her, and not helping John by drafting him as well? Are we to say instead that the government is somehow serving the goal of helping each citizen who *might* have been drafted to better conform with a background reason? Surely we make the best sense of such a case by saying, quite simply, that the government's function is to take steps to achieve the general moral goal of providing for the society's security by means of the exercise of a power to impose duties on (some) citizens. Again, this is what the task-efficacy view would say.

Assuming the political subordination thesis is true, a background reason for action, such as the postulated duty to contribute in appropriate ways to collective security, must figure in any argument that might plausibly be offered to show that the government does, in fact, possess the power to conscript in this way. This is true for both the task-efficacy approach and the NJT. But we nonetheless mis-describe the situation if we say that the possession of the power is justified because its exercise ensures that those whose normative situation is affected will better comply with that background reason than would otherwise be the case. That is why I said earlier that it may well be a necessary condition of a government's possessing legitimate authority over any particular person in regard to any particular matter that the NJT, *or some condition similar to the NJT*, be satisfied. What is arguably necessary is that, in light of the political subordination thesis, the justification of the power invokes some background reason that applies to any person whose normative situation is affected by its exercise. But it does not follow that the exercise of the power enables any such person to *better* comply with that reason. Still less does it follow that this was the purpose either of having the power or of exercising it in particular instances.

Raz recognizes that there will be cases, along the lines of the conscription example, in which burdens are imposed on a small number of persons in order to ensure that a benefit accrues to the larger community, or to some segment of it. He notes that "[t]he government has authority over [those who bear the burdens] only if they have reason to contribute to a scheme which benefits others."[102] This is true if the political subordination thesis is true; in the example, the reason in question is the duty to contribute in appropriate ways to maintaining the security of the society. Expanding on this point, Raz observes:

> It is not good enough to say that an authoritative measure is justified because it serves the public interest. If it is binding on individuals it has to be justified by considerations which bind them. Public authority is ultimately based on the moral duty which individuals owe their fellow humans.[103]

All of this is surely true, but that fact does nothing to buttress the claim that the NJT must be satisfied in order to justify political authority. Perhaps Raz might wish to say of the conscription example that, once the scheme has been put in place and it has been determined who has the legal duty to serve and who does not, each individual is, in fact, complying in the best possible fashion, all things considered, with his or her background duty to contribute in appropriate ways to the security

---

[102] Raz, *The Morality of Freedom*, supra note 2, at 71.
[103] Ibid. 72.

of the society. To interpret the situation this way sounds artificial and strained. But even beyond that, there is simply no reason to think that anything like this is in general true, as we can see by varying the hypothetical.

Suppose that the government in question permits voluntary enlistment, and only uses the conscription lottery to bring the army up to its optimal size where enlistment numbers fall short. It might well be the case that, for any given citizen, she best complies with the background duty to contribute in appropriate ways to the security of the society if she enlists, rather than simply submitting to the draft as and when required. Perhaps this is so, for example, because the act of enlistment is a public expression of one's willingness to serve one's country, and that one better complies with one's background duty by making a public declaration of this kind. To avoid unnecessary complications, assume that a person who has just been conscripted had already made the decision to enlist, but had not actually acted on the decision at the time that she was conscripted. Thus it is not true, at least of this particular person, that she is better complying with her background duty by obeying the order to report for military service than she would if she were to act on her own judgment by enlisting, and this is true even though the background duty is part of the justification for the specific duty to report for service when so ordered. Raz is correct to say that "[i]t is not good enough to say that an authoritative measure is justified because it serves the public interest," but only in the sense that appeal to the public interest is not sufficient by itself to justify the authoritative measure. The *point* of the authoritative measure is surely to serve the public interest, which here takes the form of a collective goal of ensuring general security. This is certainly how the task-efficacy view would regard the matter. Raz is also correct to say that "[p]ublic authority is ultimately based on the moral duty which individuals owe their fellow humans." Given the political subordination thesis, this presumably means that a moral duty, such as the postulated background duty to do one's part to maintain collective security, will necessarily figure in the justification of an authoritative measure such as the conscription lottery. But it does *not* mean that the point or function of the authoritative measure is to enable persons *better* to comply with that background duty.

This is perhaps a good place to point out another, related difficulty to which the service conception gives rise, insofar as it holds that the function of authority is, quite simply, to improve conformity with right reason. Raz has observed that the NJT "invites a piecemeal approach to the question of the authority of governments, which yields the conclusion that the extent of governmental authority varies from individual to individual, and is more limited than the authority most governments claim for themselves in the case of most people."[104] Thus if, to revert to an earlier example, I happen to know much more about how safely to transport a dangerous substance than does the governmental agency which has been charged with regulating such matters, the piecemeal approach suggests that the agency does not have the authority over me that it claims, and that I am not morally bound by its directives. If we say that the function of authority is, quite simply, to enable me better to conform with background reasons that apply to me, then it becomes difficult to make sense of the fact that legal systems claim virtually unlimited power to regulate any activity or aspect of life,[105] and that they do not acknowledge any exceptions to that authority which are not explicitly recognized by the law itself. No doubt Raz is correct to say that it is not a condition of adequacy of an explanation of the concept of authority that those who have authority accept, even implicitly, that the explanation is correct.[106] Even so, one would nonetheless expect any adequate explanation to make sense of, in the minimal sense of being consistent with, the behavior of those who claim authority. If the function of authority really were to enable persons better to conform with right reason, then one would expect there to be *many* cases in which the claim of authority could be justified by appeal to pure expertise.[107] One would nonetheless also expect in such cases that the law would act, as Raz has put it, "like a knowledgeable friend,"[108] acquiescing gracefully when a subject either knows more than it does or

---

[104] Ibid. 80.

[105] See supra note 5.

[106] Raz, "The Problem of Authority: Revisiting the Service Conception," supra note 81, at 1006.

[107] The very formulation of the NJT, which looks to whether one person is able to help another better to conform to right reason, should lead us to expect many pure expertise cases in the law. In fact, there are almost none. (I leave aside the issue of paternalism, which requires more in the way of substantive justification than the NJT can provide.) In his recent article restating his views on authority, Raz remarks that expertise and coordination are, in the case of political authority, usually "inextricably mixed." Raz, "The Problem of Authority: Revisiting the Service Conception," supra note 80, at 1031, 1036. This may be so, but not because pure expertise cases are, for practical reasons, say, not possible or feasible. The lack of pure expertise cases in the law is, in the end, an embarrassment for the NJT.

[108] Raz, *Ethics in the Public Domain*, supra note 15, at 332.

succeeds in finding some third party who knows more.[109] Regarded as a general response to the subjection problem, the NJT counsels me to seek assistance in conforming to right reason wherever I can find it, so that if I have good grounds for believing that I will generally do better in safely transporting a dangerous substance by following the law of California than by following the law of Pennsylvania, then I should follow the law of California. But the law of Pennsylvania does not see the matter this way. It insists that, insofar as I fall within its jurisdiction, I have a categorical obligation to follow its directives except to the extent that the law itself makes room for some exception. Far from encouraging me to seek assistance in conforming to right reason wherever I might find it, the law tells me that I am obligated to follow its directives, and that is the end of the matter. This suggests that there is an almost unavoidable tension in regarding the NJT as a full-fledged general response to *both* the subjection problem *and* the justification problem.

Insofar as he has, at least in the past, treated the service conception as a full-fledged response to the justification problem, Raz has viewed the analysis of authority as beginning with the one-to-one relation between an authority and a single person subject to the authority, so that authority over a group of persons is to be accounted for by reference to authority relations between individuals.[110] Let me call this the *aggregative* aspect

---

[109] Cf. Perry, "Law and Obligation," supra note 7, at 283–4.

[110] Raz, *The Morality of Freedom*, supra note 2, at 71. It is worth pointing out that the aggregative aspect of Raz's theory of authority arises for other theories besides his own. It arises, for example, for all so-called "voluntaristic" theories, which make the state's authority over any given individual a function of whether or not that individual has performed a certain kind of specified voluntary act. Thus it applies to the common understanding of the argument from fair play, as well as to many versions of consent theory. That this is so is illustrated by Simmons' characterization of his own, generalized version of a Lockean theory of authority. Simmons holds that an obligation to obey the law is triggered by voluntary acts of the kind just discussed. Simmons, *Justification and Legitimacy*, supra note 11, at 154–5. Since Simmons subscribes to the view that "political voluntarism [offers] the correct account of these transactional grounds for legitimacy," ibid. at 155, it follows that the legitimacy of a given state is, on his account, a function of how many individuals happen to have transacted in the right kind of way with the state. Thus although Simmons' theory of authority is quite different from Raz's—Raz at no point relies on consent or any other voluntaristic notion—both theories nonetheless hold that any legitimacy that a given state possesses *qua* state depends on an aggregation of whatever distinct authority relations happen to hold between the state and each of its subjects considered one by one. Since Simmons does not think that any state, no matter how just, has received the consent of all of its subjects, he agrees with Raz that no state is every fully legitimate or, as he puts it, legitimate simpliciter. But because the state *is* legitimate for those who have consented to it, he similarly agrees with Raz that the legitimacy of the state *qua* state can be a matter of degree.

of the service conception. More precisely, the aggregative approach means that the extent of legitimate authority in a given state is a function of (1) the total number of individuals over whom, considered one by one, the state can be said to have legitimate authority and (2) the extent of legitimate authority held over each individual. The aggregative aspect goes hand-in-hand with the piecemeal approach to political authority, which suggests, in turn, that the paradigm of an authority relation is, for the service conception, precisely a case of pure expertise. But, as we saw in the preceding section, the NJT simply cannot justify political authority based on pure expertise. If, however, we adopt the view that the principal function of political authority is not to enable individuals taken one by one to better conform with right reason but that it has the function, rather, of accomplishing, in line with the task-efficacy view, important moral goals by means of a power to impose obligations, then we are likely to see the paradigmatic instances of authority as those in which the government's actions can be understood, to borrow a term from Finnis, as intended to advance the common good. As Finnis recognizes, large-scale coordination of complex activity is perhaps the best example of how the common good can be advanced.[111] Once we reject the idea that the function of political authority is to enable individuals better to conform with right reason one by one, then we are also naturally led to the view that an exercise of political authority can probably only rarely be justified by appealing solely to expertise, or at least to expertise of the kind Raz is interested in, namely, an ability to help other individuals better conform to the reasons that apply to them. At any rate we cannot say that the possession of expertise of this kind is, as the service conception would have it, a prima facie basis in and of itself for justifying legitimate authority. It is not even a basis for a limited authority to act paternalistically, since paternalism requires more in the way of substantive moral argument than the NJT can provide.

At this point, let me return to the conceptual problem that was discussed in the preceding section. As we saw there, Raz, at least in his early work, treated the NJT as the conceptual core of legitimate authority. But the requirements of the NJT—*A* has authority over *B* if *B* will do better in complying with the reasons that apply to her if she is guided by

---

[111] Finnis, *Natural Law and Natural Rights*, supra note 62, at 153.

A's directives instead of following her own judgment—are so specific that one is naturally inclined to treat it as a substantive theory of justification rather than as the general and abstract analysis of a concept. Another way to put this point is to say that the NJT seems to be a complete theory of authority in itself, which requires nothing more in the way of substantive moral argument to reach conclusions about whether a particular de facto authority is legitimate or not; it simply requires empirical data about who can assist whom in conforming with right reason.[112] The theory's conceptual framework and its substantive justificatory claims seem indistinguishable. Furthermore, the NJT's failures as a substantive justificatory theory, documented in this and the preceding section, surely disqualify it as an analysis of the concept. If the view contains within itself a method for determining when someone is a legitimate authority for someone else, and that method does not work in a wide range of cases, then the view cannot be an acceptable analysis of the concept of authority.

However, the largest failure of the NJT, considered as an exercise in conceptual analysis, concerns its aggregative aspect. If the NJT has a conceptual core, this is it. As we have seen, Raz writes that "[t]he analysis of authority [concentrates] exclusively on a one-to-one relationship between authority and a single person subject to it," and that "[i]t is an advantage of the analysis . . . that it is capable of accounting for authority over a group on the basis of authority relations between individuals."[113] This may make some sense for very limited instances of practical authority, such as that involved in the parent–child relationship. But it cannot be true that the legitimacy of large-scale, highly complex instances of government-instigated schemes of coordination and cooperation—for example, the totality of the tightly inter-related regulatory regimes governing the airline industry, ranging from the safe design of aircraft, to safety in aircraft manufacture, to the oversight of passenger security, to the provision of rules ensuring the safe and efficient operation of airports

---

[112] This is not quite right, since sometimes the value of autonomy will win out over what would otherwise constitute legitimate authority. But this concerns a *limit* on the scope of authority; it is not part of the theory of authority itself. Autonomy plays a more integral role in Raz's response to the subjection problem, which is only natural since Wolff's anarchist challenge to the rightness of subjecting one's will to another (in *any* situation, and not just the political context) is based on a very strong conception of autonomy.

[113] Raz, *The Morality of Freedom*, supra note 2, at 71.

and flights—is determined by examining the relationship of the government (or its agencies) to each and every individual involved in these
activities on a one-to-one basis and somehow combining the results into
a comprehensive judgment about the legitimacy of the enterprise as a
whole. In fact, this overstates what the NJT is capable of even in principle. The service conception provides no algorithm or formula for
"accounting for the authority over a group on the basis of authority relations between individuals"; in its terms, the NJT applies *only* to the
normative relationships between an authority and the individuals subject to it, considered one by one. There is no room for the idea of the
enterprise *as a whole* possessing legitimate authority in any sense other
than the conjunction of statements about all such relationships.

At this point, it is natural to suggest that the NJT is not the fundamental core of the concept of authority, but rather a supplementary
constraint that is to be added to, say, the value-based conception of
authority that was introduced in section III. The NJT's task would then
be to act as a filter on background reasons that can figure in a substantive justification of legitimate authority. The claim would be that the
actual substantive theory, whatever it is, must only operate with background reasons that an individual will end up better complying with.
There are a number of difficulties with this suggestion. The first is that,
as shown by the hypothetical of the person who was conscripted after
she had decided to enlist but before she had the chance to do so, there is
simply no reason to think that a person must *better* comply with relevant
background reasons, as opposed to simply *complying* with them. Second, we already *have* an appropriate filter on reasons, which ensures
precisely that people will comply with appropriate background reasons,
but which does not insist they must better comply with them. I am
referring to the political subordination thesis, which holds, it will be
recalled, that all political reasons are subordinated to political morality.
This is a substantive moral thesis which, for purposes of discussion, I am
assuming to be true. It requires that there be, in the case of the conscription hypothetical, for example, a background reason such as the duty to
contribute in appropriate ways to the collective security of one's country.
As it happens, the service conception contains a feature, in addition to
the NJT, which is quite relevant here. The "dependence thesis," which is
very close in substance to the political subordination thesis, states that
"[a]ll authoritative directives should be based, among other factors, on

reasons which apply to the subjects of the directives and which bear on the circumstances covered by the directives."[114] It is the dependence thesis, not the NJT, which is the element of the service conception that is best suited to serve the role of a constraint on background reasons. The dependence thesis is fully compatible with the task-efficacy theory, in a way that the NJT is not.

Let me turn now to the value-based conception of a moral power that I introduced in section III. According to that conception, one person *A* has a power to effect a certain kind of change in the normative situation of another person *B* if there is reason for regarding actions which *A* takes with the intention of effecting a change of the relevant kind as in fact effecting such a change, where the justification for so regarding *A*'s actions is the sufficiency of the value or desirability of enabling *A* to make this kind of normative change by means of this kind of act. One of the central claims of this chapter is that this conception of a moral power should be regarded as the conceptual core of legitimate political authority (and most other forms of practical authority). There are a number of points about the value-based conception that should be noted. First, as I have emphasized before, the claim I am making is a piece of normative/conceptual analysis;[115] it is not intended to be a substantive theory addressed to the justification problem, nor can it operate as such. It is not self-applying; further moral argument is required to determine what kinds of value (if any) will justify *A*'s possession of such a power, as well as to determine the sufficiency of that value. This information will be provided by particular substantive theories of justification. Furthermore, given the open-endedness of the value-based conception, it can, depending on one's substantive views, be supplemented by further moral theses, such as the political subordination thesis. Second, as we saw in section III, the value-based conception provides specific criteria to judge the adequacy of substantive theories. These are the value-of-intentionality and the prospectivity conditions. Together these criteria rule out, in quite decisive ways, most of the extant theories in the field, including the argument from the natural duty of justice, the fair play principle, the associative obligations theory, and the NJT.

---

[114] Raz, *Ethics in the Public Domain*, supra note 15, at 198.
[115] Cf. Raz on "normative-explanatory" accounts of concepts. *The Morality of Freedom*, supra note 2, at 64.

Third, by virtue of the fact that it begins with the idea of a normative power that the state claims to hold over all its subjects, who may well number in the millions, the value-based conception is by its very nature a top-down affair; its most natural (although admittedly not inevitable) affiliation is with substantive theories of justification that are similarly top-down.

Let me next consider how the value-based conception works with the task-efficacy theory. It should be borne in mind that the former is a conception of the concept of legitimate authority, and the latter is a substantive theory which is addressed to the justification problem. I will use Finnis's version of the task-efficacy theory for purposes of illustration. Finnis describes the general character of the theory in the following way: "Authority (and thus the *responsibility* of governing) in a community is to be exercised by those who can in fact effectively settle co-ordination problems for that community."[116] He emphasizes the singularly important role of effectiveness—the expectation that most people will obey the de facto authority's directives—as follows: "[T]he sheer fact that virtually everybody *will* acquiesce in somebody's say-so is the presumptively necessary and defeasibly sufficient condition for the normative judgment that that person has (i.e. is justified in exercising) authority in that community."[117] To begin, notice the following three points. First, as the latter quotation makes clear, the task-efficacy theory is intended *directly* to justify legitimate authority; the argument does not proceed via an intermediate conclusion to the effect that there is a general obligation to obey the law. Second, the theory meets the value-of-intentionality requirement: It is implicit in the theory that there is (instrumental) value in the fact that someone has the effective say-so—the capacity—intentionally to solve co-ordination problems (or achieve other important collective goals) simply because people can be expected to do as he says. Third, the theory meets the prospectivity condition, since, as was explained in section III, effectiveness is most naturally understood as a present expectation of future acquiescence, rather than as future acquiescence as such.[118]

---

[116] Finnis, *Natural Law and Natural Rights*, supra note 62, at 246 (emphasis in original).
[117] Ibid. at 250 (emphasis in original).
[118] See note 63 supra.

At this point it will be helpful to recall that the value-based conception of political authority insists that the value required by the theory attaches, strictly speaking, to the possession by the state of the capacity to intentionally change the normative situation of its subjects, rather than directly attaching to, say, the states of affairs that the exercise of that capacity might bring about. But instrumentalist theories of authority such as the task-efficacy view discern a systematic link between these two kinds of value, and effectiveness clearly provides just such a link: The essence of effectiveness is the sheer fact that people will generally do what the state demands, and this fact has instrumental value precisely because it puts the state in a position to pursue important moral goals, and bring about valuable states of affairs, on behalf of its subjects. If the state in fact pursues improper or evil goals, or even if it can simply be expected to pursue improper or evil goals in the future, it will lose the legitimacy that effectiveness prima facie confers (hence Finnis's stipulation that effectiveness is only a *presumptively* necessary and *defeasibly* sufficient condition for legitimate authority).

The task-efficacy theory, insofar as it looks to effectiveness as the *sole* source of value in the justification of authority, appears to advance a very stark, and indeed, by modern standards, quite radical, view of what legitimate political authority consists in. But its starkness can be softened in various ways. First, other factors can be treated as sources of value and still fall within the spirit of the theory. For example, *expertise* on the part of the authority, such as expertise in solving co-ordination problems generally, or technical expertise concerning, for example, the safe maintenance of aircraft, seems like a very plausible source of instrumental value in addition to effectiveness.[119] A similar point holds for *efficiency* in solving coordination problems. (Expertise and efficiency differ from effectiveness because the last is defined strictly in terms of an expectation of future acquiescence.) Second, the task-efficacy theory is not limited to the solution of large-scale coordination problems. Finnis's discussion focuses on such problems, which of course figure very prominently in the modern regulatory state. But the idea of an important "collective" moral goal is meant only to capture the idea that the justification of political legitimacy must begin with the state's claim to hold

---

[119] Notice that this sense of expertise is different from that presupposed by the NJT, which is strictly reason-based and comparative in nature.

authority over a *group* of persons, namely its citizens or subjects, and that its authority over individuals is determined by their membership in this group.[120] This is just another way of saying that the legitimacy of political authority must be determined non-aggregatively. In this sense, the legal protection of the individual rights of *all* citizens,[121] or the general maintenance of public order and safety, are collective moral goals that clearly fall within the purview of the task-efficacy theory.

However, these minor modifications and clarifications of the task-efficacy theory will no doubt strike many readers as failing to get at the heart of the problem, which is that there is no room in the theory's account of political legitimacy for such values as justice, say, or democracy. For purposes of illustration, let me concentrate on democracy. There is controversy about whether democracy, or, more generally, process-based values, can be taken into consideration by the NJT.[122] But it seems clear that the task-efficacy theory has no place for democratic concerns. This is where the distinction between the concept of authority, as determined by the value-based conception of a moral power, and substantive theories of political authority, such as the task-efficacy view, becomes quite important. It will be recalled that the value-based conception of political authority insists that the value required by the theory must in the first instance attach to the possession by the state of the capacity to change the normative situation of its subjects, rather than attaching to, say, the states of affairs that the exercise of that capacity might bring about. The task-efficacy theory rightly discerns a systematic connection between the value of possessing the power and the value of

---

[120] Finnis's theory of authority is clearly non-aggregative in character, since authority is claimed by the state over a *group* of persons—in Finnis's terminology, a "complete community"—and not over individuals one by one. Finnis, *Natural Law and Natural Rights*, supra note 62, at 147–53. It is in this sense that the task-efficacy theory can be said to be top-down in nature.

[121] In note 4 supra I distinguished between theories of political authority that begin with the justification of a normative power and theories that begin with the justification of the use of coercive force, and suggested that the general claims of this chapter apply to theories of both types. Ripstein's theory, which is of the second type, takes as its starting point the protection and enforcement of individual rights, where individual rights are understood as reciprocal limits on the freedom of all. In my view, his theory falls within the scope of the claims that I am making here about the nature of legitimate authority, because it clearly adopts a non-aggregative approach to the justification of authority.

[122] Raz and Enoch say that they can. See Raz, "The Problem of Authority: Revisiting the Service Conception," supra note 81, at 1030–1; Enoch, "Authority and Reason-Giving," supra note 47. Hershovitz disagrees. See Hershovitz, supra note 75.

the states of affairs that exercising the power can bring about. *But other substantive theories of legitimate authority besides the task-efficacy theory are compatible with the value-based conception, which means that there are other sources of value besides effectiveness which can attach to the capacity to change persons' normative situation.* Thus one kind of theory would find *intrinsic* value in the fact that the possessor of this capacity was democratically elected.[123] Another kind of theory would find instrumental value in this fact, in the sense that democratically-elected authorities would be considered to be more likely to make better substantive decisions.[124] (Such theories, being instrumental in character, clearly have an affinity with the task-efficacy theory.) Mixed accounts are possible: Two substantive theories, such as the task-efficacy view and the view that democracy has intrinsic value, can co-exist under the single conceptual umbrella of the value-based conception of political authority. If that is so, political legitimacy in the substantive sense might well turn out to be a very complex matter, which would be consonant with the wide range of views that we find in the literature concerning its true character.[125] In my opinion, the task-efficacy theory has an essential role to play in any plausible comprehensive account of legitimate political authority (to the extent that any such account can be given at all), but it can be combined

---

[123] My student Douglas Weck is developing a theory of political authority along these lines. Weck's view, as I understand it, is that democratic authority can resolve reasonable moral disagreement in a way that is both fair and objective, and that has intrinsic moral value because it is partially constitutive of the moral bonds between persons. I believe that Thomas Christiano also understands democratic authority as having intrinsic value, although he does not use that term. See Christiano, *The Constitution of Equality* (Oxford: Oxford University Press, 2008), 231–59. Christiano believes that what he calls "inherent" legitimate authority involves a right to rule, where a right to rule is a claim-right that is (1) associated with a power to impose obligations and (2) correlative of a limited duty on the part of citizens to obey the law; this latter duty is owed directly to the right-holder, which for Christiano is not the state as such but rather a democratic assembly. I do not believe that legitimate authority involves a claim-right that is correlative of a duty to obey the law and that is owed directly to either a democratic assembly or the state. Where a duty to obey exists, it is owed, if to anyone, to one's fellow citizens or to the community as a whole. See further supra note 49. However, it is enough for present purposes that Christiano agrees that legitimate authority involves a power to impose obligations. He believes that "a properly constituted democratic assembly" "pools" the individual rights of citizens in such a way that each "can be said to have an equal say" over matters of law and policy. Ibid. 246–7. "Having an equal say" can only be important in this way, it seems to me, if it is regarded as possessing intrinsic value.

[124] David Estlund defends a view of this sort in David M. Estlund, *Democratic Authority: A Philosophical Framework* (Princeton: Princeton University Press, 2008).

[125] Here the Hohfeldian approach to political legitimacy intersects with other approaches, of the sort briefly discussed in section I. See note 11 supra, and accompanying text.

with, or supplemented by, theories that take account of other values, including in particular that of democracy. Defending this proposition is, however, a very large project, which cannot be undertaken here.

VII. CONCLUSION

The main conclusion of this chapter is that the value-based conception of a moral power, which holds, very roughly, that one person has practical authority over another if there is sufficient value in the former person's being able intentionally to change the normative situation of the latter, is the moral and conceptual core of the concept of legitimate political authority. As we have seen, the value-based conception generates its own adequacy conditions for substantive theories of legitimate authority, namely, the value-of-intentionality and the prospectivity conditions, which rule out some substantive theories but rule in others. For the most part the chapter has addressed itself to a set of traditional problems in political philosophy, but in concluding I would like to at least cast a glance in the direction of a distinct but related branch of philosophy, namely, jurisprudence. Jurisprudence is related to political philosophy in many ways, but the one with which I am concerned here is the close relationship which clearly exists between the concept of authority and the concept of law. I would like to conclude with the perhaps overly bold suggestion that the value-based conception of a moral power is the conceptual core and perhaps—depending on one's views about descriptive versus normative jurisprudence—also the moral core both of jurisprudence and of law itself.

Rather than attempting to provide a full defense of this claim, I would like to illustrate my point with a piece of intellectual history. When Hart first introduced the distinction between primary and secondary rules in *The Concept of Law*, he wrote that "rules of the first type impose duties; rules of the second type confer powers, public or private."[126] Later in the book, however, he wrote that secondary rules "may all be said to be on a different level from the primary rules, for they are all *about* such rules."[127] It is this second idea, of secondary rules as metarules, that comes to prevail in *The Concept of Law*, and of the three kinds of secondary rules

---

[126] Hart, *The Concept of Law*, supra note 25, at 81.
[127] Ibid. 94 (emphasis in original).

that Hart mentions, it is rules of recognition that come to predominate; the other two kinds, namely, rules of change and rules of adjudication, become less salient as Hart's discussion proceeds, and eventually all but disappear from view. The result is that the rule of recognition becomes the centerpiece of Hart's theory of law, and has been the subject of intense scrutiny among philosophers of law ever since. For example, one very familiar debate concerns whether or not rules of recognition give rise, or are capable of giving rise, to obligations or to any other kind of reason for action.

A rule of recognition is of course a duty-imposing rule (in form, at least), and rules of adjudication and rules of change are power-conferring rules. I have suggested elsewhere that, because of Hart's commitment to non-cognitivism, he had to come up with a characterization of second-ary rules as social practices, and that it is much easier to do this for duty-imposing rules than for power-conferring rules.[128] Hence the role of power-conferring rules had to be downplayed, and the rule of recogni-tion took center stage. But it is far from obvious that this order of theo-retical priority is correct. Jeremy Waldron has suggested, to my mind quite plausibly, that jurisprudence might do well to abandon the con-cept of a rule of recognition altogether.[129] Whether or not that is so, the theoretical priority that Hart eventually accords to rules of recognition over power-conferring secondary rules seems to me to be clearly in ten-sion with his fundamental insight that "the introduction into society of rules enabling legislators to change and add to the rules of duty, and judges to determine when the rules of duty have been broken, is a step forward as important to society as the invention of the wheel."[130] In other words, at the foundational level of law, it is legislative and judicial powers[131] that

---

[128] See Stephen Perry, "Hart on Social Rules and the Foundations of Law: Liberating the Internal Point of View," *Fordham Law Review* 75 (2006), 1171, at 1177–1200; Perry, "Where Have All the Powers Gone: Hartian Rules of Recognition, Noncognitivism, and the Constitu-tional and Jurisprudential Foundations of Law," in M. A. Adler and K. A. Himma, *The Rule of Recognition and the U.S. Constitution* (New York: Oxford University Press, 2009), 295, at 305–18.

[129] Jeremy Waldron, "Who Needs Rules of Recognition?" in Adler and Himma, supra note 128, 327.

[130] Hart, *The Concept of Law*, supra note 25, at 41–2.

[131] Hart speaks of power-conferring *rules*, as he must given his view that the foundations of law are constituted by social rules, which in turn are constituted by social practices. In my view normative powers need not be embodied in rules (although they can be), and they certainly do not have to be constituted by social practices.

are most important, not judicial duties. My suggestion, which I cannot defend further here, is that in order to take this analysis further, we must look to the value-based conception of a moral power and to the understanding of legitimate political authority that that conception underpins.

2

How to Hold the Social Fact Thesis:
A Reply to Greenberg and Toh[1]

BARBARA BAUM LEVENBOOK

A rough approximation of the social fact thesis is that law is ultimately entirely a matter of social fact. As Greenberg points out, many judges believe that the arguments they give to defend a position on a particular point of local law are also reasons why an alleged standard *is* the valid local law. (Greenberg 2006a, p. 239) Since appeal to morality appears in such arguments from time to time, it is reasonable to suppose that judges assume that it belongs in such proofs. If the social fact thesis is untenable, this assumption may well be correct. The tendency is to think that if the social fact thesis fails, the law exists and has its content partly in virtue of moral considerations. The very presence of moral appeals in legal reasoning would then stand in need of no special warrant. The appeals needn't be something else—departures from law or gap-filling, for example—masquerading as proof of the antecedent law. Appeals to morality *qua* appeals to morality would be relevant in all legal systems. But if the social fact thesis is tenable, it becomes an open question whether appeal to morality is ever appropriate in vindicating a claim about antecedently existing law. If it is, a further question arises, namely: what warrants that appeal? Additional warrant will be needed, and its connection to social facts will require elucidation.

---

[1] I want to thank my colleagues John Carroll, Robert Mabrito, and Michael Pendlebury for very helpful suggestions on earlier drafts of this chapter.

In short, the tenability of the social fact thesis bears ultimately on how to understand—and how to do—legal reasoning and legal justification. As is well known, Dworkin's highly influential theory of law is inconsistent with the social fact thesis. He takes himself to have given a sustained argument in *Law's Empire* for his own theory and thus against all competitors, including, of course, the social fact thesis (Dworkin 2006, p. 222). That argument has been extensively criticized, and in any case cannot be evaluated here. For the purposes of this chapter, I will assume that Dworkin has not, at least not successfully, refuted a general version of the social fact thesis.

Since the publication of *Law's Empire*, Greenberg and Toh have launched transcendental arguments against important or interesting general versions of the social fact thesis. Together, Greenberg and Toh can be read as posing a dilemma for those who hold that law is ultimately a matter of social fact. Toh provides the first horn of the dilemma. Suppose that many true propositions—or, perhaps more accurately, many correct assertions—of law are normative. Then the considerations in virtue of which they are true or correct cannot ultimately be social facts, because the derivation of any normative conclusion requires a normative premise. Greenberg, who does not assume that statements of law are normative, provides the second horn of the dilemma. Suppose that true propositions of law are not normative. Still, it cannot be true that they state or are legal facts in virtue of social facts alone. For the very nature of law requires a particular kind of rational connection between that which determines legal facts and the legal facts themselves. Social facts cannot meet this demand; (non-legal) normative facts are needed. In short, Greenberg and Toh together claim that the social fact thesis is consistent with neither the existence nor the normativity of law. This is a powerful challenge, and it requires a careful refutation. That's the purpose of this chapter.

A social fact can be roughly characterized as belonging to a subspecies of descriptive fact, a species taken, by both positivists and anti-positivists alike, to exclude moral facts. This is apparently meant to hold even if, as meta-ethical naturalists maintain, moral facts are also descriptive facts. *A fortiori*, social facts are meant to exclude satisfying moral-political standards such as democratic ideals. Social facts are also meant to exclude satisfying non-moral normative standards of prudence, rationality, economics, aesthetics or welfare. In addition, it is often assumed, especially by critics of legal positivism, that social facts cannot be normative or evaluative.[2]

The structure of this chapter is as follows. In the first section, Greenberg's argument against a metaphysical version of the social fact thesis will be sketched and criticized. Greenberg targets what I call a *constitutive thesis*, which assumes that legal facts are fixed by simpler facts (their properties and relations). This thesis may be initially formulated as the claim that legal facts are fixed by (simpler) social facts alone; though obviously refinements must be made in this formulation to accommodate the position of inclusive legal positivists. Greenberg's argument against the constitutive thesis relies upon his demand for what can be called an *internal validation* of the constitutive thesis. I shall argue that Greenberg jumps to conclusions about the tenability of an external defense of any constitutive thesis, and, more importantly, that his particular demand for an internal validation of the constitutive thesis is ad hoc. His arguments in favor of this demand are seriously inadequate. I shall show that Greenberg is hoist on his own petard, as well, because adding the kind of normative facts he advocates to the base of social facts also fails to satisfy his particular requirement of internal validation.

In the second section, Toh's argument against a justificatory version of the social fact thesis will be examined and rejected. This version may be roughly characterized as follows: a genuine reason to act in accordance with the law (and a genuine obligation to do so) obtains ultimately because of social facts alone. I shall argue that Toh understands the idea of tracing reason-giving force to social facts alone in a highly artificial way in order to make his argument. He confuses a claim about tracing justification with a claim about entailment of a normative statement from premises. When the idea of tracing reason-giving force is understood differently and more naturally, Toh has no argument against a justificatory version of the social fact thesis. I argue that Toh's under-

---

[2] I will not challenge this characterization of social facts. (But see fn. 12, below.) It isn't clear just what it takes to be a normative or a non-normative *fact*. If the view is that normative facts and non-normative facts cannot be identical, the assumption should not be accepted in the social fact thesis debate without substantial argument. For it begs the question against a combination of the view that legal facts can be normative and what I shall later call the *metaphysical reduction thesis*. See the discussion, below.

standing of what the justificatory claim entails isn't a fair interpretation of the justificatory claim, and that a fairer interpretation is of philosophical interest.

GREENBERG'S TRANSCENDENTAL ARGUMENT

The heart of Greenberg's argument appears in two articles, "How Facts Make Law," and its sequel, "Hartian Positivism and Normative Facts: How Facts Make Law II." His is a transcendental argument against a general metaphysical version of the social fact thesis. Greenberg's arguments are dense, packed with special terminology, some of it familiar to students of the philosophy of mind ("rational determination," "metaphysical determination," "constitutive determination"), and presented expansively and with much elaboration. What he means by "rational determination," "metaphysical determination," "metaphysical dependency," "constitutive determination" and other key phrases may not be clear to all interested persons.[3] However, the master argument can be simplified and reconstructed as follows:

A legal fact (such as "that contracts for sale of land must be in writing"[4]) isn't metaphysically basic.[5] If a legal fact isn't metaphysically basic, it depends for its existence on more basic facts. That means that legal facts are fixed by simpler (base) facts (their properties and relations). Suppose, initially, that these base facts are social facts alone. For example, suppose that the legal facts are fixed by such things as the fact that the legislature passed a statute that has a certain plain meaning, the fact that a court issued a decision whose text has a certain plain meaning, the fact that the legislature put a preamble into or voted down an amendment to the statute that has a certain plain meaning, the practice of using a body of judicial decisions as support for legal propositions, and

---

[3] This is one of his clearer explanations of one of his terms: "To say that the A facts rationally determine the content of the law is to say something about what *makes* the content of the law what it is...." (Greenberg 2007, p. 137).

[4] Greenberg 2006b, p. 267.

[5] Greenberg is making the assumption that there are legal facts. He further assumes they are true propositions about law, stating the content of laws (Greenberg 2006c, 114). Those who assume that (many) laws are norms and take certain views about normativity will not agree that assertions of the content of (these) laws amount to true propositions. Hence, I have treated Greenberg's arguments as the second horn of a dilemma, although he may regard his arguments as sufficient even if laws are norms.

so on.[6] Then we might imagine that there is a correct function, or mapping, from these base social facts to the content of law. This function will trace how social facts like these interact to produce specific legal content. But there must be an explanation of why this is the function that counts, rather than an alternative[7] (Greenberg 2006a, p. 231). That explanation must be in terms of reason. As judicial argumentation seems to demonstrate and clearly assumes, law has a close connection to responsiveness to reasons. Law is in some way reason-apt.[8] It follows that it cannot be just a "brute fact" that such-and-such social facts result in a law whose content is so-and-so. The content of law must be reasonable or sensible in relation to its base. That is, it must make sense when we focus on specific base facts that a particular proposition about law, and not its contradictory or contrary, is true. But no function from a base of social facts alone to the content of law can be shown to have this feature. Hence, the base facts are not confined to social facts, and the social fact thesis is untenable.[9]

Two clarifications are in order. Greenberg targets what I call the (social fact) *constitutive thesis*, which holds that legal facts are fixed by social facts alone (ultimately, if not proximately).[10] The first clarificatory point

---

[6] Greenberg makes assumptions about social facts which result in a narrower view of social facts—e.g. the fact that the legislature passed a statute is not counted by Greenberg as a social fact unless a legislature passing a statute itself obtains solely in virtue of complex social facts (Greenberg 2006a, p. 235; 2006b, p. 267 fn 9). Perhaps the same goes for the fact that a statute has a certain "plain meaning"; it is not a social fact unless the meaning and grammar rules of a language obtain in virtue of complex social facts. Greenberg seems prepared to grant that *if* the provisos are met, the complex fact that the legislature passed a statute that has a certain plain meaning counts as a social fact. He denies that the antecedent is met, however.

[7] A special case of this point is that there must be an explanation of why the correct function isn't a "bent" one (e.g. whereby some practice of deferring to, say, an administrative agency's interpretation of a given statute fixes its application to some cases but not to cases when the agency is headed by someone born on the day of Lincoln's birthday). Greenberg concludes from consideration of bent functions that (the social fact of) practices of tracing specific legal content from particular social facts cannot supply the explanation that excludes bent functions (Greenberg 2006a, pp. 248–51).

[8] This is my way of putting the matter, not Greenberg's.

[9] Greenberg goes on to argue that what is missing is consideration of (non-legal) normative facts, such as fairness or welfare. See text, below.

[10] Greenberg assigns this view to Raz 1979, Hart 1994, Shapiro 1998, Coleman 2001, and Himma 2002 (Greenberg 2006c, 114 fn. 4). Coleman is unquestionably an inclusive legal positivist, and Himma has extensively defended the view. If an inclusive legal positivist held the picture of explaining legal facts by simpler base facts, he or she would say that the type of base facts by appeal to which we can account for legal facts varies, depending on the legal system. In *some possible* legal system, the base facts are social facts. In other possible legal systems,

is that this kind of fixing, or metaphysical determining, might be thought of, roughly, as an *in-virtue-of* relation.[11] States of affairs obtain and objects exist and have properties in virtue of something, such as different states of affairs or different properties those objects possess. An in-virtue-of relation holds in all possible worlds. The relation is assumed to be asymmetric. (It has more characteristics, and there are debates about precisely which ones, but we need not go into these deep waters.)

Second, the social fact constitutive thesis isn't the only kind of metaphysical social fact thesis. I've initially characterized the social fact thesis as holding that law is ultimately entirely a matter of social fact. However, "a matter of" language obscures the difference between several claims. One of them may be called the *metaphysical reduction thesis,* or MR for short. Suppose that there are legal facts. According to MR, there isn't a difference in metaphysical levels between a legal fact and certain social facts. Legal facts are "entirely constituted," as other reductivists sometimes say, by complex social facts. One who ascribes to MR is not making a claim about an asymmetric explanatory in-virtue-of relation. Instead, the MR proponent holds that for legal facts, there is "nothing over and above" certain social facts. Such a thesis can be ascribed to Austin and Bentham, both of whom defined "a law," somewhat implausibly, in terms of a complex social fact about commands and sanctions.[12]

the base facts include non-legal normative facts. Inclusive legal positivists do not claim, and may well deny, that these normative facts obtain in virtue of social facts. However, the explanation of why such facts are included in the base appeals ultimately only to social facts.

[11] Greenberg contends that the fixing he has in mind isn't the in-virtue-of-relation, but then says that the fixing in the constitutive thesis is an "at least in part in virtue of" relation (Greenberg 2006a, p. 227, fn 8). I will ignore this complication in what follows, except to say that it's doubtful that a social fact thesis is designed to be as strong as the claim that legal facts exist solely in virtue of social facts. For on Greenberg's account, by saying that social facts alone fix the content of laws, one denies that synthetic necessary truths are necessary for the existence of legal facts (Greenberg 2006c, 114, fn. 6). It is doubtful that any social fact theorist wishes to make such a claim. He might say, however, that social facts, *along with* necessary truths, fix the content of laws (ultimately, if not proximately), or that social facts are the only sorts of *facts* that fix the content of laws.

[12] There is language in Hart's seminal work, *The Concept of Law,* which appears to identify the rule of recognition, the ultimate legal norm, with a different complex social fact, a social practice among officials, although whether this language represents his considered view is a matter of dispute (H. L. A. Hart 1994, pp. 109, 110). Coleman adds Ross to the list of legal positivists who are metaphysical reductivists (Coleman 1998, 397). Coleman denies that Hart is a reductivist concerning the rule of recognition (Coleman 2001, p. 77). Kelsen, as Green points out, rejected any sort of reduction of law to social fact (Green 2003).

Recall that Greenberg contends that any constitutive theory must explain *why* just this base fact fixes just that legal fact, rather than some other legal fact or some non-legal fact or nothing further (Greenberg 2007, p. 133). One of his ways of putting the point is to say that constitutive theories of law are subject to a requirement of "rational intelligibility" (Greenberg 2006b, p. 268; 2006c, 116). An analogous demand could not be placed on a metaphysical reduction theory of law. As Kim puts it, "Identities eliminate the logical space within which explanatory questions can be formulated" (Kim 2003, p. 570). If the identity between a particular legal fact and a particular social fact holds, it would be a brute fact that just this legal fact is identical with just this social fact. One cannot argue against the possibility of this brute fact by maintaining, as Greenberg does, that legal facts aren't metaphysically basic while also assuming that all social facts are more metaphysically basic. That begs the question against the metaphysical reduction thesis.

There is an uncontroversial idea that could be called "explicability," or even "rational intelligibility," that *can* be accommodated by a proponent of MR. Reductions have reductive theses. The success of any particular reductivist enterprise requires that the reductive thesis advanced be true or at least plausible. One might say that it should "stand to reason" that the thesis in question is true or at least plausible. One could contend, then, that any acceptable specific reductive thesis (that facts of this type described in legal language are identical to facts of that type described in non-legal and non-normative language) must be rationally intelligible. Call this *theory rational intelligibility.*[13] Further, we are entitled to demand that a reductivist thesis be defended; the thesis, cannot, in the end, be merely asserted to be a brute fact.

Defending a specific reductive thesis is, however, consistent with maintaining that the connection between any particular law L and its associated social fact Q is brute, because it is identity. It follows that, even if successful, Greenberg's argument cannot be credited with refuting

One holding MR who thought legal facts were normative could not accept the characterization of social facts as descriptive and Greenberg's characterization of descriptive facts as "non-normative" (Greenberg 2006a, pp. 225, 234; 2006b, p. 265). MR explains legal facts in terms of social facts described in non-legal and non-normative language to which legal facts, or some norms identifying legal facts, are alleged to be identical. It is the *language* describing the social facts to which legal facts are reduced that is non-legal and non-normative, not the social-legal facts themselves.

[13] I am indebted to my colleague John Carroll for this line of thinking.

the metaphysical version of the social fact thesis, but rather, one sub-version of it, the social fact constitutive thesis. Nonetheless, it is an important version, and it's fair to regard it as a central version.[14]

The reflections on MR illustrate the first real difficulty with Green-berg's argument against the social fact constitutive thesis. For something similar can be said about theory rational intelligibility for a social fact constitutive thesis. When a legal fact, such as that contracts for sale of land must be in writing, is explained by appeal to social facts, the appeal relies on a theory that social facts of that sort ground legal facts of that sort (in just this way). The general theory stands in need of defense, but if it is successfully defended, the theory is made rationally intelligible. The particular connection between a legal fact (e.g. that contracts for sale of land must be in writing) and social facts in virtue of which it is a legal fact is not inexplicable or opaque, because it follows from the theory. We understand that it cannot be anything else that's the legal fact in virtue of these particular social facts, and we understand why. Given, for example, the statute on the matter, and given a lot of other social facts, and given the truth of the theory, it can't be the case in this particular legal system that contracts for sale of land need not be in writing. It must be the case that they are required to be.

Greenberg acknowledges the point (Greenberg 2006a, pp. 254–5), but assumes that such a philosophical defense cannot be found. He selects Hart's theory of law, on the ground that it has been highly influential, interprets it as a constitutive theory, and launches a series of criticisms of it (Greenberg 2006b). Evaluating Greenberg's criticisms of Hart would take this discussion too far afield. The obvious point is that even if his criticisms were successful, his assumption that there can be no philosophical defense of any social fact constitutive theory would be under-motivated and inadequately defended.

The appeal to theory rational intelligibility is an appeal, one might say, to an *external validation* of a theory's reasonableness. In the alleged

[14] "Legal positivism is the thesis that the existence and content of law depends on social facts and not on its merits" (Green 2003). See also Shapiro 2007, p. 33: "The second thesis, [of traditional legal positivism] sometimes known as the "Social Fact Thesis," holds that the existence and content of the law are ultimately determined by certain facts about social groups." And see Dworkin's characterization of legal positivism, that "law exists only in virtue of some human act or decision" (Dworkin 1977, p. 70).

absence of an external validation of a social fact constitutive thesis, Greenberg, as I've indicated, demands an internal validation. The second difficulty with Greenberg's argument is that a social fact theory has resources that may achieve one sort of internal validation. A constitutive theory can identify intermediary facts (e.g. social rules or social institutions) fixed by the base descriptive facts yet in turn, perhaps with further social facts, fixing the legal facts (again, along with necessary truths). (These intermediary facts might be considered to be more complex social facts. They might be considered to be legal facts. Their classification does not matter for present purposes.) If, in addition, each of the subsidiary determining relations is individually more intuitive, or more plausible, or more easily defended, than the leap from the ultimate base facts to the target legal facts, the latter relation is made intelligible.[15] Developing the particulars of a constitutive thesis might, in short, supply this kind of explanation. That there has been failure to date would be sharply contended by some legal philosophers. Moreover, failure to date is not a sufficient reason to abandon the enterprise. Greenberg is not entitled to assume that no social fact constitutive theory can provide an internal validation of the connection between the content of a particular law and some particular base social facts.

The strategy envisaged, even if successful, would be rejected by Greenberg. He insists on a particular sort of internal validation in a constitutive theory: the connection between the alleged base facts and legal facts is to be explained *entirely by* the base facts. This demand is expressed in obscure language,[16] but the idea seems to be that the base facts jointly must wear their relevance to legal content on their faces. It would have to be clear to reason, *just* by examining the total set of relevant base facts, why they "make the contribution they do" to specific legal content (Greenberg 2007, p. 133).

---

[15] The resulting picture needn't be simple. There may be several layers of intermediate facts, and at each point, additional descriptive facts added to create the next layer. If the explanatory power of such a view can be demonstrated, especially its explanatory superiority, that may be all that is needed to avoid the appearance of a mysterious or arbitrarily postulated brute-fact connection.

[16] "[T]he constitutive determinants must constitute *reasons* why the legal facts obtain" (Greenberg 2006b, p. 268). "What the rational-relation requirement demands is not higher-order reasons, but determining facts that together provide reasons for the legal facts" (Greenberg 2006b, p. 271).

Greenberg points out, correctly, that non-legal, non-normative social facts cannot satisfy this demand. However, there is no need for them to do so. The most important objection to Greenberg's argument against the constitutive version of the social fact thesis is that this demand is *ad hoc*.[17] Such a requirement would be an implausible demand on a claim about, say, what fixes mental states (as it precludes claims, reductive or otherwise, about the metaphysical dependency of mental states on physical states), as Greenberg is aware and happy to admit. We are entitled to be shown why the matter should be different with respect to law.

Greenberg takes himself to do so, but fails. He contends that the need for this special kind of internal validation, this strong sense of being reason-based, is built into "our ordinary understanding "of law (Greenberg 2006a, pp. 231–2). This is a pivotal part of his case against the constitutive version of the social fact thesis, yet his arguments for this claim are few and underdeveloped. There is a short argument that begins with the observation that everyone working out the content of law gives reasons for their conclusions. Greenberg then contends that participants believe they are doing more than giving reasons for belief, more than using heuristic devices. Instead, they take themselves, at least when correct, to be citing the reasons that make the legal content what it is (Greenberg 2006a, p. 239). Suppose he is correct that at least some of the reasons given in legal argumentation are taken to be reasons why law has specific content. It does not follow that what is cited ever constitutes an account of *why* it is what determines specific content, or that it is taken to do so, or that it is expected to do so.

It is true that in legal argumentation, if someone claims that law has a particular content, he can be challenged to defend the view—that is, to give a reason. We should be wary of talking of what is part of *our* ordinary understanding of any concept, as intuitions often vary deeply. However, let us grant, for the sake of argument, that it is part of our ordinary understanding of law that a claim of law is defense-apt, reason-apt in some sense. But it's a long way from the observation that a claim of law is defense-apt to the contention that considerations that could be given in defense must make it clear why, how—or even that—they are the considerations that wholly set the content. There is nothing in legal

---

[17] Despite Greenberg's assertions to the contrary (Greenberg 2006a, pp. 231–2; Greenberg 2006b, p. 267).

argumentation or legal practice that establishes that requirement,[18] and it is not entailed by the demand to defend a contentious claim about the content of law.

In short, the argumentative nature of legal discourse provides no reason to believe that it is part of "our" ordinary understanding of law that legal content claims must be true in virtue of considerations that together wear their specific metaphysical relevance on their faces.

Greenberg also provides this passage:

In general, the large body of legal theory that has explored the question of whether law practices are capable of rendering the law determinate... presupposes that law practices determine the content of law in a reason-based way. If the relation between law practices and the content of the law could be opaque, any set of law practices would be capable, as far as we would be able to judge, of determining any set of legal propositions.[19]

Unfortunately, all that one is entitled to conclude from the "large body of legal theory" is that it presupposes that law practices determine the content of law in a way that is *rationally discoverable*, and that claims about this determination are *rationally defensible*—i.e. not arbitrary—on the basis of a theory that is itself rationally intelligible, or defensible. These presuppositions are also all one needs to avoid the kind of opacity Greenberg is describing in this passage. That determination of law content is rationally discoverable and that theories should be rationally defensible are uncontroversial assumptions; alleged presuppositions using any other sense of "reason-based" in Greenberg's passage is not. One can't generalize to other ways of being reason-based (e.g. being self-explanatory) from any of the above concessions.

The problem is not merely that the demand for Greenberg's particularly strong form of internal validation of a constitutive thesis is inadequately defended. The demand is something that he and others who reject the social fact constitutive thesis ought to hope is indefensible. For social facts are not the only candidates to fail to satisfy this demand. Let us assume, for the moment, that there are such things as normative

---

[18] For example, when reasons given in legal argumentation are challenged as not dispositive or not appropriate, the grounds are rarely, if ever, that they don't wear their metaphysical relevance to legal content on their face.

[19] Greenberg 2006a, pp. 239–40.

facts, and allow for the possibility that the legal facts that Greenberg discusses—the ones that are fixed by base facts—may themselves turn out to be normative. Then we can say that non-legal normative facts also fail to satisfy Greenberg's demand for internal validation, and for the same reason.[20] The irony is that Greenberg proposes to solve the problem of showing the reasonableness of the connection between base facts and legal facts by adding non-legal normative facts to the base. Legal facts, he argues, are partly fixed by non-legal normative facts such as fairness (Greenberg 2006b, pp. 275–6), stability, "values of democracy," or "special value facts" relative to particular legal systems (Greenberg 2006b, p. 258; 2006c, 127).[21] On the surface, appealing to fairness, for example, may appear to explain its own role, assuming it has a role, in fixing legal content, and by extension, the role of any practice fairness supports.[22] Suppose someone makes a legal content claim, C, about the law of a particular legal system. We ask, "Why is the legal content C?" and are told, "C is only fair, given this statute's plain meaning (and certain other practices, such as the practice of relying on plain meaning in the past)." That may look like an explanation, indeed, a particularly full explanation. But further examination reveals that it does not explain why what's only fair, given the statute's plain meaning, helps to determine positive law's content.

Greenberg tries to use Davidson's radical interpretation theory of mind to show that we can explain something—in that case, the attribution of beliefs and desires to an individual—by appealing to normative facts.[23] One is invited to draw the conclusion that normative facts have or at least add explanatory power. But this is an unsuccessful argument, even if Greenberg is correctly presenting Davidson's views on mental states. It is true that for Davidson, the physical constituents of beliefs and desires cannot constitute beliefs and desires of an individual unless they jointly meet some minimal (normative) standards of rationality.[24]

---

[20] In this contention, I seem to be agreeing with an earlier critic of Greenberg. The assumption at there are non-legal normative facts, such as moral facts, would be rejected by some moral philosophers (e.g. Hare).

[21] "On the face of it, facts about how law practices should contribute to the content of the law make rationally intelligible how the law practices do contribute to the content of the law" (Greenberg 2006b, p. 285).

[22] *Pace* Greenberg's claim quoted in n. 21. This claim, I argue in the text, is false.

[23] Greenberg 2006b, pp. 286–7.

[24] I'm indebted to Michael Pendlebury for the explanation of Davidson.

However, this won't help Greenberg. There is the normative fact that a certain assigned mental content under certain conditions makes a specific person's behavior more intelligible. If this normative fact helps to determine mental content, it doesn't follow that why or how this fact and others determine the mental content has been made intelligible.[25] What is needed, at the minimum, is a theory to tell us how this normative fact helps fix the mental content. At this stage of explanation, the theory's assertions operate as brute fact. Pressing matters further requires demonstrating why this theory is true or is a better theory than one that does not draw a connection between normative facts and mental content.[26] This is a demonstration of theory rational intelligibility.

Similarly, if fairness is a determinant of legal content in legal systems, *saying* that a law has the content it does in virtue, in part, of (the) fairness (of taking, for example, the plain meaning of a promulgated statute as the content of the law it lays down) doesn't make the relationship between the alleged base facts and specific legal content rationally intelligible. That requires reasons why the fairness of taking the statute that way is, happily, the way the statute creates legal content; it requires, in other words, a defense of a theory of legal content assigning fairness that role (as a necessary truth). For the kind of rational transparency Greenberg wants, in other words, theory rational intelligibility is as indispensable with respect to a claim that non-legal normative facts help to fix the content of law as it is with respect to the constitutive version of the social fact thesis.

Another way of expressing the point is as follows. Fairness, welfare, and the like are uncontroversially reasons for creating legal content of a

---

[25] Oddly, Greenberg seems aware of this point (Greenberg 2006b, p. 287, fn. 56).

[26] One who believes in the existence of normative facts can say that one alleges a normative fact of some sort when one alleges that a theory is the best theory of mental states. Analogously, one alleges a normative fact of some sort when one alleges that a social fact constitutive theory is the best theory of legal facts. A social fact theorist may consistently maintain that the successful defense of a theory's rational intelligibility entails this kind of normative claim—further, that this kind of normative claim entails that some successful defense or other is possible. In this way, the claim that it is the best theory of legal facts adds some explanatory power to an alleged connection between legal facts and social facts. But Greenberg is not addressing the issue of normative facts *about* constitutive theories of law (which would be involved in external validation). He is addressing the alleged role (or, rather, lack of role) of normative facts *within* constitutive theories of law. And for this task, Davidson's views on mental states are of no use.

certain kind in the first place. They wear their *justificatory* relevance to law or intended law or legal procedures on their face. Yet fairness and the like are not, *on their face*, reasons for the legal content being what it is, given that law is a social artifact; and that is a failing they share with social facts.[27] Having that feature is precisely what Greenberg is demanding. My point is not to criticize Greenberg for failing to establish the rational intelligibility of an alternate constitutive theory of law, one that assigns non-legal normative facts to the base. My point is that the explanatory force of citing non-legal normative facts is neither self-evident nor, if one has certain positivist intuitions, attractive or plausible, and thus cannot meet Greenberg's own demands.

In short, according to Greenberg, what are needed are reasons that are *prima facie* or self-evidently jointly explanatorily relevant to law's actual content. Non-legal normative facts, like social facts, cannot meet this demand; nor can the addition of non-legal normative facts to social facts meet this demand. This makes Greenberg's insistence on the demand itself tactically inexplicable.

I have maintained that Greenberg's argument against the constitutive thesis version of the social fact thesis fails primarily because it relies on a demand for a particularly strong kind of internal validation of the rationality of any constitutive theory, and that this demand is undefended and cannot be satisfied by his alternative constitutive theory of law or others that use non-legal normative facts in the base. I conclude that the demand is *ad hoc*. It follows that Greenberg's transcendental argument supplies no grounds for rejecting the social fact constitutive thesis.

TOH'S ARGUMENT

Greenberg's argument against the social fact thesis is careful not to rely upon any assumptions about whether law is normative or the nature of

---

[27] Greenberg asserts that "the determinants of the content of the law must include reasons why law practices make the contribution that they do to the content of the law" (Greenberg 2007, p. 133, note omitted). This claim doesn't follow from his arguments. Moreover, fairness isn't this kind of reason unless the theory that it is is the best theory of legal content. Greenberg isn't entitled to assume that it is, for that would be begging the question against the social fact constitutive thesis.

such normativity, but Toh's argument[28] is the reverse. He relies on assumptions on both points.

Toh follows Hart in recognizing both external and internal statements of law. He assumes that internal statements are normative in a very strong sense. They "purport to proffer" reasons for action.[29] From this crucial premise, the argument proceeds as follows: If an internal statement is vindicated, it must really proffer reasons for action. But from statements about non-normative social facts alone, nothing follows (deductively) that proffers a genuine reason for action. There must be a conditional premise in any such derivation whose antecedent is a statement of social fact and whose consequent is the (normative) internal statement. That conditional premise is either analytic or a norm, and it isn't analytic, so it must be a norm. Hence, from statements about non-normative social facts (and analytic truths) alone, no internal legal statement deductively follows. Hence, internal legal statements cannot be vindicated on the basis of social facts alone. Hence, the social fact thesis is false for internal legal statements.

Toh targets a justificatory version of the social fact thesis, which may be stated as follows: a genuine reason to act in accordance with the law (and a genuine obligation to do so) obtains ultimately because of social facts alone. Call this *the social fact justificatory thesis*. Unfortunately, his argument fails to refute this thesis.

First, a minor correction is in order. Internal legal statements are supposed to be statements of law made "from the point of view" of committed participants in the legal system. The assumption is that internal statements of law are normative in the very strong sense that they "purport to proffer" genuine reasons for action. This is much too crude a characterization, since it is applicable, at best, to only some normative legal statements—namely, statements of requirement and

---

[28] I mean throughout what Toh calls his "formal argument." He also produces an informal one. It is meant to show that for all normative statements, a norm must be part of its justification. It can be ignored here for many reasons, not the least of which is that the reply to the formal argument sufficiently replies to the informal one.

[29] Moreover, the reasons purportedly proffered are reasons of a certain strength, which Toh refers to as *deontic reasons*. They entail a genuine obligation. Construed in this way, Toh is joining the discussion of the alleged failure of legal positivism to account for duty-imposing laws creating genuine obligations. For the sake of simplicity, I will set aside the complications introduced by the idea of obligation in what follows.

prohibition—and not others.[30] No doubt the former is all that is intended in the discussion, but it is well to be clear at the outset. The second clarification is more important. The claim that internal legal statements proffer reasons for action is ambiguous. One sense of it will not help Toh, and should be set aside. This is the claim that (these) normative legal statements have some strong connection to proffering genuine reasons for action through the *activity* of making the statement. Consider an idea from the philosophy of language, the distinction between semantics and pragmatics. It is undeniable that at least sometimes legal officials and practitioners utter statements of legal requirement or legal prohibition under circumstances where it is also clear that the utterers believe there is a genuine reason for action in accordance with the law. One might hold that in the activity of uttering these statements—that is, through the pragmatics of legal language, rather than the semantics—the message about genuine reason is delivered. In, for example, uttering "Aing is illegal," utterers deliver the message that the addressee has a genuine reason not to A. One might explain this

---

[30] Many legal statements, made by committed persons from their point of view—e.g. "Consent is a defense to battery," "At common law, the finder of abandoned property may possess it,"—do not in any sense proffer reasons for action in accordance with them. These statements can perhaps be thought of as stating the absence of legal norms (e.g. "There is no legal duty to refrain from battery of a consenting adult," "The finder has no legal duty to possess and no legal duty to refrain from possessing abandoned property"), but we wouldn't want to conclude that they are not normative themselves, on pain of introducing an artificially restricted idea of normativity. (I've used here Raz's analysis of what he calls *weak permissions* (Raz 1990, p. 97). Toh lists among "deontic" reasons reasons of permissions (Toh 2008, 456).) Certain legal rights statements also express no reasons to act. For example, Rex Martin offers this example: "Americans have a constitutional right to free speech." Those who engage in constitutionally-protected free speech have an immunity because Congress lacks the authority to prohibit or require certain speech. Even if somehow talk about Congress could be translated into talk about reasons for members of Congress, *qua* members, to do or not do something, it is not true that the Constitution gives members of Congress a reason not to enact such laws. They simply cannot do so (Martin 2002, p. 120). [Having a right or a defense to battery might entail that someone, say a judge, has a duty under certain conditions to do certain things, such as dismiss a lawsuit or direct a verdict for the defendant. But the relevant statements do not mean such a thing. There are many conditional duties (not to mention a few permissions) that follow from these statements. Even if an antecedent of a conditional manages to list all of the conditions under which all of the (correlative) duties obtain, the result is not a claim of a reason to act.] Perhaps these consitutional rights statements, too, can be thought of as stating a combination of the absence of normative requirements and prohibitions and an absence of a normative power on the part of Congress to create certain laws. But do we really want to restrict the notion of normativity so that the rights statements aren't normative? Nothing seems to be gained by doing so.

phenomenon by holding that there is a separable illocutionary force whereby the speaker purports to proffer genuine reasons for action, just as there is an illocutionary force whereby the speaker promises. Then one can say that a reason utterances such as "Aing is illegal" sometimes— or even typically, if you like—are linked to a proffering of reasons is that in uttering "Aing is illegal" (in their official role) legal officials sometimes—or even characteristically—perform the illocutionary act (consisting of a core content uttered with illocutionary force) of proffering (what is presented as) genuine reasons for action.

Alternatively, one offering a legal pragmatics can borrow Grice's idea of implicature, which is the idea that sometimes because of the conversational context and sometimes because of convention, by uttering one message, the speaker communicates another. The view will be that there are contexts in which utterances declaring a norm, N, to be legally valid or to be "the law" communicate the message that there are genuine reasons to conform to N. An example of such a context would be when someone is trying to justify his demand that you conform to N, or justify his own actions in conformity to it, and offers as the sole reason that N is the law. This is just the sort of thing Toh focuses on as a central "use" (his term) of legal statements (Toh 2008, 455, 459–60).

These pragmatics accounts establish a connection between some legal statements (delivered on some occasions) and purporting to proffer genuine reasons for action. But I take Toh as intending something stronger, as relying on the premise that internal legal statements have proffering reasons for action as part of their *semantic* content. He needs this premise in order to have proffering genuine reasons for action cause trouble for a claim about what justifies normative legal statements, where justification is conceived of as the deduction of normative legal statements independent of their conversational contexts. For on a pragmatics account, the justification of the propositional core of the message comes apart from the justification of the entire message or the illocutionary act itself. Deducing the former isn't deducing the latter.[31]

---

[31] Appropriate adjustments could be made in the argument that follows for the assumption that Toh intends to take normative statements only in conversational contexts—e.g. as those with the implicature that there is a genuine reason for action. He might then hold that a statement with this implicature is justified only when the statement is true and there is a genuine reason for action. Then he might interpret the social fact justificatory thesis as holding that a statement with this implicature can be justified solely on the basis of social facts (and analytic truths) alone.

What supports the premise that internal legal statements have proffering reasons for action as part of their content? Toh's discussion suggests he reasons as follows: because internal legal statements are normative, they proffer a reason-giving force quite independent of their context of utterance (Toh 2008, 447, 472). This argument relies in turn on a substantive, and controversial, philosophical assumption about normativity for which Toh does not argue—namely, that all norms, or all correct norms, of requirement or prohibition must have as part of their *semantic* meaning that one has a reason to comply with them (Toh 2008, 472, 475). It follows that the normativity of law is to be explained along the lines of the normativity of moral norms, that is, as critical normativity.[32] Arguing about the nature of normativity in general or legal normativity in particular will take us too far afield. Let us grant, for the sake of argument, that laws are norms and that defending a normative legal statement, which we may call an *internal legal statement*, is justifying it in a way that shows that there is a genuine reason to act in accordance with it. In other words, let us grant the controversial premise in question. Assume that there is no showing that such an internal legal statement is correct or true without establishing that there is a reason to comply with it (and there is an obligation to comply with it).[33]

What should *not* be granted is a further assumption Toh makes: that the social fact justificatory thesis is making a claim about deduction.[34] He interprets the claim that normative legal statements (that purport to proffer reasons for action) are vindicated, or justified, ultimately on the basis of social facts alone as entailing the claim that such statements can

---

[32] As opposed to what Shiner calls "positive" normativity of law. See Shiner 2010, p. 432.

[33] Toh claims another warrant for his assumption: members of a select group of legal positivists who are his target (namely, Raz and Coleman) assume that some legal statements have as part of their semantic meaning purporting to proffer genuine reasons for action, and so does Hart. The exegetical case cannot be evaluated here, but it can be made. Raz (1979, p. 155) recognizes "committed" internal legal statements. In some of his writings, Coleman picks up the notion. Although Toh cites Green, he misses this passage: Green (2008, 1049) says: "judges speak as if their orders create reasons for their subjects to conform in the first instance, not merely reasons to conform if they happen to be followed by a further conviction for contempt, obstruction, or resisting arrest.... [L]egal obligations...purport to be categorical reasons for acting." Toh cites similar language by Marmor (2001, p. 25).

[34] Toh does not make this assumption about every sort of deduction of a normative claim. He makes it about deductions that proceed from statements of "the considerations *in virtue of* which the relevant...claim is correct or true" (Toh 2008, 446, my emphasis), from appeals "to considerations that generate or engender the normative force of that normative claim" (Toh 2008, 465).

be deduced from premises consisting of statements of social fact and analytic truths alone.

Once deduction is assumed to be at stake, it becomes difficult to resist Toh's conclusion. For Toh is correct that a conditional that links a statement of social fact to an internal legal statement (understood as a norm) is necessary in order to validly deduce the latter from the former. He argues persuasively against Searle and others that the conditional cannot be analytic if its antecedent is a factual statement and its consequent is a genuine norm. One line of this further argument invokes the possibility of disagreement over the truth of the conditional statement and the intelligibility of refusing to regard the disputants as confused about meanings of key terms (Toh 2008, 476–7). A more sophisticated argument points to our inferential practices of supporting such a conditional by appeal to substantive norms and alleges that holding that the conditional is a substantive claim is the best explanation of that practice (Toh 2008, 477).[35] It follows that no statement that social facts obtain can entail an internal legal statement. It is not possible to deduce an internal legal statement solely from statements of social facts along with analytic truths.

However, there are good reasons *not* to assume that what is at issue in the social fact justificatory thesis is a deduction. The weakest reason is that Toh cannot afford to do so. This assumption might be used to prove what Toh doesn't want it to, namely that there are *no* legal statements that can be vindicated on the basis of social facts (and analytic truths) alone.[36] Toh initially equates justifying a legal claim with providing "the considerations in virtue of which the relevant legal claim is correct or true" (Toh 2008, 445–6).[37] If providing such considerations can be accomplished for internal legal statements through valid deductions, it can be accomplished for external legal statements through valid

---

[35] In addition, at one point, Toh invokes the idea that statements of social fact don't have proffering reasons for action as part of their content, but normative statements do. (See, e.g., Toh 2008, 472).

[36] Toh thinks that "the social fact thesis" is plausible for external legal statements (Toh 2008, 447, 453). Tracing the vindication of external legal statements the way he traces the vindication of internal legal statements puts his argumentative strategy into tension with his own philosophical views.

[37] He later says that the kind of justification of a normative claim that he has in mind provides "considerations that generate or engender the normative force of that normative claim" (Toh 2008, 465).

deductions. However, by reasoning analogous to Toh's, an external legal statement (L) cannot be deduced from a statement of social fact (Q) alone. There must be a premise in the form of a conditional linking Q to L (of the form "if Q then L"). To save some form of the social fact thesis as he understands it, Toh must hold that this conditional is either a statement of a social fact itself or is analytic. However, that claim is vulnerable to doubts like those raised by his arguments against the analyticity of the conditional required for deduction of internal legal statements. The conditional is not a statement of a social fact; our inferential practices in disagreements about conditionals of this sort do not appeal primarily to evidence. So Toh must hold that it is analytic. However, specific conditionals for external legal statements have been challenged on the grounds that denying them is not, in the relevant sense, unintelligible. (Indeed, Greenberg takes just such a line with a conditional that can be constructed for Hart's theory (Greenberg 2006b, pp. 281–2).) Attempts to come up with a relevant conditional that no one can deny on pain of conceptual confusion or unintelligibility have been unpersuasive to date. Toh is not entitled to assume that there are correct analytic conditionals, and so, not entitled to assume that it is possible to deduce an external legal statement solely from statements of social facts along with analytic truths.

Moreover, despite the language of analyzing the concept of law sometimes employed in them, philosophical positions that have implied a conditional of the form "If Q, then L" appear to be allegedly informative, and to be in need of serious philosophical argument, in a way at odds with the idea of the analyticity of this conditional. More cannot be made of this point without greater discussion of analyticity than is warranted here, but it is safe to conclude that taking deduction to be at issue is problematic in a claim that justification of external legal statements is solely based on social facts (and analytic truths). The second reason to resist the deduction model is, in short, that it is problematic no matter what sort of legal statement one thinks there can be—Toh's committed internal, Raz's detached internal, or external.

The third reason, and the one that I will emphasize, to resist understanding the justification claim as entailment is that it isn't a fair reading of the social fact justificatory thesis. For on this reading, the problems to be surmounted in order for the social fact justificatory thesis to be true are twofold: first, there must be correct, or true, conditionals linking a social fact statement and a legal statement; and second, they must have the right status—namely, analyticity. It won't be a fair reading of the thesis if there is a reasonable alternative interpretation on which the social fact justificatory thesis is a less problematic view. I turn now to argue that there is.

Toh takes the social fact justificatory thesis to be embedded in, and to motivate, a project undertaken recently (and in some cases, abandoned even more recently) by self-declared legal positivists of tracing reasons to act in conformity with laws to collective agency, conventions, or the solving of coordination problems (all of them allegedly analyzable into a set of social facts and relations).[38] He is objecting to this project, and convinced that in it "the social fact thesis" has been extended too far. Indeed, he takes this project to be central to the concerns of anyone who holds the social fact thesis.[39] However, a natural interpretation of the common theme of this project, weaker than Toh's entailment version, is the following: A legal norm can be justified in its reason-giving (and perhaps even obligation-giving) status on the basis, ultimately, of social facts alone.[40] Call this the *justification basis claim.*

The justification basis claim is *not* a claim about entailment. Justification, like causal explanation, is context-sensitive, varying with the practical interests of the inquiry. A social fact theorist can assume that there are such things as non-legal moral norms and say that when a legal philosopher is trying to come up with an argument that social facts create genuine reasons for acting in accordance with law, he or she is rarely concerned to defend a claim about what the true or correct non-legal moral norms are. Usually, it is taken for granted that some plausible candidates—concerning fairness, for example, or welfare—are correct. The problem is conceived of as connecting some circumstances in which law exists with these norms, so as to show that the apparent normativity of legal language isn't misleading. Hence, some (unchanging) background non-legal moral norms are presupposed, analogous to the presupposition in common sense causal

---

[38] The legal positivists include Raz (1979), Postema (1982), and Coleman (2001).

[39] Toh takes "the social factualists' main aim" as that of "devising an explanation of how reasons and obligations for action are generated by laws that is different from, and competes with, the natural law explanation of the same" (Toh 2008, 488).

[40] Compare with one of Toh's characterizations of the social fact thesis: "...the defense of [internal legal statements]...is ultimately a matter of, and only of, appeals to some social facts" (Toh 2008, 455).

explanations of background causally relevant conditions that are, along with a necessary but insufficient condition that is identified as "the cause," jointly sufficient for the occurrence of the explained event. One cannot deduce a statement that an event has occurred from a statement of "the cause" alone (along with analytic truths), understood in this way. Similarly, one cannot deduce a normative legal statement from a statement of social facts alone (along with analytic truths). Nonetheless, in contexts of inquiry typical of the law, it makes sense to say, along with Hart and Honoré (1985), that the cause of events is (often) ultimately what is abnormal or unexpected. Something of similar form is being said about justification of internal legal norms by the justification basis thesis.

Someone holding this thesis may be perfectly willing to grant that an internal legal statement L is a norm, and that at least one other norm is involved in its full, or complete, justification (particularly, in the justification of the claim that there is a genuine reason to conform to it). Nonetheless, he or she maintains that there are genuine reasons to act in accordance with L—indeed, genuine obligations to act in accordance with L—ultimately only when and because some social fact obtains. On this account, a social fact does the work of engendering a real obligation or genuine reason to conform to a valid law. The social fact triggers the application of background norms; it is what makes them relevant to the question of whether there is any genuine reason or obligation to conform to L.[41] This is what the contention that only social facts are ultimate in the justification of some normative statement of law amounts to.[42]

This approach can be illustrated without endorsement by looking at one such specification of social facts, discussed by Toh. Postema (1982)

---

[41] A case in point is Marmor 2001, p. 28 (conventions give rise to duties to act when the convention is a coordination convention and the convention solves a problem its parties have a moral duty to solve). Marmor says something similar about constitutive conventions (Marmor 2001, pp. 29–31). His case that constitutive conventions sometimes give rise to genuine reasons is similar to Coleman's and depends upon an independent commitment by participants to the practice the conventions constitute. But conventions do not produce reasons for making that commitment, for being a participant. Hence, conventions do not furnish a complete justification for a claim that there is a genuine reason to obey a particular law.

[42] The full justification of the part of the claim that it is *law* that does the requiring may also be set against the background of philosophical but not necessarily analytical claims, such as the metaphysical social fact thesis given above. The sense of ultimacy I am talking about isn't Toh's

maintains in his earliest work on the topic that conventions at the foundation of law solve coordination problems. Let us assume that when a convention exists with a specific content, it is a social fact that it exists and has this content. A member of the group with the coordination problem has a reason to conform if he believes that common knowledge of the content of the convention will make others choose conformity as the way to solve the coordination problem. Since it is a convention, others have this common knowledge and will make that choice. If the agent is a party to the convention, he has the requisite beliefs, and he has a reason to act. Conformity is a way to satisfy preferences each of the parties have independently of the convention (Postema 1982, p. 179).

Reading Postema as an exponent of the justification basis claim yields the following specific contention: legal officials have a reason to conform to some fundamental legal norm on the basis, ultimately, of the social facts that a convention exists among officials of conforming to that legal norm and that the conformity solves their coordination problem.[43] Notice, however, that to deduce the norm itself (or, rather, its reason-giving force), we must at the minimum add to a statement of the social facts the background normative assumption that one has reason to act in ways that will satisfy one's preferences. (This assumption may itself be in need of justification by reference to additional norms.)

---

sense. Toh conceives the structure of normative argument, for the sake of his discussion, on the model of foundationalism in epistemology (Toh 2008, 468–9). This, I think, tends to make him interpret claims about what is ultimate in justification of legal and moral assertions only as claims about what is foundational in the hierarchy of norms relevant to their justification. (See, e.g., Toh 2008, 463–4, 466, and his discussion of Searle on promising, Toh 2008, 477.) Toh is aware that those with a coherence model of normative reasoning reject his foundationalism, but believes his main argument can be recast without it. It is worth adding as a side comment that even if coherentists are wrong about the structure of normative reasoning, the structure Toh postulates cannot be taken for granted. There is a long debate among moral philosophers (and political philosophers such as Hobbes) about why even the ultimate moral norms bind us, raising the possibility that what is foundational in an account of why we are bound by a behavioral requirement may not be a norm at all.

[43] Postema 1982, 178: "[The convention] need not be just, reasonable, or otherwise morally admirable independent of the context of coordination. What accounts for its...binding character is merely its present success in solving the recurring or persisting problem of coordination." Postema (1982, 179–82) goes on to add other factors that are necessary to supply a binding reason for conformity to a convention: it should be reasonable to interpret one's actions as intended to induce reliance on one's conformity and others rely to their detriment, or the undertaking should be "analogous to" one of mutual benefit. Postema makes no claim that these additional considerations are or could be social facts.

I am not contending that the justification basis claim *successfully* explains why officials or lay persons have genuine reasons to conform to legal requirements, when they do. My purpose is not to add to the defense of the social fact thesis, but to subtract from the case against it. The justification basis claim will explain why under some circumstances officials or others have genuine reasons to conform *provided* a specification of the social facts in question can produce reasons *of the right kind.*[44] It may be that such a specification cannot be produced. But Toh's deductive strategy does nothing to show that it cannot.

I have contended that interpreting what Toh calls "the internal version of the social fact thesis" as the justification basis claim makes this alleged version of the social fact thesis less problematic than Toh's entailment interpretation. Recall that the entailment interpretation is problematic on two fronts: the conditional necessary for a valid deduction must be true for some specification of the social facts involved; and this conditional must have the right status, namely analyticity. The justification basis interpretation has just one problem: the conditional necessary for a valid deduction must be true for some specification of the social facts involved. It must be true that if certain social facts obtain, from them, reasons to conform to a legal requirement follow (with the help of background norms).

So Toh's entailment interpretation of the so-called "internal version of the social fact thesis" isn't a fair one. It's a mistake to read into the social fact thesis a claim about full justification, or about social facts being what is sometimes referred to as a *complete reason* for action.[45] Suppose, however, that I am wrong and that Toh's entailment claim *is* a version of the social fact thesis. The argument above has shown that it is not the sole version.

---

[44] For example, will, reasons of instrumental rationality suffice, as in Postema's early account? If the reason boils down to what officials owe each other, is this the right kind of reason to account for a legal requirement on officials to apply or enforce the law against ordinary law subjects?

[45] What the deductive strategy adopted by Toh (and also earlier by Zipursky, on behalf of Dworkin) shows *at best* is that the full justification—mentioning every consideration necessary to the deduction of the internal legal statement or, on a coherentist model, every consideration in the mutually supporting array that supports the claim—must include another norm. See Zipursky 2001, pp. 229–30. Or, in other words, a social fact cannot be a *complete reason*, as Marmor puts it in describing conventions, Marmor 2001, p. 26.

Moreover, the argument has cast doubt on the claim that it's a central version.[46] On either possibility, it follows that any demonstration of the entailment claim's defects is not *eo ipso* a demonstration of the untenability of the "internal legal statement version of the social fact thesis."

Note that directing attention away from an entailment claim to a justification basis claim is *not* watering down an interesting claim to an uninteresting one. The justification basis claim, while weaker, is hardly a platitude, nor is its denial a platitude. The justification basis claim is a substantive philosophical claim that rejects positions associated, rightly or wrongly, with anti-positivists. It rules out the position that only the moral merits of a law can be the ultimate source of the normativity of law.[47] It rules out the position that only the moral merits of a legal system can be the ultimate source of the normativity of its laws.[48] It rules out the Dworkinian suggestion that laws have some normative claim on officials who are charged with applying them ultimately because laws result from a proper weighing of principles established in past political decisions, where it is not a social fact what the principles or their proper weights are, and the principles themselves are not (and need not accurately reflect) unchanging background non-legal norms.[49] So *if* it is of interest whether there is a viable justificatory version of the social fact thesis, the justification basis thesis is an interesting contender.

Moreover, there are at least two reasons why it is, or may be thought to be, important whether a justificatory version of the social fact thesis is viable.

---

[46] Toh 2008, 445–6 takes it as the central version.

[47] According to Toh, rejecting this view is one of the goals of "social factualists" (Toh 2008, 467).

[48] It also rules out positions associated with legal positivists. In particular, it rules out the position that the reasons for conforming to law boil down to a probable personal gain in success in moral agency. (See, e.g., Raz on authority and especially the normal justification thesis.) For Raz gives a normative account of what I have called "success in moral agency."

[49] It is worth noting that the justification basis claim needn't be confined to self-identified legal positivists. Although it is difficult to draw a sharp and uncontroversial distinction between legal positivism and natural law theory, and even though interest in the distinction has considerably waned, it's worth noting that some who may be identified as natural law philosophers can make the justification basis claim. Christiano and Sciaraffa maintain that Locke employs the fact of "unanimous voluntary consent" to ground a genuine obligation to obey law and also to delineate a legal system from other social arrangements of declaration of will by a powerful superior (Christiano and Sciaraffa 2003, 408–9). (This point seems underappreciated in the literature.) Suppose such a fact were selected as the ultimate social fact, the Q, because of a connection to certain moral norms, such as norms of (procedural) justice. The result might reasonably be regarded as a natural law theory of law.

First, those who think about law have long sought to account for the critical normativity of law, where law has critical normativity. A social fact justificatory thesis claims to give such an account by directing attention to allegedly non-normative social facts. The viability of a social fact justificatory thesis at this point in the philosophical debate directs inquiry into channels (namely, the search for the social facts in question) that would otherwise be dismissed. Second, some legal thinkers suppose that any constitutive theory of law must also account for the normativity of law, and further suppose that the normativity in question is critical normativity. On these twin assumptions, which I do not share, the viability of a social fact justificatory thesis bears directly on the tenability of a social fact constitutive thesis.

CONCLUSION

I have argued that recent attacks on the social fact thesis, the claim that law is ultimately entirely a matter of social fact, have failed. Two versions of this thesis have been examined: a constitutive version, which is a metaphysical claim; and a justificatory version, which is a normative claim. Greenberg, by attacking the constitutive version, in effect contends that the social fact thesis is inconsistent with the existence of law. Toh, by attacking the justificatory thesis (and by assuming that the normativity in question is critical normativity), in effect contends that the social fact thesis is inconsistent with the normativity of law. Both philosophers, I have argued, fail to make their case. Greenberg's argument relies on a requirement that is ad hoc, unmotivated, and unsatisfied by his own view. Toh's argument confuses tracing justification with tracking deduction. Neither philosopher can support a wholesale rejection of the social fact thesis in either version. The constitutive social fact thesis and what I have argued is the best interpretation of the social fact justificatory thesis are more resilient than these critics allow.

WORKS CITED

Christiano, Thomas and Stefan Sciaraffa. (2003) "Legal Positivism and the Nature of Legal Obligation," *Law and Philosophy* 22: 487–512.
Coleman, Jules. (1998) "Incorporationism, Conventionality, and the Practical Difference Thesis," *Legal Theory* 4 (1998): 381–426; reprinted in (2001) *Hart's Postscript: Essays on the Postscript to the 'Concept of Law'* (Oxford: Oxford University Press), pp. 99–147.

—— (2001) *The Practice of Principle* (New York: Oxford University Press).
Dworkin, Ronald. (1977) *Taking Rights Seriously* (Cambridge, Mass.: Harvard University Press).
—— (2006) *Justice in Robes* (Cambridge, Mass.: Belknap Press of Harvard University Press).
Green, Leslie. (2003) "Legal Positivism," *Stanford Encyclopedia of Philosophy.* <plato.stanford.edu/entries/legal-positivism/>.
—— (2008), "Positivism and the Inseparability of Law and Morals," *NYU Law Review* 83: 1035–58.
Greenberg, Mark. (2004/2006a) "How Facts Make Law." Originally published in *Legal Theory* 10 (2004): 157–98. Reprinted in Scott Hershovitz, ed. *Exploring Law's Empire: The Jurisprudence of Ronald Dworkin* (Oxford: Oxford University Press, 2006), pp. 225–64.
—— (2006b) "Hartian Positivism and Normative Facts: How Facts Make Law II," in Scott Hershovitz, ed. *Exploring Law's Empire: The Jurisprudence of Ronald Dworkin* (Oxford: Oxford University Press), pp. 265–90.
—— (2006c) "On Practices and the Law," *Legal Theory* 12: 113–36. Reprinted in Enrique Villanueva, ed. (2007) *Law: Metaphysics, Meaning and Objectivity.* Rodopi Philosophical Studies: Social, Political, and Legal Philosophy 2 (Amsterdam: Rodopi), pp. 95–124.
—— (2007) "Reasons Without Values?" in Enrique Villanueva, ed., *Law: Metaphysics, Meaning and Objectivity.* Rodopi Philosophical Studies: Social, Political and Legal Philosophy 2 (Amsterdam: Rodopi), pp. 133–43.
Hart, H. L. A. (1994) *The Concept of Law,* second edn (Oxford: Clarendon Press).
—— and Tony Honoré (1985) *Causation in the Law,* second edn (Oxford: Clarendon Press).
Himma, Kenneth Einar. (2002) "Inclusive Legal Positivism," in Jules Coleman and Scott Shapiro, eds. *Oxford Handbook of Jurisprudence and Philosophy of Law* (Oxford: Oxford University Press), pp. 125–65.
Kim, Jaegwon. (2003) "Supervenience, Emergence, Realization, Reduction," in Michael J. Loux and Dean W. Zimmerman, eds. *The Oxford Handbook of Metaphysics* (New York: Oxford University Press), pp. 556–84.
Marmor, Andrei. (2001) *Positive Law and Objective Values* (Oxford: Clarendon Press).
Martin, Rex. (2002) "On Hohfeldian Liberties," reprinted in Michel Troper and Annalisa Verza, eds. *Legal Philosophy: General Aspects.* Selected Proceedings of the 19th IVR World Congress, New York (1999). ARSP Beiheft 82. (Stuttgart, Germany: F. Steiner), pp. 119–27.
Postema, Gerald J. (1982) "Coordination and Convention at the Foundations of Law," *Journal of Legal Studies* 11: 165–203.
Raz, Joseph. (1979) *The Authority of Law* (Oxford: Clarendon Press).
—— (1990) *Practical Reason and Norms* (Oxford: Oxford University Press).
Shapiro, Scott. (1998) "On Hart's Way Out," *Legal Theory* 4: 469–507.

Shapiro, Scott. (2007) "The 'Hart-Dworkin' Debate: A Short Guide for the Perplexed," in A. Ripstein, ed. *Ronald Dworkin* (Cambridge: Cambridge University Press), pp. 22–55.

Shiner, Roger A. (2010) "Law and Its Normativity," in Dennis Patterson, ed. *A Companion to Philosophy of Law and Legal Theory*, 2nd edn (Malden, Mass.: Wiley-Blackwell), pp. 417–45.

Toh, Kevin. (2008) "An Argument Against the Social Fact Thesis (and Some Additional Preliminary Steps Towards a New Conception of Legal Positivism)," *Law and Philosophy* 27: 445–504.

Zipursky, Benjamin. (2001) "The Model of Social Facts," in Jules Coleman, ed. *Hart's Postscript: Essays on the Postscript to the 'Concept of Law'* (Oxford: Oxford University Press), pp. 219–70.

3

John Austin on Punishment[*]

MATTHEW H. KRAMER

John Austin is commonly (and accurately) credited with propounding a sanctions-based conception of law. Oddly enough, however, Austin did not say very much about the nature of sanctions. His remarks in *The Province of Jurisprudence Determined* are especially meager, and his somewhat more extensive and illuminating comments in his *Lectures on Jurisprudence* are pointers toward a theory of sanctions rather than a full-blown theory in their own right. Besides, much of what needs to be said about Austin's account of sanctions has already been said by H. L. A. Hart. Nevertheless, although the topic of Austin on punishment may initially seem unpromising, his thoughts about punishment are certainly worthy of scrutiny; he was, after all, a major figure in the development of the deterrence-oriented conception of punitive institutions. Moreover, his various pronouncements—even when, or perhaps especially when, they are quite misguided—can fruitfully stimulate reflection on the role of governments in responding to wrongdoing.

I. A BIT OF PRELIMINARY EXPOSITION

The importance of sanctions in Austin's thought is unmistakable. Austin repeatedly maintained that laws properly so called are general commands issued by a superior to some inferior(s) with threats of injurious

* This chapter was originally written as a paper for a conference at University College London in December 2009 to mark the sesquicentennial of Austin's death. I am grateful to Michael Freeman and Lisa Penfold for organizing the conference, and to Andrew Halpin, James Murphy, and James Penner for very useful comments. I subsequently presented an abridged version of the paper as a lecture at the University of Leicester in March 2011. I am very grateful to my hosts on that occasion, Claire Grant and Phil Cook, as well as to the other members of the audience.

consequences in the event of disobedience. Laws established by a political regime, then, are general commands issued by the regime's sovereign to the people who are subject to the sovereign's sway. Those commands are backed by threats of evil consequences—threats of sanctions—that will be carried out if the commands are not heeded. According to this theory, a legal duty is a position of fearful exposure to the imposition of a sanction by a political regime. To say that someone is under a legal duty to refrain from murdering anybody else, for example, is to say that he or she will probably undergo a feared sanction if he or she murders anybody. (The terms "fearful" and "feared" in the last two sentences indicate that, within Austin's overall theory, the fearful attitudes of the addressees of legal mandates are among the existence-conditions for any obligations imposed by those mandates. Austin sometimes omitted to mention that subjective component in his analyses of the nature of legal obligations, but especially in his *Lectures on Jurisprudence* he did refer to it at many points. Indeed, his inclusion of it in his analyses is what led him into the error that will be criticized in the next main section of this chapter. Thus, Hart was unwise to suggest—even *en passant*—that Austin had succeeded in "seeing...the general irrelevance of [a] person's beliefs, fears, and motives to the question whether [the person] had an obligation to do something."[1] On the one hand, Hart usually displayed ample awareness of the subjective element in Austin's analysis of the concept of legal duties; for example, his apt criticism of the Austinian conflation of "being obliged" and "having an obligation" derived from that awareness. On the other hand, in the paragraph from which I have quoted just above, Hart mistakenly intimated that Austin's theorizing was focused solely on the external behavior of the addressees of legal mandates. Such an intimation is puzzling, because Hart clearly knew better.)

Austin was surprisingly relaxed when discussing how likely the imposition of a sanction must be in the event of somebody's non-compliance with the laws of a jurisdiction. He initially talked of "[t]he evil which will probably be incurred in case a command be disobeyed," but he slightly later indicated that "where there is the smallest chance of incurring the smallest evil, the expression of a wish amounts to a command,

---

[1] Hart 1961, 81. For a corrective to Hart's aberrant comment, see Murphy 2005, 194–5.

and, therefore, imposes a duty. The sanction, if you will, is feeble or insufficient; but still there *is* a sanction, and, therefore, a duty and a command" (Austin 1995, 22, 23, emphasis in original). The statement in this latter quotation cannot be taken very seriously, since it would license far too many outlandish ascriptions of duties. For example, whenever a young child expresses a preposterous wish to some adults, there is a non-zero probability—however small—of their incurring some detriment, however minor, if they decline to comply with her wish. Austin's pronouncement therefore yields the conclusion that the adults are under a duty to comply with the child's ridiculous wish. To save Austin from any such ludicrous conclusion, we should not construe at face value his assertion about the smallest chance and the smallest evil. Instead, we should take him to be maintaining that a duty has been imposed by a command when there is a significant chance of the address-ee's incurring a significant harm in the event of her non-compliance with the command's terms.

2. A FIRST MISSTEP

One of the first major missteps in Austin's conception of sanctions is linked to his remarks on the probability of the incurring of evil conse-quences. As has been evident at least since the time of Hart's famous critique of Austin, the latter thinker's jurisprudential ideas are vitiated by their disregard of the normativity of laws' contents and effects. Austin regrettably sought to explicate legal relations as purely physical and psy-chological relations. That aspiration of his informed the following mis-guided assertion: "The greater the eventual evil, and the greater the chance of incurring it, the greater is the efficacy of the command, and the greater is the strength of the obligation: Or (substituting expressions exactly equivalent), the greater is the *chance* that the command will be obeyed, and that the duty will not be broken" (Austin 1995, 23, empha-sis in original). By trying to explicate legal relations as relations of threat-ened force and probabilities, Austin went astray in this passage in at least five ways.

First, the addressees of a law might be unaware of that law itself, or unaware of the nature of the sanction attached to it, or unaware of the likelihood of apprehension and conviction in the event of non-compli-ance. Moreover, even if all the addressees of some law do know of its existence, some or all of them might misinterpret its terms and might therefore misunderstand the ways in which it bears on any number of situations. Indeed, especially in a large modern legal system, ignorance and misinterpretations of some laws are virtually inevitable, as is ignorance of the specifics of the sanctions that are attached to various legal mandates. Such ignorance and misinterpretations break some of the links between (1) the severity of the sanctions that back up legal mandates and (2) the probability that the duties imposed by those mandates will go unbroken. If people are unaware of the existence of a mandate, then obviously they will not be motivated by it to conform to its requirement. (Even if the substance of the mandate fortuitously coincides with the content of some independently operative inclination of theirs, the mandate itself will not motivate their compliance with its requirement if they are unaware of its existence.) Similarly, if they are unaware of the nature of the sanction that is attached to some mandate, then the greater or lesser severity of that sanction will not affect their behavior. Homologous points can be made about the other cognitive deficiencies that have been mentioned here. In each case, the possible presence of such a deficiency thwarts Austin's effort to establish the links between the severity of sanctions and the probability of compliance.

A second obstacle to the success of his effort is that any given sanction might produce no marginal deterrent effect. If a sanction of n degrees of severity is sufficient to deter anyone who can be deterred from committing the type of crime to which the sanction is attached, then the imposition of a sanction of $n + 1$ or $n + 2$ degrees of severity will not produce any further deterrent effect. In such circumstances, then, a shift from the milder sanction to the sterner sanction will not increase the likelihood that the relevant law will be obeyed and that the relevant legal duty will go unviolated. Conversely, a shift from the harsher sanction to the more lenient sanction will not decrease that likelihood.

Third, as is recognized in a statement by John Locke which Austin quoted in Lecture V of *The Province of Jurisprudence Determined*, people inclined to disobey legal mandates are quite often under the mistaken impression that they can evade any threatened penalties for their recalcitrance: "And as to the punishments due from the law of the commonwealth, [potential lawbreakers] frequently flatter themselves with the hope of impunity" (Austin 1995, 146, quoting—or slightly misquoting—Locke 1975, 357 [Bk II, Chap. XXVIII, § 12]). If people are firmly convinced that they can avoid any sanctions attached to legal directives, then the probability of their flouting the directives is not affected by the stiffening or relaxing of the severity of the sanctions.

Fourth, a legal mandate might forbid some mode of conduct which everybody is disposed to eschew in any event. If so, then the threat of sanctions attached to such a legal ban is redundant. The unattractiveness of the specified mode of conduct in the eyes of the legal mandate's addressees is itself a sufficient deterrent. Austin at a couple of later junctures recognized this point perfectly well. In Lecture II of *The Province of Jurisprudence Determined*, for example, he wrote as follows:

There are classes of useful acts, which it were useless to enjoin; classes of mischievous acts, which it were useless to prohibit. Sanctions were superfluous. We are sufficiently prone to the useful, and sufficiently averse from the mischievous acts, without the motives which are presented to the will by a lawgiver. Motives *natural* or spontaneous (or motives *other* than those which are created by injunctions and prohibitions) impel us to action in the one case, and hold us to forbearance in the other. [Austin 1995, 44, emphases in original]

This passage, which is echoed in Lecture V (Austin 1995, 140 n9), belies the suggestion that the probability of people's compliance with the terms of a legal mandate is always perfectly correlated with the combination of (i) the severity of the sanction that is to be incurred by anyone who does not heed those terms and (ii) the likelihood of the actual imposition of such a sanction in the event of non-compliance.

A fifth reason for rejecting that misconceived suggestion was likewise glimpsed by Austin himself. He noted that legal mandates can be impotent as well as redundant. Any legal mandate is impotent if it forbids a mode of conduct which the addressees of the mandate are resolutely disposed to adopt regardless of the legal consequences (at least up to a very high level of punitive severity, and perhaps up to every such level). As Austin perspicaciously observed, the impotence of legal mandates is especially common in situations where people are motivated by religious scruples: "[I]f [a] practice is favoured by...moral or religious sentiments, the strongest possible fear which legal pains can inspire may be mastered by a stronger fear of other and conflicting sanctions" (Austin 1995, 140). The sort of sentiment that Austin here had in mind was bluntly expressed by the apostles Peter and John when they were ordered by the prevailing authorities in Jerusalem to desist from speaking and teaching in the name of Jesus: "Whether it is right in the sight of God to listen to you rather than to God, you must judge; for we cannot but speak of what we have seen and heard" (Acts 4:19–20). Given that Austin was amply aware of such sentiments, he should not have declared that the strength of a legal obligation is always the sheer inverse of the likelihood of its being breached. Insofar as a legal mandate is impotent, no inverse correlation obtains at all.

2.1. *A First Alternative to Austin's Analysis*

In sum, given these several ways in which Austin's account of the stringency of legal obligations is wide of the mark, we need to consider briefly some alternative lines of thought. Either of two analyses can displace his analysis. One approach would follow Austin in equating the stringency of legal obligations with the severity and conditional probability of the sanctions that are threatened for breaches of those obligations. Though aligned with Austin on that point, this approach would take issue with his pronouncements by insisting that the property of stringency so understood is not invariably correlated with—and is certainly not equivalent to—the unlikelihood of violations of legal duties. Any correlation between that stringency and that unlikelihood is subject to the sundry contingencies that have been tersely recounted here.

While making clear that the strength of legal obligations is not equivalent to the unlikelihood of breaches of those obligations, the first alternative to Austin's analysis does not necessarily yield the conclusion that that strength is a partly evaluative property rather than a purely empirical property. Any judgment about the property in question presupposes certain judgments concerning what is generally detrimental or beneficial for human beings, but the latter judgments can be those of the addressees of legal mandates rather than those of detached jurisprudential theorists. In other words, this first alternative can construe the strength of legal obligations as the extent to which the sanctions that enforce the obligations are feared by the people who are threatened with those sanctions.[2] So construed, the strength of an obligation is an empirically ascertainable property.

---

[2] The probability of the imposition of the threatened sanctions in the event of the addressees' non-compliance with their obligations would also have to be taken into account. I have omitted that element here and in the next paragraph for the sake of stylistic convenience.

A more sophisticated version of the first alternative to Austin's analysis would instead present the stringency of legal duties as a partly evaluative property. Specifically, it would construe such stringency as the objective severity of the sanctions that give effect to legal duties; that objective severity does not necessarily correspond to the extent to which those sanctions are feared by the duty-bearers.[3] Rather than being ascertainable through purely empirical means, a property of this sort cannot be gauged without evaluative judgments on the part of jurisprudential theorists. Without such judgments, those theorists cannot know whether one sanction is more severe than another, and indeed they cannot even know whether something is a sanction rather than a reward. Insofar as we understand the stringency of legal duties along these lines as a partly evaluative property, we would be particularly unwise to accept that that stringency is perfectly correlated with the empirically ascertainable likelihood that those duties will be fulfilled.

2.2. A Second Alternative to Austin's Analysis

A second approach would constitute an even more marked departure from Austin. Instead of cashing out the stringency of legal obligations by reference to the sternness of sanctions, we could cash out that property by reference to the gravity of the wrongs in which any breaches of those obligations consist. Such an explication would of course be normative—indeed, moral—rather than purely descriptive. Importantly, it would leave open the possibility that some legal mandates which carry stiff sanctions do not impose stringent obligations, and also the possibility that some legal mandates which carry light sanctions do impose stringent obligations. None of this would be inconsistent with legal positivism or specifically with Austin's justified emphasis on the distinction between the law as it is and the law as it ought to be. What this approach would maintain is that, whereas the existence-conditions of legal obligations are always at least partly empirical,[4] the stringency of

---

[3] Suppose, for example, that the duty-bearers do not care much about their own autonomy and are thus not very apprehensive about certain sanctions that would significantly circumscribe their autonomy. Nevertheless, such sanctions are objectively severe because of the curtailments of autonomy which they involve whenever they are imposed.

[4] My reason for inserting the qualification "at least partly" is that Inclusive Legal Positivists maintain that the existence-conditions of some legal obligations include moral principles as well as empirical facts concerning the behavior and attitudes of officials. For my principal defense of Inclusive Legal Positivism, see Kramer 2004, chaps 1–4. For some other important

those obligations is a moral matter. When stringency is so understood, it is obviously not perfectly correlated with the unlikelihood of transgressions of legal mandates. Indeed, any correlation is incidental.

3. DETERRENCE THROUGH PUNISHMENTS AND OTHER SANCTIONS

Near the beginning of *The Province of Jurisprudence Determined*, Austin indicated correctly that not all sanctions—in his sense of the word "sanctions"—are punishments. He remarked that "the evil to be incurred by disobedience is frequently styled a *punishment*. But, as punishments, strictly so called, are only a *class* of sanctions, the term is too narrow to express the meaning adequately" (Austin 1995, 22, emphases in original). Having maintained that the set of punishments is a proper subset of the set of sanctions, Austin proceeded to say nothing whatsoever about the features of punishments that differentiate them from sanctions of other types. Indeed, in *The Province of Jurisprudence Determined*, he said nothing further about sanctions of other types. He tacitly left his readers to guess what such sanctions might be.

In his *Lectures on Jurisprudence*, Austin was somewhat more illuminating. He continued to say nothing about the features of punishments that distinguish them from sanctions of other kinds, but he did at least fleetingly refer to some non-punitive sanctions. In the following sentence, for example, he listed four types of sanctions: "I am condemned to restore a house which I detain from the owner; to make satisfaction for a breach of contract; to pay damages for an assault, to the injured party; or to pay a fine for the same offence" (Austin 1885, 456). Although the last of these sanctions is a punishment, the other three are private-law remedies. The restitution of wrongly withheld property, the payment of damages for a breach of contract, and the payment of damages for a harm-causing breach of duty in tort law all count as sanctions under Austin's conception. More puzzling is Austin's slightly later statement that "certain obligations are sanctioned by nullities" (Austin 1885, 457). Exactly what Austin had in mind with this laconic formulation is not entirely plain. He supplied no elucidation of it. However, Hart took

defenses of Inclusivism, see Waluchow 1994; Coleman 2001. For some more recent elaborations of Inclusivism, see Kramer 2007; 2009.

the statement to suggest that laws impose obligations when they prescribe procedures for the exercise of legal powers, and that the otiosity of any effort to exercise a legal power without following the prescribed procedure is the sanction that enforces the power-holder's obligation (Hart 1961, 33–5). Having construed Austin's statement along those lines, Hart rightly took exception to it.

We can here leave aside the dubious claim that nullity is a sanction, and we can likewise leave aside the exegetical question whether Hart correctly interpreted Austin on that point. My concern here instead is to ponder the difficulties posed for Austin—and for other theorists who share his conception of sanctions—by the fact that not all sanctions are punishments. As we have seen, tort-law remedies are also classified by Austin as sanctions. Now, what should be noted here is that many courses of conduct punishable as crimes are also tortious, where wrongdoers who are liable to undergo punishments are also liable to pay compensation to the people who have been victimized by their misconduct.[5]

Why is the overlap between criminal law and tort law importantly problematic for Austin (and for like-minded theorists)? To discern the answer to this question, we should recall that Austin was one of the foremost figures in the development of the deterrence-oriented conception of punishments and other sanctions. *The Province of Jurisprudence Determined* and especially his *Lectures on Jurisprudence* teem with proclamations of that conception of legal enforcement. The following passage is only one of many:

> If, then, the [addressee of a law] fulfil his duty, and if he fulfil his duty out of regard to the sanction, the fact, precisely stated, is this: He is obnoxious to evil from the Law, in case he violate his duty. This conditional evil, like every possible evil, he necessarily wishes to avoid. And, in order that he may avoid the evil with which he is threatened by the Law, he wills the act, or *intends* the forbearance, which the Author of the Law commands. [Austin 1885, 446, emphasis in original]

Deterrence-oriented conceptions of legal sanctions are usually embedded in broader utilitarian theories, as was true in Austin's case. Hence, a central tenet of a deterrence-oriented theory is that the sanctions for

---

[5] Of course, some criminals are indigent and are thus not likely to be sued as tortfeasors by their victims. Numerous other criminals, however, are possessed of resources sufficiently ample to make the pursuit of tort claims against them worthwhile. Obviously, my remarks in this section pertain to cases involving criminals of the latter sort.

various violations of the law should be set at levels that optimally discourage people from committing such violations. Under a theory of this kind, deterrence is optimal if the utility-promoting effects of some type of sanction—which are due principally to its lowering the incidence of certain transgressions of the law—maximally exceed the utility-diminishing effects of that type of sanction, which are due principally to its direct infliction of pain and its diffuse engendering of fear.

The pursuit of an optimal level of deterrence is hugely complicated, if not thwarted, by the overlap between tort law and criminal law. If certain punitive measures are optimal in the absence of any tort-law sanctions, they will be excessive when combined with the tort-law sanctions—and vice versa. Either at the level of individual sentences and remedies or at the level of sentencing guidelines and compensation-awarding guidelines, a deterrence-oriented system of legal governance has to coordinate criminal law and tort law very closely. Yet that coordination, if feasible at all, will produce a number of untoward effects. Among them are awards of damages in tort law that fall far short of compensating plaintiffs for their losses; unduly lenient sentences for any serious crimes that give rise to major tort claims; markedly disparate sentences for qualitatively indistinguishable crimes; potential multi-year delays in the handing down of sentences or awards of damages, while judges wait to see whether any corresponding litigation or prosecutions will materialize and how such proceedings will be resolved (if they ever do materialize); and the vesting of tort-law plaintiffs with a significant role in determining the severity of criminal sentences. Exactly how Austin and other deterrence-oriented theorists can overcome these difficulties—difficulties that arise when tort law and criminal law are taken to serve exactly the same fundamental purpose—is not at all clear.[6] In any event, Austin himself never addressed such matters.

---

[6] Efforts by law-and-economics theorists to grapple with the relationship between criminal law and tort law have been unimpressive. For some pertinent comments, see Coleman 1988, 157–9. (In a riposte to Coleman, Russell Hardin errs by maintaining that law-and-economics theorists should hold that the distinctive purpose of criminal sanctions is to force wrongdoers to internalize certain diffuse costs such as those incurred by people throughout a society who adopt precautions in response to the occurrence of misdeeds. See Hardin 1992, 372–4. *Pace* Hardin, such costs are already taken into account by efficiency-seeking jurists when they determine whether various general modes of conduct should be classified as tortious.)

4. THE POINT OF PUNISHMENT

As readers of Austin know, he generally took the chief object of jurisprudential enquiry to be the articulation of proper definitions of juristic terms and phrases. Such a methodological ambition came under criticism from Hart, of course, who regarded it as both unrealizable and unduly confining (Hart 1961, 13–17). My concern here is not with Hart's criticism, which seems to me partly justified and partly overstated. Rather, what deserves some brief attention is the inappositeness of Austin's methodology in his elaboration of his account of sanctions.

Austin wrote as follows: "Every sanction properly so called is an eventual evil *annexed to a command.* Any eventual evil may operate as a *motive* to conduct; but, unless the conduct be commanded and the evil be annexed to the command purposely to enforce obedience, the evil is not a *sanction* in the proper acceptation of the term" (Austin 1995, 118, emphases in original). Though the main concern of Austin here was to distinguish between sanctions on the one hand and incidental evils or natural evils such as illness on the other hand, he was also articulating—in a highly compressed form—his deterrence-oriented conception of legal sanctions. That is, he maintained that the defining point or purpose of punishment resides in the use of threats of evil consequences to induce fear-based compliance with legal requirements. He presumed that this conception of punishment falls out of a proper definition of the term "sanctions."

In fact, however, any such conception of punishment is a thesis of political morality. A deterrence-oriented account of the fundamental point or purpose of punishment competes with other general accounts of punishment as a practice of retribution or denunciation or incapacitation or purgation or rehabilitation. To engage in the satisfactory championing of any one of those accounts in preference to the others, a theorist has to undertake moral argumentation rather than lexicographical explication.

For Austin, of course, the requisite argumentation consisted in his advocacy of utilitarianism. Like most other deterrence-oriented theorists, he embedded his account of punishment in a general utilitarian framework. That broader framework, however egregious its substantive shortcomings, is recognizably a moral theory. It confers intelligibility on the claim that the point or purpose of punitive institutions is to lower the incidence of criminal activity by issuing general threats of nasty consequences that will be inflicted on people who engage in such activity. Lowering the incidence of illegal misdeeds in that manner is the way in which a system of criminal justice contributes to the realization of utilitarian objectives, and is thus what morally justifies the workings of such a system (in the eyes of utilitarians).

To be sure, if the claim about reducing the rate of violent behavior and other misdeeds were to be reformulated as a thesis about a general function or effect of punishment, it would not have to be embedded in a utilitarian theory. Such a proposition about a general effect or function of punishment is a theoretical-explanatory thesis rather than a normative thesis,[7] and is thus not in need of the normative underpinnings provided by a moral doctrine such as that of utilitarianism. However, the claim attributed here to Austin is about the point or purpose of punishment, rather than simply about a function that punishment performs or an effect that punishment produces. So presented, the claim is an ethical thesis about the central feature that morally justifies the workings of a criminal-justice system.

Admittedly, not every ascription of a point or purpose to some institution is a justificatory thesis. An ascription of a point or purpose to some particular practice—rather than to a general type of practice—is typically an encapsulation of the objectives consciously pursued by the people who participate in the practice. Those objectives might or might not be morally upright, and therefore might or might not invest the practice with positive moral force. Similarly, an attribution of a point or purpose to some general type of practice (such as putting together jigsaw puzzles or tackling crossword puzzles) will not necessarily amount to a moral justification. The status of such an attribution as a moral justification depends largely on whether most instances of the specified type of practice significantly affect the interests of people other than those who directly participate therein; for example, if most instances of the activities of putting together jigsaw puzzles and tackling crossword puzzles do not significantly bear on the interests of people other than the participants, then the attribution of a non-moral point or purpose to those

---

[7] Of course, even as a theoretical-explanatory thesis, the proposition would not fall out of a definition of the term "sanction" or out of any other definition. Legal theorists are not lexicographers.

activities is entirely pertinent. Even more obviously, the imputation of a point or purpose to some wicked practice is not a moral justification of that practice. If a morally decent person ascribes a certain point or purpose to the practice of slavery or genocidal conquest, she is hardly thereby seeking to vindicate any such pattern of human interaction morally.

Nonetheless, when the matter under consideration is the existence of the punitive mechanisms of legal systems, any ascription of a point or purpose to those mechanisms is a moral ascription. Such an ascription is not an attribution of a mere effect or function, nor does it simply recount the intentions and objectives of the people who operate legal regimes. Moreover, it does not pertain to a type of institution which is intrinsically evil or which has no significant bearing on the interests of people other than those who participate directly therein. Accordingly, the imputation of a point or purpose to the punitive workings of legal systems is intelligible only as a moral thesis. In Austin's case, as has been stated, it is more specifically a utilitarian thesis.

Now, somebody might object that I am reading far too much into the two sentences from Austin which I have most recently quoted above. After all, those sentences appear to ascribe a purpose to the officials who run any legal system: namely, the purpose of eliciting obedience to legal mandates by threatening to impose sanctions on disobedient people. The quoted sentences do not appear to ascribe a purpose to the punitive mechanisms of legal systems themselves. Consequently, my remarks about the latter type of ascription may seem out of place.

Such an objection is misconceived. Austin, let us recall, insisted that nothing properly counts as a sanction unless it has been attached to a mandate for the purpose of eliciting compliance. Consequently, nothing properly counts as a legal mandate unless it carries a sanction that has been attached to it for the purpose of eliciting compliance,[8] and therefore no institution properly counts as a legal system unless its mandates carry sanctions that are attached for the aforementioned purpose. Such is the claim advanced by Austin. To see why that claim ought to be

---

[8] Austin proclaimed: "Every *law* or *rule* (taken with the largest signification which can be given to the term *properly*) is a *command*." He then indicated that a "command is distinguished from other significations of desire, not by the style in which the desire is signified, but by the power and the purpose of the party commanding to inflict an evil or pain in case the desire be disregarded" (Austin 1995, 21, emphases in original).

construed as a moral thesis about the point or purpose of legal punishment, we should ponder a variant of it that might be propounded by a
retributivistic twin of Austin (whom I shall designate as "Austin-R").

According to Austin-R, nothing properly counts as a sanction unless
it has been attached to a mandate for the purpose of responding to the
negative deserts of malefactors by inflicting upon them hardships that
are severe enough to be commensurate with the seriousness of their misdeeds. Consequently, nothing properly counts as a legal mandate unless
it carries a sanction that has been attached to it for the purpose of
responding to the negative deserts of miscreants. Ergo, no institution
properly counts as a legal system unless its mandates carry sanctions that
are attached for that very purpose. Such is the claim advanced by
Austin-R.

What plausible basis could there be for the proposition that nothing
properly counts as a legal system unless the sanctions that enforce its
mandates are invoked and applied for retributivistic purposes? Construed as an analysis of the meaning of the word "sanction" or as an
analysis of the meaning of the phrase "legal system," such a proposition
is wildly outlandish. Retributivism as an account of punishment does
not fall out of any definitions of juristic terms. Only when the proposition about what counts as a legal system is construed as a moral thesis
about the proper point or purpose of punitive mechanisms does it carry
any credibility. Though such a proposition so construed may be wrong—
and is indeed wrong or at least too sweeping, in my view—it is by no
means ridiculous. It makes sense as a moral thesis, whether or not it is
correct. Consequently, to render satisfactorily intelligible the pronouncement by Austin-R, we should conclude that (contrary to initial appearances) he is talking about the point or purpose of legal punishment at
least as much as about the purposes pursued by legal officials.

We should draw a parallel conclusion about Austin himself, of course.
Though his remarks are overtly about the purposes pursued by legal
officials in attaching sanctions to legal mandates, the remarks are plausible only when they are construed as the attribution of a moral point or
purpose to the punitive operations of legal systems. By contrast, a wood-
enly face-value reading of those remarks would render them preposterous. After all, quite preposterous is the notion that a system of governance
will not properly count as a legal system if the sanctions that back up its
mandates have been attached thereto by the system's officials for

retributivistic purposes. Perhaps there are some genuine grounds for declining to classify this or that particular system of governance as a legal regime, but the putative reason just mentioned is no genuine reason at all. Sanctions attached for retributivistic purposes can still perform the function of deterrence that is essential for the survival of any system of governance. Hence, such a system can be a full-blown legal regime even if the officials who run it are retributivistically concerned with desert and equality and moral responsibility as they carry out their official roles. Their pursuit of such ideals is not only consistent with the healthy operations of a legal-governmental system, but is also generally promotive of those operations.

Thus, if Austin's assertions about what properly counts as a legal sanction are to be colorable, they have to be construed as the imputation of a moral point or purpose to the punitive operations of legal systems as such. Instead of foolishly denying that the officials who run such a system might be animated by retributivistic preoccupations, Austin was maintaining that the fundamental moral justification for institutions of legal punishment resides in their capacity to discourage wrongdoing by threatening evil consequences for malefactors. His obfuscatory methodology, whereby he presented the exposition of that justification as an elucidation of the meaning of the term "sanctions," should not distract us from recognizing the full import of his attribution of a deterrence-oriented role to the enforcement of legal norms.

5. AUSTIN'S PSYCHOLOGICAL ACUITY

Heretofore, this chapter has been quite critical of Austin. It will thus briefly conclude with some words of well-deserved praise. Often the classical exponents of deterrence-oriented conceptions of punishment are derided as propagators of crude models of human psychology. Such derision is dubious in application to most of those exponents, and especially in application to Austin in his *Lectures on Jurisprudence*.

Austin's conception of punishment, as has been repeatedly noted in this chapter, is that of a deterrence-oriented theorist. According to such a conception, the psychological reaction on which the imposition of punishment centrally and indispensably trades for the fulfillment of a morally worthy purpose is the fear induced by the prospect of harmful consequences. Austin himself repeatedly gave voice to that understanding of the role of punishment. He wrote, for example, that sanctions are attached to any legal mandate so that each person "is restrained by his fear of the evil from doing the act which is forbidden" (Austin 1885, 444, italics removed). However, he did not simply leave things there. He went on to consider at some length how a person's habitual fear of the sanctions levied against the perpetrators of various crimes can eventually lead the person to develop genuine moral scruples about committing those crimes.

On the one hand, Austin rightly denied that somebody's fear of legal sanctions would in any credible circumstances directly and abruptly extinguish (rather than simply overmaster) his or her desire to engage in some legally proscribed course of conduct. Damascene conversions generally do not occur outside the realm of religious fantasy. On the other hand, Austin submitted that somebody's fear of legal sanctions can quite credibly extinguish his or her law-breaking inclinations through a gradual process whereby the unattractiveness of the sanctions is psychologically transferred—over a long period of time—to the legally forbidden modes of conduct themselves. As Austin wrote:

> Our necessary aversion from the evils with which we are threatened by the Law is often transferred by insensible degrees to the injuries or wrongs which might bring these evils upon us. Our fear of the sanction is changed into hate of the offence. Instead of fulfilling our duty through fear of the sanction, we fulfil our duty through that aversion from wrong which the habitual fear of the sanction has slowly engendered. [Austin 1885, 449–50]

Though Austin's account of the gradual development of favorable attitudes toward legal requirements is reliant on a rather crude associationist picture of mental functioning, it is perceptive and is largely accurate with reference to quite a few circumstances. It constitutes a notable amplification of the proposition that a legal system's central means of securing compliance with its mandates is the eliciting of fear through threats of sanctions.

Indeed, without abandoning his deterrence-oriented conception of punishment at all, Austin here went a long way toward embracing the denunciatory theory of punishment that was elaborated later in the nineteenth century by James Fitzjames Stephen. Like the deterrence-oriented approach to punishment, the denunciatory approach is consequentialist, and the two of them are compatible with each other; but they are also quite different from each other. Central to the denunciatory approach is the idea that punishments give expression to a community's detestation of the misdeeds for which the punishments are levied. Denunciatory theorists hold that the expressive role of punishment is instrumentally valuable because the manifesting of a community's attitude of revulsion toward serious crimes will help to solidify people's sentiments against the commission of those crimes.[9] Like the deterrence-oriented rationale, then, the denunciatory theory maintains that a key purpose of punishment lies in the reduction of criminal activity. However, whereas the advocates of the deterrence-oriented approach contend that the reduction will occur chiefly through the evocation of fear in people, the advocates of the denunciatory rationale contend that the crime-diminishing effect of punishment derives chiefly instead from the reinforcement and purification of people's moral sentiments. This difference between the two theories was famously captured by Stephen in the following passage:

Some men, probably, abstain from murder because they fear that, if they committed murder, they would be hung. Hundreds of thousands abstain from it because they regard it with horror. One great reason why they regard it with horror is, that murderers are hung with the hearty approbation of all reasonable men. [Stephen 1863, 99]

Now, I am not claiming here that Austin was a full-blown denunciatory theorist. However, even while retaining a primary focus on fear and deterrence as the products of legal sanctions, he grasped to quite a considerable degree the role of those sanctions in shaping and refining people's ethical outlooks. His conception of punishment, though it never amounted to a full-blown theory, was richer and more subtle than is suggested by Hart's characterization of the Austinian sovereign as a gunman writ large.

6. A TERSE CONCLUSION

The sections of this chapter are not united by a single continuous line of argument. Instead, the chapter has explored several distinct though

---

[9] Denunciatory theorists hold that a second valuable consequence of the expressive role of punishment consists in the defusing of people's vindictive impulses. By giving vent to people's feelings of hatred and resentment, the punitive sway of a legal system satisfies their instincts for revenge and thereby greatly lowers the likelihood of their resorting to private acts of retaliation. I here leave aside this second strand of the denunciatory theory.

overlapping complexities in Austin's remarks on the nature of sanctions. Some of those complexities are peculiar to his thought (with his efforts to reduce all legal relations to patterns of behavior and psychology), whereas others are of broader applicability to many deterrence-oriented accounts of punishment. Indeed, by attending to the difficulties that block the development of a successful Austinian theory of punishment, we can better grasp some of the difficulties that confront any deterrence-oriented justification of punitive institutions. Moreover, by attending to both the strengths and the weaknesses of Austin's reflections on such institutions, we can better apprehend the relations between the deterrence-oriented justification and alternative justifications. We can come to understand how best to argue for a deterrence-oriented approach, and we can discern the similarities and dissimilarities between that approach and rival positions. Hence, a study of Austin's remarks on sanctions can commend itself even to philosophers who look thoroughly askance at antiquarian ventures into the history of ideas.

REFERENCES

Austin, John. 1885. *Lectures on Jurisprudence*, Volume I. Fifth Edition. Edited by Robert Campbell. London: John Murray.

Austin, John. 1995. *The Province of Jurisprudence Determined*. Edited by Wilfrid Rumble. Cambridge: Cambridge University Press. Originally published in 1832.

Coleman, Jules. 1988. *Markets, Morals, and the Law*. Cambridge: Cambridge University Press.

Coleman, Jules. 2001. *The Practice of Principle*. Oxford: Oxford University Press.

Hardin, Russell. 1992. "The Morality of Law and Economics." *Law and Philosophy* 11: 331–84.

Hart, H. L. A. 1961. *The Concept of Law*. Oxford: Oxford University Press.

Kramer, Matthew. 2004. *Where Law and Morality Meet*. Oxford: Oxford University Press.

Kramer, Matthew. 2007. "Why the Axioms and Theorems of Arithmetic are Not Legal Norms." *Oxford Journal of Legal Studies* 27: 555–62.

Kramer, Matthew. 2009. "Moral Principles and Legal Validity." *Ratio Juris* 22: 44–61.

Locke, John. 1975. *An Essay concerning Human Understanding*. Edited by Peter Nidditch. Oxford: Oxford University Press. Fourth edition originally published in 1700.

Murphy, James Bernard. 2005. *The Philosophy of Positive Law*. New Haven, CT: Yale University Press.

Stephen, James Fitzjames. 1863. *A General View of the Criminal Law of England*. London: Macmillan.

Waluchow, W. J. 1994. *Inclusive Legal Positivism*. Oxford: Oxford University Press.

4

Publicity and the Rule of Law*

BRUNO CELANO

I. INTRODUCTION

By the 'Rule of Law' I mean, as has now become usual among legal theorists, a set of formal and institutional features the law may possess in varying degrees (see section II). These features define an ideal, which laws have traditionally been expected to live up to.

One of these features is *publicity*. Part of what constitutes the Rule of Law is the requirement that the laws should be public. This is the subject of this chapter. When it is claimed that the Rule of Law requires that the laws should be public, what is to be understood by this claim? How is the relevant notion of publicity to be defined?

The question itself raises some puzzlement. What kind of question is it? I try to handle this problem in section 2. Answering our main question requires, as we shall see, an understanding of the point, or points, of the publicity requirement, and of the Rule of Law generally. Sections 3 and 4 will be devoted to a first approximation to an answer to our main question. In sections 5 and 6 I will propose an amendment to this answer, leading (or so I hope) to a richer understanding of the point of publicity. Answering the question will also require (sections 7 and 8) focusing our attention on a particular version of the Rule of Law—I shall call it the 'Enlightenment Rule of Law'—in which legislation plays a prominent role. Section 9 will raise a further difficulty, leading to a final amendment of our proposed definition of publicity.

* I am grateful for helpful comments and criticism to J. Queralt, G. Maniaci, J. J. Moreso, G. Pino, F. Poggi, A. Schiavello, and A. Spena, as well as to L. Green, B. Leiter, and an anonymous reader for OUP. An earlier version of this essay was delivered at DI.GI.TA., University of Genoa. I am grateful to the audience there, and especially to M. Barberis, P. Chiassoni, P. Comanducci, R. Guastini, M. La Torre, R. Marra, and C. Redondo.

My main claim is that the Rule of Law requirement of publicity is best understood in terms of the notion of common, or mutual, knowledge. When it is required that the laws should be public, what should be meant by this is not only that each one of the law's addressees should know what the law is, but also that everybody should know that everybody knows what the law is, that everybody should know that everybody knows that everybody knows what the law is, and so on. This may look unnecessarily complicated. I'll try to show that this is a false impression, and that understanding the publicity requirement along these lines illuminates various aspects of the normative ideal that the publicity requirement may be taken to embody. Think of a regime in which laws are made known to their addressees by sending each one of them sealed envelopes. Everybody knows what the law is. But, would the Rule of Law requirement of publicity be met? I think many would be inclined to answer in the negative. Why? What is implied in our inclination to answer in this way?

2. UNDERSTANDING THE QUESTION

There are many different ways of understanding the phrase 'the Rule of Law'. Here I adopt the one which has become common in contemporary jurisprudence in the last forty years or so:[1] by 'the Rule of Law' (RoL, for short) I mean a loose cluster of (1) formal features of the laws (prospectivity, publicity, relative generality, relative stability, intelligibility and relative clarity, practicability,[2] consistency), plus (2) institutional and procedural desiderata (such as, for instance, that the making of particular norms, providing for individual cases, be guided by general rules; and, further, so-called principles of 'natural justice': that the resolution of disputes be entrusted to somebody not having an interest at stake in the judgment, and not being otherwise biased; the principle *audi alteram partem:* and so on).[3] Items on the list partly vary according to the accounts given by different authors. The core, however, is stable.

---

[1] Accounts in this family have the form of "a sort of laundry list of features that a healthy legal system should have. These are mostly variations of the eight desiderata of Lon Fuller's 'internal morality of law'" (Waldron 2002, 154).

[2] i.e. conformity to the principle *'ought'* implies *'can'*.

[3] For a list of these institutional and procedural requirements, see, e.g., Raz 1977, 215–18. On principles of natural justice cf. Hart 1961, 156, 202. For similar lists of the RoL requirements see Fuller 1969, ch. 2, Finnis 1980, 270–1; Marmor 2004, 5 ff.; Kramer 2007, ch. 2.

Before we venture any answer to the question of how to understand publicity, let us ask what sort of question this is. One could say that what the question calls for is stipulation; or, alternatively, an historical inquiry into what different theorists—as well as lawyers generally, and, perhaps, the public at large—mean when they claim that laws should be public. The question could, no doubt, be understood in these ways. However, I'll follow a different tack.

RoL features define an ethico-political ideal which laws are usually expected to live up to. In order to determine how each one of its features is to be understood, we have to gain some understanding of this ideal and to unravel its various aspects. We have to understand, that is, what the point, or points, of the RoL are, so as to determine what its various requirements should properly be taken to mean. At the same time, we could not gain any understanding, however rough, of the ideal without a preliminary understanding of the various requirements it encompasses. One step ahead on one count (what is the point of the Rule of Law?) is supposed to enable further steps on the other (how is this Rule of Law requirement to be understood?), and vice versa. The circle is supposed to be a virtuous one. But we have to jump in somewhere.

This is a normative, substantive ethico-political inquiry.[4] When I ask what is the best way of defining the RoL requirement of publicity, it is in this sense that the word 'best' has to be understood.

3. THE INSTRUMENTAL VALUE OF PUBLICITY

What then is valuable in publicity, from the perspective of the RoL ideal? A first answer to this question is quite simple.[5] Given what the point of

---

[4] Such an inquiry is not unrelated to the two alternatives I mentioned two paragraphs above. The outcomes of a substantive normative inquiry of the kind described can only be deemed plausible to the extent that they on the whole agree with the *endoxa* (i.e. the opinions held by all, or by those who are competent enough, or by the main authors) in the relevant field; and they must be capable of being upheld as resting on—or leading to—plausible redefinitions of the relevant concepts, given their current usage (mere stipulation is, of course, a different matter). Thus, the two alternatives mentioned (stipulation, understood as plausible redefinition of ordinarily used concepts, and critical understanding of what others have said) work as—partially defeasible—constraints on our inquiry.

[5] The arguments I shall put forward are not meant to show that publicity is always, under any circumstances, required, or desirable. They only provide *pro tanto* reasons in its support (cf. for an inventory of "the forms of legal secrecy" in the modern state Kutz 2009, 203–9). Besides, publicity is discussed, in this chapter, as part of the RoL. The RoL itself is one ethico-political

the RoL is, the value of publicity is instrumental. For the laws to achieve the end the RoL assigns them, they have to be public. Let us see why.

What is the point of the RoL? A first, rough answer to this question is close at hand. What the RoL says is, first of all, that the laws should be such that they can be followed and obeyed.

Most of the RoL features specify, more or less directly, what is instrumentally required in order to achieve an end—namely, the end of guiding human behaviour through rules.[6] Thus, many of them are features the laws must possess if they have to be capable of being followed and obeyed. So understood, the features constituting the RoL are features an instrument (laws) must possess in order to perform its function (guiding human behaviour), and to perform it well. In this way, the RoL requirements are to law what sharpness is to a knife (Raz 1977, 225).

To illustrate: if they are to be able to guide human behaviour laws have to be laid out in advance (prospectivity), and to be clear enough for their addressees to understand them (intelligibility). The same line of reasoning obviously holds for publicity: if they are to be capable of guiding human behaviour, laws have to be public.[7]

This gives us a first, obvious (though by no means unimportant) determination of what 'public' should be understood to mean here. If they are to be capable of guiding human behaviour, laws have to be *made known* to their addressees.[8]

4. PUBLICITY AND HUMAN DIGNITY

There is, however, more to publicity—understood as the laws' being made known to their addressees—than its instrumental value.[9]

ideal among many other commendable ideals; it should not be taken as setting requirements that always, under any circumstances, override any other ethico-political consideration.

[6] In Fuller's (1969, 106) phrase, "the enterprise of subjecting human conduct to the governance of rules." Cf. Raz 1977, 214.

[7] This is the main *rationale* for viewing publication as a necessary condition for enacted laws to acquire full legal validity (cf. Guastini 2010, 77–8).

[8] This holds only for what may be called 'normal', or standard, guidance—i.e. guidance through an understanding, by the agent, of what the law, according to its tenor, requires of him, and that it is required of him (Celano 2013b). All sorts of non-standard cases can be devised (e.g. parents may sometimes, in order to make their children do A, tell them not to do A, thus relying on their children's standing disposition to do the opposite of what they tell them to do).

[9] There is one aspect of the value of publicity which I take to be unproblematic, and with which I shall not be concerned here. Publicity is a necessary condition for accountability. One

This requirement of publicity also embodies a basic insight about justice: it is unjust that an agent should be judged blameworthy, and punished, for having acted against a standard of conduct—or norm (I shall use these terms interchangeably)—that was unknown to them.[10] Call this moral principle the *ignorantia legis excusat* (ILE) principle.

The status of the ILE principle is precarious. There may perhaps be good reasons (which I shall not explore here) for holding people morally blameworthy for violations of moral standards they have no knowledge of. Likewise, there may be good reasons (pragmatic or otherwise) grounding, in the legal domain (specifically, in the field of criminal law), the principle *ignorantia legis non excusat*. The moral ILE principle, however, expresses, I think, a sound default position: barring special considerations, *ceteris paribus*, etc., it would be unjust to judge an agent blameworthy, and to punish them, for having violated a norm, or normative requirement, of which they have, and had, no knowledge.[11] Quite sensibly, we may wish to amend, and weaken, the principle in order to take account of the hypothesis of faulty ignorance: *ceteris paribus*, it is unjust to judge an agent blameworthy, and to punish them, for having violated a norm, or normative requirement, they did not know, and were faultlessly not in a position to gain knowledge of (reasonable ignorance). By so weakening the principle we impose on agents the burden of doing their best in order to ascertain what the standards their behaviour is subject to are (thereby licensing a defeasible presumption: absent special evidence, the agent is supposed to know what the relevant norms are).

---

way in which the RoL "restricts the discretion of government officials, reducing wilfulness and arbitrariness," argues B. Tamanaha (2009, 7, 8), is "by insisting that government officials act pursuant to and consistent with applicable legal rules"; one way in which the law operates to obtain this benefit is this: "legal rules provide publicly available requirements and standards that can be used to hold government officials accountable during and after their actions" (this, I take it, includes judicial decisions). The case for publicity is even stronger, of course. when one looks to *democratic* accountability (Kutz 2009, 200).

[10] Cf. for a vivid illustration of this point F. Kafka's *In der Strafkolonie* (1919).

[11] The point is that ignorance is an *excuse* (and, thus, it prevents blameworthiness), although the act is, in fact, wrong (cf., on the legal count, Husak 1994, 109, 114). The principle obviously allows for cases in which, to use B. Williams's phrase (1989, 43), "it will be merely unclear what, if anything, blame [blame "in a focussed form, as opposed to its acting as a broader instrument of correction and disapproval"] is effecting" (cases in which it may be an "unintelligible mystery" what blame is up to; Williams 1989, 44).

These considerations are especially important in providing moral grounds for the legal principle *ignorantia legis non excusat*.[12] In the light of these considerations, in fact, the legal principle may itself come to be understood as a corollary of the principle of publicity: where the laws are made accessible to their addressees, *ignorantia legis* may (defeasibly) be presumed to be blameworthy.[13]

Our weakened ILE principle, it seems, neatly applies to publicity: *ceteris paribus*, it is unjust to judge an agent blameworthy, and to punish them, for having violated a norm that has not been made known to them. This only works, however, under a *proviso*. The *proviso* is that the relevant standard, or norm, be of a certain kind: it must be a norm that an agent can gain no knowledge of unless it is made known to them— i.e. a norm with which an agent cannot become acquainted unless it is somehow communicated to them.[14]

Standards of conduct that exist only if someone, individual or body, has laid them down, or more generally that exist only as the upshot of contingent human action or behaviour, I shall call 'positive'. Positive standards of conduct (including positive law) fit the relevant condition: agents whose behaviour is subject to positive norms could gain no access to such norms unless they are somehow made known or communicated to them. In their case, then, the *proviso* is satisfied. Where positive norms are concerned, it would be unjust, *ceteris paribus*, to hold an individual blameworthy, and to punish them, for having violated a norm that was not made known to them, i.e. was not public. This is what the RoL requirement of publicity expresses. Correspondingly, we can posit a (moral) right, held by individuals

---

[12] On reasonable mistake as a legal excuse, cf. Husak and von Hirsch 1993, 166–70.

[13] So that, conversely, ignorance due to failure of publicity exonerates (Husak and von Hirsch 1993, 166, 173). Cf. also Husak 1994, 115: "good citizens make an effort to learn the law of the state. But duties inhere in both directions. Good states make an effort to teach citizens the law." The presumption, and the corresponding burden, may appear especially plausible in the case of (1) power-conferring rules, specifying the procedure and formalities to be respected in order, e.g. to write a valid will; and (2) rules which apply to "people who occupy very specific roles" (cf. Goodin 2010, 620–1).

[14] This may suggest the idea (Goodin 2010) that, in order to avoid the ILE stricture, it is desirable that the law—in its duty-imposing aspect (not relating to special roles or activities)— should closely track (and be known to do so) morality, on the (both unrealistic and theoretically problematic, I think) assumption that, on the whole, the dictates of the latter are known to everybody, or at least can be easily worked out by everybody. I shall not discuss this proposal here.

subject to a given jurisdiction, that (positive) norms in that jurisdiction be at least made known to them. This is not the much stronger requirement that norms to which individuals are subject should be justifiable to them, so that they can understand and endorse the reasons supporting them.[15] It is the far more modest requirement that it should be somehow communicated to them that they are supposed to act in this or that way.

If we now ask *why* it would be unjust, *ceteris paribus*, to judge an individual blameworthy, and to punish them, for having violated a positive standard not made known to them, we find it hard to give a further answer. We seem to have reached moral bedrock. We could say, however, more or less circularly, that violations of the principle would be violations of human dignity: they would show lack of respect for human beings as responsible, autonomous agents. The argument might go like this.

Respect for human beings as responsible, autonomous agents entails taking due account of their capacity for making informed choices: leaving room for their capacity to be, in Raz's phrase, (part) authors of their own lives (Raz 1986, 369). Judging an individual blameworthy, and punishing them, for having violated a positive standard not made known to them contradicts this attitude—no choice was left to them. This is why it expresses disrespect for human dignity (cf. Kramer 2007, 151).

J. Raz has claimed that "observance of the rule of law is necessary if the law is to respect human dignity" (Raz 1977, 221). "Respecting human dignity," he argues, "entails treating humans as persons capable of planning and plotting their future. Thus, respecting people's dignity entails respecting their autonomy, their right to control their future" (Raz 1977, 221). The main way in which disregard for the RoL "violates human dignity" is by allowing the frustration of expectations the law itself has encouraged (this is, says Raz, often "analogous to entrapment"; Raz 1977, 222).

The argument for publicity (as presently understood) sketched two paragraphs above illustrates this. Punishing an individual for having

---

[15] According to J. Waldron (1987), a similar requirement, concerning the principles of government, is the fundamental ethico-political requirement at the heart of modern liberalism.

violated a positive standard not made known to them is also a sort of entrapment, showing disrespect for their status as a responsible, autonomous agents. There is something deeply misconceived in putting the blame on such an agent for having acted against a norm of conduct unknown to them (provided always that they are not at fault for their ignorance—see above). Being exposed to the possibility of such punishments generates serious uncertainty, restricting the agent's opportunities for making informed choices and planning their future—as typically do, according to Raz (1977, 222), violations of the RoL. Thus, the RoL requirement of publicity, so understood, neatly fits the picture of the RoL as a shield against (certain forms of) disrespect for human dignity.[16]

5. PUBLICITY AS COMMON KNOWLEDGE

So far, the law's being public has been understood in a way compatible with the (unrealistic) hypothesis of laws that are communicated to their addressees by way of sending each one of them sealed envelopes (section 1). But this, I argue, is too narrow an understanding of the concept of publicity. We have to enrich the set of those to whom the relevant standards should be made known, by giving it a special structure. The relevant standards are to be understood as being made known neither *to one person at a time*, nor to a plurality of persons *independently of each other*, though simultaneously. They are to be made a matter of *common*, or mutual, knowledge.

I define the notion of common knowledge thus:

It is common knowledge among A and B that p if and only if
(1) A knows that p;
(1') B knows that p;
(2) A knows that B knows that p;
(2') B knows that A knows that p;
and so on, *ad infinitum*.

---

[16] That the point of (many of) the RoL requirements is to warrant, *inter alia*, (certain forms of) respect for human beings as responsible agents, entitled to make autonomous choices, is common ground. Cf. Fuller 1969, 162–3; Finnis 1980, 272–3; MacCormick 1985, 26; Marmor 2004, 21, 32; Kramer 2007, 162, 171, 176; Waldron 2008, 76.

Or, in other words

p is common knowledge among the members of group G if and only if
each one of the members of G
(1) knows that p;
(2) knows that each one of the members of G knows that p;
(3) knows that each one of the members of G knows that each one of the
members of G knows that p;
and so on, *ad infinitum*.[17]

---

[17] On the notions of common, or mutual, knowledge see respectively Lewis 1969, 52 ff.;
Schiffer 1972, 30 ff. (differences between the two notions need not detain us here). The connection between common knowledge and publicity is no surprise. In fact, the notion of
common knowledge is supposed to capture "the idea that some fact is 'out in the open' or
'entirely public' with respect to certain individuals" (Gilbert 1987, 188; cf. also Chwe 2001,
13). A number of caveats are in place here. (1) In the text common knowledge is defined in
terms of a hierarchy of epistemic iterations. This is the simplest and intuitive way of introducing the phenomenon; the definitions provided by the main authors usually have, however, a different structure—such that they entail, or otherwise generate, epistemic iterations
of the kind indicated. (2) Its being common knowledge that p requires, apparently, an infinite set of epistemic states, or unbounded computational capacities, by the relevant individuals; and, it is argued, since human cognitive capacities are limited, common knowledge
is impossible. This objection can be met (various strategies have been proposed; cf. Vanderschraaf and Sillari 2007, sections 2.2, 2.5, 4). But, even if it can be, (3) it remains true that
"it is almost impossible for something to become common knowledge in a large society"
(Binmore 2008, 17, 23). I assume that some suitable notion of *approximate common knowledge*, or "ordinary common knowledge" (Paternotte 2010), can be built, by weakening some
of the conditions for common knowledge proper, thus overcoming this and similar objections. (4) Here, and in the next section, common knowledge is presented as a necessary
condition (for the law to be efficacious in its intended way, here; for it to respect human
dignity, in the next section). Strictly speaking, I do not show this (specifically, I do not
demonstrate that the series of higher-level epistemic iterations is bound to be closed, in
whatever way it is supposed to be closed when common knowledge proper obtains). I show,
rather, that common knowledge proper, or some suitable form of approximate common
knowledge, is a necessary condition for those feats to be achieved. (5) Highly sophisticated
formal definitions of the concept of common knowledge (and of approximate common
knowledge) have been worked out (cf. for a survey Vanderschraaf and Sillari 2007, section
2). An assessment of these proposals is both beyond my competence and unnecessary here.
For our purposes, an intuitive grasp of the phenomenon is all that is needed. It is an
undoubtedly real phenomenon (cf. Chwe 2001, 77–9), which the definition given in the
text, though informal and imprecise, vividly depicts. (6) I talk, following the tradition, of
common *knowledge*; the distinction between knowledge and belief is, however, of obvious
importance in this context. Under this respect, too, I leave matters undetermined, relying on
entrenched ways of characterizing the phenomenon. It should be stressed, however, that
common 'knowledge' is usually the upshot of guesswork by the individuals involved, and a
defeasible achievement.

The best way of understanding the RoL requirement of publicity is in terms of such common knowledge.[18] There are three reasons for this. The first concerns the efficacy of the law, and will be discussed in the present section. The second and the third will be discussed, respectively, in sections 6 and 7. A fourth reason for requiring that the laws should be commonly known among their subjects goes beyond the RoL ideal, and involves further ethico-political assumptions (section 8).

Let us return to our understanding of publicity as instrumentally valuable—indeed, necessary—in order for the laws to achieve their intended (normal) purpose (section 3). If laws are to provide guidance for human behaviour, as we have seen, they have to be made known to their addressees. But efficacy also requires mutual knowledge, in two ways.

First, as noted by H. H. Clark and T. B. Carlson (1982), when what is required is a "joint act," shared beliefs *among the addressees* is crucial. By a 'joint act' is meant "an act by two or more people who must, in general, intentionally co-ordinate their separate actions in order to succeed" (Clark and Carlson 1982, 2).[19] When for example, X tells A and B to shake hands "for [X] to expect [A and B] to be able to carry it out, he must intend each of them to recognize not only what he asked of *him* but also what he has asked of the other. If they are told separately and have no guarantee the other has been told, they should realize they cannot carry out that joint act without further negotiation" (Clark and Carlson, 1–2; cf. also Chwe 2001, 9, 111).

The law may enjoin a plurality of addressees to perform joint acts. Think, for example, of regulations that assign tasks to collegial bodies, or set up the provision of public services. In such cases, it will not be enough that the relevant directive be made known to each of the addressees separately (as with the sealed envelopes). It will also be necessary, if the directive is to guide behaviour in the intended (standard) way, that

---

[18] For a suggestion in this sense (regarding public policies), cf. Luban 1996, 170. According to Rawls (1971, 48), it is a "reasonable simplifying assumption" (for the purposes of a theory of justice) to see publicity as common knowledge as a defining property of the rules constituting an institution; accordingly, the law is characterized as a system of "public rules" (Rawls 1971, 207; Rawls, however, does not use the phrase 'common knowledge').

[19] Examples include "shaking hands…, rowing a boat, speaking and listening, driving down a highway, signalling in Morse code, walking in a crowd of people, meeting, and dancing" (Clark and Carlson 1982, 2).

it becomes common knowledge among them. In such cases, then, what the RoL requires, by way of publicity (making positive laws known to their addressees), is common knowledge.[20]

But, second, this turns out to be true of a huge number of legal requirements,[21] including cases of actions each one of us can perform on our own (not involving coordination in the above sense), under a certain plausible condition.

Consider a group of individuals G, all addressees of a positive requirement R, such that, for each member of G, part of the reason for complying with R is the expectation that the other members of G will comply (because they have this expectation, because they expect the others to have this expectation, and so on). Everybody is expected to comply because, *inter alia*, each expects the others (to expect the others...) to comply; everybody complies, in part, because each has this set of expectations about the others' expectations and conduct.

The condition under which our finding turns out to be true of many positive laws is that, where a legal system exists (which requires its being generally efficacious), the population of its addressees is, to a varying extent, a group of the kind described. This may be understood in two ways.

First, it may be a matter of the actual subjective motivations of the addressees. Where (nearly) all (nearly) always comply because (*inter alia*) they are disposed to comply on condition that they expect the others to comply, and they in fact expect the others to comply because they expect them to expect the others to comply (and so on), the laws cannot guide behaviour (in the standard way) unless they are matters of common knowledge.[22]

It may also be understood, second, as a matter concerning what (objectively) good reasons each addressee has for complying. Many legal requirements are such that it would make no sense to comply with them

---

[20] A special case is when the law enjoins the performance of a set of actions providing the solution of a coordination problem in the strict, game-theoretical sense. In order to work, in this way, as solutions to coordination problems laws have to be common knowledge among their subjects (cf. generally Lewis 1969). In such cases the law works as a mere indicator. Once one of the many equilibria available is made salient to the parties by being singled out by the law, all individuals involved will, by hypothesis, do their part in it (cf. Ullmann-Margalit 1981; Green 1988, 111–15).

[21] Bentham's idea (cf. Postema 1986, 246).

[22] Remember, here and in what follows, caveat (4) in n. 17.

unless one expected most of the others to comply as well. Examples range, it may be argued, from complying with many traffic regulations to paying taxes or, on some accounts, keeping one's word. It is, in general, the case with legal directives that can plausibly be explained as attempted solutions to multilateral Prisoner's Dilemmas and similar sorts of collective action problems. In such cases, it is necessary for the addressees to have reason to comply that it is common knowledge among them what the requirements imposed by the laws are. In this interpretation, then, what the RoL requirement of publicity expresses is the idea that, in order for the laws to provide good reasons for action to their subjects, they should be common knowledge among them.

6. COMMON KNOWLEDGE AS A PRECONDITION FOR CERTAINTY

Once again, however, the common knowledge requirement is not merely a matter of the law's being efficacious. Here too publicity is a matter of respecting human dignity.

Why? Because in order for each individual to enjoy—or to have the opportunity of enjoying—his status as a responsible, autonomous agent, it is not enough that the way the legal system will react to his actions be predictable to him (on the basis of his own knowledge of the laws). It is also necessary that he is in a position to predict, with reasonable confidence, how it will react to *the other citizens'* behaviour. It is necessary, generally, that he be able to form reasonable expectations about how the others will act in response to the existing legal standards; and, once again, how they act will depend in part on how they expect the legal system to react to their behaviour, and that of others. Thus, in order for the laws to make room for their subjects' autonomy it is necessary for them to be common knowledge.

Observance of the RoL is necessary if the law is to respect human dignity, because laws meeting RoL conditions will guarantee a measure of certainty in the relations between the law and its subjects (thus making room for their autonomous choices) and do not act as 'entrapment' devices (section 4). This applies to individual citizens in their relation to the government. But it also applies to citizens in relation to each other; or, better, to each individual citizen's relation to the government in relation to *the other citizens'* relation to the government. Certainty, and the avoidance of 'entrapment', will only be possible if the laws work as commonly known social interaction devices that are a common focus for relatively stable mutual expectations. Only laws meeting the condition of publicity understood as common knowledge are apt to give rise to a stable, reliable set of concordant mutual expectations at all levels, thus guaranteeing a measure of firmness and predictability in the interaction of rulers and ruled, and of law's subjects with each other.

To sum up. Certainty of the relations between the law and its subjects requires that an individual can form reliable expectations about the behaviour of government's officials and of the other citizens (and of government's officials in relation to other citizens, and vice versa), in respect of existing legal standards; this holds for all alike (and each is aware of this...). It is only by being public in the deeper sense of being a matter of common knowledge that law contributes to the establishment, among its subjects, of a system of relatively stable and relatively reliable interlocking mutual expectations. And this is a necessary condition if the law is to show respect for the subjects' ability to make meaningful autonomous choices.

7. THE RULE OF LAW AS THE RULE OF LEGISLATION

Let us now ask ourselves what kind of norms are best able to satisfy the publicity condition in the sense of common knowledge. The answer is, it seems to me, *prescriptions*.[23]

Prescribing is, roughly, the purposive activity of trying to get people to do something by telling them to do it. Prescribing has several formal features. As with any other purposive, goal-oriented activity some of these express the requirements that the activity has to fulfil in order to achieve its constitutive purpose. Some of these features instantiate elements of the RoL ideal. This is no surprise, of course, since, as I remarked in section 3, most of the RoL conditions follow from what is instrumentally required when we want to subject human behaviour to the

---

[23] "Prescriptions are *given* or *issued* by someone. They 'flow' from or have their 'source' in the will of a norm-giver... They are, moreover, addressed at some agent or agents, whom we shall call norm-*subject(s)*" (von Wright 1963, 7; further features which he sees as "characteristic of norms which are prescriptions" (von Wright 1963, 7) are of no interest for us here).

guidance of rules; and prescribing just *is* trying to subject human behaviour to the guidance of rules.[24]

So, for instance, prescriptions typically have to be prospective and intelligible if they are to be capable of achieving their purpose of guiding human behaviour. Further, the activity of prescribing is subject to rational pressure in favour of conformity to the principles that '*ought*' implies '*can*' (practicability), and that conflicts are to be avoided (consistency).[25]

A conceptual connection between the issuing of prescriptions and a constraint of common knowledge is not hard to find. When prescriptions are issued, what happens between lawgiver and addressee is out in the open among them.[26] A prescription is typically issued with a certain intention and its workings rest on a complex set of interrelated intentions, and their successful expression and detection (Grice 1957; Strawson 1964, 256–7; Schiffer 1972, 19; Celano 1990, 127–51, 205–13; cf. also Raz 1996, 283). The lawgiver normally has, first, the intention to make the addressee perform a certain action; and, second, the intention to make the addressee perform a certain action as a consequence of his uttering a sentence. Third, he intends to make the addressee perform a certain action (as a consequence of his uttering a sentence) by virtue of the recognition, by the addressee, of these very same intentions.

In issuing a prescription, then, the lawgiver assumes his addressee to be capable of detecting—and of expressing her detection of—a complex set of nested intentions. The addressee is presumed to be capable of understanding: (1) that the speaker wants her to behave in a certain way; (2) that he wants to make her behave in the desired way; (3) that he wants to produce this outcome as a consequence of his uttering a sentence; (4) that he wants to produce this outcome by virtue of her recognition of these intentions, (1) to (4). It follows that for a prescription to affect its addressee's conduct in the way it is intended to, it is necessary that the

---

[24] This should be qualified. Prescribing is not necessarily the issuing of *general* directives, or of 'rules' proper. Under this respect the requirements of the RoL do not apply to prescribing as such. But we may abstract from this, and focus on the respects in which prescribing does indeed instantiate the kind of activity RoL requirements apply to.

[25] Cf. Celano 2013b. These are all features that prescriptions *typically* exhibit, and pressures prescriptions are *standardly* subject to. The possibility of non-standard prescriptions is not ruled out. These will be cases of abuse of the institution of prescribing.

[26] Cf. for a detailed treatment of this point Celano 2013a, section 6.

addressee understand that her understanding of the prescription is itself a necessary condition for it to produce the desired outcome. A prescription is a kind of tool that works (in the way it is intended to work) only if the object it causally affects understands that it is so working. It also follows that the operation of a prescription—Y's conduct being guided by X's uttering a sentence—is grounded on X's anticipating Y's practical reasoning, including Y's representation in her practical reasoning of X's practical reasoning, and of this very anticipation.

So, in order for the lawgiver to achieve his aim, it is necessary for him to make his intention of making the addressee perform a certain action through the utterance of a given sentence known to the addressee (this is our first notion of publicity; see section 3). This is not, however, sufficient. If odd or deviant ways of influencing others' behaviour are to be ruled out (Strawson 1964, 256–7, 263; Schiffer 1972, 30), a condition of common knowledge also has to be satisfied. In prescribing, the lawgiver intends to make the addressee perform a given action by virtue of the recognition, by the addressee, of this very intention. Thus, an utterance may count as a prescription only if the addressee believes that the lawgiver has the relevant intentional structure, if she believes the lawgiver to believe that she believes he has it, and so on. Likewise, it is necessary that the lawgiver believes that the addressee recognizes this structure, that he believes her to believe that he believes this, and so on. In short, a prescription only has been issued if it is common knowledge among lawgiver and addressee that it has been issued.

Let us return now to the law. What kind of legal standards most naturally fit this model? The answer may appear obvious: statutes—i.e. the upshots of legislative activity. (I do not mean to claim that statutes are the only kind of legal standards that may fit this picture, but that they are the ones that most naturally come to mind and are good candidates.) At a first glance legislation plainly *is* the issuing of prescriptions.[27] So the kind of positive law the RoL requirement of publicity as common knowledge most naturally applies to is statutes, the product of legislation. Admittedly, prescriptions must be common knowledge *between lawgiver and addressee* and the RoL requirement of publicity, as presently understood, requires that the laws be common knowledge (also) *among their addressees*. This is a further step. But prescriptions (and thus,

---

[27] But see the last paragraph of this section.

statutes), given the role common knowledge plays in their coming into existence and in their intended (normal) workings, will typically meet this further condition. Prescriptions are thus doubly public. Under normal conditions, prescribing is a procedure openly and publicly directed at the issuing of public directives. Where prescriptions are involved not only the standard itself, but also its mode of birth, are normally out in the open. As noted by J. Waldron, legislation is 'transparent': the legislature "is an institution set up explicitly to make and change the law.... [L]aw-making in a legislature... is law-making through a procedure dedicated publicly and transparently to that task" (Waldron 2007, 99).[28]

So understood, legislation is a special kind of power. When the government exercises that power over its subjects, it addresses them as adults: it accords them the dignity of beings worthy of being publicly, openly addressed, and of being guided through their understanding of the way in which power is being exerted over them. In short, it treats them with and shows them *respect*.

This way of exercising power over a human being is different from the way in which people sometimes try to guide children's behaviour—distorting reality, or trying to manipulate, unknown to hem, the environment or their preferences, by working behind their back. These, of course, are ways in which even adult men and women are often treated—and sometimes wish to be treated (or have to be treated). But they are not respectful ways.[29]

In short, then, to the extent that they are all addressed as the addressees of prescriptions, individuals are treated with *equal respect*. This concerns, of course, only the form of the relationship, not the content of the prescription. It is compatible with all sorts of disrespect and unjust discrimination.[30] But it positively is, it seems to me, a further aspect involved in the point of the publicity (common knowledge) requirement.

All this gives a legislative twist to the RoL. The RoL has to be understood—according to the understanding of the requirement of publicity

---

[28] Cf. also Waldron 1999b, 12; and 2009, 693.

[29] Remember that we are dealing, here, with standard cases. Abuses are possible (n. 25).

[30] Orders may be harsh, brutal; they may be wielded as weapons by people intending only to make other people do certain things—or positively aiming at humiliating them. Prescriptions, as discussed in the text, are an ideal communicative type.

we are now considering—as the rule of legislation. This is a specific version of the ideal of the RoL, whose building blocks were laid down, roughly, in European legal culture in the 18th and 19th centuries. I shall call it 'Enlightenment RoL' (ERoL for short). ERoL gives pride of place, in the development and operation of law, to legislation.[31]

This version of the RoL raises several problems. I simply note some of them here, deferring to another occasion any attempt at solving them.

(1) The RoL is often depicted as a spontaneous, non-manufactured, unintended, gradually evolving order of human interaction whose administration and piecemeal development is entrusted to the collective, 'artificial' reason of the judiciary. Obviously, ERoL does not fit this picture.

(2) The notion of a legislation-oriented RoL—ERoL—runs counter to the well-established contrast between 'the Rule of Law' and 'the rule of men'.[32]

(3) The most serious problem is, I think, raised by the apparently obvious claim that legislation plainly is the issuing of prescriptions, that statutes are prescriptions. Legislation proper, as it occurs in developed legal systems, has many complex, articulated procedural and institutional features, which have no obvious equivalent in the case of simple acts of prescribing. Most important, there is no obvious way in which a multi-membered legislature, composed of individuals and groups who sharply disagree with each other on the relevant issues, and making decisions on the basis of majority rule, may be assimilated to an individual, enacting his own will by expressing it in the form of a prescription (Waldron 1999a, part I; 1999b, 26–8).

8. THE ENLIGHTENMENT PROJECT

There is, then, a conceptual connection holding (via the centrality of legislation) between ERoL, on the one hand, and an understanding of

---

[31] A commitment to ERoL is conceptually linked to the endorsement of normative legal positivism—the view that it is a good and desirable thing that the laws have easily identifiable, readily accessible, as far as possible non-controversial social sources (Celano 2013a).

[32] This is noted in Raz 1977, 212, and explained in Waldron 1999b, 24; 2007, 101–4. For a discussion, cf. Celano 2013a, section 5.

publicity as common knowledge, on the other hand. This connection points to a further reason—a fourth reason (section 5)—for understanding the RoL (specifically, ERoL) requirement of publicity as a requirement of common knowledge. It rests on some aspects of what I shall rather loosely call, with no pretentions of historical exactness, 'the Enlightenment project'. The endorsement of ERoL is one of its main components; some of its further facets will emerge in what follows. The connection between the Enlightenment project and publicity as common knowledge goes beyond the ideal of the RoL (and ERoL), as here understood. It comes into light when ERoL is seen as an element in the Enlightenment project.

The Enlightenment project, as I understand it, involves a set of substantive ethico-political assumptions concerning the status and the rights of citizens of a republican political community. They can be best spelt out in broadly Kantian terms. I list those that are relevant to our inquiry: members in a just political community are free and equal; as autonomous agents, they are entitled to being subject to laws that they at least understand and recognize as such, and they have a right to criticize freely these laws. I am not going to defend these views here. In this section, the RoL publicity requirement will be worked out within the framework of these assumptions. I argue that, in this framework too, publicity is best understood as common knowledge.

It is part and parcel of the Enlightenment project that positive laws should be fully accessible to all. This requires that their existence be ascertainable by each of their addressees (this is, as we shall see in a moment—section 9—the offspring of publicity in our first sense). It also requires that they be intelligible to common human understanding. The laws must not be the jealous possession of (in Bentham's phrase) "Judge & Co," purportedly requiring, for their knowledge and understanding, a special, 'artificial' reason, which is somehow beyond the capacities of all cognitively normal adult human beings. Lawyers should not function as priests having unique access to the sacred books.

But the Enlightenment project also requires that the law should be public in a further, stronger sense. The laws must be such that they can be the subject of public discussion, and the object of open criticism. They are meant to constrain the actions and interactions of free and equals; and only laws that can be openly discussed and criticized are compatible with the status of individuals as free and equal.

This, once again, requires that the laws should be not merely known to each addressee, but also common knowledge among them. In one sense, this is a trivial point. Only standards of conduct commonly known can be the object of public critical debate.[33] But why, one may wonder, are only laws that are public, in this way, fit for free and equals?

Part of the answer follows from what I have said already about common knowledge as a condition for the law's respecting the dignity of responsible, autonomous agents. In order for each individual to enjoy that status it is necessary that the laws may become the common focus for relatively stable mutual expectations (section 6). Government by prescriptions (and thus by legislation) shows respect for its subjects (section 7). Moreover—and this is the present point—autonomous individuals have, as such, a right to openly criticize any claim, doctrine, theory or institution (especially so, when it purports to guide them, and it claims the authority for doing so), including, of course, their own views, laying down their criticism under the eyes of the public at large—that is, in the public sphere (Kant 1781, AXI, A738-9/B766-7; Kant 1784). And only laws that are public—i.e. commonly known—can be so criticized (non-public laws would *eo ipso* lose their status in the process).

The point can be elaborated. The Enlightenment project includes a commitment against secrecy of laws, and of governmental action, as a general principle (Bobbio 1980, 94; Luban 1996, 154–7). It includes, for example. a rejection of the Platonic Noble Lie (Plato, *Resp.* 414b–c), *arcana imperii.* or 'Government House utilitarianism'.[34] Why? Because free individuals are subject to public laws: their being subject to the constraint of a law is only compatible with their autonomy if they openly and frankly acknowledge it, under everybody else's eyes.[35] It must be out in the open that something is required, as must what is required, and

---

[33] On publicity as a condition for the "public scrutiny" of the laws, cf. Kramer 2007, 151–2 (but cf. also Fuller 1969, 51).

[34] This is part of what J. Waldron (2009, 693; see also 2001, 418), following Rawls, calls "the liberal principle of publicity": "the idea that the legitimacy of our institutions should not depend upon any widespread public misapprehension about the way they operate."

[35] According to Waldron (2009, 693, "transparency" (i.e. conformity to the principle of publicity; see this chapter, n. 34) "conveys the idea that the law in some sense *belongs* to the members of the public. It is *their* law."

what is supposed to follow as a consequence of behaviour not conforming to the requirement. Free people do not hide their subjection. Their right to criticize freely presupposes this openness of acknowledgment.

I assume that individuals in a political community are free and equal only if they recognize each other as free and equal. And, given that being subject to a law is only compatible with autonomy if openly and frankly acknowledged, under everybody else's eyes, individuals can only recognize each other as free and equal, when subject to a set of laws, if these laws are common knowledge among them.[36]

Thus, in a community of free and equal people under law it is out in the open what the laws they are subject to are. (This can be accomplished, as we have seen—section 7—through a Gricean structure of interrelated intentions extended to encompass common knowledge of the laws among addressees.) Free and equal people can only be subject to forms of power that satisfy this condition, and this is the kind of power that the Enlightenment project distinctively supports.

Let us now take stock. Publicity (common knowledge) is a necessary condition if the law is to respect the autonomy of its subjects (section 6). It is an essential element in ERoL, accounting for the way in which laws meeting the ERoL ideal show respect for their subjects as adult human beings (section 7). And it stands out as a prominent desideratum when the RoL (specifically, ERoL) ideal is seen, as it is in this section, as part of the Enlightenment project. The RoL (ERoL) is essentially a form of *public* power, whose operations are commonly known among its subjects, as contrasted with forms of power that operate 'behind the back' of individuals (by manipulating, unknown to them, their environment, preferences, or beliefs). And, for this reason, it is a mode of power which fits the dignity of adult, responsible, autonomous agents.[37]

---

[36] If publicity is understood as common knowledge, the RoL condition of publicity corresponds to Rawls's "first level" of publicity concerning the acceptance of the principles of justice in a well-ordered society (cf. Rawls 1999, 292–3, 324). (The assumption that in a well-ordered society principles of justice should be public in this sense is there already in *A Theory of Justice*, Rawls 1971, e.g. at 48–9; cf. Larmore 2003, 369–75.) Further, when seen in the light of the Enlightenment project, the requirement of publicity (common knowledge) sets the stage, or prepares the ground, for what Rawls (1999, 293, 324) calls "full publicity"—a much more exigent condition, concerning the shared *justification* of the relevant standards.

[37] This is why ERoL is germane to a critique of power: an anatomy, and exposure, of the mechanisms distinctive of forms of power not compatible with the autonomy of subjects. The import of the publicity condition in this regard is shown in the fact that some of these mechanisms are refuted—both made ineffective, and shown to be disreputable—by their being laid

9. PUBLICITY FOR OFFICIALS?

But, it will be objected, all this is too naive. In modern states, citizens do not know much of the law, let alone its complexities and intricacies. And it is extremely unrealistic to think that it could be otherwise. The division of labour applies to the legal domain, too. Detailed knowledge of the law is the lot of a specialized profession. How could it ever be otherwise?

This pessimism is reflected in contemporary jurisprudence. As noted by J. Waldron (2009, 692), rules of recognition are typically thought of, following Hart, as stating the criteria *officials* are supposed to avail themselves of in identifying valid legal norms. The identification of the law is a task that, it is assumed, belongs primarily if not exclusively to officials and to professional lawyers. At the limit, perhaps, a legal system could exist where only officials have cognizance of the law.[38]

Moreover, if we follow the lines of Hart's (1961, 89–95) conceptual genesis of developed legal systems, the views about publicity laid out in the previous sections look less plausible still. It is precisely in a (hypothetical) 'primitive', pre-legal society—a closely-knit community whose members share a *Weltanschauung*, ruled by a regime of social rules of obligation only—that individuals all know, with confidence and in some detail, what the existing rules are, and what they require. (And, we may add, only in such a society do individuals also know that the others know...what the rules are.) It is precisely where, as a consequence of social development and of changing circumstances, uncertainties as to what are the rules of the group arise and become endemic that secondary rules are needed, and a legal system comes into being. Publicity, as here understood, is it seems distinctive of a *pre-legal* community. By definition, where law exists, knowledge of it is the more or

out in the open, and made explicit. Think, for example, of religious indoctrination, when prompted by the unstated assumption that widespread religious belief, no matter whether true or false, is necessary for the maintenance of a stable social order.

[38] Publicity for officials only may lead to non-standard forms of guidance of citizens' behaviour (cf. Kramer 1999, 45–6; Kutz 2009, 210). There may be sound ethico-political reasons favouring "selective transmission" of some legal standards (specifically, some criminal law decision rules) to officials only, keeping citizens unaware of their existence ("acoustic separation," Dan-Cohen 1984). It is debatable (to say the least) whether, as Dan-Cohen argues (1984, 667–73; cf. also Kutz 2009, 210), this is compatible with the RoL. Be that as it may, as I remarked (n. 5) the RoL should not be taken as an ideal that always, under any circumstances, overrides all other relevant ethico-political considerations.

less exclusive possession of a restricted class (officials, professional law-yers) employing special, technical tools (rules of recognition) in order to find out what it is.[39]

It would be foolish to deny the main claims upon which the objection rests. True, one could reply that the ideal of publicity, as here under-stood, is precisely that: an ideal. An ideal's realization need not be an easy matter. But an ideal must be such that its realization has at least a minimum of plausibility. Rather, replying to the objection calls, I think, for a revision, and weakening, of our understanding of the ideal of pub-licity. The needed revision is not dramatic. Law, in contrast to a regime of customary rules of obligation, is characterized by rules that make pos-sible deliberate changes of existing rules—i.e. the deliberate modifica-tion or destruction of previously existing rules, and the deliberate creation of new ones. Hart calls such secondary rules "rules of change"; where such rules exist, the rule of recognition of the system will neces-sarily refer to them (1961, 93). Only in following these rules can people make (or change) positive laws (section 4). We should modify our claim to hold that publicity requires that *these rules*—i.e. the procedures for making positive law—be, at least in their rough outlines, common knowledge among the citizens, that an official, reliable, public record of the outcomes of the activities they define (i.e. legislation) should be available and that the existence of a device for publication of the laws itself be common knowledge among the citizens.

---

[39] Cf. Waldron 1999b, 13–14. So far, I have been talking of publicity as a matter of the laws being (commonly) known *by their addressees*. But who are the addressees of the laws? Officials, or the citizenry at large? Considerations along the lines set out in the text may lead to an option for the former hypothesis. More generally, many legal theorists (notably Kelsen) have held, for various reasons, that what legal norms purport directly to guide is the behaviour of officials only. Such views press us further away from the understanding of the ideal of publicity I have been defending—indeed, in the opposite direction. True, we might content ourselves with the claim that what the RoL requires is that laws, understood as directives addressed to officials, should be common knowledge among the latter, This would be a way of meeting—in fact, of eluding—the objection discussed in the text. A mistaken way, however. It is true that, if rules of recognition are to be understood, along the lines of Hart's *Postscript* (1994), as conventions of official behaviour (which is by no means devoid of problems; cf. Green 1996, 1695–7; Celano 2003; Dickson 2007), then it might perhaps follow, by definition, that they are com-mon knowledge among officials (it all depends on how the concept of convention is moulded). But this has little to do with the ideal of the RoL, as usually understood. The RoL—and, *a fortiori*, ERoL—is a set of ethico-political requirements concerning basically the law in its relationship to ordinary people.

Prescribing is a procedure publicly directed at the issuing of public directives: both the created norms and their mode of birth are out in the open (section 7). This—plus an official, accessible, public record of the prescriptions issued—is what the publicity of legislation consists in.[40] It is true that laws cannot literally be *made known* (section 3) each one of them to each one of their addressees; nor can they, one by one, in detail, literally become common knowledge among them. But by such means they can become *ascertainable* by those whose conduct they purport to rule—with the aid, no doubt, of professional lawyers.[41]

Is this enough? It still remains true that few citizens know even a few statutes; they are not assiduous readers of official records of legislative proceedings (Guastini 2010, 83). Where ERoL, and the Enlightenment project generally, have gained some footing, however, records of the relevant legal material are there and available to everybody. Rough knowledge of the ways in which laws are created and applied is a matter of basic civic education . And legal education is, in principle, open to all, on an equal footing; you do not have to prove allegiance to a church or party, nor special personal qualities or family descendance, in order to have access to it. In principle, anybody can acquire it.

REFERENCES

Binmore, K. 2008 'Do Conventions Need to Be Common Knowledge?', *Topoi* 27.

Bobbio, N. 1980 'La democrazia e il potere invisibile', in Bobbio, *Il futuro della democrazia*, Einaudi, Turin 1984, 1991.

Celano, B. 1990 *Dover essere e intenzionalità. Una critica all'ultimo Kelsen*, Giappichelli, Turin.

Celano, B. 2003 'La regola di riconoscimento è una convenzione?', in M. C. Redondo (ed.), *Il 'Postscript' di H. L. A. Hart*, *Ragion pratica* 21 (monographic issue).

Celano, B. 2013a 'Normative Legal Positivism, Neutrality, and the Rule of Law', in J. Ferrer Beltrán, J. J. Moreso, and D. M. Papayannis (eds.), *Neutrality and Theory of Law*, Springer, Dordrecht.

[40] Cf. Waldron 2009, 692–3.
[41] Realistically, ascertainability with the aid of legal experts is what the RoL requirement of publicity, in the end, boils down to (Kramer 2007, 115–17, 150). Accessibility of legal advice to all citizens may be taken to be one of the main institutional RoL desiderata (this chapter, n. 3).

Celano, B. 2013b 'Law as Power: Two Rule of Law Requirements', in W. Waluchow and S. Sciaraffa (eds.), *Philosophical Foundations of the Nature of Law*, Oxford University Press, Oxford.

Chwe, M. S.-Y. 2001 *Rational Ritual. Culture, Coordination, and Common Knowledge*. Princeton University Press, Princeton (N. J.).

Clark, H. H., and Carlson, T. B. 1982 'Speech Acts and Hearers' Beliefs', in N. V. Smith (ed.), *Mutual Knowledge*, Academic Press, London 1982.

Dan-Cohen, M. 1984 'Decision Rules and Conduct Riles: On Acoustic Separation in Criminal Law', *Harvard Law Review* 97.

Dickson, J. 2007 'Is the Rule of Recognition Really a Conventional Rule?', *Oxford Journal of Legal Studies* 27.

Finnis, J. M. 1980 *Natural Law and Natural Rights*, Clarendon Press, Oxford.

Fuller, L. L. 1969 *The Morality of Law*, revised edn, Yale University Press, New Haven.

Gilbert, M. 1987 'Modeling Collective Beliefs', *Synthese* 73.

Goodin, R. E. 2010 'An Epistemic Case for Legal Moralism', *Oxford Journal of Legal Studies* 30.

Green, L., 1988 *The Authority of the State*, Oxford University Press, Oxford.

Green, L. 1996 'The Concept of Law Revisited', *Michigan Law Review* 94.

Grice, H. P. 1957 'Meaning', in *Studies in the Way of Words*, Harvard University Press, Cambridge (Mass.) 1989.

Guastini, R. 2010 *Le fonti del diritto. Fondamenti teorici*, Giuffrè, Milan.

Hart, H. L. A. 1961 *The Concept of Law*, Clarendon Press, Oxford.

Hart, H. L. A. 1994 'Postscript', *The Concept of Law*, second edn, Clarendon Press, Oxford.

Husak, D. N. 1994 'Ignorance of Law and Duties of Citizenship', *Legal Studies* 14.

Husak, D. N., and von Hirsch, A. 1993 'Culpability and Mistake of Law', in S. Shute, J. Gardner, and H. Horder (eds.), *Action and Value in Criminal Law*, Clarendon Press, Oxford 1993.

Kant, I. 1781 *Kritik der reinen Vernunft*, ed. R. Schmidt, Meiner, Hamburg 1926, 1976.

Kant, I. 1784 'Beantwortung der Frage: Was ist Aufklärung?', *Berlinische Monatsschrift* 4.

Kramer, M. H. 1999 *In Defense of Legal Positivism: Law without Trimmings*, Oxford University Press, Oxford.

Kramer, M. H. 2007 *Objectivity and the Rule of Law*, Cambridge University Press, Cambridge.

Kutz, C. 2009 'Secret Law and the Value of Publicity', *Ratio Juris* 22.

Larmore, C. 2003 'Public Reason', in S. Freeman (ed.), *The Cambridge Companion to Rawls*, Cambridge University Press, Cambridge 2003.

Lewis, D. 1969 *Convention. A Philosophical Study*, Blackwell, Oxford.

Luban, D. 1996 'The Principle of Publicity', in R. E. Goodin (ed.), *The Theory of Institutional Design*, Cambridge University Press, Cambridge 1996.

MacCormick, N. 1985 'A Moralistic Case for A-Moralistic Law?', *Valparaiso University Law Review* 20.

Marmor, A. 2004 'The Rule of Law and Its Limits', *Law and Philosophy* 23.

Paternotte, C. 2010 'Being realistic about common knowledge: a Lewisian approach', *Synthese* 183(2): 249–76.

Plato *Respublica*, in *Platonis Opera*, ed. J. Burnet, vol. IV, Clarendon Press, Oxford 1902.

Postema, G. J. 1986 *Bentham and the Common Law Tradition*, Clarendon Press, Oxford.

Rawls, J. 1971 *A Theory of Justice*, Oxford University Press, Oxford, rev. edn 1999.

Rawls, J. 1999 *Collected Papers*, ed. S. Freeman, Harvard University Press, Cambridge (Mass.).

Raz, J. 1977 'The Rule of Law and Its Virtue', in *The Authority of Law: Essays on Law and Morality*, Clarendon Press, Oxford 1979.

Raz, J. 1986 *The Morality of Freedom*, Clarendon Press, Oxford.

Raz, J. 1996 'Intention in Interpretation', in *Between Authority and Interpretation: On the Theory of Law and Practical Reason*, Oxford University Press, Oxford 2009.

Schiffer, S. 1972 *Meaning*, Clarendon Press, Oxford, second edn 1988.

Strawson, P. F. 1964 'Intention and Convention in Speech Acts', in *Logico-linguistic Papers*, Methuen, London 1971.

Tamanaha, B. 2009 'A Concise Guide to the Rule of Law', in G. Palombella and N. Walker (eds.), *Relocating the Rule of Law*, Hart Publishing, Oxford.

Ullmann-Margalit, E. 1981 'Is Law a Co-ordinative Authority?', *Israel Law Review* 16.

Vanderschraaf, P., and Sillari, G., 'Common Knowledge', in E. N. Zalta (ed.), *The Stanford Encyclopedia of Philosophy* (Spring 2009 edn), <http://plato.stanford.edu/archives/spr2009/entries/common-knowledge>.

von Wright, G. H. 1963 *Norm and Action: A Logical Enquiry*, Routledge & Kegan Paul, London.

Waldron, J. 1987 'Theoretical Foundations of Liberalism', in *Liberal Rights*, Cambridge University Press, Cambridge 1993.

Waldron, J. 1999a *Law and Disagreement*, Oxford University Press, Oxford.

Waldron, J. 1999b *The Dignity of Legislation*, Cambridge University Press, Cambridge.

Waldron, J. 2001 'Hobbes and the Principle of Publicity', *Pacific Philosophical Quarterly* 82.

Waldron, J. 2002 'Is the Rule of Law an Essentially Contested Concept (in Florida)?', *Law and Philosophy* 21.

Waldron, J. 2004 'The Rule of Law as a Theatre of Debate', in J. Burley (ed.), *Dworkin and His Critics*, Blackwell, Oxford 2004.

Waldron, J. 2007 'Legislation and the Rule of Law', *Legisprudence* 1.

Waldron, J. 2008 'Hart and the Principles of Legality', in M. Kramer et al. (eds.), *The Legacy of H. L. A. Hart: Legal, Political, and Moral Philosophy*, Oxford University Press, Oxford 2008.

Waldron, J. 2009 'Can There Be a Democratic Jurisprudence?', *Emory Law Journal* 58.

Williams, B. 1989 'Internal Reasons and the Obscurity of Blame', in *Making Sense of Humanity and Other Philosophical Papers 1982–1993*, Cambridge University Press, Cambridge 1995.

5

Hart and Kelsen on International Law*

MICHAEL GIUDICE

Hans Kelsen is responsible for introducing one of the most intriguing claims in analytical jurisprudence in the twentieth century: not only are national law as well as international law prominent forms of law, they must form one and only one legal system. The idea that laws exist as part of legal systems is of course a familiar one. Most contemporary analytical legal theorists see the key to explanation of a large part of the nature of law in explanation of the nature of legal systems. For example, in an article devoted entirely to setting out the core problems of legal theory, Joseph Raz asserts that all laws, for example, Canadian laws, German laws, and English laws, form part of legal systems, in these instances, Canadian law, German law, and English law.[1] And H. L. A. Hart, of course, developed his account of the concept of law by introducing the notion of a rule of recognition—a system-constituting social rule practised by judges and other officials of a legal system, which specifies the membership conditions of all legal norms of the system. Neither Raz nor Hart, however, ever went as far as Kelsen's remarkable view that all laws in the world must form a unity in one legal system. While Raz says very little about international law, his writing on the identity of legal systems, and especially the relation between law and state, shows that he must reject Kelsen's view: there is no cosmopolitan political society to underpin a world legal system (yet).[2] Hart did take up Kelsen's view about the relation between national law and international law, but only to show that when tested against the facts it could serve no useful

* I owe thanks to Keith Culver and Talene Thomasian for helpful discussion, and especially Les Green for valuable comments on an earlier draft.
    [1] Raz, 'The Identity of Legal Systems', in *The Authority of Law* (Oxford: Clarendon Press, 1979), 78–121.
    [2] Ibid.

purpose in adequately describing or explaining international law. In Hart's view, there are international legal obligations but no international legal system; international law lacks the secondary rules of a legal system and so exists only as a primitive legal order composed entirely of primary rules of obligation.

More than forty years on, few analytical legal theorists have subjected Hart's account to assessment, and none have questioned whether his own account of international law escapes all of the problems he identifies with Kelsen's view. In light of the flourishing of analytical legal theory since Hart, some insist that lack of critical analysis of Hart's view of international law is unacceptable. In a recent paper, Jeremy Waldron writes:

> Those international lawyers who do bother to read Hart's chapter on international law usually come away with the impression that Hart, like Austin, did not believe there was any such thing as international law. That is not quite correct, but Hart did say that international law is like a primitive legal system—all primary norms and no secondary norms. And that characterization was wrong in 1960 and it is certainly wrong now.[3]

Waldron does not provide an argument for why Hart's view is wrong, but this is not his aim; his message is that the issue has been all but entirely neglected, and without good reason. Yet if he is right in supposing that Hart's view is wrong, then analytical legal theory may indeed be in a truly bad state regarding international law. The reason is simple: if Hart's influential criticisms of Kelsen's view are successful, but Hart's alternative explanation is mistaken, then analytical legal theory would appear to be without an adequate account of the nature of international law.

The aim of this chapter is to take a first step towards reviving analytical work on international law.[4] To do so I will revisit the Hart–Kelsen debate on international law—the debate that could have been—and see

---

[3] Waldron, 'Hart and the Principles of Legality, in Matthew H. Kramer, Claire Grant, Ben Colburn, and Antony Hatzistavrou, eds., *The Legacy of H. L. A. Hart: Legal, Political, and Moral Philosophy* (Oxford: Oxford University Press, 2008), 67–83, 68. More strongly, Waldron adds: 'Those who regard themselves as working to protect and develop Hart's legacy have shown little interest in subjecting Hart's claims about international law to any sort of careful scrutiny or revision. The neglect of international law in modern analytic jurisprudence is nothing short of scandalous. Theoretically it is the issue of the hour.' Ibid, 69.

[4] See also Samantha Besson and John Tasioulas, eds., *The Philosophy of International Law* (Oxford: Oxford University Press, 2010).

what kind of light it can shed on understanding international law. This point of departure seems to me to be justified as it represents the most sophisticated analytical disagreement about the nature of international law, even if over forty years old now. My view is that the disagreement has much illumination to offer, but only once one of its key terms is recast: both Hart's and Kelsen's central use of 'legal system' as a tool in explanation of international law obscures more than it reveals.

The chapter is organized as follows. In the first section I will set out some of the main elements of Kelsen's vast account of international law, and how, in his view, international law must relate to national law. In the second section I will examine Hart's criticisms of Kelsen's view. While these are many, I will focus on three in particular: (i) that Kelsen's methodological requirement of completeness is misguided; (ii) that it is mistaken to suppose that international law must contain a system-constituting basic norm, and (iii) that a relationship of validating purport is insufficient to explain the unity of international law and national law even if they were connected by a single basic norm. The purpose of the second section will be to show that while Hart's criticisms are illuminating, they are not uniformly decisive. There is much to gain by holding on to certain elements of Kelsen's view. In the third section I will move from consideration of the differences and disagreement between Hart and Kelsen to consider a distinctively common feature of their accounts of international law: their views exhibit a shared commitment to the explanatory tool of 'legal system' in attempting to make sense of international law. In the fourth section I shall identify some of the core features of international law which show why a system-based explanation is ill-suited to explanation of international law. Here I will argue that while viewing international law from the lens of system brings some benefits, these must be weighed against—and are ultimately outweighed by—associated costs.

I. KELSEN: THE UNITY OF INTERNATIONAL LAW
AND NATIONAL LAW

There is a tendency in analytical legal theory to focus entirely on the nature of state legal systems as key to understanding the nature of law. Such was Hart's focus, but this characteristic approach was made most explicit by Raz. In explaining the criteria of adequacy of a legal theory, Raz adopts what he calls an assumption of 'the importance of municipal law':

In pursuing such investigations [into the nature of municipal legal systems] it may turn out that municipal systems are not unique, that all their essential features are shared by, say, international law or by church law. If this is indeed so, well and good. But it is not a requirement of adequacy of a legal theory that it should be so or indeed that it should not be so. It is, however, a criterion of adequacy that the theory will successfully illuminate the nature of municipal systems.[5]

On Raz's view, a very common view, accurate explanation of international law is a separate task, and one safely detachable from the task of addressing the core problems of legal theory. As Kelsen saw things, however, there could be no such view of separable tasks, and for the following reason. There are several municipal or state legal systems in the world, and if each is to be viewed or understood as a legal system—as a system of valid norms—there has to be some way of explaining the relation between these. Otherwise, Kelsen thought, we would have to assume the existence of one state legal system but deny the existence of all others, since other legal systems, if unconnected or unauthorized by one's legal system, could only be viewed as unlawful or illegal, and so not of the nature of law. The way out of this problem, Kelsen maintained, is to view the relation between state legal systems in terms of international law. On this account, it is a requirement of completeness that general jurisprudence take as its object of explanation both municipal law[6] and international law, and especially their relation. For ease of reference I will call this the *methodological requirement of completeness*.

In the simple observation of many national legal orders in the world we also have the germ[7] of the motivation behind Kelsen's epistemological postulate of unity: 'to understand all law in one system—that is, from one and the same standpoint—as one closed whole. Jurisprudence subsumes the norms regulating the relations between states, called international law, as well as the norms of national legal orders under one and the same category of law. In so doing it tries to present its

[5] Raz (note 1 above), 105.

[6] 'Municipal law' will be used interchangeably with 'state law' and 'national law'.

[7] Or at least one of the germs. Kelsen's postulate of unity is also inextricably bound to his view of normativity. See Raz, 'Kelsen's Theory of the Basic Norm', in *The Authority of Law* (Oxford: Clarendon Press, 1979), 122–45.

object as a unity.'[8] Several features of Kelsen's postulate of unity merit explanation.

First, in Kelsen's view the unity of national law and international law requires the absence of conflict or contradiction between the norms of international law and national legal orders. Otherwise, 'only a dualistic or pluralistic construction of the relation between international and national law would be possible.'[9] A no-conflict requirement for explanation of the relation between national and international law might strike some as absurd, but Kelsen gives it considerable plausibility by suggesting, by analogy to unconstitutional laws within states, that many apparent conflicts or contradictions are not really conflicts or contradictions at all, which are logically irresolvable, but only grounds for 'annulment' whereby one norm is subject to invalidation by an appropriate institution but nonetheless remains valid until invalidated.[10] So, for example, to say that the norms of a state legal system are inconsistent with the norms of international law might often be better understood as an observation that there is a reason for invalidating or annulling the offending state legal norms.

Second, the epistemological postulate of unity is a presumption or hypothesis, not an attempt to account for any facts without addition or remainder. Kelsen explains:

The entire legally technical movement, as outlined here, has—in the last analysis—the tendency to blur the border line between international and national law, so that as the ultimate goal of the legal development directed toward increasing centralization, appears the organizational unity of a universal legal community, that is, the emergence of a world state. At this time, however, there is no such thing. Only in our cognition of law may we assert the unity of all law by showing that we can comprehend international law together with the national legal orders as one system of norms, just as we are used to consider the national legal order as a unit.[11]

As others have observed,[12] Kelsen believed that international law was in a process of growth towards greater centralization and unity, but at the

---

[8] Kelsen, *Pure Theory of Law*, 2nd edn, trans. Max Knight (Berkeley and Los Angeles: University of California Press, 1967), 328.

[9] Ibid., 329.

[10] Ibid., 330–1.

[11] Ibid., 328.

[12] See Hedley Bull, 'Hans Kelsen and International Law', in R. Tur and W. Twining, *Essays on Kelsen* (Oxford: Clarendon Press, 1986), 321–36, 325–6.

time he was writing, there was not yet any such centralization or unity which would constitute a universal or world legal system. In this way the postulate flows from the broader methodology of Kelsen's 'pure' theory of law, a theory which aims to be free from political, ethical, and sociological considerations.[13] It is an epistemological postulate for knowing or cognizing law: in Kelsen's view, it is only by postulating the unity of national and international law that the existence and nature of law can be truly known.

Third, international law and national law, while they form a unity, are not identical in structure. For Kelsen, an essential feature of law is its coercive nature. In national law, enforcement is centralized through the existence of distinct law-applying and law-enforcing institutions. Unlike national law, the enforcement of international law is decentralized, with its characteristic lack of centralized courts and enforcement institutions. Sanctions at the international level are very much a matter or 'technique of self-help' for states.[14] As we will see below, the decentralization of international law is what ultimately led Kelsen to the conclusion that international law, in fact, only amounted to a primitive legal order.

Fourth, the relation between international law and national law is one of complementarity, in which I believe three dimensions can be distinguished. Along the first dimension, what we might call the *dimension of specification*, the norms of international law are given further content or specification by national law. A fairly straightforward example will illustrate this aspect of the relation between international law and national law. A norm of international law provides that states have the right to territorial integrity, which among other things protects states' rights to create and operate a system of legislative, judicial, and executive institutions. While this is a universal norm of international law, it is up to particular states to decide issues at various lower levels, ranging from fairly general levels (such as what specific kinds of institutions to have, or what precise relations or divisions of power to establish) to particular levels (such as speed limits on roads or voting ages).

The second dimension of complementarity is what we might call the *dimension of hierarchy*. This dimension of the relation of complementarity identifies the direction of delegation or authorization

---

[13] Kelsen (note 8 above), 1.
[14] Ibid., 323.

between international law and national law. Here, however, the relation of hierarchy can be viewed in either of two different ways. On one possibility, national law might be viewed as primary, in which case international law is to be viewed as subordinate or delegated law. Alternatively, international law might be viewed as supreme or primary, in which case national law is to be viewed as authorized or delegated by international law.

Although in early work Kelsen appeared to think that the primacy of international law was the juridically correct view,[15] in later work he settled on the view that both perspectives are equally possible, as both allow the possibility to know both national and international law as a unity and without contradiction.[16] This did not mean, however, that nothing turned on the choice when viewed from outside the perspective of jurisprudence. Politically, the choice is very important as the different perspectives represent very different moral and political commitments. The primacy of national law is associated with a nationalist or imperialist political attitude, while the primacy of international law represents a pacifist or cosmopolitan political attitude in international affairs and relations.[17]

The third dimension of complementarity is what we might call the *institutional dimension*. While the dimensions of specification and hierarchy show separation but also connection between national and international law, this dimension signifies the distinct overlap or interdependence between national and international law in the institutions whose operations contribute to the unity of law. More simply stated, national institutions have an essential and large share of the responsibility for applying international law.[18] Kelsen presents the idea by characterizing States as 'organs' of the international legal order:

---

[15] Kelsen, *Introduction to the Problems of Legal Theory*, trans. B. L. Paulson and S. L. Paulson (Oxford: Clarendon Press, 1992), 116–25.

[16] Kelsen (note 8 above), 339–47; Kelsen, *General Theory of Law and State*, trans. Anders Wedberg (Cambridge, Mass.: Harvard University Press, 1945), 386–8; and Kelsen, *Principles of International Law* (New York: Rinehart and Company, 1952), 428–38.

[17] Kelsen (note 8 above), 347.

[18] For example, the International Criminal Court's relation to state courts is characterized explicitly in terms of a principle of complementarity, whereby the ICC will only assume jurisdiction to prosecute international crime where the relevant state or states are somehow unwilling or unable to do so themselves. See Benjamin N. Schiff, *Building the International Criminal Court* (Cambridge: Cambridge University Press, 2008), 114–17.

An aspect of this unity [of national and international law] is the fact that the States as acting persons are organs of international law, or of the community constituted by it. The creation and execution of an order are the functions of its organs and the international legal order is created and executed by States. It is especially the creation of international law by treaties that clearly reveals the States as organs of the international community.[19]

This dimension of complementarity is best termed an institutional dimension as it is clear that it is institutions within or of the state, rather than the state itself, which are largely responsible for the application and enforcement of treaties which vary in subject-matter. So, for example, a labour treaty will create duties for the labour institutions of states (e.g. a ministry of labour, labour boards, etc.), a treaty regulating environmental issues will create duties for environmental institutions and actors (e.g. a government department of environment, manufacturing industries, energy providers, etc.), and a transnational crime treaty will create duties for national police institutions to share information, evidence, and deliver offenders. In addition to topic-specific institutions, courts at various levels within states will also bear the brunt of applying international law in cases of dispute, especially in cases where state institutions are accused of having failed to meet international obligations to their citizens.

One final element completes the account we need of Kelsen's view of international law and its relation to national law. This is Kelsen's important notion of the basic norm: the foundational, system-constituting norm which provides the reason for the validity of all other norms of the system by identifying the system's historically first constitution. Here is Kelsen's argument for the basic norm:

If we ask for the reason of the validity of the constitution, that is, for the reason of the validity of the norms regulating the creation of the general norms, we may, perhaps, discover an older constitution; that means the validity of the existing constitution is justified by the fact that it was created according to the rules of an earlier constitution by way of a constitutional amendment. In this way we eventually arrive at a historically first constitution that cannot have been created in this way and whose validity, therefore, cannot be traced back to a positive norm created by a legal authority; ... [i]f we ask for the reason of the validity of the historically first constitution, then the

---

[19] Kelsen (*General Theory of Law and State*, note 16 above), 351.

answer can only be...that the validity of this constitution—the assumption
that it is a binding norm—must be presupposed...[20]

Kelsen adds,

Since the reason for the validity of a norm can only be another norm, the presupposition must be a norm: not one posited (i.e., created) by a legal authority,
but a presupposed norm...Since it is the basic norm of a legal order (that is, an
order prescribing coercive acts), therefore this norm, namely the basic norm of
the legal order concerned, must be formulated as follows: Coercive acts ought
to be performed under the conditions and in the manner which the historically
first constitution, and the norms created according to it, prescribe. (In short:
One ought to behave as the constitution prescribes.)[21]

So in the same way and for the same reason that the unity of law is postulated or presupposed, so is the basic norm. The content and place of
the basic norm also varies depending on which type of law is taken as
primary. If national law is primary, then the basic norm of all law is the
norm that identifies the state legal order (and especially its historically
first constitution) as the supreme and foundational source of all law. If
international law is primary, then the basic norm of all law is the norm
identifying the international legal order as the supreme and foundational source of all law. While there is little evidence that Kelsen thought
international law had a historically first constitution similar in nature to
a state's historically first constitution,[22] it is well known that he settled
on the norm 'States should behave as they have customarily behaved'[23]
as the basic norm of international law. Indeed, in one place Kelsen
simply describes the basic norm of international law itself as the constitution of international law in a 'transcendental-logical sense'.[24]

2. HART'S CRITICISMS

With an account of Kelsen's view of international law in hand, we can
now turn to Hart's criticisms. As I noted in the introduction, I shall

---

[20] Kelsen (note 8 above), 200.
[21] Ibid., 200–1. [Translation slightly modified. Compare with Kelsen (*General Theory of
Law and State*, note 16 above), 116.]
[22] Although Kelsen's did say that he considers the Charter of the United Nations to be 'of
decisive importance.' Kelsen (*Principles of International Law*, note 16 above), vii.
[23] Kelsen, (*General Theory of Law and State*, note 16 above), 369.
[24] Kelsen (note 8 above), 216.

distinguish and focus on three of Hart's criticisms: (i) that Kelsen's methodological requirement of completeness is misguided; (ii) that it is mistaken to suppose that international law must contain a system-constituting basic norm, and (iii) that a relationship of validating purport is insufficient to explain the unity of international law and national law even if they were connected by a single basic norm. My aim here is to show that Hart's criticisms are not nearly as uniformly successful as those working in the analytical tradition have supposed, but their shortcomings are nonetheless instructive.

(i) The methodological requirement of completeness is misguided

Recall that in Kelsen's view, from the fact of a multiplicity of legal systems in the world there arises a requirement to view these as a unity: if each system is to be viewed as a system of valid norms, each must be viewed as connected to the rest in a way which constitutes a unified and closed whole. The problem, and task for legal theory, then, is to demonstrate how this could be so. Kelsen's solution is of course the epistemological postulate of unity. Not everyone agrees, however, that there is any problem here to solve. Hart writes:

The...argument reduces to the contention that all law forms a single system because there is a form of knowledge ('jurisprudence' or 'connaissance juridique') or a science of law which studies both international law and municipal law as falling under the single description 'valid laws' and thus represents 'its object' as a unity... Surely we might as well attempt to deduce from the existence of the history of warfare or the science of strategy that all wars are one or all armies are one.[25]

Hart's criticism only works, of course, if the analogy does as well, but there is good reason to follow common sense and think that law and war, for example, are not relevantly similar. The unity doctrine flows from Kelsen's account of the logic of norms and the nature of normativity. But there is no reason Kelsen need be committed to a similar account where it simply has no application, as in warfare (as distinct from the law or morality of warfare).

More importantly, it is not difficult to see why the nature of municipal law might not be adequately explained in isolation from international

[25] Hart, 'Kelsen's Doctrine of the Unity of Law', in *Essays in Jurisprudence and Philosophy* (Oxford: Clarendon Press, 1983), 309–42, 322.

law, or at least in isolation from an account of international conditions. All principles of sovereignty in international law define or regard sovereign statehood partially in relational terms. For instance, consider the elements of statehood laid out in the Montevideo Convention of 1933. To be a state there must be a territory, a permanent population, and an effective government capable of governing the territory and population and entering into international relations.[26] The benefits of sovereignty include quite naturally the right to territorial integrity and freedom from intervention which come from recognition by other states (although such freedom is increasingly becoming subject to institutionally recognized moral conditions, especially human rights conditions[27]). Indeed, the social practices of surrounding states, especially their recognition and cooperation, matter very much to the existence and operation of municipal legal systems. It would be folly to ignore the social fact that the sovereignty of Canada, for example, and so the existence of its legal system (while perhaps not the content of its particular legal norms, though even here there is likely influence), depends a great deal on the US government's recognition of Canada's government, borders, and citizens, among other things. Any social fact account of a state legal system would have to admit as much.

(ii) International law need not contain a system-constituting basic norm

Hart's second criticism is less methodological, and based more on an account of the facts of international law as he sees them. In the final chapter of *The Concept of Law*, Hart takes issue with Kelsen's claim that international law must contain a basic, system-constituting rule. In Hart's view,

There is indeed something comic in the efforts made to fashion a basic rule for the most simple forms of social structure which exist without one. It is as if we were to say that a naked savage *must* really be dressed in some invisible variety

---

[26] The Montevideo Convention is discussed in Allen Buchanan, *Justice, Legitimacy, and Self-Determination* (Oxford: Oxford University Press, 2004), 264. On the essentially relational quality of sovereignty, see also Timothy Endicott, 'The Logic of Freedom and Power', in Besson and Tasioulas (note 4 above), 245–59.

[27] See, for example, Michael Reisman, 'Sovereignty and Human Rights in Contemporary International Law', *American Journal of International Law* 84 (1990), 876. For illuminating discussion, see Joseph Raz, 'Human Rights Without Foundations', in Besson and Tasioulas (note 4 above), 321–37; and Raz, 'Human Rights in the Emerging World Order', *Transnational Legal Theory* 1 (2010), 31–47.

of modern dress. Unfortunately, there is also here a standing possibility of confusion. We may be persuaded to treat as a basic rule, something which is an empty repetition of the mere fact that the society concerned (whether of individuals or states) observes certain standards of conduct as obligatory rules. This is surely the status of the strange basic norm which has been suggested for international law: 'States should behave as they have customarily behaved.' For it says nothing more than that those who accept certain rules must also observe a rule that the rules ought to be observed. This is a mere useless reduplication of the fact that a set of rules are accepted by states as binding rules.[28]

We can distinguish two claims in this passage. One is the claim that the norm 'States should behave as they have customarily behaved' has no content, and so goes no distance in showing that a distinct, system-constituting rule exists above and beyond what Hart calls primary rules of obligation at the international level. This is a mistake worth correcting. Hart's focus on the abstractness of Kelsen's formulation of the basic norm unfortunately leads Hart to overlook the actual content of the basic norm Kelsen has in mind. Here is Kelsen's full statement:

The basic norm of international law...must be a norm which countenances custom as a norm-creating fact, and might be formulated as follows: 'The States ought to behave as they have customarily behaved.' Customary international law, developed on the basis of this norm, is the first stage within the international legal order. The next stage is formed by the norms created by international treaties. The validity of these norms is dependent upon the norm *pacta sunt servanda*, which is itself a norm belonging to the first stage of general international law, which is law created by custom constituted by acts of States. The third stage is formed by norms created by organs which are themselves created by international treaties, as for instance decisions of the Council of the League of Nations, or of the Permanent Court of International Justice.[29]

This account of a hierarchy of norms follows an exercise in tracing the validity of a low-level norm of international law. More importantly, it looks very much like the kind of system-constituting hierarchy we would expect to find in a Hartian municipal rule of recognition, which identifies the sources of law in a legal system and ranks them. Hart's charge of emptiness seems even more misguided when we notice that it is also easy

---

[28] Hart, *The Concept of Law*, 3rd edn (Oxford: Clarendon Press, 2012), 236.
[29] Kelsen, (*General Theory of Law and State*, note 16 above), 369–70.

to formulate Hart's idea of a conventional rule of recognition in abstract terms which invite the same charge of empty repetition or mere useless reduplication: *unless they are required to do otherwise by valid positive law, officials must apply as valid the norms of their own customary behaviour (and not, for example, norms of other people's customary behaviour, or moral norms, etc.).* Kelsen might have reached the wrong formulation of the basic norm, for example, by incorrectly identifying the hierarchy or missing some sources. But it is no more accurate to say that his attempt amounts to an empty repetition than it would be to say that Hart's notion of a rule of recognition amounts to an empty repetition.[30]

The second claim in the passage quoted above is more interesting, and likely more successful, but not for Hart's reasons and not without further explanation to come in the next section. As I will return to it below, I will simply introduce the claim here. In Hart's view, international law does not amount to a legal system, but neither does it need to. As the account of primitive legal orders show, fully binding legal obligations can exist in the absence of system-constituting rules and institutions.[31] All that is required is a regular pattern of conduct held to be obligatory, from an internal point of view, by the relevant participants. International law, then, resembles in structure a primitive legal order in which there are no secondary rules of recognition, adjudication, and change, but only primary rules of obligation which can be seen in the normative practices of states.

At this point it might be tempting to suppose that Hart and Kelsen radically disagree on the nature of international law. Such a view would only be partly true. Kelsen certainly believes that legal obligations, at national or international levels, can only exist if valid according to a basic, system-constituting rule, while Hart maintains that primitive, socio-legal obligations can exist even in the absence of basic, system-constituting rules, provided the conditions of a social rule of obligation exist. However, there is a second dimension to the contrast between

---

[30] I am of course assuming that the rich influence of Hart's notion of a rule of recognition somewhat demonstrates that the notion is not an empty repetition or useless reduplication. But see Jeremy Waldron, 'Who Needs Rules of Recognition?' in Matthew D. Adler and Kenneth Einar Himma, eds., *The Rule of Recognition and the U.S. Constitution* (New York: Oxford University Press, 2009), 327–49, in which Waldron claims that the notion of rules of change seems to (and can) do all the work a rule of recognition is meant to do.

[31] Hart (note 28 above), 91–2.

Kelsen's view and Hart's view which suggests they have significantly different aims. Consider the following passage from Hart:

> Again once we emancipate ourselves from the assumption that international law *must* contain a basic rule, the question to be faced is one of fact. What is the actual character of the rules as they function in the relations between states? Different interpretations of the phenomena to be observed are of course possible; but it is submitted that there is no basic rule providing general criteria of validity for the rules of international law, and that the rules which are in fact operative constitute not a system but a set of rules, among which are the rules providing for the binding force of treaties.[32]

Hart adds the observation that the facts might someday change, such that an international rule of recognition might emerge. But until then, all that exists is a primitive set of international laws. Nonetheless, what is important to notice here is that Hart's insistence that we give up the assumption of a basic norm and turn instead to the facts is very different from Kelsen's commitment to understand how both national law and international law can and must co-exist. Kelsen did not, as we saw above, deny that in fact there is no such international legal system as things actually stand. Perhaps, then, Kelsen and Hart are at cross-purposes: Kelsen aims to understand the conceptual possibility of international law and its relation to national law, whereas Hart is concerned with explaining the reality of international law as it actually exists. Kelsen's 'pure theory' approach certainly exhibits some distinctive methodological commitments, so there is no doubt some truth to this observation. As Hart's next criticism shows, however, even if there is an element of cross-purpose, this would not resolve (or dissolve) the disagreement.

(iii) A relationship of validating purport is insufficient to show the unity of law

What if the facts did match Kelsen's view? What if, that is, there were centralized judicial, legislative, and executive institutions all authorized by a historically first international constitution, which in turn claimed to provide the reason for the validity of all national legal orders?[33] Would

---

[32] Ibid., 236.
[33] And, vice versa, what if all national legal orders did in fact claim to provide the reason for the validity of international law, and in turn, the validity of each other's national legal orders?

this make a difference to the success of Kelsen's theoretical explanation of the unity of law? Hart did not think so. In his 1968 article 'Kelsen's Doctrine of the Unity of Law' he deepens his rejection of Kelsen's view by moving beyond the observation that the facts are on his side. As Hart argues, not only is a basic rule for international law unnecessary, its associated epistemological postulate of unity—even if also a true description of how international law actually is—is bound to distort understanding of the relation between systems of norms. Hart offers the following analogy to show that while one system's norms might refer to the norms of another system, and so purport to provide the reason for their validity, it is still not possible to presume, as Kelsen's epistemological postulate of unity does, that the norms all belong to one system.

Suppose the question arose whether I, Hart, wrote this paper in obedience to someone's order that I should write it. Let us assume that evidence is forth-coming that just before I sat down to write this paper the Vice-Chancellor of Oxford University dispatched to me a document purporting to order me to write a paper on Kelsen's Doctrine of the Unity of Law. It is plain that whether or not I wrote this paper in obedience to that order could not be settled by comparing the contents of the order ('Hart: write a paper on Kelsen's Doc-trine of the Unity of Law') with a true description of my later conduct ('Hart wrote a paper on Kelsen's Doctrine of the Unity of Law'). This comparison would indeed show correspondence between the content of the order and the description of my conduct, in that the action-description contained in the order is applicable to my subsequent conduct. But though in order to estab-lish that I did write this paper in obedience to this order it would be *necessary* to show this correspondence between the content of the order and the descrip-tion of my conduct, plainly this would not be *sufficient*.[34]

What is missing, Hart observes, is consideration of the context, specifi-cally, consideration of any facts of recognition of the order:

It would also be necessary to establish certain facts that have to do not with the content of the order, but with the circumstances surrounding the issue and reception of the order, involving consideration of such questions as the following. Did Hart receive the Vice-Chancellor's missive? Did he recognize it as an order? Did he write the paper in order to comply with this order? Did anyone else give such an order? If so, whose order did Hart intend to obey? A

---

[34] Hart (note 25 above), 312–13.

'pure theory' of imperatives that ignored such facts and circumstances surrounding the issue and reception of orders, and restricted itself to the characterization of the relationships between the contents of orders and the description of actions, would necessarily be incompetent to settle the question whether any person had obeyed a particular order.[35]

Hart's conceptual claim, illustrated by this analogy, that a relationship of validating purport is insufficient to show that norms belong to the same system, quite readily explains much of international law whereby norms of international law might claim to bind all states but may not in fact form part of a single system with the legal orders of all states.[36] The Universal Declaration of Human Rights, for example, certainly claims, through its universal (or near universal) set of state signatories, universal application to all states, but it is a sad reality that not all states observe or recognize the universal rights in their domestic affairs (or if they recognize rights of the Universal Declaration, they may not recognize all of them). Alternatively, even if a state's legal system did recognize human rights which match in content the human rights of the Universal Declaration, as, for example, many of the rights contained in the Canadian Charter of Rights and Freedoms do, this would also be insufficient to show that the Universal Declaration and the Canadian Charter form part of one unified legal system.

To summarize, there is much in Kelsen's view that survives Hart's criticisms, and serves well to explain the relation between national law and international law. In particular, the view that the nature and existence of state law cannot be explained in isolation from explanation of the nature and existence of international law is likely sound,[37] and the associated account of their complementarity is certainly very plausible. Further, the presumption that international law has a basic norm, while it encounters other difficulties to be discussed below, is far from a useless reduplication or empty repetition of a set of primary social practices of international law as Hart charges. However, it is Hart's third criticism, more so than the first two, which is successful. Even if there is unity of the kind Kelsen has in mind between international law and national law, that is, if international law referred to and purported to provide the

[35] Ibid., 313.
[36] For a similar criticism, see Raz (note 7 above), 127–8.
[37] See section 2(i) above.

reason of the validity of the norms of national legal orders (or vice versa), and the norms of the national legal orders matched or could be viewed to complement the norms of international law (or vice versa), as Hart shows such reference and identity or continuity of norms is not enough to show that norms do in fact belong to one and the same system. What is missing is the identification of institutional practices of recognition—facts of recognition—to show that norms are systemically connected.

3. UNDERSTANDING INTERNATIONAL LAW THROUGH THE LENS OF LEGAL SYSTEM

It might be easy from reading Hart's critique of Kelsen's account of international law to get the impression that Hart saw little value in keeping any of the elements of Kelsen's view. I hope the foregoing shows why we ought not to follow Hart on this score. But a reconstruction of the Hart–Kelsen debate also shows that, despite disagreement on various issues, Hart and Kelsen share a similar view: on the facts, international law only exists as a kind of primitive legal order. Their reasons are remarkably similar. Hart maintains that international law lacks secondary rules, and by association, secondary institutions such as courts and legislatures of the right kind. In Kelsen's view, international law is decentralized, as it contains no tribunals or institutions capable of independently applying and enforcing international legal norms. For both Hart and Kelsen, then, international law is in fact primitive because nonsystemic. In what follows I want to put the differences between Hart and Kelsen aside and assess this shared view. In particular, I shall argue that the choice between characterizing international law either as a primitive legal order or as an international legal system is a false dichotomy created by an inappropriate reliance on the idea of legal system as a tool of explanation.

Let's return to the importance of legal system in explanation of law. As we saw above, many suppose that the key to understanding law in its typical and primary form is to view laws in terms of systems, for as Raz suggests, all laws come in the form of systems. What are the core features of such a commitment? Several are important. The first is that the idea of a legal system makes it possible to conceive of the membership of all norms within some domain. For example, we can conceive of Canadian laws because there is a Canadian legal system which applies to all norm-subjects of the Canadian state. Similarly, to raise the question of the legal status of international norms in an international domain is to ask if there is an international legal system which defines the membership of those norms. A second related feature of the concept of legal system is the idea of sources of law. Laws exist within some domain if they have been created or recognized by authoritative institutions within some legal system. In this way, a legal system also requires, or defines, the membership not just of norms but also of institutions or officials.[38] A third typical feature of legal systems is the hierarchy of norms it observes as well as a hierarchy of institutions or officials it establishes. While it may be possible to imagine a legal system with no hierarchy of norms or officials or institutions, much like one might imagine a legal system without coercion which applied to a society of angels, such a legal system would certainly be an unfamiliar one. Fourth, legal systems also typically claim supremacy for their norms, such that norms from other, non-legal or foreign legal sources must be viewed as subordinate or inapplicable altogether. Fifth, legal systems also typically claim a kind of comprehensiveness, both in the range of subject-matter or social issues they address, as well as the territorial or spatial domain over which they apply.

These features are certainly found in—at least in the idea of—the modern sovereign state, in which the creation, application, and enforcement of law are centralized, and there is no appeal or reliance on extra-state institutions or rules for validation or authorization. The degree to which sovereign states meet such conditions is a separate question, and it is certainly up for debate whether the law in federal or other forms of states where sovereignty is in some way shared or divided requires an alternative explanation. What is important for our purposes, however, is the extent to which both Kelsen and Hart deploy the idea of legal system in explanation not of state legal systems, but in explanation of international law.

---

[38] There is of course a problem of circularity looming here, as the norms of a legal system appear to determine who the officials and institutions are but the officials and institutions are responsible for determining which norms are legal norms of the system. For an assessment of the problem of circularity, and its associated problem of indeterminacy, see Keith Culver and Michael Giudice, *Legality's Borders: An Essay in General Jurisprudence* (New York: Oxford University Press, 2010), ch. 1.

Consider Kelsen first. As we saw, he pursued an explanation of the unity of all of international law, without distinction, with national law, such that international law, as well as national legal orders, could only exist if viewed as a whole, closed system. He was of course willing to suppose that the supremacy of a world legal system might lie either at the international level or some particular national level; but in either alternative, comprehensiveness of regulation and a hierarchy of legal orders are clearly part of his view. His account of the basic norm, which identifies custom, treaties, and decisions of particular international institutions, also serves to show the commitment to systemic sources of law; all international laws must have their source in one of these forms of international law-making. Finally, Kelsen's no-conflict requirement of law shows that other norms are either irrelevant (as are moral norms from a juristic point of view), or subordinate if not a basic norm.

Hart's reliance on the notion of legal system in explaining international law is also evident, but in a much more indirect way, as his emphasis lies in the observation that there is no international legal system. In this way, Hart's application of the idea of legal system to international law shows international law to be defective as a system, which in turn means that if there is any international law at all, it must only be primitive law. But notice the nature of Hart's question: is there an international legal system for *all* of international law? Put in other words, from a view comprehending the whole domain of international relations, does international law amount to a legal system? I think the following passage helps to show that for Hart an international legal system was an all-or-nothing matter, either there is a legal system for all of international law or there is no international legal system at all:

It is true that, on many important matters, the relations between states are regulated by multilateral treaties, and it is sometimes argued that these may bind states that are not parties. If this were generally recognized, such treaties would in fact be legislative enactments and international law would have distinct criteria of validity for its rules. A basic rule of recognition could then be formulated which would represent an actual feature of the system and would be more than an empty restatement of the fact that a set of rules are in fact observed by states.[39]

[39] Hart (note 28 above), 236. In a couple of articles David Lefkowitz suggests that at least customary international law is systemic in Hart's sense. See Lefkowitz, '(Dis)solving the Chronological Paradox in Customary International Law: A Hartian Approach', *Canadian Journal of*

Treaty-making rules might seem to be best characterized as secondary rules of change in Hart's framework, but they would only constitute systemic or genuine secondary rules of change if their recognition is general and widespread; two states, or any group of states (it is difficult to specify the size Hart has in mind to exclude by reference to general recognition), cannot create or practise systemic, secondary rules of change. Secondary rules of any kind, after all, would require an ultimate, system-constituting rule of recognition.[40] As we will see in the next section, this is a rather odd view. Multilateral treaties, and the obligations they give rise to, for instance, are no doubt very strangely explained as primary obligations, once we observe that treaty obligations rest on deliberate, traceable acts of creation.

Hart did not, then, see any general criteria of validity or systemic sources. By association neither did he see a hierarchy of legal norms or institutions. It is more difficult to say, however, whether he thinks the remaining primary international rules of obligation are supreme, or even claim supremacy. In one sense international rules limit the sovereignty of states, so they might be viewed to be at least among the supreme criteria of state law, but in another sense states are relatively free to choose to recognize international law or not, which makes international law more subordinate than supreme. Perhaps the more accurate explanation is that some rules of international law are supreme, such as those delimiting the territorial borders of states, but other rules are not, such as international environmental laws, which rest more so on the individual practices of states. Distinguishing supreme from subordinate international laws is no doubt a difficult task, but thankfully it is not necessary to undertake it here.

Seeing the absence of the core marks of a legal system, both Hart and Kelsen suppose that international law at best amounts to a primitive legal order. But is this the best conclusion to reach about international law? We have now seen some reasons to be sceptical. In the next section

---

Law and Jurisprudence 21 (2008), 129–48; and Lefkowitz, 'The Sources of International Law: Some Philosophical Reflections', in Besson and Tasioulas (note 4 above), 187–203. It is not clear, though, whether Hart would have endorsed such an approach, especially as customary rules resemble most closely primary social rules of obligation, which can exist in the absence of a legal system according to Hart.

[40] See Samantha Besson, 'Theorizing the Sources of International Law', in Besson and Tasioulas (note 4 above), 163–85.

I want to pursue Hart's approach of subjecting theories of international law to the facts. I aim to show, however, that such an exercise shows that while there is no international legal system of the sort Kelsen and Hart imagine, neither is there a primitive legal order. The facts are more complex.

4. SOME FACTS OF INTERNATIONAL LAW

Before moving on we should note at this point two options not taken in assessing Hart's criticisms of Kelsen. One way to defend Kelsen's view would be to defend his methodology: in explaining law we must attend to the logic of a juristic point of view—a point of view from which we attempt to understand law entirely on its own terms—without attention to any facts. I share doubts about such a methodology, and the possibility of a purely 'pure' theory of law, so this will not be my approach.[41] A second line of defence would be to argue that Kelsen's account of the unity of international and national law is best viewed, or necessarily viewed, as a defence of an important moral ideal.[42] In my view this is not really a competing approach at all to Hart's, but more so a change of questions.[43] Instead, I aim to stick to Hart's approach of testing theories against facts, but most importantly to show that Hart's own view of international law does not escape the most problematic feature of Kelsen's view—its reliance on the idea of 'legal system' to characterize all law.

What, then, are some prominent facts of international law with which to test the theories of Kelsen and Hart? Two are especially important.

(i) Fragmented, but not primitive

Earlier we noted in discussion of the institutional dimension of complementarity in Kelsen's account of the epistemological postulate of unity that international laws typically require the aid of state institutions to be applied and enforced. If no state which signed and ratified an environmental treaty in effect carried out the terms of the treaty, or

---

[41] For critical discussion of Kelsen's methodology, see Raz, 'The Purity of the Pure Theory', in *The Authority of Law*, 2nd edn (Oxford: Clarendon Press, 2009), 293–312.

[42] See Lars Vinx, *Hans Kelsen's Pure Theory of Law: Legality and Legitimacy* (Oxford: Oxford University Press, 2007).

[43] It is also doubtful it could be an intelligible interpretation of Kelsen's view.

displayed any intention to do so, not only would the treaty fail to achieve its goal, we would have good reason to doubt whether any law had been created at all. The same is no doubt true of treaties governing other subject-matters, from labour to security to human rights. In other words, while some international institutions are often formed by treaty, such as the North Atlantic Treaty Organization and the World Trade Organization, such institutions are ill explained if their existence and nature is conceived to be distinct and independent from member state institutions. As Kelsen says, unity 'tends to blur the distinction between international law and national law'. On this score, at least, the institutional dimension of complementarity of Kelsen's epistemological postulate of unity seems to fare quite well when used to explain the facts.

Where Kelsen's theory of unity fares less well, however, is in handling the widespread fragmentation of international law.[44] The sheer number of treaties and treaty-based regimes is enough to warrant scepticism regarding the unity of international law, but it is their distinct operations and relative isolation from each other which demonstrates disunity. An example familiar to public international lawyers will serve to illustrate. The World Trade Organization regulates and decides matters of trade among member states, but typically does not recognize, let alone enforce, international human rights law found within the many international human rights declarations and conventions.[45] In this way, as many have observed, international law tends to be topically or sectorally delimited.[46] But even on a single topic or within a single sector of international law there is fragmentation. Consider the question of international authorization of the use of force. The UN Security Council

[44] For useful discussion see the various contributions in Jeffrey L. Dunoff and Joel P. Trachtman, eds., *Ruling the World? Constitutionalism, International Law, and Global Governance* (Cambridge: Cambridge University Press, 2009).

[45] For analysis see Jeffrey L. Dunoff, 'The Politics of International Constitutions: The Curious Case of the World Trade Organization', in Dunoff and Trachtman (note 44 above); Joel P. Trachtman, 'Constitutional Economics of the World Trade Organization', in Dunoff and Trachtman (note 44 above); Donald H. Regan, 'International Adjudication: A Response to Paulus—Courts, Custom, Treaties, Regimes, and the WTO', in Besson and Tasioulas (note 4 above), 225–41.

[46] See Gunther Teubner and Andreas Fischer-Lescano, 'Regime Collisions: The Vain Search for Legal Unity in the Fragmentation of Global Law', *Michigan Journal of International Law* 25 (2003–4), 999–1043.

claims to be the sole institution capable of authorizing the use of force[47], but its decisions (or non-decisions) are sometimes ignored by other key institutions or organizations, such as the North Atlantic Treaty Organization.[48] Such lack of coordination and cooperation raises serious doubts about the systemic role the Security Council claims to play. The issue of the authorization of force is also complicated in two further ways: first, even single member states often act without the support or coordination of the UN Security Council and NATO, as, for example, the US often does. It might be objected that this cannot be so, at least in the case of the US, since the US is also a member of both the UN Security Council and NATO. To this we might simply respond, heeding Hart's lesson, that the US's membership in multiple international institutions ought not to be presumed to provide any unity, as often it contributes more to disunity and fragmentation of international law.[49] Second, alongside UN law on the use of force sits general customary international law on the use of force.[50] Customary international law is constituted by two elements, a material element (state practice) and a normative element (*opinio juris*), and as such brings a host of ontological difficulties in determining when a customary rule has crystallized into existence and what its precise content is, but most importantly it also shows that there are other sources of international law on the use of

---

[47] Article 24(1) of the United Nations Charter states that the 'Members confer on the Security Council primary responsibility for the maintenance of international peace and security, and agree that in carrying out its duties under this responsibility the Security Council acts on their behalf.' Reproduced in Ian Brownlie, ed., *Basic Documents in International Law*, 6th edn (Oxford: Oxford University Press, 2009), 8.

[48] On NATO's intervention in Kosovo, see Philippe Sands and Pierre Klein, *Bowett's Law of International Institutions*, 6th edn (London: Sweet and Maxwell, 2009), 37, 339. For evidence of cooperation between the Security Council and regional organizations, see See Rebecca M. M. Wallace and Olga Martin-Ortega, *International Law*, 6th edn (London: Sweet and Maxwell, 2009), 304–7.

[49] Fragmentation of the sort identified in this paragraph also shows why Kelsen's methodological requirement of completeness, which I argued earlier does not succumb so easily to Hart's objection, nonetheless ultimately fails. While it is true that national law cannot be understood apart from international law, since the existence of states and state legal orders requires explanation of surrounding state and international social practices, it does not follow that *all* international practices of recognition of states and international organizations are systemically connected to the degree required to establish world unity of the kind Kelsen has in mind.

[50] For insightful discussion of the customary law on the use of force in the context of the Nicaragua cases, see John Tasioulas, 'In Defence of Relative Normativity: Communitarian Values and the Nicaragua Case', *Oxford Journal of Legal Studies* 16 (1996), 85.

force besides UN and NATO law and no settled relation between these.[51]

Perhaps Hart is right, then, that international law is really simply a primitive legal order, where there are only primary rules of obligation but no system-constituting basic rule or norm. But here we can see the error in Hart's account as well. A lack of systematicity does not mark the presence of a mere primitive legal order. Several treaty-based organizations and unions, such the WTO and the EU, exhibit characteristics which demonstrate development far beyond that of a set of socially accepted primary rules of obligation, a set marked by the absence of secondary rules of recognition, change, and adjudication and associated secondary institutions, and whose obligations only exist in long-standing customary practices and so can only change with gradual shifts in those customary practices. Both the WTO and the EU contain rules for the deliberate change of rules, as well as institutions distinctly charged with the creation of rules and the settlement of disputes. It is therefore possible to pull on the chain of validity of WTO and EU rules, and see (at least some) cases about the meaning or application of these rules resolved. There is something quite odd, then, about characterizing the WTO and the EU as instances of primitive law, consisting entirely of primary rules of obligation and so lacking any secondary rules.

Might we not then say that while there may be no legal system for all of international law, contra Hart and Kelsen there are nonetheless many international legal *systems*: a WTO legal system, an EU legal system, a NAFTA legal system, a MERCOSUR legal system, and so on? If by such characterization we mean simply to say that these various organizations and unions are constituted partly by primary rules of obligation as well as secondary rules of recognition, change, and adjudication, then perhaps this is fine, but notice that much of the original idea of a legal system is lost, in particular, the ideas of comprehensiveness, supremacy, and distinct borders for norms and institutions. Many international organizations and unions are topic-specific, dealing only with security, trade, or intellectual property, for example. They also depend to varying degrees on state institutions and norms to complement their international norms and apply and enforce these in member states, so their

---

[51] See Wallace and Martin-Ortega (note 48 above), 9–20.

domains are mixed between international and national levels and their relative force is uncertain. But perhaps the greatest reason why the idea of legal system is misplaced in thinking about particular international organizations is that the very idea of a legal system, with its focus on distinct conditions of membership and distinct sources of law in the form of authoritative officials and institutions, naturally invites questions of determination and exclusion: which norms are part of the system and which ones are not?; which institutions are part of the system and which ones are not?[52] International rules and organizations, because of their relative non-independence from state laws and institutions, are best characterized as overlapping and connected rules and institutions; in other words, inter-dependence seems to be their nature, not closure in the form of determination and exclusion.[53]

(ii) Non-state sources of international law

The discussion so far has focused on what we might call classic public international law, international law created by and applicable to states. As persons, groups, businesses, and other institutions acting internationally know, however, focus on this kind of international law leaves many obligations and sources of obligation out of the picture. There are countless non-governmental organizations, multi-national corporations, institutions of various industries, and other groups whose practices which cross state borders typically amount to rules of obligation coupled with dispute-settlement processes.[54] Such 'transnational law', as it is

---

[52] See, for example, Julie Dickson, 'How Many Legal Systems? Some Puzzles Regarding the Identity Conditions of, and Relations Between, Legal Systems in the European Union', *Problema: Annuario de Filosophia y Teoria del Derecho* 2 (2008), 9–50.

[53] Just what are the limits to the idea of legal system in explanation of law? To be clear, the claim I am advancing in this section is that in non-state areas of law that nonetheless fall within the province of jurisprudence (whether or not they produce clear cases of law) less is explained by the idea of a legal system than many (including Hart and Kelsen) suppose. International law is one such area of law in which there are many non-primitive legal orders even in the absence of central, system-constituting secondary rules. But I also believe, though I cannot argue for the claim here, that less is explained by the idea of legal system in the context of municipal or state law as well than is commonly thought. See Culver and Giudice (note 38 above).

[54] Two useful collections on transnational law are Gunther Teubner, ed., *Global Law Without a State* (Aldershot: Dartmouth, 1997), and A. Peters, L. Koechlin, T. Förster, and G. F. Zinkernagel, eds., *Non-State Actors as Standard Setters* (Cambridge: Cambridge University Press, 2009).

often called, often emerges where reference or reliance on state or public international law or institutions is simply too costly, time-consuming, inefficient, or even unnecessary. Transnational law naturally raises questions of legitimacy, as the actors responsible for its creation are often unrepresentative and not democratically accountable. But such moral and political defects do not taint the legal quality of the rules and institutions of transnational law.

Neither Kelsen nor Hart mentioned let alone considered transnational law, even though its existence is not terribly new. The challenge, however, that transnational law poses for system-based legal theory is clear. Transnational law, like international law and especially treaty-based regimes, is fragmented but often developed in topic-specific contexts far beyond custom-based social practices consisting solely of slow-growing and slow-decaying primary rules of obligation. And even though transnational law and institutions do sometimes come to interact in various ways with state and international law and institutions,[55] often they do not; in this way the unsystemic nature of transnational law is only compounded by lack of connection to or authorization by state or international law and institutions.

A likely objection should be considered here. Someone might deny that transnational law is really law at all, existing as it does in the shadows of state and international law and sometimes in conflict with these as well. If the objection amounts to the claim that transnational law is not really law because it is unlike state law, then the response is to resist state-based legal theory: while state law is prominent, it is not the only kind of law. If the objection amounts to the related claim that transnational law is not law because it is unsystemic, the response is likewise to question the presumption—or postulate, since that is what it is—that all law is systemic. If there is a lesson here it might be formulated as follows: legal systems might be prominent forms of law, but when they exist they must be understood as part of the facts to be explained, and not as a necessary part of the theoretical apparatus or tools used to explain law wherever and whenever it is exists. And if we are to pursue Hart's approach of testing theories against the facts, in

---

[55] See, for example, Janet Koven Levit, 'Bottom-Up International Lawmaking: Reflections on the New Haven School of International Law', *Yale Journal of International Law* 32 (2007), 393–420.

the case of transnational law I think the facts must reign: transnational law is real.[56]

In the final section of 'Kelsen's Doctrine of the Unity of Law' Hart explains that part of the value in subjecting Kelsen's view to scrutiny is the need it shows for analytical jurisprudence to further investigate theories of deontic logic and the nature of recognition of legal norms and legal systems. Regarding recognition, he identifies three issues which will need to be addressed. First, since international law lacks authoritative law-applying and law-enforcing agencies—agencies to whom we can look in municipal legal systems for evidence of recognition—we will need to face problems in defining what kind of recognition is sufficient in a decentralized community. Second, and relatedly, without effective international courts whose practices could confirm the existence and membership of international laws, we will need an account of recognition capable of specifying the conditions for the creation of international laws in the absence of application by courts. Third, and finally, Hart observes that we will need some way to distinguish cases where courts *apply* domestic law from cases where courts merely *recognize* foreign law in deciding matters of private international law.[57] The problem such cases are meant to reveal is the problem of explaining when recognition of different legal norms shows that those legal norms belong to the same system. In earlier argument I offered reasons why the costs of employing the notion of legal system in explanation of international law likely outweigh the benefits, so I think we have good reason here to resist the terms in which Hart identifies the problems of recognition. All of this is to show that the problems of recognition in international contexts are no doubt more complicated than Hart (and Kelsen) realized. Much work is left to be done.

[56] One final observation should decide the case for transnational law. As Hart notes in explaining the 'choice' between a wide positivist concept of law, which includes within the category of law morally evil but legally valid rules, and a narrow natural law concept of law, which excludes from the category of law morally evil rules, he appeals to two success criteria for theories or concepts of law: 'If we are to make a reasoned choice between these concepts, it must be because one is superior to the other in the way in which it will assist our theoretical inquiries, or advance and clarify our moral deliberations, or both.' Hart (note 28 above), 209. I think it would be difficult to deny the gains for theoretical and moral inquiries by including transnational law within the concept of law. For theoretical consideration, see Roger Cotterrell, 'Transnational Communities and the Concept of Law', *Ratio Juris* 21 (2008), 1–18.

[57] Hart (note 25 above), 341–2. Hart introduces, albeit very briefly, the distinction between 'original' recognition and 'derivative' recognition, though he admits that it needs much elaboration.

6

Relational Reasons and
the Criminal Law[1]

R. A. DUFF

I. RELATIONAL REASONS

Some reasons for action are relational. I have a relational reason to Φ when I have reason to Φ in virtue of a relationship in which I stand, or a role that I fill; absent that relationship or that role I would not have that reason to Φ; others who do not stand in that relationship or fill that role do not have that reason to Φ. I have a relational reason to feed this child—that he is my child: absent that parental relationship, I might still have a reason to feed him, as might others who are not his parents— for instance that he is starving; but absent that relationship, I would not have and others cannot have that specific relational reason to feed this child. I have a relational reason to respond to this person's philosophical queries—that she is my student: absent that pedagogical relationship, I might still have reason to respond to her questions, as might others who are not her teachers—for instance that it is good to help such seekers after philosophical insight; but absent that relationship, I would not have and others cannot have that specific relational reason to respond to her queries. I have relational reason to pay John £10—that I borrowed it from him and promised to repay him today: absent that promissory relationship I might still have, and others might have, reason to give him £10—for instance that he is impoverished and I am (or they are) rich; but absent that promissory relationship, neither I nor others could have that specific relational reason to give him £10.

Where there are relational reasons, there are relational values. If I have relational reason to feed my child, there is relational value in such parental

[1] Versions of this chapter were given at Washington University, the University of Minnesota, the Hebrew University Jerusalem, and the UK Association for Legal and Social Philosophy; I am very grateful to the participants in those discussions for helpful comments and criticisms.

feeding. If I have relational reason to respond to my student's philosophical inquiry, there is relational value in such pedagogical responsiveness. If I have relational reason to pay this debt, there is relational value in such promissory fidelity.

That there are relational reasons, of these and other kinds, is not controversial. What is controversial is the status of relational reasons, and whether they are always derivative from, or reducible to, other kinds of reason or value that are not in this way relational. We can note two possible kinds of derivation here.

First, and modestly, it might be argued that what underpins my relational reason to feed my child is a more general, less personal, value—that children be cared for by their parents. I have this relational reason to feed this child only because it is good that children be cared for by their parents. Similarly, perhaps I have this relational reason to respond to this person's philosophical question only because it is a relational good that teachers be responsive to their students' intellectual inquiries; and I have this relational reason to pay John £10 only because it is a relational good that promises be kept by those who make them (who are of course the only agents who can keep them).

Second, and more radically, it might be argued that even such general relational values and reasons as these are not rationally basic, but are dependent on or ultimately reducible to other, wholly non-relational, kinds of reason. On this view, the ultimate value that my feeding my child realizes is not the relational value of children being cared for by their parents, but rather the non-relational value of children being nurtured (or even the yet more general value of the vulnerable being cared for): I have this specific relational reason to feed my child only because parents in general have relational reasons to care for their children; and parents have such relational reasons only because, we have found, they are especially well placed to realize the value of children being cared for. Similarly, the value underpinning a teacher's relational reason to respond to her student's philosophical questions, and teachers' relational reasons to respond to their students' intellectual queries, might be that people be educated, or that those who seek wisdom be helped to gain it: such relational reasons for teachers (indeed, the role of 'teacher' itself) are generated by that value if that value is well served by people filling such roles and coming to have such relational reasons.

In what follows I will not be much concerned with the first kind of argument. In one way it is uncontroversial, since if I have a relational, parental reason to feed my child, it must be true that parents generally have relational reasons to care for their children, though we might argue about the logical ordering as between the particular and the general case: should we see the individual parent's reason as grounded in or dependent on the more general value; or do we articulate the more general value only as a way of summarizing what we can recognize in a range of particular cases?[2] I will be more concerned with the second kind of argument, and with the adequacy of this kind of reductive explanation of relational reasons; and I will attend to one implication of the second kind of argument (which could also on some readings be an implication of the first).

The implication concerns the reasons for action that others might have who do not stand in the particular relationship, or play the particular role, that gives me my relational reason. That relational reason speaks directly to me, and only to me (unless others stand in the same relationship—it would also speak to the child's other parent, or the student's other teachers): other people cannot have that relational reason to feed the child or to respond to the student. But this does not rule out the possibility that the source of my relational reason for action is also a source of other reasons for action for other people; and if values speak, in the language of practical reason, to all who can assist their realization, that possibility is an actuality.[3] If it is good that children be cared for by their parents, all rational agents have reason to do what they can to realize, or assist the realization of, that good. Only parents can of course realize it directly, by caring for their children; but others can assist its realization by encouraging and helping parents to care for their children, or perhaps by criticizing them if they fail to do so. Even more obviously, if the basic value is that children, or the vulnerable, be cared for, this is a source of reasons for action for all rational agents. If it is true that parents are best placed to realize that value directly in relation to children, other people (in

---

[2] Debates about moral particularism are in the background here: see also L. Blum, *Moral Perception and Particularity* (Cambridge: Cambridge University Press, 1994).

[3] See J. Gardner, 'Relations of Responsibility', in R. Cruft, M. Kramer, and M. Reiff (eds), *Crime, Punishment, and Responsibility* (Oxford: Oxford University Press, 2011), 87, at 89–91; also J. Gardner, 'Complicity and Causality', *Criminal Law and Philosophy* 1 (2007), 127.

principle, all other rational agents) have reason to help, insofar as it lies within their power, to bring it about that parents discharge that derivative responsibility. We can also now say, however, that others could in principle directly realize that basic value, of children or the vulnerable being cared for, since it is not internal to that value itself that the caring be done by the parents; and that they might indeed have good reason to do so, if they are able to do so and a child's parents are absent, or unable or unwilling to discharge their parental duties themselves.

The difference between these two perspectives, one of which takes relational values to be foundational, the other of which appeals to non-relational foundational values, should not be overstated. Those who take the relational view would no doubt agree that even if the value of parents caring for their children is an ultimate, irreducibly relational value, that children are cared for is also an important value; and even if parental care is given priority, if parents are unwilling or unable to fulfil their role, others have reason to step in to care for the children. Depending on how parenthood should be understood, it might be possible to replace absent parents (by adoption, for instance): or it might be possible only to provide proxy parents (by fostering, for instance); or only to provide non-parental care, which realizes a different value from that which the parents can realize. But there remains this key difference between these two understandings of the ultimate value that is realized in parental care for a child. On the relational view, only parents can directly realize the ultimate value: all that others can do is to assist parents to realize that value, or try to realize a proxy or substitute value in the parents' absence. On the non-relational view, by contrast, others could in principle realize the value that parents realize when they care for their children—that children be cared for. They might generally do better to leave the direct realization of that value to the parents, if parents are generally better placed to realize it: but that is a contingent rather than a conceptual matter, and if the parents are unavailable, unwilling, unable, or incompetent, others might be able to step in and—with skill and luck—realize the very value that the parents failed to realize.

My concern in this chapter is with the ways in which these issues play out in the particular context of the criminal law, to which we must now turn.

2. RELATIONAL REASONS AND THE CRIMINAL LAW

This chapter's questions concern the kinds of reason that the criminal law of a tolerably just society offers those whom it claims to bind. They are questions about normative reasons, rather than about motivating reasons: what kinds of good reason, reasons by which we should be guided, does the criminal law claim to offer us? We might put this question by asking what normative reason we have to obey the criminal law, but to avoid what we will see later to be significant confusions, we will do better to ask two more precise questions. First, what reason do we have not to act in ways that the substantive criminal law defines as criminal? Second, what reason do we have to submit ourselves to the criminal process of trial and punishment?[4] The distinction between substantive criminal law and criminal process will be important later.

Such questions about reasons are also questions about authority: in asking what reasons the criminal law offers us, we are also asking what kind of authority it claims over us. This is not simply a particularized version of the general question about the kind of authority that the law claims—although it cannot but be connected to that question: for we will see that the criminal law's claimed authority is of a quite distinctive kind.

In answering these questions, I will defend three claims. First, the normative reasons we have for obeying the criminal law are, typically or paradigmatically, relational and civic: in a liberal republic, of the kind in which contemporary democrats should aspire to live, they are grounded in our relationship not to the law or the state as such, but to our fellow citizens as members of the polity whose law it is; we should obey the criminal law because that is what we owe to our fellow citizens—and because it is our law.[5] Second, we do not typically have such relational reasons for obeying the substantive criminal law: indeed, we do not typically have any normative reason to obey the substantive criminal law, nor does that law seek our obedience. Third, the criminal law's authority does not consist in the power to make wrongful conduct that

---

[4] I will hereafter refer simply to 'reasons'; they should be understood as normative reasons unless otherwise described. I will also take for granted the qualification 'in a tolerably just society'.

[5] I will not comment here on what normative reasons, if any, members of non-democratic or illiberal polities may have to obey the criminal law of their polity: I certainly do not assume that they can have no reason to do so, nor that the criminal law would then lack authority; but their reasons will certainly be different.

was not already independently wrongful: it rather lies primarily in its procedural dimension, as the power to call alleged wrongdoers to public account, to judge their conduct, and to condemn and punish their criminal wrongdoing; and that authority is relational, in that it depends on the criminal law's status as the law of a political community whose members can collectively claim such authority over each other.[6]

In arguing for these claims I will be arguing against some common (albeit often implicit) assumptions: assumptions about the nature of the substantive criminal law, in particular that it essentially consists in prohibitions—in proscriptions or more rarely prescriptions that we are required to obey; about the grounds of retributive punishment—that its normative appeal is grounded in an impersonal demand of justice that the guilty suffer for their crimes); about the significance of the criminal process and the criminal trial—that their essential purpose is an instrumental one, to identify those who are eligible for punishment. These assumptions have, I will suggest, distorted our understanding of the normative significance of the criminal law: of the reasons we have for respecting or obeying it, of the authority that it can properly claim.

I will begin to explain and defend my claims by looking (in the next two sections) at the substantive criminal law. Section 5 will deal with the criminal law's procedural dimension, and its distinctive authority. Finally, in section 6, I will note two apparently problematic cases for my account—cases that actually show the merits of that account.

3. THE SUBSTANTIVE CRIMINAL LAW (I): *MALA IN SE*

The substantive criminal law defines a range of specific offences (and defences), as well as various general conditions and principles of criminal liability: I focus here on the 'special part', in which specific crimes are defined, individuated, and categorized. Some crimes are so-called '*mala in se*': they consist in conduct that is purportedly wrongful independently of and prior to its definition as criminal. The distinction between '*mala in se*' and '*mala prohibita*' is neither uncontroversial nor sharp, and some deny its utility altogether.[7] This might, however, be

---

[6] The qualifications 'typically' and 'paradigmatically' will be explained in what follows.
[7] See J. Bentham, *A Comment on the Commentaries* (1776), in J. H. Burns and H. L. A. Hart (eds), *Collected Works of Jeremy Bentham* (London: Athlone Press, 1977) iii, 63, on this 'acute

partly because they mistakenly suppose it to be a distinction between conduct that is, and conduct that is not, wrongful prior to its criminalization, rather than between conduct that is, and conduct that is not, wrongful prior to its legal regulation.[8] As should soon become clear, the distinction need not be neat or sharp to serve its essentially expository purpose, since both *mala in se* and *mala prohibita* consist in conduct that is supposedly wrongful independently of the *criminal* law, and it does not matter if there are borderline cases in which it is not clear whether the conduct's wrongfulness is altogether independent of its legal proscription. For present purposes, however, we can focus on the range of uncontroversial *mala in se* that includes murder, rape, and other serious attacks on the person.[9]

A relational account of our reasons for obeying the criminal law lacks plausibility in this context: if we ask why we should obey the laws that define murder and rape as criminal, the answer is surely not that we should obey them because we owe it to our fellow citizens. Apart from anything else, such an answer might imply that the murder or rape of a non-citizen is a different (perhaps lesser) wrong than the murder or rape of a citizen: we owe it to our fellow citizens to obey the laws that prohibit us from murdering or raping them, but we do not owe this to people who are not our fellow citizens. Perhaps such an answer need not imply this: perhaps we could argue that we owe it to our fellow citizens to obey the laws that prohibit the murder or rape not just of fellow citizens, but of anyone. But what is more deeply wrong with such an answer is that it portrays the laws that define such crimes as a set of prohibitions, and thus portrays our refraining from such wrongs as a matter of *obeying* those laws (obedience is what prohibitions seek). One implication of such a portrayal is that in defining such wrongs as crimes the criminal law offers us new normative reasons for refraining from the conduct it thus prohibits. That is what authoritative prohibitions

---

distinction ... which being so shrewd, and sounding so pretty, and being in Latin, has no sort of occasion to have any meaning to it'.

[8] See further R. A. Duff, *Answering for Crime* (Oxford: Hart Publishing, 2007), 89–93. More precisely, what matters is the conduct's purported wrongfulness: in a system that unjustifiably criminalizes homosexual conduct because it is wrongly supposed to be immoral, homosexual conduct will count as a *malum in se*.

[9] Property crimes constitute one kind of borderline case, since their definitions depend on the (non-criminal) law's definitions of property: but we need not worry about whether their wrongfulness depends on a legal *proscription* of the conduct they involve.

purport to do: whatever reasons we may have had for Φ-ing, the prohibition gives us new, perhaps peremptory or exclusionary, reason not to Φ. But that is not what the criminal law, in its substantive mode, typically says to us in its definitions of *mala in se* (it would be a strange message to a potential rapist that, whatever reasons he might have had to commit rape in the absence of the criminal law, respect for the law should restrain him).

The law rather presupposes that we already had amply sufficient, normally conclusive,[10] moral reasons to refrain from such wrongs—reasons to which it does not purport to add. Its definitions of such wrongs as crimes constitute not prohibitions but declarations: not to the effect that these are wrongs, since that is what it presupposes, but to the effect that these are public wrongs—wrongs that properly concern the polity as a whole, and for which we will be called to public account through the polity's courts. The substantive criminal law draws the boundary between 'public' and 'private' realms of wrongdoing, between those wrongs that are, and those that are not, the business of the polity: it marks out the kinds of (pre-criminal) wrong of which the polity will take formal public notice through its criminal courts.[11] This shows us the element of truth in Kelsen's notorious claim that law is addressed to the courts—that it is 'the primary norm which stipulates the sanction'.[12] The key point is not that the criminal law is addressed to the courts rather than to the citizens: it is, rather, that the central purpose of the criminal law is revealed not in its substantive dimension but in its procedural dimension; the substantive criminal law serves to mark out those kinds of conduct to which the criminal law's procedural provisions will be applied.

It is of course also true that the substantive criminal law can be seen as offering us new, prudential reasons for refraining from what it defines as crimes. The prospect of conviction and punishment might deter from

---

[10] Only normally sufficient, because through its specifications of general defences the criminal law recognizes that we can exceptionally have good reason to commit a *malum in se*.

[11] See further S. E. Marshall and R. A. Duff, 'Criminalization and Sharing Wrongs', *Canadian Journal of Law & Jurisprudence* 11 (1998), 7; Duff (n. 8 above), ch. 4.

[12] H. Kelsen, *Allgemeine Staatslehre* (1925; translated by A. Wedberg as *General Theory of Law and State*; Cambridge, Mass.: Harvard University Press, 1945), 63; see H. L. A. Hart, *The Concept of Law*, 2nd edn (Oxford: Oxford University Press, 1994), 35–42.

crime those who are not sufficiently motivated by the pre-criminal moral reasons for refraining from such wrongdoing, and if we think that deterrence has any proper role among the aims of a system of criminal law and punishment, we will take it that part of the point of the substantive criminal law is precisely to provide citizens whose moral motivation is inadequate with such (supplementary) prudential reasons for what would now count as obedience to its prohibitions:[13] 'refrain from Φ-ing or else' is a sanction-backed prohibition on Φ-ing. This does not, however, undermine my claims that the primary purpose of the substantive criminal law is declaratory rather than prohibitory, and that it does not offer us new normative reasons for refraining from the conduct it defines as criminal. For, first, the prudential reasons offered by the law in its deterrent mode are not normative reasons: the law does not tell us that we ought to refrain from what it defines as crimes to avoid punishment; it offers such reasons as reasons that might in fact motivate those who are insufficiently moved by the normative reasons on which it rests. Second, the legitimacy of deterrence depends on there already being sufficient, non-deterrent, normative reasons for us not to do what the law seeks to deter us from doing: if the criminal law is to have more normative authority than the gunman who coerces us to act as he wishes, what it seeks to deter us from must be something that we anyway, independently of its deterrent threats, have good normative reason not to do. A legitimately deterrent criminal law does not say to us simply 'refrain from Φ-ing, or else': it reminds us first that we ought not to Φ, and then adds a supplementary deterrent reason for those unmoved by that (precriminal and non-deterrent) 'ought'.

Victor Tadros has offered a counter-example to my claim that the substantive criminal law must presuppose, and cannot create, the wrongfulness of the conduct that it criminalizes. Suppose that we aim to reduce the harm caused by the misuse of knives, and realize that an effective way to do this would be to bring it about that no or very few people carry concealed knives. But we also realize that if we just declare that no one should carry a concealed knife, or pass a non-criminal regulation

---

[13] I take no view here on whether or how deterrence is a proper aim of the criminal law: see further A. von Hirsch, *Censure and Sanctions* (Oxford: Oxford University Press, 1993), ch. 2; R. A. Duff, *Punishment, Communication, and Community* (New York: Oxford University Press, 2001), 82–8.

banning such carrying, many people will not be dissuaded from carrying concealed knives; and that even given such a regulation, it would be wrong to carry a concealed knife only if most other people were not carrying them (for if many others do carry them, it will be legitimate to carry one as a defensive precaution). The only way to make an anti-knife regulation effective is to make it a matter of criminal law; only if knife-carrying is made criminal will enough people desist from it, and only then will it be wrongful for any individual to carry one. This, Tadros argues, is a case in which criminalization might be justified, if it would be an efficient way of reducing the harms caused by knife misuse, but in which the conduct to be criminalized is not wrongful prior to its criminalization.[14] I am not persuaded. Even if it is not wrong for people to carry knives in advance of regulation, once a legitimate regulation is in place it is wrong for us (note the collective plural) to carry knives, and that wrongfulness justifies criminalizing the breach of the regulation. A defendant could still justify carrying a knife by showing that, since others were not obeying the regulation, he needed to carry one in self-defence: but that would be to justify his commission of a wrong, not to show that it was not a wrong. The criminal law could recognize such a justification; but this is not a case in which it criminalizes conduct that was not already wrongful.

I have talked so far only about the terms in which the substantive criminal law 'typically' speaks to us: for in at least two kinds of case (cases that also bear on the question of who the 'us' are to whom the criminal law is to speak) the law cannot speak so simply of pre-criminal wrongs from which its addressees already have good reason to refrain.

The first kind of case concerns those who dissent from the values that the criminal law declares, and deny the wrongfulness of the conduct that it defines as criminal.[15] I have talked so far as if the criminal law can simply presuppose the wrongfulness of the conduct that it criminalizes—on the basis either of a dogmatic moral realism, or of a deep and broad moral consensus among members of the polity whose

---

[14] V. Tadros, 'Wrongness and Criminalization', in A. Marmor (ed.), *Routledge Companion to Philosophy of Law* (London: Routledge, 2012) 157, at 169–72.

[15] Another kind of dissenter denies that the criminalized conduct constitutes a public wrong; but if she admits that the conduct is wrongful, she agrees that she has good reason to refrain from it, though denying that that reason concerns the criminal law; her case therefore does not concern us here.

law it is; but no such presupposition seems viable in our morally plural, fractious contemporary societies. This is not the place to discuss just how deep those fractures are, save to note two points: first, that if they run so deep as to make it impossible (factually or morally) to identify a set of values as 'our' values, values that make a legitimate claim on the allegiance of all members of the polity, then criminal law (as distinct from some uneasy *modus vivendi*, or the mere exercise of coercive power by some over others) is impossible; second, that whilst 'our' values might, in a context of profound substantive moral disagreements, be partly procedural, about the procedures through which we are to decide on our collective rules, they cannot be purely procedural, since any set of process values must depend on some set of substantive values concerning the status of and the dealings between those who are party to the procedures. What we cannot deny, however, is that while criminal law might be possible, it cannot presuppose complete moral consensus. Even if we constrain it within as narrow a scope as is feasible (alert to the multiple dangers of overcriminalization),[16] even if we try to avoid criminal laws whose content is deeply morally controversial, the criminal law must sometimes take a controversial moral stand. It must, for instance, declare either that all forms of euthanasia are criminal, or that some are not: it will in either case be at odds with the deeply held moral views of some citizens, either declaring to be wrongful conduct that they believe to be morally permissible, or not declaring to be a public wrong conduct that they believe to be deeply wrong—for reasons given which it is a public wrong if it is wrong at all. So too, to take a less dramatic example, with fox-hunting:[17] the criminal law must either declare it to constitute a public wrong, as against the views of those who regard it as at least permissible, perhaps even as a public good; or (if only through its silence) declare or imply that it does not constitute a public wrong, as against the views of those who regard it as involving a wrongful maltreatment of animals that should be seen as a public wrong.[18]

---

[16] See D. Husak, *Overcriminalization: The Limits of the Criminal Law* (Oxford: Oxford University Press, 2008).

[17] See Hunting Act 2004, criminalizing (most) hunting of mammals with dogs.

[18] On some of the problems that normative dissent and difference create for liberal criminal law, see N Lacey, 'Community, Culture, and Criminalization', in Cruft et al. (n. 3 above), 292.

It might be tempting to say that the question raised by such examples is what 'we' should say to such dissenters; but that would beg important questions about the identity and scope of the 'we'. To put the question in those terms implies that 'we' are those whose values the law expresses, confronted by a 'them' who dissent; but of course 'we' could be the dissenters. We will do better to ask what the criminal law should say, in what terms, to those who dissent.

In some cases, the law should surely speak robustly of what is a public wrong, and say to the dissenters that they are wrong. Some men no doubt still believe that it is a husband's right to beat (or, as they might say, to 'chastise') his wife, or at least that such treatment of a wife by her husband is not the law's business: in such cases part of the point of criminal law is to declare authoritatively that this constitutes a public wrong, whose perpetrators will be called to public account. Although the law might also function as a deterrent, offering prudential reasons for what will then count as obedience to men who are insufficiently motivated by its moral message, its primary meaning is still declaratory: it does not claim that husbands ought to refrain from beating their wives out of respect for the law that prohibits such conduct; it rather defines such conduct as a public wrong from which they already had conclusive reason to refrain—reason that the law presupposes and recognizes rather than creating.

In other kinds of case, however, the law should perhaps recognize that the dissent is not unreasonable. It must still take a stand, since to remain silent is also to take a stand, and if the stand it takes (through an appropriate process of democratic deliberation) is that the conduct that many regard as a public wrong should not be criminal, what it says to the dissenters need only be that, whilst they can disapprove of the conduct morally, and criticize it informally, they cannot look to the criminal law to condemn it, or seek forcibly to prevent it as they can legitimately seek to prevent crime. But what can it say if the stand it takes is to criminalize conduct that dissenters wrongly but not unreasonably, in the eyes of those whose values it represents, regard as morally permissible? Here perhaps the criminal law offers us normative reasons for obeying its requirements. Rather than declaring that the dissenter's conduct is an incontrovertible public wrong from which she already had conclusive reason to refrain, and for which she is now called to public account and censure, the law can speak in the terms in which a liberal law is often said to address conscientious dissenters and civil disobedients: 'unless and until you can secure a change in the law through the democratic political process, you should respect the results of that process, and obey the law that it produces even if you disagree with the content of that law'.[19] That, it can be said, is something that the dissenter owes to her fellow citizens as members of a democratic polity: the reasons offered, that is, are relational and civic, in that they depend upon the dissenter's relationship as a citizen to her fellows; non-citizens cannot have *that* reason for acting in conformity to a polity's criminal law.[20] What she now owes, however, is indeed obedience. The claim is not, or not simply, that she already had conclusive reason to refrain from what the law now defines as a crime, since it is recognized that she does not accept that she has such reason, and that she might not be unreasonable in that denial. The claim is rather that, even if she can see no sufficient pre-criminal reason to refrain, she ought to see the fact that the conduct has been criminalized as a reason to refrain from it: as a reason, that is, to obey the law that criminalizes it—to refrain from the conduct because it is criminal.[21]

My suggestion that we should distinguish these two ways in which the criminal law can and should speak to dissenters raises three further questions which I cannot pursue here. First, how can we distinguish the cases: why should we say, as seems plausible, that the law should speak in the former, unqualified way to a person who sees nothing wrong in beating his wife, or in defending his daughter's 'honour' by killing the man of a different race or religion who dares to woo her; but in the latter, more nuanced way to one who believes that certain forms of requested euthanasia are justifiable and should be legal, or that fox-hunting is a legitimate sport? On what grounds can we distinguish 'unreasonable' from 'not unreasonable' views? One possibility might be to distinguish cases in which dissenters can be seen as offering an interpretation of

---

[19] The normative force of this response depends, of course, on the extent to which the current law is the result of a genuinely democratic process, and to which there is a public political process through which dissenters can argue their case and can be heard.

[20] The reasons they can have will be discussed later.

[21] Some might express this distinction as one between the 'content-dependent' reasons that we normally have to refrain from criminalized conduct, and the 'content-independent' reasons that in this kind of case the law offers the dissenter; but I prefer not to become embroiled in the problems that distinction raises (on which see P. Markwick, 'Law and Content-Independent Reasons', *Oxford Journal of Legal Studies* 20 (2000), 579).

values that we share as part of our civic tradition, from those in which their claims cannot be seen as an interpretation of, or a variation, on those values.[22] Some hunters appeal to a moral conception of our relationships with other animals that takes animal cruelty seriously as a wrong, but portrays hunting as something that need not be cruel and that can be pursued without denying the hunted animal's moral significance. Proponents of some forms of requested euthanasia can claim to be interpreting the central value (even the sanctity) of human life. But no such argument can be made by the wife-beater or the 'honour' killer.

Second, if the law should speak to some dissenters in the terms suggested here, that must make some difference, if not to the label of the offence for which they are to be convicted, at least to their sentence: they should be censured now not as citizens who have committed an unarguable substantive public wrong, but rather as citizens who have shown a lack of proper respect for the democratic process by committing what they know that their fellow citizens have (after a process in which their dissenting voices were or could have been heard) deemed to be a public wrong. I cannot discuss this further here.

Third, the tones in which I have suggested the criminal law should speak to a reasonable dissenter might seem more appropriate in some cases, such as hunting, than in others, such as euthanasia. It seems legitimate to say to the fox-hunter that he should, despite his sincere and not unreasonable belief that hunting should not be criminal, refrain from it out of respect for the democratically made law that criminalized it; but can we honestly say something similar to someone who has come conscientiously to believe that she must provide her terminally ill loved one with the help that he has so earnestly requested to achieve the death that he wants? Can we respect her motives for such an action, and yet tell her that she should refrain out of respect for the criminal law: or should we recognize that respect for the law or the democratic process is not a reason that we could expect to outweigh, cancel or exclude the reasons that motivate her to commit euthanasia? One crucial difference between her and the hunter is that she regards her action not merely as morally permissible, but as something that she must do, so that in saying that she should obey the law we ask her to act against her conscience; but the

---

[22] Thanks to Sandra Marshall for this suggestion.

mismatch between what motivates her to commit euthanasia—the moral significance and depth of that motive—and the reasons we offer her to obey the law is also important. If this is right, perhaps in cases such as this (we cannot discuss here which other kinds of case might be 'such as this') the criminal law cannot seek respectful obedience: it must either declare the action to be wrong, and its agent wrong to think it right; or provide a 'conscience clause' that allows an agent with deep conscientious objections to refraining from what the law defines as criminal to avoid criminal liability for acting in accordance with her conscience.[23]

The second kind of problem case raises related, though importantly different, issues: it is that of a non-citizen who is temporarily within the jurisdiction of a polity's criminal law, and who, acting in accordance with his own values (values reflected in his own polity's criminal laws) commits what, as he knows, 'our' laws define as a crime.[24] What should the law say to him? Here again we must distinguish two kinds of case, to which different responses will be appropriate.

Sometimes the criminal law should speak robustly of the public wrong that the visitor has committed. If a wife-beater or 'honour' killer is visiting from a country where such conduct is both morally and legally sanctioned, we should not say to him that he should respect our local customs and obey our local laws whilst he is here; we should say that his conduct constitutes a public wrong for which we will call him to account if he commits it in our country. We do not call him to public legal account for that conduct if he commits it outside the ambit of our criminal law, since wife-beating or 'honour' killing committed abroad is not the business of our courts, and is not a crime under our law: but it is important to be clear that in saying that he is not, on that basis, guilty of a crime under our law, we are not saying that what he does is not wrong. Our law is silent on wife-beating committed abroad, not because it declares such conduct to be permissible,

---

[23] Another issue is whether such a conscience clause should be seen as providing a justification or an excuse. The DPP's 'Policy for Prosecutors' on assisted suicide, which in effect (despite the DPP's formal denial) decriminalized compassionate assistance to suicide by private individuals, provides a useful starting point here <http://www.cps.gov.uk/publications/prosecution/assisted_suicide_policy.html>.

[24] I assume knowledge of the law here to avoid entanglement with issues about ignorance of law.

R. A. Duff

but because such conduct is not its business: the collective voice in which our law claims to speak, the voice of the citizens of the polity, is not a relativist voice that portrays the wrongness of wife-beating as conditional on local cultural norms; but it is a voice that recognizes the limits of its authority. What makes wife-beating a crime here but not abroad is not that it is wrong because, or only when, it is committed here, but that only then is it the business of our courts and of the law that they apply. As moral agents, we can comment on the morality of such conduct wherever it is committed: but what gives us the standing to pass legal judgment on it as criminal is that is committed within our polity.[25]

Sometimes, however, a recognition of cultural differences might give us reason to speak to the visitor in different tones. We might recognize, for instance, that her conduct reflects her and her culture's conception of what counts as honest dealing or fair competition in business matters, or of what counts as offensive or inoffensive conduct in public places—a conception that we should not condemn as unreasonable. This does not imply that she must therefore be acquitted, through a version of the 'cultural defence', for conduct that is properly criminal in this polity; but it does suggest that if she is to be convicted, the basis for her criminal liability should not be that she committed a substantive public wrong, but that she failed to respect the local conventions and understandings that the local law expresses. Here we might mobilize a 'When in Rome' slogan, and might talk (as we would not in the former case) of the normative reason that she has to obey the local criminal law: whether or not she should see her conduct as independently wrongful, the fact that it is defined as a public wrong by the criminal law of the country she is visiting gives her reason to refrain from it (to obey that law). That reason is also, however, a relational reason. She does not owe such obedience as a citizen, to her fellow citizens—for she is not a citizen of this polity; but she is a guest in this polity, and we can say that as a guest she owes it to her hosts to respect the local conventions in this way.

My account of the substantive criminal law, insofar as it deals with *mala in se*, can thus deal with both these apparent problem cases. I can

---

[25] This jurisdictional point, given which the crime committed abroad is not the business of our law, will be explained and argued more fully in section 5 below.

still maintain that we do not typically have (and that the criminal law does not typically offer) normative reason to obey the substantive criminal law; and that when we do have such reason to obey the law, the reason is relational, grounded either in our relationship, as citizens, to fellow citizens of the polity whose law it is, or in our status as guests in the polity.

However, the realm of *mala in se*, though salient in both theoretical and public discussion of the substantive criminal law, constitutes a relatively small proportion of the law, since the majority of criminal offences do not consist in clearly pre-legal wrongs; I must therefore turn now to the realm of so-called *mala prohibita*, which might seem much more problematic for the kind of account I am offering.

4. THE SUBSTANTIVE CRIMINAL LAW (2): *MALA PROHIBITA*

Paradigmatic *mala in se* consist in conduct that is supposedly wrongful independently of and prior to not only its definition as criminal, but any legal proscription. Paradigmatic *mala prohibita*, by contrast, consist in conduct that is wrongful (if at all) only because it is legally proscribed. Indeed, the conduct that constitutes a *malum prohibitum* is often not possible, let alone wrongful, prior to its legal regulation: I cannot, for instance, fail to display a tax disc on my car, or submit a false income tax return, absent the laws that create and maintain a system of car registration or of taxation.

Now in the context of *mala prohibita* we should indeed talk, as I have argued we should not typically talk in the context of *mala in se*, of the normative reasons that we have to obey the law; it is also true, as we will shortly see, that those reasons are by no means always civic relational reasons, grounded in our relationship as citizens to the polity to which we belong and to fellow members of that polity. However, and quite apart from the fact that the reasons for obeying the law are in this context quite often relational reasons, the key point is that we are still not obeying, and still do not have normative reason to obey, the substantive criminal law: the law that we obey and ought to obey is not the criminal law. I can therefore maintain my claim that the substantive criminal law is not a source of reasons for action, and does not seek our obedience. Its role is still to mark out certain pre-existing wrongs as 'public', and the difference between *mala in se* and *mala prohibita* is that the latter kinds of wrong, whilst pre-criminal, are not pre-legal.[26]

To understand this point, we must realize that the criminalization of a *malum prohibitum* involves what is logically a two-stage process. First, we see good reason to regulate a certain kind of conduct: to create, for instance, a system of taxation to generate money for the public purse, or a system of rules to regulate motor vehicles. Such regulatory systems require those whom they bind to refrain from certain kinds of conduct that might not be wrongful prior to the system's creation: they demand that we obey their rules, even if the conduct prohibited by the rules was not already wrongful. Once the rules are in place, and if they have a legitimate claim on us (for instance as marking a good faith attempt by a legitimate government to make regulations that will serve some aspect of the common good), we have reason to obey them—and obedience is indeed what is now involved: I display this disc on my car, I send this form to the tax office, because that is what the law (the road vehicle or tax regulations) requires of me. The normative reason that I have to obey is not simply that this is what the law requires, but that it is what the law requires is integral to my reason for action, in a way in which the fact that the law defines wounding as a crime is not part of my reason for refraining from the conduct thus defined as criminal.

Sometimes our reasons for obeying such regulations are relational and civic: an account of why I should pay my taxes, for instance, would plausibly talk of how I owe it to my fellow citizens to make a fair contribution to the public purse which pays for the public goods of the polity—goods in which I also share.[27] Sometimes my reasons for obedience have nothing to do with my role as a citizen: if the driving regulations specify that we should drive on the left, any road user in that jurisdiction has the same reason to drive on the left, that this is (usually) an efficient way to safely coordinate the activities of drivers in this area.

---

[26] That is why it is important to define a *malum prohibitum* not as an offence consisting in conduct that is not wrongful prior to its criminalization (were that so, a criminal law whose function is to mark out certain pre-existing wrongs could include no *mala prohibita*), but as an offence consisting in conduct that is not (or might not be) determinately wrongful prior to its legal proscription: on this point and its complications, see Duff (n. 8 above).

[27] This implies that non-citizens who are temporarily in a country do not have the same kind of reason as do citizens to pay whatever taxes they are liable to pay—which seems to me to be true.

A visitor has just the same reason as any citizen to obey such regulations, and commits the same wrong if she fails to obey them.[28] Those who take a deeply relational view of reasons might say that even here our reasons are relational: that we owe it to each other, as human beings who recognize each other's vulnerability, to take such care not to endanger each other. But the relevant point here is that our reasons are not the kinds of relational reason, grounded in our role as citizens, that I have claimed ground our obedience to the criminal law. Whatever reasons for obedience we have, however, they are not reasons for obeying the criminal law, since the regulations that we are obeying are not (yet) part of the criminal law: they are road traffic regulations, or tax regulations, and the criminal law has not yet entered the picture.

The criminal law enters the picture only when we ask how these regulations ought to be enforced—how we should respond to breaches of them. Quite different kinds of response are possible, including the absence of any formal legal response (giving the regulations a purely exhortatory legal character), a system of administrative penalties which are not presented as punishments for criminal offences, and a system under which civil suits are brought by those who think that they have been injured by the breach of the regulations. What would make it appropriate to criminalize such breaches would be that they constitute wrongs that the polity should mark and respond to as such: not only, that is, that they constitute wrongs which are in the relevant sense 'public', but that our response to them should make that aspect salient, by calling those who commit them to public account, and censuring them if they cannot provide an exculpatory answer.

Of course, if the regulations are properly justified as having been created by a democratic process, and as serving (or being reasonably claimed to serve) an aspect of the common good, the breach of them is a public wrong: a wrong, because a breach of regulations that we have good reason to obey; a public wrong, because a breach of regulations that serve the common good. We therefore have reason to criminalize the breach of any justified regulation. But this does not trivialize my claim that we have here a two-stage process of criminalization.[29] First, that we have

---

[28] See Gardner, 'Relations of Responsibility' (n. 3 above), at 95: he is right about this kind of case, but wrong to generalize from this kind of case to all others.

[29] Thanks to Ken Waters for pressing this point.

reason to criminalize breaches does not entail that we always have conclusive reason to do so: we might still see better reason to favour one of
the other kinds of response noted above. Second, even when we do
decide to criminalize, it is important to be clear about the logic of that
decision. Deliberation about criminalization must begin by asking
whether we have any reason to criminalize the conduct in question. We
have reason to criminalize it, I have argued, only if it constitutes a public
wrong—a wrong whose character as wrong and as public must be independent of its criminalization. In the case of *mala prohibita*, the conduct
is wrong as the breach of a legitimate regulation which we ought to
obey: the existence of the regulation, its legitimate claim on our obedience, and the wrong involved in breaching it, are therefore presupposed
by the criminal law that defines such breaches as criminal; which is to
say again that the substantive criminal law functions not to create
wrongs, but to mark certain pre-existing wrongs as public wrongs.

So far, I have tried to explain and defend the second of the three
claims sketched above in section 2, and aspects of the first and third
claims: that we do not typically have relational reasons to obey the substantive criminal law, because we do not typically have any normative
reason to obey it; that when we do have reason to obey it, that reason is
relational and civic, in that we owe such obedience, as citizens, to the
fellow members of our polity (or, if we are guests, to our hosts); and that
the criminal law's authority does not include or consist in the power to
make wrongful conduct that was not already wrong. The authority of
the substantive criminal law lies rather in defining certain pre-existing
wrongs as 'public' wrongs—as wrongs which properly concern the whole
polity. The force and the implications of so defining a wrong as a public
wrong are made visible in the criminal process, in particular in the criminal trial: in the procedural-punitive dimension of the criminal law,
which gives institutional form and effect to the conception of crimes as
public wrongs. It is to that dimension of the criminal law that we must
therefore now turn, to ask what kind of authority it can claim, and what
reason we can have to submit ourselves to it.

5. THE CRIMINAL PROCESS

Theorists often describe the criminal process in instrumental terms: it
is a mechanism that connects crime to punishment, by enabling the

identification (without intolerable inaccuracy) of those who, having committed crimes, are now eligible for punishment. The process might be constrained by non-instrumental principles (those captured by the notion of 'due process') which function both to protect those subjected to it from hasty and unreliable findings of guilt and to rule out practices that violate other rights or values; but its essential justifying aim is instrumental—to identify those who are to be punished. I have argued elsewhere that this is an inadequate view of the criminal process, and will not repeat the argument here;[30] but I do need to summarize its main claims.

The criminal trial is best understood (as a matter of rationally reconstructive normative theory, not of empirical description or socio-legal analysis) as a process of calling to account: as a formal public process through which those alleged to have committed public wrongs are called to answer, through the court, to their fellow citizens. The defendant is called, initially, to answer *to* a charge of wrongdoing: he faces an indictment which alleges that he committed a specified criminal wrong, and he is expected to respond to that indictment either by a plea of 'Guilty', which admits his culpable commission of the offence and accepts the authority of the court to censure and sentence him; or by a plea of 'Not Guilty', which whilst not perhaps constituting a claim of innocence, at least challenges to the prosecution to prove his guilt. If the prosecution proves that he did commit the offence charged, he is expected to answer *for* that commission, either by offering a defence which claims that his commission of it was not culpable,[31] or by accepting conviction and the censure that conviction conveys. If we ask why we should collectively respond in this way to alleged commissions of public wrongs, the answer is not that this is the most efficient way of identifying the perpetrators who are then to be punished (though of course it matters that those convicted committed the relevant crimes); it is rather that this is the appropriate way for a liberal polity to respond to alleged violations of its public values. It is appropriate because it takes the wrong seriously

---

[30] See R. A. Duff, L. Farmer, S. E. Marshall, and V. Tadros, *The Trial on Trial (3): Towards a Normative Theory of the Criminal Trial* (Oxford: Hart Publishing, 2007).

[31] On the distinction between offences and defences, and on how we should draw it, see J. Gardner, 'Fletcher on Offences and Defences', *Tulsa Law Review* 39 (2004), 817; V. Tadros, *Criminal Responsibility* (Oxford: Oxford University Press, 2005), ch. 4; Duff (n. 8 above), ch. 9.

as a violation of the polity's core values, and because it thus also does justice to the victims (when there are any), by recognizing that they have been not just harmed (if they have been harmed), but wronged: we show our concern for the wrong that a fellow has suffered by trying to call its perpetrator to account. It is also appropriate as doing justice to the alleged offender—both to innocents who are charged with wrongs that they did not commit, and to the guilty: to call someone to answer for alleged wrongdoing is to treat her as a responsible fellow member of a normative community (in this case, the polity), by whose values she is both bound and protected.

Seen in this light, the criminal trial is perhaps the central feature of a system of criminal law, and provides the central justifying purpose of the substantive criminal law. That is, the (or at least a) central function of the substantive criminal law is to identify the wrongs whose perpetrators are to be called to public account in this way: the substantive dimension of the criminal law must be understood and rationalized in terms of the procedural dimension that it exists to serve. We can also now see that the authority that the criminal law claims resides in its procedural dimension, as the authority to identify those wrongs whose perpetrators will be called to account in this way, and to call them to account.[32]

But what gives the court the right, the standing, to call an alleged wrongdoer to account in this way, or the right to judge her and to censure her? By what authority does the court call the defendant to answer to the charge, and pronounce a verdict of guilt or of innocence at the end of the trial?[33] What could ground the defendant's duty (if she has such a duty) to respond to the charge and to accept the court's verdict? Such questions are salient in cases in which a defendant refuses to enter a plea because she denies the court's authority or legitimacy: for to enter a plea is to accept the court's authority as the body by and through which I am properly called to answer this charge—which is something that a defendant might want to make clear she denies. But it is a question that is raised by all criminal cases, and the answer to it cannot be a purely legal one. We could rehearse the legal basis of the court's opera-

---

[32] And, of course, to punish them; I discuss punishment briefly below.

[33] A verdict of 'Not Guilty' is not as such a finding of innocence: it requires only a failure by the prosecution to prove guilt beyond reasonable doubt. But it still amounts to a verdict of innocence, since it amounts to a finding that the presumption of innocence, to which every citizen is entitled, has not been defeated.

tions, and show how it has the legal authority to try this defendant: but the deeper questions that concern us here are about the moral authority of the court and of the law in whose voice it speaks.

Any answer to these questions must be able to explain (or to show that we should reject) the essentially local authority claimed by the domestic law and courts of contemporary nation states—the fact that English courts will try, as a crime under English law, a theft committed in England, but will claim no authority over a theft committed in Brazil by a Brazilian citizen against another Brazilian citizen.[34] What gives the English court authority over the thief who stole in England, but not over the Brazilian thief?

One kind of answer to such questions about the criminal court's authority makes the local character of that authority an essentially contingent, pragmatic matter: it ultimately grounds it not in any relational, civic reasons, but in the impersonal, universal demands of justice, and in the contingent fact (when it is a fact) that the domestic courts of nation states are best placed to satisfy those demands. Justice demands that wrongdoers be called to account and punished (the passive voice matters here). That demand speaks to all rational agents, and gives reasons for action to any who can act so as to assist its satisfaction.[35] We must all recognize the value in thieves being brought to justice, wherever and from whomever they steal. We should hear the demand that they be punished, and have reason to create and maintain institutions that can satisfy that demand. Within a state, we therefore have reason to maintain a system of criminal law that will call such wrongdoers to account; and since the demands of retributive justice are universal rather than local, we have reason to give our domestic law and our domestic courts jurisdiction over wrongs committed not only within our territory, but

---

[34] The references to the citizenship of offender and of victim are necessary because some states operate with a principle of 'nationality', which gives domestic courts jurisdiction over crimes committed abroad by the state's citizens, or of 'passive personality', which gives domestic courts jurisdiction over crimes committed abroad against the state's citizens. See, e.g., French *Code Pénal*, art 113.6–7; German *Strafgesetzbuch*, s 7.1–2, Sex Offenders Act 1997, s 7. See generally M. Hirst, *Jurisdiction and the Ambit of the Criminal Law* (Oxford: Oxford University Press, 2003), ch. 5. I comment below on exceptions to such limits marked by claims of 'universal jurisdiction'.

[35] For this view of reasons for action, see, e.g., Gardner (n. 3 above); M. M. Dempsey, 'Public Wrongs and the "Criminal Law's Business": When Victims Won't Share', in Cruft et al. (n. 3 above), 254.

anywhere in the world. English criminal law and its courts can therefore in principle claim jurisdiction over Brazilian thefts. However, this is not to say that we have conclusive reason to give our courts such an extensive jurisdiction. In deciding how we should act in relation to a value or demand that we recognize, we must ask how we can most efficiently serve the realization of that value or the satisfaction of that demand, and whether others are better placed to realize it or to satisfy it; we might conclude that we should make no direct efforts to realize it or to satisfy it, because we are not well-placed to do so efficiently, or because others are better placed to do so. When we ask how we should act in relation to the demands of retributive justice, we might conclude that where there are nation states with effectively functioning systems of criminal law, they are best placed to satisfy those demands in relation to wrongs committed within the territory over which they exercise effective authority; and for reasons both of efficiency and of respect for national sovereignty (itself a value that we should preserve), nation states should not generally claim jurisdiction over wrongs committed within another state's territory. So what gives English law and English courts the right to call English citizens to account for crimes they commit in England is not any deep relationship between them, as citizens, and this law and these courts as their law and their courts; it is the fact that such a jurisdictional ordering is an efficient way to satisfy the demands of justice.[36]

There are obvious attractions to this account. It accords with the passive voice in which we sometimes talk about serious wrongs: the founding statute of the International Criminal Court 'affirm[s] that the most serious crimes of concern to the international community as a whole must not go unpunished and that their effective prosecution must be ensured';[37] this leaves open the question of who is to ensure that 'effective prosecution' and punishment. It makes sense of the Principle of Territoriality by which the jurisdiction of domestic criminal courts is often defined:[38] given the scope of the effective authority that nation states typically wield, we can expect that their courts will be best placed

---

[36] See A. Altman and C. Wellman, *A Liberal Theory of International Justice* (Oxford: Oxford University Press, 2009), esp. ch. 4; also C. Wellman, 'Piercing Sovereignty', in R. A. Duff and S. P. Green (eds), *Philosophical Foundations of Criminal Law* (Oxford: Oxford University Press, 2010), 461.

[37] Rome Statute of the International Criminal Court (1998), Preamble.

[38] See Hirst (n. 34 above), ch. 1.

to deal with wrongs committed in their territory. This account also provides a straightforward rationale for the authority of the International Criminal Court, and of other international tribunals set up to deal with atrocities committed in, for instance, Rwanda and what used to be Yugoslavia,[39] and for the 'universal jurisdiction' over international crimes claimed by some domestic legal systems:[40] although nation states should normally be left to deal with crimes committed within their territory, if the domestic legal system and its courts are unwilling or unable to do so, and the crimes are so grave that the demands of retributive justice become insistent, international bodies or other states might be justified in intervening to ensure that justice is done. For the justice that needs to be done can, in principle, be done by anyone with the capacity to do it: it is a contingent fact that it is usually best done by the domestic courts of the state in whose territory the crime occurs; when that fact does not obtain, others may intervene.

However, such an account of the criminal law's authority also has some more disturbing implications. In particular, first, it might open the door, at least in principle, to vigilantism—to the private imposition of punishment (or 'punishment') by those who are frustrated by the failure of their local courts to do what justice requires. Whether that door is even in principle opened depends, of course, on how we should understand punishment and punitive justice. It might seem that if we follow the orthodox route in defining punishment, according to which punishment must be imposed 'by an authority',[41] vigilantism is ruled out in principle, since a vigilante mob counts as vigilante precisely because it lacks authority: but that would be too quick, since we must first ask what value punishment is to serve. If we begin, as retributivists sometimes begin, with the intuition that the guilty 'deserve to suffer', and see punishment as a formal way of imposing such suffering on them, a vigilante mob could in principle do the work that punishment is to do, and realize the value (the proportionate suffering of the guilty) that

---

[39] The International Criminal Tribunals for Rwanda (1994) and for the former Yugoslavia (1993), on which see A. Cassesse, *International Criminal Law* (2nd edn; Oxford; Oxford University Press, 2008), 324–35.

[40] See L. Reydams, *Universal Jurisdiction* (Oxford: Oxford University Press, 2003).

[41] See A. Flew, 'The Justification of Punishment', *Philosophy* 29 (1954), 291; H. L. A. Hart, 'Prolegomenon to the Principles of Punishment', in *Punishment and Responsibility* (Oxford: Oxford University Press, 1968), 1.

punishment is to realize; even if what the mob does cannot count as 'punishment', such a definitional stop cannot rule out the claim that the mob might achieve what criminal courts, on this view, aim to achieve by punishment. This is not to suggest that those who offer such an account of the criminal law's authority are committed to permitting vigilantism: they can plausibly argue that vigilantism so often causes such serious harm (and commits such serious wrongs), and so rarely imposes duly proportionate suffering, that it should never be tolerated. The fact remains, however, that if the value to be realized is that the guilty undergo suffering proportionate to their desert, vigilantism could in principle serve that good.

Second, such an account underplays the oddity of the idea that English law and English courts might claim jurisdiction over the Brazilian thief. It would normally, on this account, be inadvisable to claim such extensive jurisdiction: inadvisable because usually unnecessary, if the courts of the state in whose territory the crime occurred are operating effectively; and also because an attempt to enforce such a claim would violate the other state's sovereignty, which is something that states normally have very good reason to avoid. But it would not be absurd to make, or to contemplate making, such a claim, since it would not be absurd to argue, or to consider whether there are adequate grounds for arguing, that by making and enforcing such a claim we could best serve the ends of justice. Surely, however, there would be something very strange—much stranger than this view suggests—about the United Kingdom parliament debating whether a Theft Act should 'extend' not just to England and Wales, or to Scotland as well, but to Brazil, or to the whole world.

The previous two paragraphs were not intended as arguments against the account under discussion here, but only as ways of raising some doubts about it. To see why it is wrong, we must attend to two essential aspects of the criminal law, and of criminal responsibility, that it fails adequately to recognize.

First, it does not take seriously enough the essentially political character of criminal law. Were the criminal law an attempt to give the moral law institutional form and force, were it for instance an attempt to ensure that moral wrongdoers receive the suffering they supposedly deserve, such an account would have more plausibility. For the moral law speaks to all moral agents; we all have reason to do what we can to make sure that it is fulfilled. If the criminal law aspires to be an institutional manifestation of the moral law, it can therefore in principle claim authority over all moral agents everywhere. There might be pragmatic reasons to limit the reach of a nation state's criminal law, or principled reasons to do with the values (such as national sovereignty) that an attempt to extend its reach beyond national boundaries would infringe; but those are reasons for not actually claiming the extensive authority that it could in principle claim. However, the criminal law is not the moral law. It is part of the structure of the polity as a political community; it addresses those whom it claims to bind not (merely) as moral agents, but as citizens of the polity. We must therefore ask what kind of remit a polity and its criminal laws can properly claim over the lives of its citizens; which aspects of those lives fall within the civic realm that is the polity's business? As citizens of a polity, we are engaged together in a civic enterprise of living together: of living together not as friends, or lovers, or colleagues in a business or profession, but precisely as citizens, whose civic life is only one aspect of their lives. In a democracy, a crucial task for those engaged in the civic enterprise is to work out, through a robust public deliberation, the nature of that enterprise, and what belongs to it:[42] to work out, for instance, which aspects of sexual life fall within the civic enterprise as public matters; whether only what is non-consensual is a public matter, because what is consensual is always a private matter. Once they have determined the scope and content of the civic enterprise, they can identify a class of public wrongs: wrongs which impinge on or fall within that enterprise, which they therefore have reason to criminalize as wrongs whose perpetrators can in principle be called to account through the criminal courts.

Now a polity and its members might of course take a profoundly non-liberal view of the public realm, and arrive at a classical form of legal moralism according to which every kind of moral wrongdoing is as such the polity's public business, and thus in principle the business of the criminal law: nothing in the logic of the conception of criminal law sketched here rules out that kind of view (though it is one I would argue against in the political debate about how we should understand our civic enterprise). All that I want to argue here is that both the legal moralist's

---

[42] See A. Harel, 'The Triadic Relational Structure of Responsibility', in Cruft et al. (n. 3 above), 103.

view, and the views of her liberal opponents, must be grounded in an account of the nature, scope and content of the civic enterprise, which is a matter of political rather than of purely moral theory. Some versions of legal moralism, as portrayed by both advocates and critics, suggest that debates about the scope of the criminal law begin with the whole realm of moral wrongdoing, and then look for ways in which we can limn a more restricted subset of wrongs as properly criminalizable; this approach might also be suggested if we say that moral wrongdoing is a necessary but insufficient condition of criminalization. We should instead, however, begin with a conception of the civic enterprise; only those wrongs that fall within that enterprise or impinge on it will figure at all in debates about what we should criminalize.[43]

The authority of a polity and its laws is limited to what falls within the civic enterprise in which its citizens are collectively engaged. On any but the most oppressively communitarian conception of the civic enterprise, it is therefore limited in two ways. It does not extend into, because the civic enterprise does not involve, all aspects of citizens' lives: a distinction will be drawn between the public and the private realms, and what occurs within a private realm, however wrong it might be, is not the polity's business, and not even in principle a candidate for criminalization.[44] As citizens, the logic of our thought about private immoralities should not be 'It's wrong, but on the other hand it's not our business', as if the wrongfulness of the conduct gave us some reason to intervene—a reason that is then outweighed or excluded by the conduct's private character; it should be something more like 'It's a private matter, so it's not our civic business to judge whether it's right or wrong'. Nor does the civic enterprise or the polity's authority normally extend beyond the polity's boundaries. English law is properly silent about, it claims no authority over, Brazilian thefts: not because the English collectively recognize that the Brazilian criminal justice system can deal with such

---

[43] It is worth noting that even Lord Devlin, who is so often portrayed as a legal moralist, implicitly accepted this: his argument was not that the immorality of any kind of conduct gave us some reason to criminalize it, but rather that, given the dependence of society (of the civic enterprise) on a shared morality, the *perceived* immorality of any kind of conduct might impinge destructively on the civic enterprise.

[44] I should emphasize that that distinction is a matter for deliberation, and will not match the geographical distinction between what is done 'in public' and what is done 'in private'. As feminist theorists remind us, that deliberation will need to be sensitive to the dangers of being too quick to classify matters as private.

thefts more efficiently, nor because they tolerate such thefts or regard them as less serious than thefts committed in England, but because the English polity, its citizens qua citizens, have no standing to judge or respond to them. As moral agents we may have an interest in thefts committed anywhere by or against anyone: I leave open here the question of whether all moral wrongs are in principle of concern to all moral agents. But as citizens, wearing our civic uniforms, our interest is normally limited to what belongs to or impinges on the civic enterprise of our polity.[45]

The second aspect of criminal law and criminal responsibility that points towards a more thoroughly relational conception of the criminal law's authority is the relational character of responsibility itself, and of punishment. We can understand moral and criminal responsibility, when their ascriptions bring the prospect of moral blame or criminal condemnation, as matters of answerability: to hold A responsible for some untoward Φ is to hold that A must answer for Φ on pain of being blamed or condemned for Φ if he cannot offer an exculpatory answer. But we do not answer into a void: we answer *to* some person or some body, and can be expected to answer only to one who has the standing to demand it of us. Responsibility-answerability is therefore a three-way relationship: A is responsible for Φ to some B, and the justifiability of such ascriptions of responsibility depends not merely on A's relationship to Φ (on which discussions of responsibility typically focus), but on B's relationship to A and to Φ, in virtue of which B has the standing to call A to answer for Φ. It follows from this, first, that when I say, in the third person, that A is responsible for Φ, it is always proper to ask to whom A is responsible for Φ; and that when, speaking in the second person, I

---

[45] Two glosses on this claim should be noted. First, the jurisdictional principles of nationality and of passive personality are consistent with such limits of a polity's authority: they mark an expansive understanding of the boundaries of the polity, as enfolding all citizens wherever they are; what is done anywhere by or to a fellow citizen is on this view our civic business. Second the qualification 'normally' is important: I am not suggesting that polities have no responsibilities beyond their own borders—that they should never take an active interest in, for instance, the serious deprivations, or the large scale wrongs, suffered by members of other polities. But such responsibilities, on the view sketched here, must mark extensions, evoked by urgent need or emergency, to the polity's normal concerns—whereas on the universalist or cosmopolitan view to which mine is opposed, what I count here as the polity's 'normal' concerns rather mark a narrowing of the in principle concern for the whole world from which we should begin.

hold *A* responsible for *Φ* or call on *A* to answer for *Φ*, I must be able to justify that holding or that calling by showing why I have the standing to call *A* to account. It also follows that *A* can ward off my criticism of him for *Φ*-ing without denying his relationship to *Φ* as its author, and without offering an exculpatory explanation of his *Φ*-ing, if he can argue that his *Φ*-ing is not my business—if he can claim that, whilst there might be others to whom he is responsible and must answer for *Φ*-ing, he is not answerable to me.[46]

A similar point holds for punishment. Theorists discussing the justification of punishment often focus on what is done to whom, or suffered by whom, without attending sufficiently to the question of who is doing it or inflicting it. Retributivists might start, for instance, from the slogan that 'the guilty deserve to suffer', and explain criminal punishment as the infliction of that deserved suffering; although they may also define punishment as something imposed by an authority, that easily becomes a secondary issue that is not seen as bearing on the meaning or the fundamental justification of punishment. That is why such theorists open up a logical space for vigilantes. If a vigilante group locks an offender up, in conditions materially similar to those he would have suffered in prison, for term as long as the prison sentence that a court would have imposed; or takes from him the amount of money a court would have imposed as a fine; or forces him to work at the kind of work, for the same period, as a court would have imposed as a Community Payback sentence: it seems that he has received the punitive suffering he deserves. He might not, strictly speaking, have suffered a *punishment*, if punishment is the infliction of hard treatment by an authority; we would also have good reason to criticize the vigilante group, in part because it was too much a matter of chance that they inflicted just the amount of suffering that the offender deserved: but it does seem that, if only by lucky chance, the vigilantes could have achieved what punishment aims to achieve.

If, however, we ask more carefully just what it is that offenders could plausibly be said to deserve to suffer, we can avoid this unwelcome implication, and provide a better account of why criminal punishment must be imposed by the polity, and cannot be imposed by vigilante

---

[46] See further Duff (n. 8 above), ch. 1.

groups. An appropriate response to wrongdoing, if the wrongdoing is our business, is to try to hold the wrongdoer to account—to call her to answer for her wrongdoing: for that takes both the wrong and its victim seriously, and takes the wrongdoer seriously as a responsible agent and fellow member of the normative community. This is an essential aim of the criminal trial, as a process through which the polity calls alleged wrongdoers to answer to charges of public wrongdoing, and to answer for those wrongs if they are proved.[47] We can understand criminal punishment as continuous with the criminal trial: as a forceful way of trying to persuade the offender to confront the wrong that she committed (to answer adequately for a wrong must involve facing up to it), and to make appropriate moral reparation to those she has wronged.[48] But if we should understand criminal punishment in such communicative terms, then its very meaning must depend not merely on what is being communicated, to whom, but on who is communicating: in this context as in many others, the meaning of a communication depends essentially on who is communicating with whom and on the relationship between them. What the offender deserves is not simply some quantum of suffering that mysteriously matches, or wipes out, or counterbalances the wrong she committed; she deserves to be called to account by those who business that wrong is, to suffer the forceful communication of the censure that they have the standing to administer, and to be required to make appropriate moral reparation to them. We must therefore ask who has the standing to call criminal wrongdoers to account for their crimes: to whom must a criminal offender answer?

As we have noted, it might be argued that as a moral agent who has committed a moral wrong (for I have argued that what is properly criminalized must be morally wrong), he must be ready to answer to any and every other moral agent: for moral wrongs are the business of all members of the universal moral community. Even if that is right, however,[49] our concern here is not with the moral wrongs of moral agents, but with

---

[47] See at nn. 30–2 above.

[48] See Duff (n. 13 above). The same point is implied by other accounts which focus on the communication of censure to the offender, and explain the hard treatment dimension of punishment in deterrent terms: e.g. A. von Hirsch and A. J. Ashworth, *Proportionate Sentencing* (Oxford: Oxford University Press, 2005).

[49] And it seems to me at best highly arguable, at least in relation to less serious and more intimate wrongs: see Duff (n. 8 above), 25–6.

the criminal wrongs committed by citizens of a polity: wrongs defined as public wrongs (i.e. as the business of the polity) by its criminal law. If we ask who has the standing to call citizens to account for such wrongs, or to whom they must answer as citizens for their public (i.e. civic) wrongs, the answer must be 'the polity', that is, their fellow citizens: it is to them that a criminal wrongdoer must answer, it is they who have the standing to call him to account, to them that he must make apologetic reparation. Both his trial and his punishment, as communicative endeavours, must speak to him in the voice of his fellow citizens, since only in that voice can they have the appropriate meaning that renders them legitimate; trial and punishment must, therefore, be administered by or with the authority of his fellow citizens. But vigilante 'punishments' lack this essential legitimizing dimension: they cannot do what justice demands, or impose what the wrongdoer deserves. Vigilantes might claim that they are calling wrongdoers to account, especially if the 'punishments' they impose flow from a kangaroo court; they might even claim to be acting in the name and on behalf of the polity whose criminal justice system has (they argue) failed to bring this wrongdoer to book: but they lack the standing to do this.

An offender must answer for her criminal wrongs to her fellow citizens, whose business those wrongs are as public wrongs. This is a relational demand: it generates relational reasons for her fellow citizens to call her to account (reasons that they do not have to call wrongdoers outside the polity to account, and that others outside the polity do not have to call this person to account), and relational reasons for her to answer to her fellow citizens through the polity's courts (reasons she does not have to answer to bodies outside the polity, and that wrongdoers outside the polity do not have to appear in its courts). This is not to deny that that relational good can be a source of reasons for action for other agents: other polities, and their citizens, might have good reason to assist this polity in calling its wrongdoers to account, for instance by being willing to extradite offenders who flee the jurisdiction in which they are summoned to trial. But there is a crucial difference between extraditing an alleged offender to be tried in another country, and putting him on trial in the country to which he fled: extradition respects the relational character of criminal responsibility, given which the Brazilian thief who flees to and is arrested in England is answerable not in the English courts but in the Brazilian courts; by contrast, to put him on trial in an English court for his Brazilian theft would be to claim an authority over him—the authority to call him to account for this wrong—that English law and English courts lack.[50]

In this section I have explained and defended the third of the three claims sketched in section 2 above: the criminal law's authority lies primarily in its procedural dimension, as the power to call alleged wrongdoers to public account, to judge their conduct, and to condemn and punish their criminal wrongdoing; and that authority is relational, in that it depends on the criminal law's status as the law of a political community whose members can collectively claim such authority over each other. Finally, however, I must comment briefly on two cases that might seem to pose problems for my account—and with which the kind of non-relational account of the criminal law's authority that I have opposed can deal very easily.

6. TWO PROBLEM CASES?

The first case has already been mentioned—that of non-citizens who are temporarily in a country as visitors, as refugees, or as workers.[51] On a non-relational account, they are bound and protected by the country's criminal law, since its authority is determined territorially;[52] but how do they fare on my account? If we emphasize citizenship as I have done, and portray the criminal law as essentially a law for the citizens of the polity, does this not exclude non-citizens from its protective reach? I do not deny that there are dangers here—that citizenship can be a dangerously exclusionary, as well as a pleasingly inclusionary, idea; but the dangers can be avoided if we take seriously the idea of being a guest.[53] Guests have a particular status in relation to their hosts, a status that brings with it both rights and responsibilities. What is relevant here is that guests are

---

[50] On extradition law see C. Nicholls, C. Montgomery, and J. B. Knowles, *The Law of Extradition and Mutual Assistance* (2nd edn; Oxford: Oxford University Press, 2007). We cannot pursue here the various questions that arise about the conditions under which extradition is or is not morally legitimate; all I need assume is that it is sometimes legitimate.

[51] See at nn. 24–5 above. I cannot discuss here the question of how citizenship should be acquired, or how easy its acquisition should be; the issue at stake here would arise so long as there are temporary residents in the country who do not even seek to become citizens.

[52] See at n. 38 above.

[53] See further Duff, 'Responsibility, Citizenship and Criminal Law', in Duff and Green (n. 36 above), 125, at 141–3.

protected by their hosts' criminal law in that crimes committed against them will be the polity's business, and that their perpetrators will be called to account; and that they are also bound by the criminal law, in that they must answer in the hosts' courts for wrongs they commit while guests. The law that protects and binds them is not their law, the courts that call them to answer are not their courts, speaking in the voice of their fellow citizens; but their distinctive role as guests puts them in a particular relationship to that law—one that gives them distinctive relational reasons to respect it, and gives its citizens relational reasons to hold them to account for their actions as guests.

The second case is that of international criminal law in its various manifestations: as we saw above, a non-relational account can readily explain the authority of international criminal tribunals, as well as the claims to universal jurisdiction made by some national systems;[54] but how could a relational account explain them? There are two possible lines of argument here; I remain unsure which is more plausible (perhaps each is plausible in different contexts; more worrying would be the possibility that neither is plausible).[55] We could, first, see international tribunals, or domestic courts claiming universal jurisdiction, as acting on behalf of the local political community to which the wrongdoer is properly answerable, when that community's courts and legal system cannot or will not call them to account. Or we could, second, argue that for some crimes, notably those that are classed as 'crimes against humanity', the relevant community to which the wrongdoer must answer is not (merely) his particular polity, but all of humanity—the 'community of nations'. Each answer is problematic, and I recognize that much more work is needed to establish whether either is plausible.

---

[54] See at nn. 39–40 above.

[55] See further Duff, 'Authority and Responsibility in International Criminal Law', in S. Besson and J. Tasioulas (eds), *Philosophy of International Law* (Oxford: Oxford University Press, 2010), 589.

7

Fairness and the Justifying Aim of Punishment

C. L. TEN

Retributive and utilitarian theories of punishment are often regarded as attempts to provide mutually exclusive and sufficient single justifications for punishment. As such, both theories fail to be convincing. But mixed or compromise theories, which seek to locate utilitarian and retributive considerations at different levels in the practice of punishment, do not seem to fully capture their significance. The crucial aspects of the practice of punishment, round which any adequate justification should be built, are that punishment seeks to reduce crime in a manner that is fair. Crime reduction and fairness should both be included in what Hart calls the General Justifying Aim of punishment, or the aim of justifying the practice of punishment, where those who violate certain rules are subject to punishment, as distinguished from issues of Distribution, which involves the reasons determining who may be punished, or the amount of punishment.[1] Although Hart himself finds room for both crime reduction and fairness in his theory of punishment, he includes only crime reduction in the General Justifying Aim, and relegates fairness to the level of Distribution. I shall return to his view, which makes a careful attempt to identify the notion or notions of fairness which feature in the Distribution of punishment, while still resisting the idea that fairness in Distribution introduces any retributive consideration into the Justifying Aim of punishment. I shall argue that fairness must ultimately be included in the Justifying Aim.

---

[1] H. L. A. Hart, *Punishment and Responsibility*, Clarendon Press, Oxford, 1968, ch. 1, esp. pp. 3–17.

Consider first the failure of retributive theories in justifying punishment. They are resolutely insensitive to the effects of punishment on crime reduction, focusing instead on the desert of offenders. For example, some retributivists support capital punishment for murder as an appropriate, or perhaps even the only appropriate penalty, irrespective of whether capital punishment is a greater deterrent than alternative forms of punishment. In his instructive survey of the evidence, Hart concludes that the statistical evidence does not show that the death penalty is a superior deterrent to imprisonment. He then discusses the other kind of "evidence" which is based on the "common sense" view that the fear of death is greater than that of any other penalty, and that therefore "it *must* be a stronger deterrent than imprisonment."[2] As against this, Hart points out that "theories that the death penalty may operate as a stimulant to murder, consciously or unconsciously, have some evidence behind them."[3]

Of course the psychological facts to which Hart alludes are somewhat speculative. But suppose that the claims about the attractive force of the death penalty are established as indisputable facts, and they show that the imposition of capital punishment sharply increases the murder rate. This would still not alter the retributive support for such punishment. Kant famously declared, "Even if a civil society were to dissolve itself by common agreement of all its members (for example, if the people inhabiting an island decided to separate and disperse themselves around the world), the last murderer remaining in prison must first be executed."[4] But evidence-insensitive retributivists would have to go well beyond Kant in recommending execution even if it is generally known that it would immediately trigger off numerous additional murders before the dissolution of civil society. The question then arises as to whether execution would serve the cause of justice, or receive the consent of members of the society. Imagine further that it is a well-established fact that punishment through imprisonment has the effect of greatly increasing serious crime. On what basis can it be claimed that major offenders should be imprisoned when no one would prefer it to some alternative which does not increase crime? Certainly, no one would benefit from the

---

[2] Ibid., p. 86.
[3] Ibid., p. 88.
[4] Immanuel Kant, "The Right to Punish," in Jeffrie Murphy (ed.) *Punishment and Rehabilitation*, Wadsworth, Belmont, 1973, p. 37.

imposition of punishment in these circumstances. Even the most obvious beneficiaries of punishment in normal circumstances, the victims of crime and their friends and relatives, would not opt for such punishment of offenders, knowing that this would increase crime, and the probability of their being the future victims of crime. Law-abiding citizens generally would suffer from an increased sense of insecurity if punishment were imposed. Any immediate satisfaction they would enjoy at the prospect or the reality of the punishment of wrongdoers would soon dissipate when they are properly focused on the dire effects of punishment in the circumstances envisaged.

The bases of retributive punishment rest on either some claim about the intrinsic value of the punishment of wrongdoers, or on an appeal to fairness in the distribution of the costs and benefits of social life. In the first case, unlike utilitarians, retributivists do not regard the harm of punishment as intrinsically bad. On the contrary, the harm of punishing deserving wrongdoers is intrinsically good. But even so, it would be odd to ignore the undeserved harm suffered by innocent victims as a result of punishment-induced increased crime. There are several ways in which one might seek to balance the good and bad of punishment. Certainly, the utilitarian method of aggregation, of maximizing the total good and minimizing the total bad, is not the only method of balancing. Nor is it the case that the only alternative is a more limited aggregation which Nozick calls "utilitarianism of rights," which involves the minimization of rights-violations, rather than the maximization of utility, however construed.[5] But whatever the basis of balancing, it is clear that *some* balancing is required. An evidence-insensitive retributivist, who simply ignores as irrelevant the harm suffered by the innocent through increased crime, does not have a plausible view. There is just too much undeserved suffering to be simply set aside.

The other retributive approach of appealing to fairness in the distribution of costs and benefits is also inadequate. The unfairness generated by crime lies in the extra benefits that criminals have gained, and punishment is supposed to rectify the unfair distribution of costs and benefits. There are difficulties in identifying the relevant benefits gained, and in explaining how punishment rectifies the unfair distribution. The

[5] Robert Nozick, *Anarchy, State, and Utopia*, Blackwell, Oxford, 1974, pp. 28–9.

details of these difficulties depend on the specific retributive theory under consideration, and I have discussed them elsewhere.[6] But a more general problem applies to all such theories: how can punishment rectify the unfair benefits acquired by offenders in circumstances when it increases crime, and thereby imposes further harms on law-abiding citizens? The rectification by punishment depends at the very least on punishment removing from offenders these benefits of crime, without at the same time generating additional harms on the innocent. This condition does not apply when punishment itself increases crime and thereby deprives law-abiding citizens of some of their original pre-punishment benefits. Punishment would then produce a greater sense of apprehension and insecurity, and more innocent people will be harmed by criminal acts.

So the possibility of punishment stimulating crime undermines the claim of evidence-insensitive retributivism to be the General Justifying Aim of punishment. On the other hand, the utilitarian theory is also inadequate because, by focusing solely on maximizing the aggregate good and minimizing the aggregate harm, it is insensitive to the way in which benefits and burdens are distributed between offenders and law-abiding citizens, so long as the distribution does not deviate from the optimal aggregate. The suffering or good of the innocent, taken on its own, is no worse or better than the similar suffering or good of the offender. Thus among the commonly raised objections to the utilitarian theory of punishment are that it permits or requires, in appropriate circumstances, the punishment of the innocent and punishment that is disproportionate to the character of the crime committed, and that it is unable to provide a proper basis for legal excuses.

Given their general approach, it is surprising that utilitarians have not been more inclined to adopt a theory of treatment, such as that of Wootton.[7] The utilitarian-minded Wootton seeks to replace a theory of punishment with her theory of treatment precisely because her theory better serves the aim of crime prevention. She maintains that the function of

---

[6] See C. L. Ten, *Crime, Guilt, and Punishment*, Clarendon Press, Oxford, 1987, pp. 52–65; C. L. Ten, "Positive Retributivism," *Social Philosophy and Policy* (1990), esp. pp. 196–200; and C. L. Ten, "Deserved Punishment and Benefits to Victims," *Utilitas* (2000), pp. 85–90.

[7] Barbara Wootton, *Crime and the Criminal Law*, Steven & Sons, London, 1981; and Barbara Wootton, *Crime and Penal Policy*, Allen & Unwin, London, 1978. I critically discuss Wootton's views in detail in *Crime, Guilt, and Punishment*, pp. 110–22.

the criminal law is to prevent or reduce socially harmful acts, and not to punish moral wickedness. Given that socially harmful acts are committed by people in all sorts of difficult-to-ascertain mental states, and not just by those who intentionally cause harm, it is a mistake to exempt from compulsory treatment those who have excuses in the sense that they are morally blameless. Their treatment may still be effective in preventing a recurrence of the harm. She mentions in particular the grave harms caused by motorists and mentally abnormal killers. One of her telling statistics is that in England and Wales in 1975, 486 persons were convicted for causing death by dangerous driving as against 369 persons convicted for either murder or manslaughter.[8]

Wootton's proposal is that at the conviction stage in a criminal trial, all that is needed is to establish that the person charged has committed a legally prohibited act. The offender's guilt does not depend on whether he acted intentionally, recklessly, or in any mental state that makes him morally culpable. In effect this means that the offence is one of strict liability in which no excuses are accepted for the commission of the prohibited harmful act. She notes that it is very difficult to establish an offender's mental state at the time when he committed the act. (She actually claims that it is "not possible" to do so, but this is needlessly too strong.)[9] Her proposals therefore have a practical advantage in avoiding certain difficulties of proof. But more importantly, she believes that it is a rational and more effective response to crime, and it better serves the aim of reducing social harm caused by it.

At the sentencing stage, the issue is how to treat the offender in a manner that best prevents a recurrence of the offence. Similar future harmful acts could result from the behaviour of other offenders, but because of the uncertainties about general deterrence, Wootton concentrates on the future conduct of the convicted offender. The aim then is "to take *the minimum action which offers an adequate prospect of preventing future offences*" (Wootton's emphasis).[10] The prevention of recidivism, rather than general deterrence, is the point of the treatment. Since we cannot be sure what form of treatment would be most useful, Wootton believes that maximum effectiveness is served by sentences

[8] *Crime and Penal Policy*, p. 211.
[9] *Crime and the Criminal Law*, p. 78.
[10] Ibid., p. 97.

that are indeterminate with respect to their duration or the "places of safety" to which offenders are confined. These places of safety could be either prisons or hospitals.[11] To her, the current distinction between prisons, where criminals are confined, and medical institutions, where the ill are treated, is unimportant. Both are simply places where different kinds of treatment are given, as appropriate.

Wootton's system of treatment resembles medical treatment more than it resembles punishment. First, medical treatment is determined by the nature of the illness and the response of the patient to various forms of treatment, and not by whether the patient is responsible for her medical condition. On the other hand, the degree of punishment is not simply dependent on the harm caused by the offender, but it is also affected by the mental state of the offender, such as whether there was an excusing or mitigating factor. The second difference is that in Wootton's system, treatment is individualized even for those who have committed similar offences, and there is no value in equality of treatment as such. This is again close to the medical model of treatment in which the type of treatment given for two patients with the same illness might vary greatly, depending for example on whether they are allergic to a particular drug. Similarly, for Wootton, offenders who have committed similar crimes might receive treatments which vary greatly in severity because of their different reactions, and the varying likelihoods of their repeating their offences in future.

However, although Wootton does not explicitly discuss this, there is still a different notion of proportionality which limits the kind of treatment regarded as appropriate, as there is in medical treatment. In medicine, we are governed by the maxim that the cure should not be worse than the illness: no brain surgery, for example, to cure a minor illness, even if such surgery is highly effective. So too for Wootton: once she has ruled out general deterrence, it is presumably unacceptable to inflict greater harm on the offender than the harm of his criminal conduct if he is left untreated, or incompletely treated. But without appealing to general deterrence, there is no place for the equivalent of exemplary punishment. What limits the extent of treatment is not any moral objection to such exemplary treatment, but rather the uncertain evidence, as she sees it, of the effectiveness of general deterrence.

---

[11] Ibid., p. 82.

But the notion of proportionality that limits the extent of Wootton's treatment is quite different from other familiar notions of proportionality. For example, because of the individualized nature of the treatment, an offender who is guilty of a serious offence could still be given a very mild treatment, or even no treatment at all. Thus a murderer, who is unlikely to kill again, would not require any treatment. He could be set free, even though many minor offenders are appropriately subjected to fairly demanding forms of treatment in order to prevent them from repeating their respective offences. The appropriate treatment for any offender in Wootton's system is not determined on a comparative basis, but depends instead on what works for the specific subject of treatment.

Wootton seeks to blur, and ultimately eliminate, the distinction between punishment and medical treatment precisely because her account of the criminal law includes different responses to harmful conduct, whether they are punitive or not. However, she ignores the fact that punishment is the expression of condemnation or disapproval of the offender for the violation of a standard of conduct that is regarded as desirable. If then the offender had an excuse, such as reasonable mistake or accident, the condemnation or disapproval is inappropriate. When, on the other hand, we use quarantine to prevent the spread of an infectious disease, we do not thereby condemn the persons quarantined for the breach of a desirable standard of conduct. This is the case even when the quarantine involves as severe a restriction of freedom as some instances of imprisonment for criminal conduct. Similarly, a fine imposed on a speeding motorist, or on a person who violates a water or electricity restriction in a period of shortage, is regarded differently from an equivalent amount in goods and services tax imposed on someone who enjoys a restaurant meal. There is no suggestion that the tax is imposed for the breach of a socially desirable standard of conduct.[12] The tax is a revenue-raising device, and it would be regarded as a failure if it led to a significant reduction in the frequency of restaurant meals. But, other things being equal, fines which resulted in a considerable reduction or even total elimination of the relevant conduct would be regarded as great successes. So the assimilation of punishment to just another

---

[12] For the distinction between a tax and a sanction, see H. L. A. Hart, *The Concept of Law*, Clarendon Press, Oxford, 2nd edn 1994, p. 39.

form of treatment overlooks the function of punishment as a response to conduct regarded as wrong or undesirable. This does not mean that we are punishing people simply for their moral wickedness, and not for the social harm they have done, as Wootton seems to suggest. The notion of punishment as a response to wrongdoing is quite compatible with the idea that the only wrongdoings that should be punished are socially harmful, and that punishment should only be imposed when it is effective in reducing such social harm. Harm caused by wrongful conduct is viewed differently from harm brought about in other ways, as for example through illness or sheer bad luck. So the aim of using punishment to reduce one source of social harm is not the same as a more general practice of reducing social harm, however it is caused, and by whatever means that are most effective and economical.

Hart has given several reasons for insisting that punishment should be restricted to cases where the offender has "the capacity and a fair opportunity or chance to adjust his behaviour" to obey the law.[13] He calls this the ideal of "fairness or justice to individuals."[14] It rewards self-restraint by making the fate of persons depend on their choices. Individuals are empowered to identify in advance when they will be free from future interference by the law, and to exclude such interference by their choices. Hart also points out that the law should reflect "distinctions which not only underly morality, but pervade the whole of our social life."[15] In their social life, persons are not only interested in the harmful effects of their conduct on one another, but they are also concerned with whether these effects are the manifestations of intentions and choices. They react differently to one another, depending on whether the conduct is voluntary, deliberate, or accidental. "This is how human nature in human society actually is and as yet we have no power to alter them."[16]

Hart is not suggesting that if we could we would change this basis on which our social relations are based. The distinctions to which he has drawn attention "pervade the whole of our social life," including aspects that we greatly value. There is no need nor desire to change them. Hart also points out that the conditions of the "moral licence" we need to

[13] *Punishment and Responsibility*, p. 181.
[14] Ibid., p. 201.
[15] Ibid., p. 183.
[16] Ibid.

punish offenders who break the law will confine punishment to voluntary wrongdoers, who have the normal capacity and a fair opportunity to meet the requirements of the law. But he maintains that the licence "may still be devoted solely to preventing future crimes."[17] So he does not think that the conditions of the licence qualify his account of the General Justifying Aim of punishment. Instead, restrictions, like that on not punishing the innocent or offenders who have certain excuses, are answers to the question of who may be punished. He is fully conscious of the possibility that the principle of fairness, when in place, could lead to increased crime, a utilitarian loss, because of successful fake pleas for excuses.[18] He refers to "two distinct principles" between which we may sometimes have to choose.[19] The principle of fairness, unlike the utilitarian principle, is not an aggregative principle, but a principle concerned with the protection of individuals from the claims of the rest of society for protection. It is also the case that the values underlying the two principles are different. The utilitarian principle seeks the protection of society from the harm of crime, whereas the fairness principle promotes choice and individual freedom.

Sometimes Hart notes how the excusing conditions derived from the principle of fairness maximize the individual's choices and power of prediction. As he puts it, the conditions provide mechanisms for "maximizing within the framework of coercive criminal law the efficacy of the individual's considered choices in determining the future and also the power to predict the future."[20] He also mentions the satisfaction of choice. Under a system of excuses, if individuals who break the law are punished for the conduct, then they can treat "the pains of punishment" as "the price of some satisfaction obtained from breach of law."[21] But it is not his intention to reduce the benefits of choice and freedom to the satisfactions obtained from their exercise which would offset the pains of punishment. This is the utilitarian approach of maximizing the common currency of satisfaction or happiness, but it is not Hart's. The point he is making is the limited one that the satisfactions obtained are genuine, but there is no attempt to reduce all the different values he has

[17] Ibid., p. 208.
[18] Ibid., p. 78.
[19] Ibid.
[20] Ibid., p. 46.
[21] Ibid., p. 47.

invoked to the respective levels of satisfactions they each generate. Elsewhere, he has criticized Rawls's claim that liberty may be restricted only for the sake of liberty itself, and not for the sake of increases in other goods, such as income and wealth.[22] Hart argues that unrestricted liberty, including liberty to inflict harm, might, in cases where the physical harm is serious, lead to restrictions on the liberty of the victims of such harm, who are incapacitated through physical injuries, or the liberty of potential victims, whose actions are inhibited by the apprehension and uncertainty of being injured. But such harmful conduct, which restricts the victim's actions, also causes pain, suffering, and distress. Hart thereby resists any attempt to reduce pain and suffering simply to a loss of liberty. He would similarly repudiate the reduction of the value of freedom and choice to the satisfactions and pleasures which their exercise would undoubtedly produce.

So Hart is right in insisting that the utilitarian principle and the principle of fairness are distinct, and that the latter restricts the application of the former. But he also maintains that the utilitarian's General Justifying Aim of reducing crime remains. More generally, he maintains that the principle of fairness answers a different question, Who may be punished? This is a question about the Distribution of punishment, and not its Aim. The values which are invoked in answering this question are not based on, or derived from, the values defining the General Justifying Aim of punishment, be those values utilitarian or retributive. Certainly, he succeeds in showing that if the General Justifying Aim is formulated in purely utilitarian terms, then it cannot include the principle of fairness. But it remains unclear why the principle of fairness cannot qualify the General Justifying Aim and dictate a reformulation of the Aim in a manner that is neither wholly utilitarian nor retributive.

Hart asserts that the principle of fairness is a qualification of utilitarianism, but it does not provide a different basis for the practice of punishment.[23] He thinks that it is quite consistent to maintain that the Justifying Aim of punishment is its beneficial consequences, while at the same time conceding that the pursuit of that Aim is restricted by a principle of Distribution. The principle of fairness is such a principle of

[22] "Rawls on Liberty and Its Priority," in H. L. A. Hart, *Essays on Jurisprudence and Philosophy*, Clarendon Press, Oxford, 1983, esp. pp. 238–41.
[23] Ibid., p. 82.

Distribution that restricts the extent to which the General Justifying Aim may be pursued at the cost to individuals.[24] It ensures that the competing claims of those who are subject to punishment are treated fairly against the claims of the rest of society to be protected from harmful conduct. The principle may be viewed from two perspectives. The first is the point of view of the rest of society who are harmed by an offence. The suffering of punishment is imposed on those who have voluntarily harmed others. The significance of this is that the principle lays down fair terms for the pursuit of the Justifying Aim of punishment, rather than entering into the formulation of that Aim itself. The other perspective is that the principle offers fair terms for the protection of individuals by laws conferring reciprocal rights and duties. Within this framework, each person has a fair opportunity either to obey the law, or breach it and pay the penalty.[25]

However, if the principle of fairness restricts or qualifies the pursuit of the Justifying Aim, then it seems to change that Aim to the extent that the original, unqualified Aim is no longer appropriate in dictating what may be done. For example, there is a difference between a Justifying Aim that simply seeks to reduce crime, and one that seeks to reduce crime in a fair manner, thereby disallowing certain effective but unfair policies of reducing crime. If the pursuit of the General Justifying Aim is qualified in this manner by a principle of fairness, why then is the principle not incorporated into a reformulated Aim? What is the substantive difference between an Aim whose *pursuit* is limited by fairness, and a qualified Aim that incorporates the principle of fairness?

Hart rejects attempts to show that a system that recognizes legal excuses can be explained by reference to a purely utilitarian General Justifying Aim. But this does not show that an explanation in terms of a more complex Justifying Aim will also fail. He believes that an acceptable account of the institution of criminal punishment "must exhibit it as a compromise between distinct and partly conflicting principles."[26] At the same time he also asserts that it is not the case that there is a plurality of different values answering a single question about the justification of punishment. Rather, there are different questions to be answered. The

---

[24] Ibid., p. 17.
[25] Ibid., pp. 22–3.
[26] Ibid., p. 1.

assumption here seems to be that different values are needed to answer different questions, and there is no one set of partly conflicting values which answers any particular question. The conflict is between the values answering different questions, and not between the values which apply to the same question. This rules out from the start a mixed Justifying Aim, or an Aim that is complex in that it represents "a compromise between distinct and partly conflicting" values. The restriction seems simply stipulative, and not clearly motivated by any deeper theoretical considerations.

But perhaps we can get a better picture of what is at stake if we consider a specific case in which a single value is proposed as the Justifying Aim of punishment, and this single value is pursued without the constraint imposed by any other value. In his early paper, "Two Concepts of Rules," Rawls distinguishes between the justification of a rule, or practice, or institution, which is the concern of the legislator, and the justification of a particular act falling under such a rule, practice or institution, which is the province of the judge.[27] Thus in the case of punishment, the judge justifies the punishment of a particular offender on the retributive basis that he has breached a legal rule. But the ideal legislator would adopt a utilitarian justification for all the rules. On utilitarian grounds, a practice of punishment which prohibits the punishment of the innocent would be preferred to a practice that Rawls calls "telishment," in which officials are authorized to use their discretion in order to try and condemn an innocent person in the best interests of society. The fear and apprehension generated by the practice of "telishment" would rule it out from the utilitarian point of view, and the alternative practice of punishment would be adopted.

Rawls and Hart agree that there are different questions in the justification of punishment. Rawls's legislative level justification of a practice, with its utilitarian underpinnings, seems to resemble Hart's account of the General Justifying Aim. Rawls's judicial level justification of an act falling under a rule seems to resemble what Hart sometimes calls Retribution in Distribution, which is the same as the principle of fairness. But a difference emerges between them in that, whereas Hart thinks that

[27] John Rawls, "Two Concepts of Rules," *The Philosophical Review*, Vol. 64 (1955), pp. 3–32. Reprinted in part as "Punishment as a Practice," in Jeffrie G. Murphy (ed.) *Punishment and Rehabilitation, op. cit.* pp. 83–91.

the answer to the question of Distribution qualifies the pursuit of the Justifying Aim, and is not derived from it, Rawls believes that the judge at her level of justification has to apply rules selected by the legislator on the basis of purely utilitarian considerations. In Rawls's scheme therefore what happens at the judge's level depends on the results at the legislator's level: judges have no rules to apply until legislators make the selection. The opposite seems to be the case in Hart's account, where the principle of fairness at the level of Distribution influences how the Justifying Aim is to be pursued.

Hart believes that even if we acknowledge that a purely utilitarian justification of the practice of punishment could confine punishment to the guilty in accordance with the principle of fairness, the Rawlsian approach is still inadequate. This is because the importance of the principle of fairness is not that it serves the goal of reducing crime, or other similar utilitarian goals. Rather, it has a non-utilitarian significance, and even if we override the principle of fairness in some extreme cases for substantial utilitarian gains, "we should do so with the sense of sacrificing an important principle. We should be conscious of choosing the lesser of two evils, and this would be inexplicable if the principle were itself only a requirement of utility."[28]

Hart is right. But what this shows is that without the inclusion of the principle of fairness, the justification of the practice of punishment is incomplete. It does not show that the principle of fairness is not part of the justification of the practice. If Hart's Justifying Aim is not qualified by the principle of fairness, it would not be different from Rawls's account of punishment. A single-value Justifying Aim may, as Hart suggests, allow for some ad hoc exceptions to its pursuit in deference to great gains in other external values which are not part of the Justifying Aim. But the systematic shaping of the practice of punishment by the principle of fairness suggests that the principle is part of the Justifying Aim, rather than external to it. Again, without the limitations systematically imposed by the principle of fairness, we would not be able to distinguish between the practice of punishment, as Hart conceives of it, and Wootton's scheme of treatment, whose aim is simply to reduce crime. Indeed, the difference between Wootton and the early Rawls, in so far as they are both guided by solely utilitarian considerations of

---

[28] *Punishment and Responsibility*, p. 12.

crime reduction, is not one of fundamental principle, but rather a matter of factual disagreement about the consequences of adopting various rules or practices. On the other hand, Hart has a principled disagreement with both of them. Hart is particularly keen to show that Retribution does not feature in the Justifying Aim of punishment. We can evaluate this claim by first considering whether Hart's notion of Retribution in Distribution, or the principle of fairness, provides a positive reason for punishing. Quite clearly no positive reason for punishment has been given when punishment is confined to the guilty, or to those who lack an excuse. Rather, these provide constraints on who may be punished. The removal of a constraint on punishment does not provide a new positive reason for punishment

Nigel Walker suggests that the relevant notion of fairness that applies to the justification of punishment is distinct from the notion of retribution, nor is it utilitarian in character.[29] He appeals to Rawls's concept of "fairness" in which self-interested people in a hypothetical state choose the basic institutions of their society from behind a "veil of ignorance" which conceals particular facts about themselves, including their talents and abilities. Walker applies the idea of choosing behind a veil of ignorance in a more specific manner, such that persons are ignorant of whether they will be "incarcerated as a law-abiding citizen or as a law-breaker."[30] They are then offered a choice between a society N in which people would be penalized only for offences for which they are genuinely responsible, and a society Q, in which they would be penalized both for their offences as well as for some of those done by others. A rational person would choose Society N where, unlike in society Q, if he were to turn out as a law-abiding citizen, he would be safe from punishment. He would be more apprehensive and insecure in Society Q. The deterrent effect of the law-enforcement policy in Q would also be minimized, rather than maximized.

Walker argues that similar considerations would lead ignorant, rational, self-interested individuals, who are unaware whether they are going to be offenders or law-abiding citizens, to choose Society B, which recognizes various legal excuses, to Society S, "a strict liability society"

[29] N. Walker, *Why Punish?*, Oxford University Press, Oxford, 1991, p. 92.
[30] Ibid., p. 93.

that does not allow any legal excuses. This is because the chances of being penalized in S would be much greater than in B, unless one makes a totally unrealistic assumption that there are many more excusable offences than inexcusable ones.

Walker believes that the choices of these rational, self-interested persons capture a notion of fairness that does not involve a retributive concept of desert. The choices maximize their power to avoid being penalized. However, the crucial notion of fairness relevant to punishment seems to be an account of how some people are to be treated relative to others who play different and unequal roles, and this comparative notion is not well captured in a device showing how a rational, self-interested person would choose. Such a person's choices are intended to minimize her chances of being penalized, without regard to the claims of others, or the source and character of the penalties. But in the context of punishment, some of the penalties are imposed for criminal or wrongful conduct, and these penalties cannot be assumed to carry the same normative weight as other kinds of penalties.

So perhaps we should adopt a different starting point that criminal acts are wrong and, other things being equal, a reduction in crime is desirable. If we had a choice between reducing crime by punishing offenders, thereby causing them suffering, and dispensing with punishment and allowing an increase in crime, causing an equivalent amount of suffering to innocent victims of crime, we would adopt the former course of action. Punishment is the preferred alternative because the suffering of innocent victims of crime is worse than the quantitatively equivalent suffering inflicted by punishment on offenders.

This account of the unequal negative values of the suffering of victims as compared with that of offenders goes against the Benthamite approach of treating them as having equal intrinsic value. Thus Mill describes Bentham's approach of not taking for granted even "the most acknowledged truths" about the wrongness of such acts as murder. Instead, Bentham would first consider all the different "mischiefs" of the crime. He would show that even the sufferings of the immediate victim alone would on average "greatly outweigh the pleasure reaped by the offender, much more when all the other evils are taken into account."[31] The

---

[31] John Stuart Mill, "Bentham," in *Essays on Ethics, Religion, and Society, Collected Works of John Stuart Mill*, Vol. X, University of Toronto Press, Toronto, 1969, p. 83.

Benthamite approach might be appropriate when we are deciding what acts are appropriately subject to punishment by the state. Thus the famous Devlin–Hart debate is about the legitimacy of using the criminal law to enforce the shared morality of society.[32] Some liberals maintain that unless an act harms others without their consent, it should not be subject to criminal punishment, even if it is widely regarded as wrong. The issue of justifying the practice of punishment arises only after we are agreed that certain acts fall within the legitimate scope of state punishment. When the question of the scope of punishable acts has been settled, these acts are regarded as wrong. Other things being equal, a reduction in their incidence is desirable. Offenders perform acts that are wrong and ought to be discouraged, whereas victims are wrongly harmed. We do not treat their respective sufferings as of equal negative value.

However, to reject Bentham's offender-victim egalitarianism is not to embrace a version of retributivism which treats the suffering of offenders as intrinsically valuable. In claiming that the suffering of victims is worse than the same amount of suffering of the offender, one is of course not claiming that any suffering as such is intrinsically valuable. So we are still very far from the retributive view that the suffering of the offender, unlike the suffering of the victim, is intrinsically desirable. We do not as yet have any positive reason for punishing. What we have is a reason for condemning the offender. But punishment is not the only way in which we can express such condemnation. A more usual, and less costly, way is to express verbal condemnation, which can be graded in accordance with the gravity of the crime. Punishment, which involves the infliction of suffering, calls for greater justification. Unless we can show that punishment is more effective in reducing crime than alternative public expressions of condemnation, we have not established a case for it.

But because of the different weights given to the suffering of the innocent victim as opposed to that of the offender, we would, in certain circumstances, choose to punish, even though not punishing, or punishing to a lesser extent, would minimize the aggregate suffering. Now, fairness in distribution does provide a positive reason for punishment. One such

---

[32] See Patrick Devlin, *The Enforcement of Morals*, Oxford University Press, London, 1975; and H. L. A. Hart, *Law, Liberty, and Morality*, Oxford University Press, London, 1981.

case is where punishment has a general deterrent effect, but only if it is of a certain level of severity. Suppose that an increase by one year in the duration of imprisonment of an offender, who has been convicted for seriously assaulting several persons, will act as a general deterrent against another potential offender assaulting a victim. Let us assume that, even with the additional one year, the punishment is not disproportionate to the nature of the offence committed. The additional one year is not needed for any other purpose except general deterrence. We make the further assumption that the harm inflicted on the offender by a year's additional imprisonment is the same as that which would be suffered by the victim of the potential offender. So the choice is between punishment, thereby inflicting a certain amount of harm on the offender, and no (additional) punishment, resulting in there being a new victim of crime who suffers the same amount of harm as that of punishment.[33] Those who give greater negative weight to the harm suffered by the victim as compared with the harm of the offender would then choose punishment. It also seems unfair that the potential innocent victim should be made to suffer in order that a guilty offender be spared an equal amount of additional harm. The offender had the opportunity to avoid the harm of punishment if the range of punishment for the crime had been publicized, and he lacks any of the normal excuses. He had been given fair warning, and could have avoided the penalties imposed. On the other hand, the victim could not reasonably have avoided the harm suffered through a criminal act committed while she was going about her normal activities. The justification for punishment in these kinds of circumstances is different from the usual utilitarian or retributive grounds. It is based on what may be called distributional fairness, and this idea of fairness is not merely a constraint on who may be punished, but it is also, in some situations, a positive reason for punishment. We may treat the excusing conditions as removing the inequality between the offender and the victim. When an offender acts with an excuse, then he could not reasonably be expected to heed the warning given by the law and avoid the legally prohibited act. In that respect he is like the victim of crime who could only have avoided being harmed by taking extreme precautions.

---

[33] See my discussion of dangerous offenders in *Crime, Guilt, and Punishment*, pp. 134–40, and of general deterrence in "Positive Retributivism," pp. 205–8.

A similar inequality in the sufferings of offenders without excuses compared with those of victims of crime has also been invoked to justify capital punishment for murder, on the assumption that there is no clear evidence for or against the deterrent effect of capital punishment. Given the choice between having capital punishment, thereby risking the sacrifice of the lives of murderers for no additional deterrent effect, and not having capital punishment, and thereby risking the lives of potential victims, whose lives would have been spared if executions deterred future murderers, some would prefer capital punishment. As van den Haag puts it, "I value the life of innocents more than the life of murderers. Indeed, I value the life of murderers negatively. Wherefore I prefer over- to under-protection."[34] (The remark about valuing the life of murderers negatively is not part of the idea of distributional fairness, and is irrelevant in this context.) The issue can be presented in a slightly different way by supposing that the evidence is different, and it now *conclusively* establishes that every execution of a murderer deters one future murderer, thereby sparing the life of one potential victim. In such a situation distributional fairness provides a positive reason for capital punishment. Given that one life will be lost either way, it is better, other things being equal, that it be the life of the murderer rather than the life of the innocent victim. Of course this does not show that the case for capital punishment is conclusive, for there could be other reasons, apart from distributional fairness, for opposing it, such as it being "something absolutely evil which, like torture, should never be used however many lives it might save."[35] There is also a version of the doctrine of double effect which some might regard as relevant here. Capital punishment is the intentional killing of the convicted murderer, whereas the policy of not having capital punishment, in the imagined circumstances, has the foreseen, but unintended, consequence of there being additional murder victims.

If distributional fairness generates a positive reason for punishing offenders, then one more barrier to its inclusion in the Justifying Aim falls. We noted earlier that even when his notion of fairness sets constraints on who may be punished, Hart still resists the incorporation of

---

[34] Ernest van den Haag, "Refuting Reiman and Nathanson," in Robert M. Baird and Stuart Rosenbaum (eds.) *Philosophy of Punishment*, Prometheus Books, Buffalo, 1988, p. 145.
[35] *Punishment and Responsibility*, p. 72.

fairness into the Justifying Aim. This is understandable to the extent that the important role of fairness in his account can perhaps be adequately captured at the level of Distribution. But once fairness introduces a new positive reason for punishment, including a justification for the use of general deterrence in reducing crime, there is a compelling case for reformulating the Justifying Aim of punishment in order to do justice to its crucial role. No doubt there is more to be said about the role of fairness, and about the extent of the offender–victim inequality. It seems clear that we have to move away from a purely utilitarian Justifying Aim, but perhaps without invoking any recognizable notion of retribution.[36]

---

[36] In late 1985, when I was in Oxford, I showed Hart the manuscript of my book on *Crime, Guilt, and Punishment*. We discussed it over lunch, and he gave me many valuable comments. One issue which particularly interested him was my attempt to formulate a compromise between the utilitarian and retributive justifications for punishment. He cross-examined me closely on where exactly I disagreed with him. From past discussions with him on other issues, I knew that his primary interest was not our disagreement as such, but it was about the truth of the matter. Hart had the rare and remarkable ability to consider and discuss his own published works with complete objectivity and detachment, as if they were the works of another person. Indeed, he was sometimes too quick to concede mistakes when in fact there were none. He had a very modest view of his own achievements. On more than one occasion, he told me that he wished that all his works would totally disappear after about thirty years from their publication dates, so that he would not be expected to endorse and defend everything he wrote in the past. While I was convinced that there was a substantial, although still rather limited, disagreement on punishment between us, all my attempts failed to locate the precise disagreement. He said of some of my efforts that he still could not see where we disagreed. With others, he said that they were not sufficiently clear for him to determine whether or not we disagreed. Under the intense pressure of his persistent questioning, I finally said words to the effect that, whereas he thought that retributive and utilitarian considerations operated at different levels, I believed that sometimes they came into conflict at the same level. I did not say very much more, but the effect on him was complete, thoughtful silence for what seemed to be a very long time. Then he remarked simply, "I am not sure, I am not sure whether you are right." After a further pause, he moved on to discuss other issues in the manuscript. I made some revisions to the manuscript before publication, but I did not have another opportunity to discuss the issue further with him. I regret very much that it has taken so long for me to return to the topic of our disagreement, and I am not sure to what extent, if at all, he would agree with my current criticisms of some of his published views on punishment. However, what is clear is that his works have endured, and they continue to influence, inspire, and provoke well past the thirty years' limit he had set for them. As a cherished friend and teacher, he is still greatly missed.

8

The Embedding Social Context of Promises and Contracts

HANOCH SHEINMAN[1]

This chapter discusses the social context of promising. It takes for granted the intuitive distinction between central and non-central cases. To say that X is the social context of promises/contracts, is to say that, in their central case, promises/contracts are embedded in some X context; promises/contracts that are embedded in some non-X context are imperfect promises/contracts: they fall outside the central case. This chapter raises some doubts about the notion that promises/contracts have a non-trivial social context. It rejects the view that the context of promises is *relational* and the opposing view that it is *transactional*. It then rejects the view that the context of contracts is transactional and the opposing view that it is relational. It recommends a pluralistic view in which the social contexts in which promises and contracts are embedded in the central case cuts across the relational-transactional divide.

ROADMAP

The chapter uses the central case method to discuss the question of the context of contrasts/promises. The conclusion is broadly pluralistic. **Section 1 (The Central Case Method)** explains that method. **Section 2 (The Organizing Example)** frames the issue in terms of the distinction between relational and transactional contexts. **Section 3 (Promissory Relationalism)**

[1] I would like to thank the participants in the contract and promise workshop at Georgetown Law for their many useful comments. For valuable comments, many thanks to David Enoch, Ruth Halperin-Keddari, Alon Harel, Les Green, Dori Kimel, Greg Klass, Shahar Lifshitz, Eyal Zamir, and an anonymous referee for this volume.

presents the view that promises are in the central case relational. **Section 4 (Promissory Transactionalism)** presents the view that promises are in the central case transactional. **Section 5 (The Plural Social Context of Promises)** rejects promissory relationalism and transactionalism in favor of pluralism about the context of promises. **Section 6 (Contractual Relationalism)** presents the view that in the central case contracts are relational. **Section 7 (Contractual Transactionalism)** presents the view that in the central case contracts are transactional. **Section 8 (The Plural Social Context of Contracts)** rejects contractual transactionalism in favor of pluralism about the context of contract. **Section 9 (Conclusion)** brings together the pluralistic conclusions of the previous sections.

Suppose we all agreed on the best characterization of the speech acts of promising and contracting. Apparently, we could still meaningfully disagree about the social *contexts* of these speech acts. Someone might stake out the following claim: In their central case, contracts are embedded in cold-ish relationships; promises, in warm-ish relationships. We can imagine someone else staking out the exact opposite of this view: In their central case, promises are embedded in cold-ish relationships; contracts, in warm-ish relationships. No one actually holds these particular views. I find these views intriguing, in spite of the fact that no one actually holds them. More to the point, they are just simplistic renditions of actually held views. Some recent work on promises and contracts appears to revolve around the question of social context. This is what some recent disagreement about contracts and promises appears to be *about*. This chapter is an attempt to make sense of the question of context.

To say that a promise/contract is embedded in some social context is to say that it is embedded in some human relationship. Now promises and contracts *are* themselves relations; they are trivially embedded in themselves. But arguably there is always some *other* relationship in which the promise/contract relation is embedded. The embedding relationship can be minimal, beginning only when the promise/contract is made and ending as soon as it is kept/performed. But the embedding relationship is not the same as the promise/contract relation itself (the relation in which the promise/contract *consists*). At a minimum, every contract is embedded in the relationship involved in its mutual performance.[2]

---

[2] For example, a sales contract is embedded in the sales relationship it enables: the exchange of payment for goods.

What is it for some context/relationship X to be *the* context of promising/contracting? On a strong reading, it is to say that (necessarily) successful promising takes place in some X context. But this is not a charitable interpretation of the question of context. It is a platitude that we successfully promise/contract in many contexts; it is just hard to believe that any context/relationship X is such that we *cannot* promise/contract outside it.

In this chapter, I will try to make sense of the question of context by reading it as a question about the *central case* of promising/contracting. To say that X is the context of promising/contracting is to say that, in their central case, promises/contracts are embedded in some X context.

I. THE CENTRAL CASE METHOD

This reading of the question can only be as attractive as what I shall call the central case method in philosophy. The most general idea is that explanation goes beyond analysis (necessary and sufficient conditions). We start with Aristotle's discussion of friendship in Book VIII of the *Nicomachean Ethics*. Aristotle notes that in some friendships, the friends value each other intrinsically (intrinsic friendship); in others only instrumentally (instrumental friendship). For Aristotle, intrinsic and instrumental friendships are both successful friendships. Aristotle would say, I surmise, that the necessary and sufficient conditions of friendship are met in both cases. But Aristotle took pains to say that intrinsic friendship is superior to instrumental friendship. And he did not simply say that intrinsic friendship is superior; he basically said that it is superior *as friendship*; he called it 'complete friendship,' 'friendship without qualification,' or 'friendship most of all.' Aristotle would not object, I think, if we took him to maintain that, *in the central case*, friends value each other intrinsically. Similarly, Aristotle said that instrumental friendship is an inferior kind of friendship. But he didn't just say it is inferior; he basically said it is inferior *as friendship*; he called it 'coincidental friendship,' 'friendship by similarity,' or 'friendship to a lesser extent.' I do not think he would object if we took him to maintain that instrumental friendship is a non-central case of friendship.[3]

---

[3] Aristotle (1999: 124; [NE, Bk. VIII, Ch. 4]).

You might think that I am saddling Aristotle with a category mistake. To say that instrumental friendship is friendship implies that it is not a marginal case of friendship, something that is neither friendship nor non-friendship. But on my reading of Aristotle, instrumental friendship is a non-central case of friendship. What is a non-central case if not a marginal case?! My reading of Aristotle is contradictory. It says that instrumental friendship is both a marginal and a non-marginal case of friendship.

That is not so. The central case method focuses exclusively on non-marginal cases, cases that fall squarely within the relevant concept rather than on its margin (borderline). The idea is that not all cases that fall squarely within the extension of a concept are created equal. That something is determinately F does not make it a central case of F. How is this possible? This is the wrong question. Why think it is *not* possible?

Speech Acts

We are getting closer to home. J. L. Austin famously distinguished between different kinds of infelicities in speech acts. Sometimes you try to do something but fail, completely. I try to promise but I find myself unable to speak. The act does not 'come off' or is not 'achieved.' This is a case of 'misfire.' Or suppose we make an agreement for the sale of land but do not put it in writing, as required by law. There is no contract to speak of. In all these cases, a necessary condition goes unmet (or we cannot tell that it is met). Austin's more interesting observation concerns other, lesser forms of infelicities, cases in which the act is successful but nevertheless defective in some interesting way. These are cases of 'abuse.' Suppose I promise to meet you at Starbucks, intending not to do so. Then I successfully promise to meet you, but 'abuse the procedure.'[4]

Austin is applying the central case method to promising. On the one hand, a lying promise is a successful promise, not a marginal or borderline case. On the other hand, it is it not a core promise, either; as a promise, it is rather imperfect. Now unlike Austin, I do believe that we can provide this result with further explanation. But I also think it is independently plausible. So plausible in fact that it seems to me to shift

---

[4] (1962): 16. Searle regards insincere promises as genuine yet 'defective' promises (1969: ch. 3). See also Kimel's distinction between necessary and normal conditions of promising in (2003: ch. 1).

the burden of proof to those who think that a lying promise is either not a promise at all or one that is perfectly good as a promise.

Sincere and Insincere Promises and Contracts

So the central case method seems to deliver the judgment that, *in the central case, promises are sincere*; insincere promises (and therefore lying promises) are somewhat imperfect as promises. (Something exactly similar should be said of contracts.) I now offer some additional explanation of this judgment by answering the two questions that it raises: If lying promises are problematic as promises, why say they are *promises*? And if they are promises, why say they are problematic *as promises*?

1. Why say that a lying promise is a *promise* at all? Why not say that it is not the case that it is a promise (because it is a non-promise or because it is neither a promise nor a non-promise)? Now to my mind, promises are a special case of assertion. But even if you disagree, the case of the lying promise seems strictly analogous (exactly similar to) the case of a lying assertion. So we can ask: Why say that a lying assertion is an *assertion*? In short, why say that a lie is an assertion? Because if it were not an assertion, it could not be a lie. To lie just is to *assert* that p and believe that not-p (without at the same time believing that p). If you don't assert, you don't lie. Here is a somewhat less circular answer. Why is a lie an assertion? Because, necessarily, the person who lies that p represents herself as knowing that p. The best explanation of this fact is that she asserts that p and, necessarily, one who asserts that p represents oneself as knowing that p. Knowledge is the constitutive norm of assertion and assertion only.[5] Now to my mind, the argument applies *directly* to promises. **To promise that one shall do X just is to assert that one shall do X as a result of this very assertion.**[6] On this view, a lying promise is a promise because (1) a lying promise is a lying assertion (a lie) and (2) a lie is an assertion. But even if you disagree, I hope you agree with me that it would be extremely surprising to learn that a lying assertion is an assertion but a lying promise is not a promise. I have no argument for this conviction. I imply find the following self-evident: *If a lying assertion is a genuine assertion, a lying promise is a genuine promise.* If you disagree, we have a stalemate. In the end, it comes down to linguistic

---

[5] See Williamson (2000: ch. 11).
[6] I defend this view elsewhere.

intuition. My linguistic intuition could not be stronger: a lying promise is a genuine, successful, complete promise; it is *within* the border of the concept *promise*; is not *on* the border and certainly not outside the border. This leads us to the next question.

2. Why say that a lying promise is problematic *as a promise*? Why not just conclude that a lying promise is a perfectly promissory promise, one that falls in the core or central case? Consider again the analogy with assertion. Intuitively, a lying assertion (lie) is not just a morally bad assertion; it is defective *as assertion*. Why? Because it violates the constitutive norm of assertion. One's assertion that p is warranted if and only if one knows that p. If one lies that p, not only does one not know that p (asserts without warrant); one also knows that one does not know that p (knowingly asserts without warrant). This is not simply a case of bad assertion; it is a case of badness as assertion. Again, I personally think that this argument applies directly to the case of the lying promise, but you might disagree. In that case, I would retreat to argument by analogy. It would be extremely surprising to discover that a lying assertion is problematic as assertion but it is not the case that a lying promise is problematic as promise.

There is also a broadly Kantian argument for the same conclusion.[7] Intuitively, lying promises (and insincere promises generally) presuppose, or are parasitic upon, sincere ones. On the face of it, you can have sincere promises without lying promises at all, but not lying promises without at least some sincere promises. If this is right, then it seems that sincere promises enjoy an explanatory priority over insincere promises. Critics of Kant have claimed that a society with only lying promises is conceivable. But such promises would still represent themselves as sincere. If this intuition is basically right, sincere promises enjoy explanatory priority.

Stephen Darwall (2011: 269) has recently provided another example of the central case method in the context of promises. He claims that inherent in the idea of promising is the notion that the promisor is entitled (has authority) to promise without coercion or manipulation. Darwall acknowledges that a promise *can* be made or accepted under duress, but he clearly thinks that, as a promise, it is imperfect:

---

[7] Kant (1998 [1785]: 15). Kant's own argument was designed to illustrate the categorical imperative in morality. The Kantian argument I present in the text is designed to illustrate the central case method in philosophy.

Promises under such conditions may not completely 'misfire,' as Austin put it, but they nonetheless constitute an 'abuse' in his terms (1962: 18). They violate 'felicity conditions' that are part of our very idea of the speech act.

Like insincere promises, coerced promises are successful promises that fall outside the central case.

Generalization

Applied to promises/contracts, the central case method says that some clear-cut cases of promises/contracts enjoy explanatory priority over others; these are the core or central cases, the cases of promissory/contractual perfection. As Austin noted, the distinction is 'not hard and fast' (1962: 16), but it is intuitive enough and might help us make sense of the question of context. My hypothesis is that competing views about the embedding context of promises/contract are best understood as competing views of their embedding context in *the central case*. **Rather than saddling someone who seems to be saying that the context of promises/contracts is X (e.g. hot/cold relationship) with the claim that you cannot promise/ contract outside some X-ish context, we take that person to claim that promises/contracts made in some non-X context are somewhat imperfect as promises/contracts or presuppose those made in some X-ish context. Unlike the former claim, the latter has a shot at being plausible.**[8]

Notice that the examples I brought to illustrate the central case method in relation to promises/contracts—sincerity and coercion— have nothing to do with the embedding *context* of the promise/contract. Promises/contracts that fall within the central case—or *perfect* promises/ contracts—are always sincere and uncoerced, regardless of their embedding context. I will entertain the possibility that the centrality or perfection of promises/contracts also depends on their embedding context. Whether this is so remains to be seen.

2. THE ORGANIZING EXAMPLE

To illustrate competing answers to the question of context and streamline the discussion we avail ourselves of Ian Macneil's well-known distinction

---

[8] The first application of the central case method to the question of context belongs to Kimel (2003).

between relational and transactional contexts (1974, 1980, 2000). As I shall understand it, this is a distinction between *two contrasting social contexts or human relationships in which promises/contracts can be embedded; to the extent that a promise/contract is embedded in a relational context/relationship, it is not embedded in a transactional context/relationship.*

The distinction is fluid; there are many equally correct ways of drawing it. This is not a problem. The only obvious problem I see with using the distinction is trivializing interpretations (aided by the admittedly imperfect terminology). We have already seen that, in a trivial sense, every promise/contract is relational: it *is* a relation (the promise/contract relation). We can now add that, in a trivial sense, every promise/contract *is* transactional: it *is* a transaction (the promise/contract transaction). So on one interpretation of the distinction, every promise/contract is both relational and transactional. This makes nonsense of the distinction.

Relational and transactional contexts must be thought of as contrasting contexts or relationships. Consider the contrast between hot and cold contexts/relationships. We can say that a relationship is relational to the extent that it is hot and transactional to the extent that it is cold. In this way every embedding context/relationship lies on a continuum between the relational (hot) and transactional (cold) extremes. We could then conveniently say that promises/contracts whose embedding contexts/relationships are closer to the relational/transactional pole are relational/transactional. The heat model is too simple not because we cannot take the temperature of a context/relationship, but because the embedding contexts/relationships of promises are more interestingly described in terms of multiple criteria.

We first illustrate the approach by using a two-criteria definition according to which relational contexts/relationships are personal and moral and transactional contexts/relationships are non-relational (namely impersonal and non-moral). On this definition, we get four kinds of context, which can be represented on a continuum (as in Table 1, where the relational- and transactional-making properties are in black and white letters, respectively).

There is of course nothing canonical about this or any other characterization of the distinction. To illustrate this point, I choose a different, tripartite definition: *Relational* contexts/relationships are close, personal, and ongoing; *transactional* contexts are *non*-relational, namely distant, impersonal, and discrete. Familiar examples of relational contexts include good relationships between family members, lovers, or friends.

Table 1: Relational vs. Transactional (Twofold Definition)

Fully Relational	Relational-Transactional	Fully Transactional
Personal	Personal	Impersonal
Moral	Moral	Non-moral
	Non-Moral	
	Impersonal	

Table 2: Relational vs. Transactional (Threefold Definition)

Fully Relational	Mostly Relational	Mostly Transactional	Fully Transactional
Close	Close	Distant	Distant
Personal	Personal	Impersonal	Impersonal
Ongoing	Discrete	Ongoing	Discrete
	Distant	Close	
	Personal	Impersonal	
	Ongoing	Discrete	
	Close	Distant	
	Impersonal	Personal	
	Ongoing	Discrete	

Familiar examples of transactional contexts include the sale of the Empire State Building, a one-off market exchange between strangers, a sale of stocks. This characterization of the distinction yields eight kinds of context, which can be represented on the continuum (as in Table 2, where the relational- and transactional-making properties are again in black and white letters, respectively).

The table illustrates the platitude that we successfully promise in very different contexts, for clearly we promise in contexts that fall in all four columns. But more important, the table illustrates the possibility of interesting views about the context of promises/contracts. Yes, we do promise/contract in all these cases, but maybe only some of these cases are privileged when it comes to promising/contracting. Maybe only promises that are embedded in a fully relational context (leftmost column) fall within the *central case* of promising; maybe those that are embedded in a fully transactional context (rightmost context) fall outside the central case of promising. Maybe contracts exhibit a very different pattern. These possibilities are consistent with the said platitude.

The following sections elaborate on such relational/transactional views of the context of promising/contracting. Competing as these views are, they share the premise that, by their very nature, promises/contracts belong to some social sphere. Again, this is not the implausible idea that successful promising/contracting cannot occur outside this privileged sphere; it can successfully occur outside that sphere. The idea is that promises/contracts made outside the privileged sphere are problematic *as promises/contracts,* or fall short of the promissory/contractual ideal. They are, in a way, *imperfect* promises/contracts.

3. PROMISSORY RELATIONALISM

Consider

Promissory relationalism. **Perfect or paradigmatic promises are relational. In the central case, promises are embedded in some relational social context. Promising in transactional or nonrelational contexts is nonparadigmatic or imperfect as promising; it presupposes promising in relational contexts.**[9] (See diagram 1.)

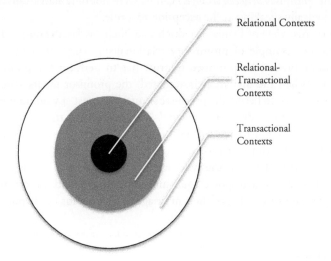

Diagram 1: Promissory Relationalism

Outer doughnut represents the zone of promissory imperfection.
Inner doughnut represents the zone of partial promissory perfection.
Inner doughnut hole represents the zone of promissory perfection.

[9] For views in this vein, compare Raz (1982), Kimel (2003, 2007), Shiffrin (2008), and Darwall (2011).

Let me mention three partially overlapping versions of this general view.

Trust relationalism. Philosophers generally agree that promises invoke trust, but there is little agreement about the kind of trust invoked. According to Dori Kimel, the trust at play in promising is not simply a disposition to believe that the promisor will keep the promise; it is a disposition to believe that she will do so for the right sort of reasons. Reasons of the right sort have to do with the promisor's moral character. Promises are normally embedded in a context of personal and moral trust, whose 'expressions are intended as weighty, sweeping statements about a person's character or moral worth' (2003: 59–60). While not a necessary condition of promising, such 'profound' trust is a 'normal condition' of promising. Thus promises between strangers, who do not already trust each other profoundly are somewhat abnormal.[10] They derive their practical force 'from the normal operation of the practice in the framework of on-going relationships, under the conditions of preexisting trust.'[11] Again, 'promises *between strangers* can be seen, not only statistically, but also logically speaking as the exception to a rule.'[12]

The trust view of Daniel Friedrich and Nicholas Southwood (2011) is another example of promissory relationalism. They claim that the promisor invites the promisee to trust her to perform the promised action. When the invitation is accepted, the promisor incurs a moral obligation not to betray the promisee's trust. The trust at work in promising is said to be distinctly *personal*: 'For someone to trust one to do something she must have a certain *faith* or *optimism* in one's character insofar as one's doing it is concerned' (278). For example, to trust her husband to be faithful, the wife 'must regard him in a certain light, namely, as someone disposed to be moved by certain kinds of reasons: a recognition of the value of their marriage, a concern for her happiness,

---

[10] The 'normal' circumstances for promising contrast with those that are 'marginal, esoteric, atypical' or 'epitomize the margins of the practice, but not its core' Kimel (2003: 7, 20).

[11] (2003: 20–31).

[12] (2007: 251). But cf. Kimel (2007: 257), where he seems to *reject* 'relational theory of promise' for the reason that it confuses promises with the background relations in which they are embedded. This is hard to square with his claim that promises outside the relational context are exceptional 'logically speaking' (251), and especially with the account in Kimel (2003), where the normal intrinsic function of promises is said to facilitate relations through the expression of personal and moral trust and respect. In any event, Kimel's (2003) account is clearly relational.

a respect for her as his wife, and so on' (278). The trust at work in promising is also said to be a *moral* attitude: the promiser displays her willingness (conditional upon the promisee's acceptance or nonrejection) 'to be party to a certain kind of relationship with the promisee, namely one in which the promisee has a certain faith or optimism in the promiser's character that the promiser will perform some action that is of importance to the promisee. In so doing, and having the overture accepted (or not rejected), the promiser incurs an obligation to the promisee not to betray the trust she has invited. The distinctive wrong involved in breaking a promise is precisely a matter of violating this obligation' (280).

Notice that the kind of trust that animates promising according to Friedrich and Southwood is not quite as personal or robust as the one that animates promising according to Kimel. According to Kimel, trust in the robust sense is not something you can have toward strangers; only those who are already quite close can be trusted in that sense. Friedrich and Southwood on the other hand think that you can trust someone you have never met. That is why they think that farmers who are all but strangers can exchange perfectly good promises (2011: 290–1 n. 6).

Strawsonian relationalism. I have already mentioned Darwall's claim that coerced promises are genuine yet imperfect promises as an example of the central case method. Darwall also provides a good example of promissory relationalism. He claims that '[p]romises have an essentially second-personal character' (2011: 268; see also 2006: ch. 8). Darwall shares the now-common view that promising is an exercise of a normative power, or *authority*, to create a package of rights the promisee would not otherwise have, including the right to have the promise kept, to demand its performance, to waive these rights, criticize nonperformance, and receive an apology.[13] He also shares the nearly universal view that promising consists of undertaking an obligation to perform the promised action: A promises B to do X when A undertakes an obligation to B to do X. Following a view he finds in Mill and Strawson, Darwall claims that this relational or directed obligation—

---

[13] This package-of-rights view of promises was first offered in by Hart (1955).

A's obligation *to* B—consists of the fact that A's failure to do X warrants us in having some negative reactive attitude such as moralized guilt (on A's part), resentment (on B's part), and indignation (on the part of some third party C).[14] On Darwall's view, all such 'second-personal' attitudes are *moralized* ones, involving some sort of evaluative judgment of moral blameworthiness, implying the person is 'morally accountable.'[15]

In what sense are the second-personal attitudes *personal*? There is a sense in which they are all personal: they all involve an 'implicit address' by one individual (the promisor) to another (the promisee), making 'a claim on that person's will and conduct.' In that sense, all second-personal attitudes are opposed to what Strawson called the *objective* attitude. When you take the objective attitude toward someone, you treat that person as an object/instrument of social policy, something to be managed, handled, or indeed protected, perhaps with a view to regulating behavior in socially desirable ways. Strawson (2008 [1962]: 9, 22, 24). There is also a sense in which only some second-personal attitudes are personal. Imagine that the promisor's action expresses ill will toward the promisee, and that the promisor and promisee *take things personally*, and react with moralized guilt and resentment (respectively). These attitudes are highly personal in the sense that one can only experience (indeed suffer) them on one's own behalf. But a third party to the promise can also experience a moralized or second personal reaction in the form of indignation or condemnation. These attitudes are somewhat *detached*; they are experienced or suffered vicariously, on behalf of someone else (here, the promisee). That said, we can focus exclusively on the attitudes of the participants of the relevant interaction (in our case, the promisor

---

[14] Cf. Strawson (1962/2008: ch. 1).

[15] Notice the reference to the claim of *legitimacy* involved in a second-personal address:

[M]oral obligations are, as a conceptual matter, standards we are aptly held responsible for violating, by ourselves and others, through reactive attitudes like guilt, indignation, and moral blame.... reactive attitudes are distinguished from other critical responses by their 'second-personal character,' that is by their invariably involving an implicit address of a putatively legitimate claim or demand. Moral obligations are what we can legitimately demand and hold ourselves and one another responsible for (Darwall 2011: 263).

Incidentally, Darwall seems to deviate from Strawson here. Strawson did not think that all reactive attitudes are moralized or imply a judgment of blameworthiness; Starwson's 'personal reactive attitudes,' such as resentment, are *not* moralized (see, e.g., 2008: 5). Second, Strawson did not think that the reactive attitudes admit of any *external* justification (see 2008: 25). Cf. also, Deigh (2012).

and the promisee). The crucial point for our purposes however is this. According to Strawsonian relationalism, the participants themselves react to promise-breaking with fully involved second personal or reactive attitudes: the promisor reacts with moralized guilt; the promisee, with moralized resentment. These attitudes betray *emotional vulnerability to the other party*.[16]

To my mind, Darwall's second-personal view of promises is best understood as a view of the central case of promises: Promises are *paradigmatically* embedded in a relationship in which the parties take highly personal moralized attitudes toward one another, and so cannot help reacting with moralized guilt and resentment to promise-breaking; in the central case, they cannot help being vulnerable to suffering these emotions. Now that does not mean that parties *cannot* promise while taking *less* personal attitudes such as detached moralized indignation, or even the entirely impersonal non-moralized objective attitude. As Strawson famously noted, responsible adults sometimes take the objective attitude toward one another if only as a refuge 'from the strains of involvement' (2008: 10, 13). However, Darwall's view does seem to imply that such promises fall outside the central case; they are somewhat defective as promises.[17]

What is the relation between Strawsonian relationalism and trust relationalism? Both views say that, in the central case, the relationships that embed promises are animated by *distinctly moral and personal* attitudes, but while trust relationalists emphasize the positive attitude of trust, Strawsonian relationalists emphasize *negative* reactive attitudes (e.g. moralized guilt, resentment, and blame). These views can be bridged by adding the positive attitude of trust to the list of second-personal attitudes, and noting that breach of trust expresses ill will that triggers negative second-

---

[16] On the personal nature of the participatory reactive attitudes Darwall follows Strawson, for whom the attitudes of 'offended parties or beneficiaries' (he called them 'the personal reactive attitudes') are 'essentially personal' (2008: 5, 10–12). As remarked in the previous note, Darwall seems to differ from Strawson on the *moralized* nature of these attitudes.

[17] This is reminiscent of Strawson's claim that we can suspend the personal reactive attitudes, and take the objective attitude instead, toward normal adults *in some particular cases* but not in general. Looking on everyone exclusively in an objective eye 'is, for us as we are, practically inconceivable' (2008: 12). '[W]e cannot, as we are, seriously envisage ourselves adopting a thoroughgoing objectivity of attitude to others' (2008: 14). [Our natural human commitment to ordinary inter-personal attitudes] is part of the general framework of human life, not something that can come up for review as particular cases come up for review within this general framework' (14).

personal attitudes.[18] Note that in one respect, Darwall's Strawsonian relationalism is like the trust relationalism of Friedrich and Southwood but unlike that of Kimel: the reactive attitudes animating the embedding relationship extends to strangers (as in the case of Hume's farmers).[19]

4. PROMISSORY TRANSACTIONALISM

Contrast promissory relationalism with

Promissory transactionalism. Perfect or paradigmatic promises are transactional or nonrelational in context. In the central case, promises are embedded in some transactional social context. Promising in relational contexts is nonparadigmatic or imperfect as promising; it presupposes promising in transactional contexts.[20] (See diagram 2.)

Let me briefly present two versions of this view.

Humean promissory transactionalism. Hume said that there are 'two different sorts of commerce, the interested and the disinterested,' and promises are 'invented for the former,' namely the 'self-interested commerce of men.' His discussion emphasizes promising made in the context of market exchange, where the parties are specifically said not to be close or caring. In Hume's famous example, farmers exchange promises to exchange their produce. Each takes this attitude: 'I have no kindness for you, and know you have as little for me.' They are rational maximizers of their own interests. This commercial context contrasts with 'the more generous and noble intercourse of friendship and good offices.'[21]

Annette Baier endorses this view of the context of promises: 'strangers will be the ones Humeans reserve their promises for.' Promises generate trust by subjecting the promisor to the practice-dependent threat of

---

[18] This seems particularly natural on Friedrich and Southwood's view. They adopt the view that trust entails *vulnerability to betrayal*, as opposed to mere disappointment. This requires the participant attitude. (The point is sometimes put by saying that a trickster who reliably predicts that his would-be victim will cooperate does not yet *trust* that person; if the would-be victim does not cooperate, the trickster would feel disappointed but not betrayed).

[19] Strawson (2008: 6–7) said that the personal relationships animated by the reactive attitudes extends to 'chance parties to an enormous range of transactions and encounters...raging from the most intimate to the most casual.'

[20] For views in this vein, compare Hume (2006 (*Treatise*, Bk. III, Pt. II, Sec. V)), Baier (1985: ch. 10 and 1994: 110–20), Macneil (1974 and 1980), and Markovits (2011).

[21] Hume (2006: 114 (*Treatise*, Bk. II, Pt. II, Sec. V)).

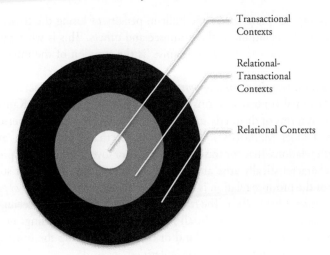

Transactional
Contexts

Relational-
Transactional
Contexts

Relational Contexts

Diagram 2: Promissory Transactionalism

Outer doughnut represents the zone of promissory imperfection.
Inner doughnut represents the zone of partial promissory perfection.
Inner doughnut hole represents the zone of promissory perfection.

'victim-initiated general withdrawal of trust.' Indeed, trust between self-interested strangers requires precisely such a threat.[22] By contrast, trust between intimates (family, friends, or neighbors) does not depend on such a threat. 'Those who take advantage of this sophisticated social device will be, mainly, adults who are not intimate with the one another.'[23]

This picture of the context of promises contrasts with the one presented in the previous section. There is nothing especially personal or moral about the attitudes animating market exchange. For all we know, the farmers in Hume's example had no previous interaction. Their mutual trust cannot reflect their views of each other's character, let alone moral character. Their promise-exchange is primarily animated by self-interested considerations. Each keeps his promise to the other 'without bearing him any real kindness,' because it is good for business. Promise-breaking is costly,

[22] Baier (1985: 188–91).
[23] Baier (1994: 112). Hume thought that paradigmatic promising is self-interested, and that parties to close personal relationships often act 'without any prospect of advantage.'

subjecting the promisor to the built-in penalty of losing the trust, and therefore cooperation, of the promisee and others. This is what Hume means when he writes that a promise 'is the sanction of the interested commerce of mankind.'[24]

Kantian promissory transactionalism. While Humeans characterize the transactional context in terms of largely prudential attitudes, Kantians do so in terms of distinctly moral attitudes, albeit avowedly *im*personal ones. Daniel Markovits for example writes that promises are 'arm's length relations' that contrast with intimate or love relationships: 'promises characteristically arise among strangers and... the immanent structure of the promise relation is in itself distancing, which is to say *opposed to intimacy*' (2011: 295). The recognition of intimacy involves seeing the other as *the* person she is, in all her particularities; promising, on the other hand requires another kind of recognition: seeing the other as *a* person, abstracting from her particularities:

> *the promise in itself is not a case of seeing the promisee... with the vividness that love requires.* Once true love has been achieved, promises between lovers wither away; and making new promises introduces a distance, a form of alienation even, into the love relation. Indeed, the genetic structure of promissory recognition is impersonal and in this sense *opposed* to intimacy. Promises prototypically do not promote intimacy, but rather an arm's length relation. (2011: 303)

Markovits concludes that 'promise's highest form will be achieved not in personal promises—which are embedded in intimate relations whose own immanent structure... competes with promissory appreciation—but in promises among strangers, that is, among parties whose engagement arises entirely at arm's length' (313–14).

For all their differences, Kantians and Humeans characterize the central case of promising in terms of some distinctly impersonal attitude. They both hold versions of promissory transactionalism.

5. THE PLURAL SOCIAL CONTEXT OF PROMISES

Promissory relationalism and transactionalism share the premise that there is some non-trivially characterizable social context to which promises belong by nature: perfect promises are either all relational in context

---

[24] Hume (2006: 114–16).

or else they are all transactional. This seems to underestimate the social adaptability of promises. I will try to show that *perfect* promises—promises that fall within the central case—can be embedded, and play a paradigmatic role, in relational *and* transactional contexts. The only truth in promissory relationalism (transactionalism) is the falsity of promissory transactionalism (relationalism): Perfect promises can be embedded in relational and transactional contexts.

Promissory Transactionalism Questioned

Promissory transactionalism mischaracterizes promising in the context of close, personal, and ongoing relationships as less than perfectly paradigmatic. Take Kantian transactionalism. The linchpin of Markovits's view is the claim that 'the immanent structure of the promise relation is in itself distancing, which is to say *opposed to intimacy*.' But this does not ring true. Parties to a loving relationship (however intimate) need to coordinate over time, and what better way to achieve this than by giving or exchanging promises? If promises promote coordination between parties to a loving relationship, then they promote the loving relationship itself. Why treat such promises as damaged goods or otherwise less than the real article?

Markovits seems to anticipate this objection. He acknowledges that 'promises and love are not strictly incompatible,' because parties to a loving relationship make 'trivial promises' as well as promises that 'are not trivial at all' (309). He does not see a problem here however, for

these possibilities concern the consequential or extrinsic interactions between promise and love. And even if the two relations can make room for each other or indeed support each other causally, they remain intrinsically—which is to say, in their immanent structure—opposed. Where love involves an emotional opening up or intimacy or vulnerability, promising closes off vulnerability. Promise is in its immanent structure opposed to intimacy; and promises characteristically arise at arm's length. (310)

But this passage cites no independent reason to believe its conclusion, namely that the immanent structure of promises is distancing and opposed to intimacy. Since promissory coordination is typically conducive to intimate relationships, any opposition between promises and intimacy seems contingent ('consequential and extrinsic') rather than essential ('intrinsic' or 'immanent'). Of course promises can be abused, as when one solemnly promises her unsuspecting partner to be faithful tonight.[25] But the possibility of such abuse is not special to promising; any speech act can be abused in a similar way. All it shows is that we should not make the wrong promise, question, or request at the wrong time. I conclude that, whether some particular promise is at odds with intimacy is a contingent matter; nothing about promises as such is distancing or opposed to intimacy or love.

Consider next Humean transactionalism. It depends on the threefold idea that (1) promising depends on the operation of self-interested motivation (it is 'the sanction of the interested commerce of mankind'); (2) close personal relationships depend on 'the more generous and noble' motive of benevolence and friendship; and yet (3) self-interest and benevolence are mutually exclusive. I shall grant (1) and (2) and question (3). Notice that Humean transactionalism depends on the mutual exclusiveness assumption (3). If self-interested and benevolent motives do not exclude each other, then you can keep your promise to your loved ones for self-interested *and* benevolent reasons; put another way, you can keep your promise both for the sake of your loved one and *and* for your own sake. In that case, there would seem to be absolutely no tension between your promise and your close relationship (even on the twofold assumption that (1) promises depend on self-interest and (2) close relationships depend on benevolence).

Joseph Butler persuasively questioned the exclusiveness assumption (1983 [1726]). Butler's thought is that these motives are genuinely different, or irreducible to one another, but are psychologically and morally compatible.[26] This sounds exactly right. Is it not eminently plausible to believe that what motivates us in our relationship with our loved ones is a mixture of considerations, including both self- and other-regarding ones? But this tends to undermine Humean promissory transactionalism. If you ever asked me whether I kept my promise to take my son to watch basketball for his sake or for mine, wouldn't the most credible answer be that I did it for the sake of us both? And unless we are given some reason to think that my motivation in this case is less than perfectly

---

[25] See Friedrich and Southwood (2011: 289).

[26] Butler makes at least three claims about the relation between self-love and benevolence (or love of one's neighbor). First, while different/irreducible, these motives are compatible (not 'opposed'). Second, just as interested motivation does not make action bad/wrong, disinterested motivation does not make it good/right. Finally, these motives are mutually reinforcing ('coinciding').

appropriate, we have no reason to think that there is anything less than perfectly paradigmatic about promises in a highly relational context.

I conclude that the case for promissory transactionalism—the notion that promises between friends, intimates, or lovers are imperfect as promises—is yet to be made out. We can formulate the rejection of this view in *functional* terms. Promises are all-purpose cooperation devices; they serve to promote various forms of interpersonal cooperation over time. The need for such cooperation is as acute in the most relational of contexts as in the most transactional or least relational ones. Therefore, relational promises can promote a paradigmatic (if not the paradigmatic) function of promises. There is no reason to treat such promises as imperfect or less than perfectly paradigmatic.

Promissory Relationalism Questioned

These problems with transactional accounts of the context of promising naturally steer us in the direction of relational accounts. I will now claim that relational accounts mischaracterize promising in the context of distant, impersonal, or discrete relationships as less than perfectly paradigmatic.

The problem is particularly serious in the case of Kimel's trust relationalism. Recall his claim that promising depends on robust personal-moral trust or respect, and that the normal function of promises is to promote close, personal, and ongoing relations by expressing such trust or respect. But if this claim were right, then the promises exchanged by Hume's farmers would be defective as promises. Recall that Hume's farmers have no knowledge or opinion of each other's moral character; they make and keep their promises primarily for reasons of self-interest. Since their promises do not promote close, personal, and ongoing relations by expressing personal-moral trust, we are forced to conclude that their promises do not fulfill the normal function of promising. But this looks like a prima facie *reductio* of Kimel's trust relationalism. The promises here clearly do seem to fulfill a major and perfectly normal function of promising: interpersonal cooperation over time. So the promotion of personal relations through the expression of personal-moral trust and respect cannot be the sole normal function of promising.

Kimel can respond that interpersonal cooperation over time is an instrumental function of promises, and his is a view about the *intrinsic* moral function of promises (2003: 27–9, 57–64). But this claim presupposes some reason for treating the expression of personal trust or respect as intrinsic to promising and the promotion of interpersonal cooperation as merely instrumental. Indeed, the very distinction is questionable. Arguably, one can value interpersonal cooperation instrumentally, for its contribution to the independently valuable relationship (say), as well as intrinsically, for its own sake. See Kagan (1998) and Frankfurt (1999: ch. 7). Indeed, cooperation seems to belong to the kind of things we value intrinsically because we value them instrumentally. In any event, there is no obvious reason to treat interpersonal cooperation as less intrinsic to promises than the expression of various positive attitudes.

The other versions of promissory relationalism I have mentioned are immune to this objection, for they do not insist that promises are paradigmatically animated by attitudes that are typically confined to some already close personal relationship. Hume's farmers for example present no obvious problem to the trust relationalism of Friedrich and Southwood or to Darwall's Strawsonian relationalism. For arguably, a stranger can accept my invitation to trust (Friedrich and Southwood) and can resent or blame me for breaking my promise (Darwall). So what is the problem?

If the problem with Kimel's trust relationalism is that it overpersonalizes promises, the problem with the trust relationalism of Friedrich and Southwood, and Strawsonian relationalism of Darwall, is that they *overmoralize* promises.[27] These views make promises that do not create a moral obligation that makes it appropriate to react to promise-breaking with *moralized* guilt or blame substandard, *not just morally speaking but as promises*.[28]

Start with the stock problem of the immoral promise, one it is immoral to make or keep, for example: Tony Soprano's promise to kill someone. Now it is not implausible to maintain that even such promises create at least some sort of obligation that is outweighed by others.[29]

---

[27] Thanks to Les Green for reinforcing my overmoralization worry. For his own overmoralization worries in another context, cf. Green (2012). For an attempt to demoralize promises, see McNeilly (1972).

[28] Notice that promises are hardly the only speech acts Darwall's relationalism overmoralizes. He claims that 'promising is but one species of a genus of second-personal *transactions* in which one person comes to have an obligation to another by virtue of a second-person interaction' (2011: 268). Other second-personal transactions include agreement, invitation, and request (see p. 270).

[29] Darwall acknowledges the distinction between moral and other genuine obligations, for example obligations of etiquette (2006: 98–9).

It is however harder to maintain that these promises create genuine *moral* obligations the violation of which makes moralized guilt or blame appropriate. One may or may not think that Tony's failure to kill as promised makes him morally praiseworthy for his conduct, but it is hard to believe that it makes him morally blameworthy for his conduct (even just a little bit blameworthy). While this claim is not obviously right, it has been explicitly endorsed by at least one proponent of Strawsonian relationalism. Gary Watson (2009) has recently claimed, with some force, that such immoral promises create absolutely no moral obligation or reason for action, and warrant no moralized guilt or blame. On this view, the normative power to create obligations or practical reasons by promising is constrained by moral considerations.[30] If this constrained authority view is right (as it seems to be), then Darwall's characterization of paradigmatic promises does not hold in such cases. Tony lacks the second-personal authority to promise. Since he is acting *ultra vires*, his promise creates no (directed) moral obligation, confers no moral right on the promisee, and authorizes no one to react with the second-personal attitudes.

But if this is right, then I think Strawsonian relationalism à la Darwall is committed to the view that Tony's promise is substandard, not just morally speaking—this much is trivially true—but also *as a promise*. And that does not seem right. After all, Tony's promise functions in much the same way perfectly moral promises do. It allows the parties to achieve precisely what they want or intend to achieve, promoting interpersonal cooperation in the process. Nor does Tony's promise seem bereft of normative implications; the constitutive norms of promising seem to apply. On the face of it, if you do not keep your promise, you fail to comply with the constitutive norms of promising; immoral promises are no exception. That Tony's failure to kill opens him up to no *moralized* guilt or blame does not mean that he complies with the constitutive norms of promising; it is just that the constitutive norms of promising need not be second-personal or otherwise moral.[31]

---

[30] As Watson notes, examples of promised moral misdemeanors are more forceful arguments for his 'constrained normative power view' than heinous promises (2009: 172).

[31] An analogy might help. Suppose that the constitutive norm of assertion is truth. Then your assertion is warranted if and only if it is true. That does not imply that your failure to speak truthfully opens you up to *moralized* guilt or blame. In my intuition, no moralized

Immoral promises are not the only promises that make trouble for Strawsonian relationalism. Let us contemplate a pair of perfectly moral promises. Consider first Hume's farmers one last time. Suppose that they keep their promises for a mix of self- and other-interested reasons. More to the point, suppose that *if* one of them broke his promise, the other would be disappointed, even angered, but would neither feel nor express moralized resentment. Instead, he would do whatever he thinks would improve things (from asking the other to deliver to threatening to disengage). Consider second your promise to meet me for lunch. Suppose that you keep your promise for a mix of considerations, prominent among which is your sympathetic concern for me. More to the point, suppose that *if* you broke your promise, you would feel or express no moralized guilt, and I would feel or express no moralized resentment or blame.

These cases seem to me entirely possible, familiar, and indeed innocent; nothing wrong seems to be going on in them. We do not always, or even typically, react to the violation of interpersonal norms with moralized guilt or resentment; we often have other—and better—ways to respond at our disposal. This seems as true in our personal lives (as in the meeting example) as in our economic lives (as in the farmers example). The promises in these cases strike me as perfectly paradigmatic.

The Strawsonian relationalist can deny this last claim and insist that the promises in these cases are, rather, degenerate or deviant. He could argue, in a Strawsonian vein, that while we can temporarily suspend the moralized personal reactive attitudes on some particular occasion (such as the abovementioned examples), doing so wholesale is neither psychologically possible nor desirable. (1) Given human nature, regarding people exclusively with the objective eye is 'practically impossible' (2008: 12). (2) It is also undesirable or impoverished. In one view, it would make for 'a tragic world of human isolation.'[32] The Strawsonian relationalist might take this to show that (3) perfectly paradigmatic promises are

---

blame is appropriate when you tell a lie to avert great harm. If this is right, the constitutive norm of assertion is not particularly moral. For a non-moral view of the norms of assertion, see Williamson (2000: ch. 11).

[32] Wolf (1981: 400). She 'hopes it is obvious why the words "friendship" and "love" would take on a hollow ring under the objective attitudes' (391).

given in the context of the moralized reactive attitudes. My main difficulty with this response concerns the inference to the conclusion. I start by raising some questions about the premises, however.

The premises (1) and (2). As Tamler Sommers (2007) has argued, neither premise is obviously right. The impoverishment claim (2) in particular seems questionable. *If* it is true that moral responsibility is a matter of susceptibility to moralized reactive attitudes, then a world in which we do not feel or express moralized guilt and blame might be a world in which we are not morally responsible to anyone for anything. But there is no obvious reason to think that we could no longer love, befriend, or have sympathetic concern for one another in such a world. Nor is there a reason to doubt that we could be virtuous, for arguably we could still love the good and hate the bad.[33] Finally, what reason do we have for thinking that the shallowing effect of going objective outweighs the notoriously painful effects of moralized guilt and resentment?

The psychological impossibility claim (1) is admittedly harder to dispute. It is hard to deny that we are in some way committed to seeing ourselves and others as appropriate objects of the personal reactive attitudes. But this claim is rather general and admits of different interpretations. Strawson for example thought that our susceptibility to the reactive attitudes is analogous to our susceptibility to induction: they are 'in no way something we choose or could give up' (2008: 28 n. 7). But other analogies might prove even closer to the mark. It might be that our commitment to the reactive attitudes is more like religious belief than inductive reasoning. It might be that we could not give it up entirely, or all at once, but can do so partially and incrementally.[34] Another interpretive question concerns the scope of our commitment to the reactive attitudes. In particular, does our most basic commitment extend to *moralized* attitudes? The question arises because in principle you can feel or express a reactive attitude that does not imply

[33] The following passage from Sommers (2007: 326–7) is an antidote to the bleak picture of objectivity of attitude:

When you take the objective attitude toward other human beings, you do nothing more than see them as natural things. But a human being is still a human being—the most exciting, infuriating, unpredictable, lovable, loathsome natural thing in the world. ... Nothing in the objective attitude prevents us from recognizing, appreciating, *cherishing* the rich and wonderful qualities of another person. ... The better the objective attitude is understood, I believe, the less 'gruesome' it will appear.

[34] See in this respect the suggestive comments in Sommers (2007: 336–40).

any moral judgment. (Apparently, this is how Strawson thought about resentment).

The conclusion (3). Suppose however that the Strawsonian relationalist is correct to claim that adopting an *exclusively* objective view of people, that is without ever feeling or expressing personal reactive attitudes, is both (1) psychologically inconceivable and (2) impoverishing. Why take this to show that (3) promises that do not invoke moralized or second-personal reactive attitudes are *deficient as promises*? Indeed Strawson acknowledges that we occasionally take the objective attitude and suspend the reactive attitudes for good reasons. Similarly Darwall never claims that appropriate interaction with others always requires viewing them from the second-person viewpoint. Thus the sheer fact that the parties to some promise would not react to the failure to keep it with moralized guilt or resentment is no reason to doubt the appropriateness of that promise. But then it is not clear in what respect such non-moralized promises are deficient as promises.

Promissory relationalism overpersonalizes promises, overmoralizes them, or both. While promise relationalism might appear somewhat more natural than promise transactionalism, I see no more reason to accept it.

Promissory Pluralism

Beginning to emerge is the following view:

Promissory pluralism. Perfect or paradigmatic promises are relational or transactional in contexts. In the central case, promises are embedded in some relational, transactional, or mixed relational-transactional. (See diagram 3.)

Notice that promissory pluralism is not the rather pedestrian observation that promises are in fact made in all these contexts; it is the stronger claim that promises are neither *primarily* relational (and only secondarily transactional) nor *primarily* transactional (and only secondarily relational). There is no interesting priority between these contexts of promising, one way or the other. When it comes to embedding social context, the core (inner doughnut) of promises is split. The claim is potentially interesting because it controverts promissory relationalism and transactionalism, two conflicting and potentially interesting outlooks variations on which can be found in the literature. If these outlooks ultimately fail, their failure can illuminate promises.

Just how pluralistic promissory pluralism is depends on our working conception of the relational–transactional distinction. I cannot exclude

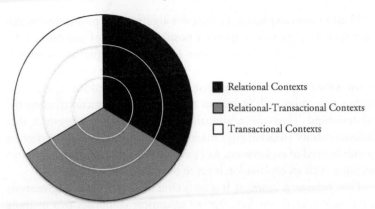

Diagram 3: Promissory Pluralism
Outer doughnut represents the zone of promissory imperfection.
Inner doughnut represents the zone of partial promissory perfection.
Inner doughnut hole represents the zone of promissory perfection.

the possibility that promissory pluralism comes out false under some interesting interpretation of that distinction; all I can say is that it seems to hold under a wide range of plausible interpretations of that distinction, including, as we saw in previous sections, some that can be found in the literature.[35] That being said, it is hard to see how that the result of our discussion could be different if we defined the relational-transactional distinction in terms of somewhat different pairs of contrasting contexts/relationships, such as caring–uncaring or non-economic–economic. In each case, I can only surmise, we will be able to find perfectly functional promises in both contexts/relationships.

However understood, the relational–transactional contrast is not hard and fast; most social contexts/relationships are mixed. But hybrid cases require no separate discussion. It is eminently plausible to predict that, if perfect promising can find place within two polar contexts, they can also find place anywhere in the middle. Consider for example promises we give/receive in mixed personal–impersonal relations—say, to/from our business partners or nannies. So long as these promises are sincere and voluntary, it is hard to fault them *as promises*.

---

[35] It is, of course, easy to falsify promissory pluralism by vindicating promissory relationalism (transactionalism) under some all-encompassing interpretation of relationality (transactionality). This falsification would trivialize the vindicated views.

None of this can provide a conclusive argument for promissory plural-ism; such an argument requires a positive account of promises. I do, however, believe that the discussion in this and the previous section is sufficient to shift the burden of proof onto the other side. The starting point is the simple observation that promises are embedded in, and seem to function quite well, in various relational and transactional contexts/relationships. Thus the relationalist (transactionalist) suggestion that transactionality (relationality) marks a certain promissory imperfection stands in need of explanation. As I have tried to show in the previous two sections, such an explanation is yet to be offered.

From promises to contracts. It is fairly clear that promises and agreements are closely related—in fact, that an agreement comprises two or more promises. Of course, an agreement is *more* than two promises. Arguably, an agreement consists of exchanged or interdependent promises, promises that depend on one another in some causal-motivational way. An agree-ment, in short, is a *joint* promise.[36] Here I want to focus on one particular kind of agreement, namely legally binding agreements or *contracts*.

Assume that contracts are legally binding agreements and that agree-ments are joint promises. Then contracts are *legally binding joint prom-ises*. This is one way to understand the familiar claim that contracts are legally binding promises.[37] As in the case of promises, some claim that contracts have their own privileged embedding context, namely that perfectly good contracts are embedded in some non-trivially describable context or relationship. As before, I illustrate these views by reference to the conveniently fluid relational-transactional distinction.

6. CONTRACTUAL RELATIONALISM

Consider

Contractual relationalism. Perfect or paradigmatic contracts are relational or nontransactional in context. In the central case, contracts are embedded in some relational social context. Contracting in transactional contexts is nonparadigmatic or imperfect as contracting; it presupposes contracting in relational contexts.[38] (See diagram 4.)

[36] See Sheinman (2011).
[37] See Fried (1981, 2007).
[38] For views in this vein, compare Macaulay (1963, 2003), Macneil (1974, 1980, and 2000), Campbell (1996, 2001), and Leib (2009).

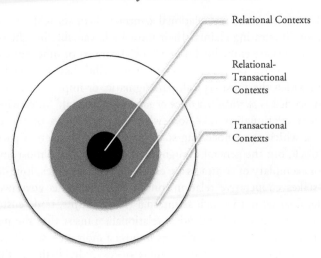

Relational Contexts

Relational-
Transactional
Contexts

Transactional
Contexts

Diagram 4: Contractual Relationalism

Outer doughnut represents the zone of contractual imperfection.
Inner doughnut represents the zone of partial contractual perfection.
Inner doughnut hole represents the zone of contractual perfection.

Indeed, it is in the context of offering a relational account of contracts that Ian Macneil introduced the relational–transactional distinction (1974). Macneil and friends of his relational contract theory repeatedly stress the social *embeddedness* of contracts, the fact that all contracts are embedded in *some* social context of relationships, institutions, and norms or other. They are obviously right about that. Indeed even the simplest of contracts *presupposes* such major social institutions as language, law (and therefore regulation), and property. The idea of socially unemended contracts—of contracts that float free of extra-legal norms or legal regulation—is a chimera.[39] But then the social embeddedness of contracts is a truism.[40] There is no reason to

[39] A special case of this chimera is that of the *unregulated* contract. Contracts are creatures of the law, and the law cannot fail to regulate contracts, if only by setting preconditions for their formation. By setting such preconditions, the law already regulates some agreements by recognizing them and not others. All contracts are subject to regulation in the form of legal rules as to their formation, content, performance, and administration. Different contracts may be regulated more or less extensively, or in different ways, but there is no such thing as unregulated contracts.

[40] It would remain a truism even if some crazy classical contract theorist denied or failed to appreciate its implications.

dwell on this claim, for relational contract theorists make stronger and more interesting claims. Their most basic valuable insight is not that contracts are embedded in *some* social context or other (of course they are), but the potentially controversial claim that the social context in which the most typical, paradigmatic, or important contracts are embedded is *particularly thick or robust* ('relational,' 'intertwined').

Different relationalists take somewhat different views of the exact sense in which the embedding social context of contracts is particularly thick, but the general thought seems to be that the most important or exemplary of contracts are embedded in a complex, long-term, high-stakes cooperative relation, one moreover that is governed by non-legal social norms such as internal rules of firms, trade customs, and etiquette. Macneil and other relationalists insist that the norms governing these relational contracts impose a more-or-less collectivist ethic of solidarity, as opposed to a more-or-less individualistic ethic of profit-maximization.[41]

An example of a highly relational contract is a supply agreement between a smelting plant and a coalmine.[42] The parties to such an agreement have typically had at least some interaction before, and in any event, they typically expect to establish a fairly long, stable, and amicable economic relationship. The relationship is expected to have multiple dimensions and require constant adjustments to the changing circumstances and needs of the parties. As the relationship evolves, the expectations arising from the contract will be adjusted by mutual consent. Since the overarching goal is continued cooperation, the parties will accommodate each other without resort to the law.[43] At the limit, the contract will amount to little more than an insurance policy for the end-game contingency (the end of cooperation). Bernstein (1996).

The basic descriptive claim of the relational contract school seems to be that such contracts are the central case or paradigm of contracts; its

---

[41] For criticism from a liberal perspective of the communitarian aspect of relational contract theory, see Barnett (1992).

[42] The example belongs to Macneil. For references and discussion, see Campbell (2001: 16–18).

[43] Macaulay (1963) has famously found that non-legal norms seem to provide the parties with at least as much guidance as does the contract (plus contract law). Contractual parties are generally reluctant to invoke the contract or remedies for its breach in the course of their relationship.

basic prescriptive claim is that the law should take account of this fact. This last claim is hardly a call for radical law reform. Indeed, relationalists often tell us that the law *already* takes the relationality of contracts into account (this being part of the evidence for their claim that contracts are paradigmatically relational). The fact that the law extensively regulates contacts of various types (e.g. insurance, employment, sale) is exhibit number one; the legal duty to perform in good faith is exhibit number two.

So contractual relationalists envisage a spectrum of embedding social contexts stretching from the highly transactional or discrete pole to a highly relational or intertwined pole, and make the non-trivial and potentially controversial claim that representative, paradigmatic, or important contracts fall closer to the relational pole than to the transactional pole. To be sure, there is no denial that highly transactional or discrete contracts *exist*; the stock example of transactional contracts is the spot purchase (at a gas station, for example). The claim is rather that such transactional or discrete contracts are the exception rather than the general rule. And this, I take it, is not just a statistical claim, but also a conceptual claim that employs the central case method: Paradigmatic, perfectly contractual contracts tend to fall closer to the relational or intertwined pole of the embedding social context spectrum than to its transactional or discrete pole. And the law should take account of this fact.[44]

---

[44] Proponents as well as critics of relational contract theory sometimes associate it with such claims as: 'every transaction is embedded in complex relations' (Macneil, 2000: 881), 'exchange of any importance is impossible outside a society. Even the purest "discrete" exchange postulates a social matrix' (Macneil, 2000: 884), 'there are no truly discrete contracts' (Campbell, 2001: 45), 'all contracts are relational' (Scott, 2000: 852), 'we are all relationalists now' (Scott, 2000: 852), 'discrete contracts—contracts that are *not* relational—are almost as imaginary as unicorns' (Eisenberg, 2000: 816). But these claims simply insist on the social embeddedness of contracts. To avoid trivialization of relational contract theory, we must take seriously the relational–transactional distinction and therefore the possibility of genuinely transactional contracts. Here is a more sympathetic reading:

It is Macneil's major achievement to have shown that open minded analysis of contracting reveals a class of relational contracts in which action predominantly is so oriented in the minds of the parties towards conscious co-operation that a contract of this class 'no longer stands alone as in the discrete transaction, but is part of the relational web'. All the negotiating tactics adopted by the parties, concerning formulation, performance, variation, termination and application of remedies, can be explained only as being informed by this co-operative attitude. (Campbell 2001: 18; references omitted)

7. CONTRACTUAL TRANSACTIONALISM

Those who reject contractual relationalism might naturally try to go all the way in the other direction to espouse

Contractual transactionalism. Perfect or paradigmatic contracts are transactional or nonrelational in context. In the central case, contracts are embedded in some transactional social context. Contracting in relational contexts is nonparadigmatic or imperfect as contracting; it presupposes contracting in transactional contexts.[45] (See diagram 5.)

Two rather similar examples of this view are worth noting.

Contract as detachment. We have already noted Kimel's promissory relationalism; we now note his contractual transactionalism. Kimel sees 'contract essentially as a tool for dealing at arm's length.' He believes that 'the main' role of contract law is that of facilitating arm's length transactions,' and that 'the institution's main preoccupation is with facilitating

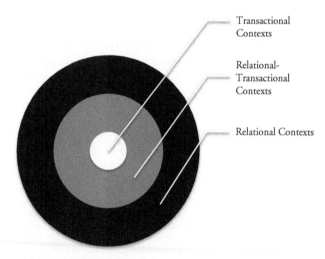

Transactional
Contexts

Relational-
Transactional
Contexts

Relational Contexts

Diagram 5: Contractual Transactionalism

Outer doughnut represents the zone of contractual imperfection.
Inner doughnut represents the zone of partial contractual perfection.
Inner doughnut hole represents the zone of contractual perfection.

---

[45] For views in this vein, compare Baier (1985: 110–20); Kimel (2003, 2007); Bagchi (2009); and Markovits (2011).

and regulating transactions outside of the framework of already-existing relationships characterized by trust, interdependence and earnest cooperation' (2007: 242–3).[46]

In Kimel's discussion, 'contract emerges not as *promise*, but as a *substitute* for promise' (2003: 79). Kimel does not really wish to deny that contracts consist of 'exchanged' promises; what he does seem to deny is that the promises of which contracts consist are very *good* ones—that they are 'normal' promises. Contracts are somewhat imperfect promises. Contracts and promises, he maintains, have 'diametrically opposed' intrinsic functions. As we have seen, he thinks that the intrinsic normal function of promises is the promotion of personal relations through the expression of robust, personal-moral trust and respect. The intrinsic normal function of contracts on the other hand is the facilitation of personal *detachment* (65–90). Personal detachment and personal relations are mutually exclusive ('diametrically opposed') (78–80)—a social practice that promotes personal detachment relative to some personal relation does not also promote these relations (and vice versa).[47] Call this picture of contracts the *detachment thesis*.

Kimel has three arguments for this thesis, two positive and one negative. These arguments all depend on the plausible claim that what makes contractual promises contractual is the fact that they are legally enforceable. Specifically, they are enforceable in the sense that the law provides a battery of remedies for their breach. While these remedies may be reparative rather than punitive, they also serve as a deterrent. By making contracts *sanction-enforceable*, the legal system

[46] Kimel (2007) stops short of asserting that contracts are paradigmatically transactional; he wishes to leave open the possibility that contracts have no single paradigmatic context. But he seems to close this possibility, as he insists that the transactional or discrete context is 'more central' to contracts than the relational context, and that the transactional model—to wit the view that contract law's main role is to facilitate arm's length transactions outside the relational context—is 'more illuminating' than the relational one (235). In any event, I will focus on Kimel's most elaborate treatment of this issue (2003). Kimel (2003) clearly treats relational contracts as less than perfectly normal—to wit as at least somewhat 'marginal, esoteric, atypical.' See, e.g., pp. 7, 20.

[47] "[Promises and contracts are] practices that are capable of promoting only one of [personal relations and personal detachment]—and not the same one" (79). Contracts "facilitate not personal relations but personal detachment" (4). Notice that the promotion of personal detachment, like that of personal relation, is said to be an 'intrinsic' rather 'instrumental' function. The implication seems to be that a personal detachment is valuable intrinsically, and apart from its contribution to some personal relation. (Otherwise, the function of its promotion would be instrumental).

makes the consequences of breach of contract significantly costly to the parties. Kimel assumes that the legal threat of sanction is *effective*: the threat itself is public, clear, and credible; breach of contract is highly likely to result in sanction. He further assumes that this credible threat of legal sanction is normally sufficient to deter breach *by itself* (37, 54–8, 75–6).

Kimel's first argument for this thesis is that the sanction-enforceability of contracts provides even perfect strangers with whatever assurance they need to co-operate successfully, and can therefore allow parties— give them the *option*—to co-operate and pursue valuable goals in transactional ('discrete') contexts, outside the context of meaningful personal relationships and their attendant attitudes of profound trust and respect (54–64, 81–2).[48] A second argument for the detachment thesis (which lies implicit in Kimel's discussion) is that parties to meaningful personal relations, with their attendant attitudes of robust trust and respect, have no *need* for contracts, because they have no need for sanction-enforceability. The constitutive attitudes of these relations provide the parties with all the assurance they need to cooperate successfully.

Kimel's third and main argument for his detachment thesis is largely negative.[49] It seeks to establish that contracts are 'singularly inadequate' to fulfill the function for which promises are 'uniquely suited,' namely the promotion of meaningful personal relations, and are at odds with the personal-moral trust that epitomizes such relations; contracts may 'positively damage, rather than reinforce, the relationship' (2003: 76–7, 56, 29). The key idea is this. The sanction-enforceability of contracts (the credible threat of sanction for breach) creates independent reasons for performance that are meant to be, and usually are, sufficiently strong to outweigh conflicting reasons, and motivate performance by themselves. Hence the sanction-enforceability of contracts 'casts a thick and all-encompassing veil over the motives and the attitudes toward each other attributable to parties to contracts.' Specifically, a party to a contract can never be sure that the other party performs the contract for the kind of reasons that are right for personal relationships—which for Kimel are reasons to promote the personal relationship by expressing profound, personal-moral trust or respect. A party to a contract cannot exclude the possibility that

---

[48] Kimel regards this as 'the trivialization of the role of trust' in contracts.
[49] For a general version of the argument, see Dan-Cohen (2002: ch. 3). For an alternative version of the argument as applied to contracts, see Bagchi (2009).

the other has performed the contract for fear of sanction. And such performance is 'largely devoid of expressive content' (cannot express personal-moral trust or respect).

We can summarize the argument thus.

(1) Significant personal relationships require motivational transparency: parties to such a relationship must be able to ascribe motives and attitudes to each other with a reasonable degree of success, and specifically the ability to tell that the other has acted from robust trust or respect for the other. (2) Yet by generating sufficient self-interested reason/incentive to perform, the sanction-enforceability of contracts creates *motivational opacity*: for all that a party to a contract knows, the other party's performance has been motivated by fear of sanction.[50] (3) Therefore, contracts are singularly inadequate for the promotion of personal relationships.

Contract as Arm's-Length. We have already noted Markovits's transactionalist view of promises. We now note that he also holds a transactionalist view of contracts. Like Kimel, Markovits characterizes the paradigmatic embedding social context of contracts as that of transactions that arise at 'arm's length,' and outside the context of intimate personal relations. He thinks that *all* perfect promises (including non-contractual ones) are arm's-length relations involving a distinctly impersonal moral attitude of recognition or respect for person(hood). Since contracts are a special case of promises, they are also arm's-length relations involving the same impersonal moral attitude. Markovits goes further to claim that contracts involve the said impersonal moral attitude *to the highest degree*; contractual promises are a *better* example of arm's-length relations than noncontractual ones. Hence contractual promises are the best example of promises: the practice of contract 'represents promise's highest and most complete expression' (2011: 296).

Markovits's reasons for thinking that contracts are paradigmatically arm's-length are somewhat different from Kimel's. According to Markovits, there are three ways in which contracts are particularly congenial to impersonal recognition. First, the *self-interested* nature of contractual

---

[50] This echoes Meir Dan-Cohen more general point that 'when sanctions are clearly announced compliance can no longer carry the significance it otherwise would have had as an expression of respect. For all we know...compliance was motivated by fear of sanction, and is therefore devoid of expressive content' (2002: ch. 3).

motivation helps to secure impersonal respect for personhood by excluding other, distinctly personal attitudes, such as sympathetic concern and paternalism (315–16). Second, contracts are *reciprocal*. For the most part, they are agreements, and an agreement consists of an exchange of promises. This 'formal equality' means that each party obligates itself to, or authorizes, the other, and each party authorizes the other partly because the other authorizes it. And this makes for a particularly complete case of the impersonal respect for person(hood) that Markovits finds in promises generally: not only does each party recognize the personhood 'or authority' of the other; she also recognizes her own personhood or authority. Finally, contracts are creatures of *positive law*, and are enforceable in the law courts. This makes the abstract public reasons generated by contractual promises concrete (318). In all these respects, 'contract perfects the recognition associated with promise.'

Notice that the main difference between Kimel and Markovits is not in their view of contracts but in their view of the relation between contracts and promises. For Markovits, the three respects in which contracts are particularly transactional or arm's length rather than relational or intimate are also the three respects in which contracts are said to be the most perfect promises. This second claim—which is captured by Markovits's slogan that contract 'represents promise's highest and most complete expression'—is not simply a consequence of his contractual transactionalism; it also requires his *promissory* transactionalism (which I questioned in section 5). Kimel on the other hand rejects promissory transactionalism, and therefore Markovits's claim that contracts are the most perfect of promises. For all that, Kimel and Markovits are both contractual transactionalists who share the belief that perfect contracts are transactional in context and arise at arm's length.

Contract as Imperfect Promise

We can also cross contractual transactionalism with promissory relationalism. Together, these views seem to entail

Contract as imperfect promise. Contractual promises are imperfect promises.[51] (See diagram 6.)

---

[51] For views in this vein, compare Kimel (2003) and Raz (1982: 928–31).

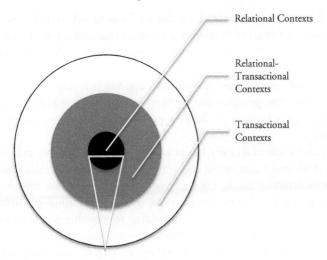

Diagram 6: Contract as Imperfect Promise

Outer doughnut represents the zone of contractual imperfection.
Inner doughnut represents the zone of partial contractual perfection.
Inner doughnut hole represents the zone of contractual perfection.

Narrowest segment of triangle area represents the zone of contractual perfection.
Middle segment represents the zone of partial contractual perfection.
Widest segment represents the zone of contractual imperfection.

Now we have already seen one way to question contract as imperfect promise, namely by questioning promissory relationalism.[52] In the next section we shall see another way of questioning the same view, namely by questioning contractual transactionalism.

8. THE PLURAL SOCIAL CONTEXT OF CONTRACTS

I question both contractual relationalism and contractual transactionalism.

Contractual Relationalism Questioned

We can be brief here, for the considerations adduced in section 5 to argue against promissory relationalism apply with even more force to contractual relationalism. The problem is not simply that many con-

---

[52] Markovitz (2011) provides a nice example of someone who rejects contract as imperfect promise because he rejects promissory relationalism.

tracts are embedded in relatively distant, impersonal, and discrete relationships, a fact sensible relational contract theorists acknowledge. The problem is also that contracts that fall much closer to the transactional or discrete pole of the spectrum than to the relational or intertwined pole seem perfectly desirable, appropriate, and functional; in promoting interpersonal cooperation over time, these highly transactional contracts seem to fulfill a perfectly paradigmatic contractual function.

Take the sale of a candy bar or a share of stock. Arguably the parties here enter into a contract of sale. If the seller fails to deliver the goods or delivers defective goods, for example, he can be liable for breach. But when things go as they should, there is barely any time-gap between entrance and performance; the embedding relationship is as brief as can be. As contracts go, these are highly transactional. And yet these contracts operate exactly as they should, allowing us to exchange goods on the market without as much as knowing each other or having to forge meaningful personal or economic relationships of any significant depth or duration.

The contractual relationalist can object that this is not a good example. What we have in these cases is not a genuine contract but an instantaneous exchange of goods. A contract is a bridge between the present and the future; it requires at least some time-gap between entrance and performance.

We can handle this objection by pointing that even brief encounters take time (if only seconds). Suppose the contract is entered into when I point to the candy I want. Then the seller performs his part of the deal one second later by handing it to me, and I perform mine another second later by paying. But I do not think the case against contractual relationalism depends on examples of near-instantaneous exchange. A sale that takes days, weeks, or even months to complete can still fall closer to the transactional end of the spectrum. Take the contract we sign when we sell our house or buy a new one. Like all contracts, these too are socially embedded, legally regulated, and require the parties to cooperate for several weeks or months. However, the contract does not typically anticipate any robust long-term cooperative relationships (personal or economic). In a typical case, the buyer and seller have not known each other from Adam, and will have no further dealings after this one is complete. And their relationship is largely confined to one dimension: property. However you understand the relational–transactional distinction, this is not an example of a highly relational contract, one that is embedded in a long-term robust multidimensional relationship. And yet these contracts operate exactly as they should, allowing us to cooperate with perfect strangers, fellow travellers, and chance partners on mutually beneficial terms without having to forge or maintain any close, long-term, personal, or multidimensional relationship.

There is a good explanation why contracts routinely function perfectly well in transactional settings. What makes agreements or exchanged promises contractual is their *legality*, the fact that they impose legally binding and enforceable obligations. The legal system provides a set of public rules for the regulation of contracts, a battery of remedies for breach of contract, and a system for their administration, namely the law courts. This legality of contracts provides parties with excellent reasons and motives to make, rely upon, and keep their contract, reasons and motives they would not have if their promises were non-contractual. Perhaps the most obvious such reasons and motives come of the legal *enforceability* of contracts. Thus the threat of being found in breach of contract and ordered to pay compensation provides parties with at least one good reason to perform their contracts. These reasons and motives are relatively insensitive to the embedding social context of contracts; they do not depend on the exact nature of the relationship the parties already have or expect to develop. In particular, they do not require a significant close personal relation; they apply to strangers and spot transactions. This is one fairly obvious explanation of the fact that contracts routinely promote cooperation in transactional social settings. Notice that the law does not simply give actual parties reasons to perform their contracts; it also gives potential parties reasons to *enter* into (or avoid entering into) contractual relations. The law does so by giving potential parties the *option* to subscribe to a framework of rules as to the formation, content, interpretation, performance, and enforcement of contracts. Subscription to the framework can streamline interpersonal cooperation by saving recourses and adding a measure of stability and predictability to their cooperative efforts. These reasons and motives do not typically require the parties to have a robust long-term cooperative relationship. **All in all, appeal to the legality of contracts can explain why they routinely promote interpersonal cooperation over time in highly transactional settings.**

Contractual Transactionalism Questioned

All this is bread and butter of contractual transactionalists such as Kimel and Markovits. Contractual transactionalists are right that many contracts are embedded in some relatively transactional (non-relational) social context, one in which the parties take a detached attitude toward one another or deal at arm's length. The spot contract between strangers is a perfectly familiar phenomenon. They are also right to insist that taking these detached or impersonal attitudes is perfectly appropriate in the transactional circumstances, and does not prevent contractual parties from cooperating on mutually beneficial terms. They are right to think that transactional or discrete contracts are often perfectly paradigmatic contracts. Yet this conclusion falls short of contractual transactionalism; it is consistent with the claim that *many perfectly paradigmatic contracts are highly relational.* In what follows, I try to support this last claim.

Islamic law (sharia) provides one potential counterexample to contractual transactionalism.[53] Under Islamic law, marriage (nikah) is not a sacrament but a private legal agreement, namely a contract. While Islamic law determines some of the terms of the contract, either party is free to modify some and insert others (with the other's consent). The marriage contract typically envisages a long-term and intimate personal (including sexual) relationship, and regulates various aspects of that relationship, including the country of residence, education and career, visitation with in-laws. It also 'obligates each spouse to treat the other well.'[54] The marriage is expected to be 'permanent,' unless the contract explicitly stipulates a fixed duration. Now I think we can say two things about such contracts. First, it seems like a perfectly paradigmatic, appropriate, and functional contract. It is bound to be among the two or three most important contracts one enters into in one's entire life, a contract that comes close to being a *precondition* for having intimate partnership in traditional Muslim society. And second, the contract seems highly relational, embedded as it is in a marriage relationship and Islamic spousal law. So Islamic law seems to counterexample contractual transactionalism.

The contractual transactionalist might retort that Islamic law is not law, so that agreements that constitute valid contracts under Islamic law

---

[53] Thanks to Ruth Halperin-Keddary for the example.
[54] Kecia (2008).

are not genuine contracts. The idea might be that Islamic law is just too simple to count as a legal system because it only has first-order rules of conduct, no second-order rules for making new rules or changing old ones by enactment. Echoing H. L. A. Hart's comments about 'primitive communities' (1992: 91–2), one might argue that the rules of Islamic law lack a *rule of recognition*, that legendary adhesive that is necessary to unify a set of conduct rules into a full-fledged legal system. Now it is not entirely clear why we should take this argument to establish its conclusion as to the legality of Islamic law rather than to question its premises,[55] but the response fails for the simpler reason that Islamic law has been incorporated into the law of some modern states. The nikah is a valid contract under Saudi law, for example (Wynn 2008).

We can now imagine the response that contractual transactionalism is a thesis about *liberal* legal systems. Islamic law might enforce spousal contracts, but liberal legal systems are properly reluctant to do so for the reason that such enforcement would compromise the personal autonomy of the partners. But this claim is not generally true. The attitude of the liberal state to spousal contracts is rather complex, and its readiness to enforce them appropriately varies with the *specific kind* of contract or contractual provision at issue.[56] For example, liberal legal systems are typically reluctant to enforce prenuptial contracts regulating how the partners lead their everyday lives (their sexual life, for instance), but are often happy to enforce prenuptial or postnuptial contracts regulating the division of property upon divorce or separation. (In my opinion, contracts that regulate the end of a close, long-term, and personal relationship are still embedded in these very relationships—and are for that reason largely relational. True: they are designed to persist through the unhappy yet realistic breakdown contingency, in which case their embedding relationship will *become* transactional. But they are hardly designed to produce or otherwise facilitate this contingency. In fact, they can reduce the likelihood of the unhappy contingency by making the parties feel more secure.)

Let us now look at a more mundane example. I previously noted that the typical sale of house contract is rather transactional or discrete,

---

[55] For the idea that 'primitive' law is law, see Hoeble (1954).

[56] For the different attitudes modern law takes to different spousal contracts, see Lifshitz (2012).

which makes trouble for contractual relationalism. It is time to add that this is not an essential feature of such contracts. The social context or relationship in which sales contracts are embedded can be as robustly relational as can be. Suppose that Jo has a close and involved relationship with her father. For all that, if she wants to buy her father's dwelling house, she must do so by executing a written contract. The contract in such a case would be embedded in a close, long-term, and personal relationship between father and daughter. Are we to say that the relational environment makes the contract somewhat defective as a contract?

Next consider the kind of contracts relational contract theorists like to emphasize, for instance employment, franchise, and supply contracts. To be sure, the relationships anticipated by such contracts are not particularly personal (they are mainly economic), but they are surely complex, long-term, cooperative, and take on significant personal dimensions as they evolve. Surely these are paradigmatic examples of contracts, agreements that are contracts if any are?

A contractual transactionalist can respond by saying that relational contracts are not particularly good examples of contracts because they are *heavily regulated*. Indeed, part of the reason why spousal, employment, fiduciary, franchise, and insurance contracts are often said to be relational is precisely the fact the law regulates them more heavily than other contracts. But we need to distinguish between the contract and its embedding relation. It may well be plausible to say that, as employment contracts become more heavily regulated (as the law determines more aspects of the relation between employers and employees regardless of their contract), employment relations become less contractual. But this does not make it plausible to say that, as employment contracts become more regulated, employment *contracts* become less contractual. The fact that contracts of type X are regulated more heavily than contracts of type Y has no tendency to show that contracts of type X are less paradigmatically contractual than contracts of type Y. Presumably if contracts of type X are more heavily regulated, then the conditions of forming such contracts are more demanding. But by hypothesis, contracts of type X fully meet the conditions set by law, however demanding. Surely the fact that a contract meets more demanding legal conditions does not make it *less* contractual. Similarly, there is no reason to believe that heavy regulation of type X contracts reflects law's reluctance to enforce them. It only reflects law's reluctance to enforce unregulated type X contracts.

I conclude that as relational contract theorists have long argued, many perfectly representative contracts are embedded in robust long-term personal and economic relationships and extra-legal social norms. I now remark on some arguments for contractual transactionalism mentioned in the previous section.

Detachment. Recall Kimel's first argument for his detachment thesis: the sanction-enforceability of contracts enables parties (avails them of the option) to co-operate and pursue valuable goals in transactional/ discrete contexts. This is exactly right, but it provides no support for the detachment thesis, the view that personal detachment is the main, intrinsic, or normal goal of contracts or contract law. It is compatible with the view that some perfectly good contracts are highly relational in context.[57]

Kimel's second, implicit argument for the detachment thesis is that significant personal relations provide parties with all the assurance they need to cooperate as they wish. But isn't sanction-enforceability some-times necessary for cooperation in highly relational contexts? For one thing, the parties might want to insure against the breakdown of their relationship. For another, they might generally trust each other in the robust sense and still lack confidence that the other will perform certain specific actions.

The cogency of the detachment thesis then turns entirely on Kimel's negative argument from motivational opacity. I want to grant its first premise and question its second, largely empirical premise, that by generating sufficient self-interested reason/incentive to perform, the sanction-enforceability of contracts creates motivational opacity: for all that a contractor knows, the other contractor's performance has been motivated by fear of sanction. My main worry is that to deliver the conclusion, the premise must be read to imply that if you are in no position to tell that I have kept our contract *other than from* fear of sanction, you are also in no position to tell that I have done so *from* robust respect for you. Otherwise, you could reasonably ascribe me

---

[57] It is not clear whether Kimel still holds that personal detachment is *the* intrinsic normal function of contracts. He recently describes personal detachment simply as 'one of the most important functions of contract law' (2007: 247). This threatens to trivialize the detachment thesis, and repudiate Kimel's claim that promise and contracts have 'diametrically opposed' normal functions (relation vs. detachment). It is compatible with the claim that personal relation is among the intrinsic normal function of contracts.

the right sort of motive, after all. But the said assumption is a close relative of the view rejected in section 5, namely that one cannot perform an action from both self-interested and benevolent reasons. In fact, your interests or our relationship might generate a sufficient reason for me to keep the contract, alongside the one generated by the law. Similarly, I can keep my contract out of fear of sanction *and* robust respect for you. But then you might in principle know for a fact that I have performed (partly) from fear of sanction *and* that I have done so (partly) out of robust respect for you. *A fortiori*, your presumed inability reliably to exclude the former possibility does nothing to exclude the latter.

The empirical premise of the argument from motivational opacity is problematic for another reason: it assumes that the sanction-enforceability of contracts provides or should provide sufficient reason to keep them, a self-interested reason strong enough to motivate performance by itself. But at least in Anglo-American legal systems, remedies for breach are often insufficient to deter breach apart from other reasons to perform, such as dependence on the continued cooperation of the other party. Nor can we salvage this assumption by interpreting it as a conceptual claim about *ideal* contract systems. There is no obvious reason to want contract remedies that motivate performance by themselves, rather than together with other self and other-regarding reasons. More to the point, why not think that optimal contract remedies are those that suffice to motivate performance in conjunction with other factors *if performance is desirable?*

The detachment thesis—the notion that perfect contracts promote personal detachment—is only as persuasive as the argument from motivational opacity. But that argument is based on questionable assumptions.

Arm's Length. Recall the three marks of perfect contracts according to Markovits: self-interest, reciprocity, and positive law. Markovits claims that these three features of contracts make them inherently distancing. That is why contracts are a particularly central case of arm's-length relations. But none of these features seems *inherently* inimical to intimate personal relationships. Consider self-interest. In a significant long-term personal relationship, we often act for the sake of the other or the relationship. But as just noted in relation to the detachment thesis, such action does not exclude self-interest. The merging of self- and other-regarding attitudes is the mark of loving or caring relationship. In such relationship it is both common and appropriate to act for the sake of the other *as well as for your own sake.*

Something similar can be said about reciprocity. Contacts are reciprocal in the sense that each party commits in exchange for the other's commitment. But notice that if this sort of reciprocity is in any way inimical to intimacy or significant long-term relationships then *all* agreements are. For all agreements are reciprocal in this way. And I see no more reason to think that agreements as such are inimical to intimacy than to think that promises are. There is nothing less than perfectly paradigmatic about agreements in highly relational contexts. Even parties to the most intimate of personal relations must cooperate, and agreements are excellent cooperation devices. Indeed there is something counterintuitive about the thought that *non*reciprocal—or unilateral—promises are *more* suitable for intimate relations than reciprocal promises (agreements).

Finally, is positive law inherently distancing or otherwise inimical to intimacy? The example of Islamic marriage contracts (and enforceable spousal contracts generally) suggests not; it suggests that the relation between positive law and intimacy is merely contingent. There is no denial that the legality of contracts is relevant to the advisability or adequacy of entering into them, as well as to the advisability or adequacy of contractualizing (making enforceable) certain types of contract (contracts regulating sexual life in detail, say). What I deny is only the notion that legally binding contracts are *inherently* opposed to intimacy.

Contractual Pluralism

Beginning to emerge is

Contractual pluralism. Perfect or paradigmatic contracts are relational or transactional in context. In the central case, contracts are embedded in some relational, transactional, or mixed relational-transactional context. (See diagram 7.)

Notice again that this goes beyond the observation that contracts are in fact made in all these social contexts; it also makes the stronger claim that both relational and transactional contracts can be perfectly paradigmatic—that the central case of contracts (the inner doughnut in the diagram) is split. Put negatively, the claim is that contracts are neither *primarily*-relational-and-secondarily-transactional nor *primarily-*

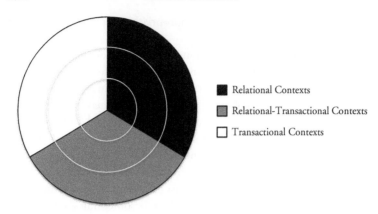

Diagram 7: Contractual Pluralism

Outer doughnut represents the zone of contractual imperfection.
Inner doughnut represents the zone of partial contractual perfection.
Inner doughnut hole represents the zone of contractual perfection.

transactional-and-secondarily-relational. The claim is potentially interesting because it runs counter to potentially interesting relational and transactional theories of contracts.

Now just how strong or pluralistic contractual pluralism is depends on our working conception of the relational–transactional distinction. I cannot exclude the possibility that the view comes out false under some plausible interpretation of that distinction. At the same time, I also cannot think of a plausible interpretation of the distinction under which contractual pluralism comes out false. It clearly seems to me to come out true under a wide range of plausible interpretations of the relational-transactional distinction, including, as I have tried to show, some of those currently on offer in the literature.

9. CONCLUSION

I close by bringing promissory and contractual pluralism into contact. After all, I have suggested (without argument) that contracts are agreements and that agreements are joint promises. What emerges is a picture in which the diversity of contractual promises reflects the diversity of agreement promises, which in turn reflects the diversity of promises. Consider

Wide promissory pluralism

(1) Promises are relational or transactional in context. In the central case, promises are embedded in some relational, transactional, or mixed relational-transactional context.

(2) Agreement promises are relational or transactional in context. In the central case, agreement promises are embedded in some relational, transactional, or mixed relational-transactional context.

(3) Contractual promises are relational or transactional in context. In the central case, contractual promises are embedded in some relational, transactional, or mixed relational-transactional context.

(See diagram 8.)

Promises, understood broadly to include agreement promises and contractual promises, emerge from the discussion as a highly adaptable social animal, one that can function perfectly well in radically different social habitats. On this picture, we make promises in pretty much every social context, be it relational, transactional, or anywhere in between. Different promises are made under different promising practices, animated by

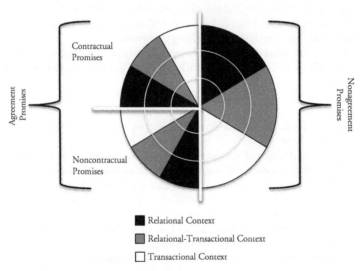

Diagram 8: Wide Promissory Pluralism
Outer doughnut represents the zone of promissory imperfection.
Inner doughnut represents the zone of partial promissory perfection.
Inner doughnut hole represents the zone of promissory perfection.

different attitudes, and governed by different social norms. Promises can play a proper role in all these settings, if only by promoting all-purpose interpersonal cooperation over time.

REFERENCES

Aristotle. 1999. *Nicomachean Ethics* T. Irwin (trans.), Indianapolis: Hackett Publishing.

Austin, J. L. 1962. *How to Do Things with Words*. Cambridge, MA: Harvard University Press.

Bagchi, A. 2009. 'Contract versus Promise,' in R. Barnett (ed.), *Perspective on Contract Law*. Austin: Walters Kluwer.

Baier, A. 1985. *Postures of the Mind*. Minneapolis: University of Minnesota Press.

Baier, A. 1994. *Moral Prejudices*. Cambridge, MA: Harvard University Press.

Barnett, R. 1992. 'Conflicting Visions: A Critique of Ian Macneil's Relational Theory of Contract,' *Virginia Law Review* 78: 1175–1206.

Bernstein, L. 1996. 'Merchant Law in a Merchant Court,' *University of Pennsylvania Law Review* 144: 1765.

Butler, J. 1983 [1726]. *Five Sermons*. Hackett Publishing Company.

Campbell, D. 1996. 'The Relational Constitution of Discrete Contracts,' in D. Campbell and P. Vincent-Jones (eds.), *Contract and Economic Organization*. Aldershot: Dartmouth Publishing Company.

——2001. 'Ian Macneil and the Relational Theory of Contract,' in *The Relational Theory of Contract: Selected Works by Ian Macneil*. London: Sweet & Maxwell.

Dan-Cohen, M. 2002. *Harmful Thoughts*. Princeton: Princeton Universtiy Press.

Darwall, S. 2006. *The Second-Person Standpoint*. Cambridge, MA: Harvard University Press.

——2009. 'Authority and Second-Personal Reasons for Acting,' in D. Sobel & S. Wall (eds.), *Reasons for Action*. Cambridge: Cambridge University Press.

——2011. 'Demystifying Promises,' in Sheinman, *Promises and Agreements*.

Deigh, J. 2012. 'Reactive Attitudes Revisited,' in C. Bagnoli, (ed.), *Morality and the Emotions*. Oxford: Oxford University Press.

Eisenberg, M. 2000. 'Why There Is No Law of Relational Contracts,' *Northwestern University Law Review* 94(3): 805–21.

Frankfurt, H. 1999. *Necessity, Volition, and Love*. Cambridge: Cambridge University Press.

Fried, C. 1981. *Contract as Promise*. Cambridge, MA: Harvard University Press.

——2007. 'The Convergence of Contract and Promise,' *Harvard Law Review* 120: 1–9.

Friedrich, D. and Southwood, N. 2011. 'Promises and Trust,' in Sheinman, *Promises and Agreements*.

Green, L. 2010. 'Two Worries about Respect for Persons,' *Ethics* 120: 212–31.

Hart, H. L. A. 1955. 'Are There Any Natural Rights?' *Philosophical Review* 64: 175–91.

—— 1992. *The Concept of Law*. Oxford: Oxford University Press.

Hoeble, E.A. 1954. *The Law of Primitive Man*. Cambridge, MA: Harvard University Press.

Hume, D. 2006. *Moral Writings*. Indianapolis: Hackett Publishing Company.

Kagan, S. 1998. 'Rethinking Intrinsic Value,' *Journal of Ethics* 2: 277–97.

Kant, I. 1998 [1785]. *Groundwork of the Metaphysics of Morals*. (M. Gregor, ed.) Cambridge: Cambridge University Press.

Kecia, A. 2008. 'Marriage in Classical Islamic Jurisprudence,' in A. Quraishi & F. Vogel (eds.), *The Islamic Marriage Contract*. Cambridge, MA: Harvard University Press.

Kimel, D. 2003. *From Promise to Contract*. Oxford: Hart Publishing.

—— 2007. 'The Choice of Paradigm for Theory of Contract: Reflections on the Relational Model,' *Oxford Journal of Legal Studies* 27: 233–55.

Leib, E. 2009. 'Relational Contract Theory: A Sympathetic Reconstruction,' in R. Barnett (ed.), *Perspective on Contract Law*. Austin: Walters Kluwer.

Lifshitz, S. 2012. 'The Liberal Transformation of Spousal Law,' *Theoretical Inquiries in Law* 13: 15–73.

Macaulay, S. 1963. 'Non-Contractual Relations in Business,' *American Sociological Review* 28: 55–69.

—— 2003. 'The Real and the Paper Deal,' in *Implicit Dimensions of Contract*, D. Campbell, H. Collins, and J. Wightman (eds.) Oxford: Hart Publishing.

Macneil, I. 1974. 'The Many Futures of Contract.' *Southern California Law Review* 47: 691–816.

—— 1980. *The New Social Contract*. New Haven: Yale University Press.

—— 2000. 'Relational Contract Theory: Challenges and Queries,' *Northwestern University Law Review* 94: 877–907.

Markovits, D. 2011. 'Promise as an Arm's-Length Relation,' in Sheinman, *Promises and Agreements*.

McNeilly, F.S. 1972. 'Promises De-Moralized,' *Philosophical Review* 81: 63–81.

Raz, J. 1982. 'Promises in Morality and Law,' *Harvard Law Review* 95: 916–38.

Scott, R. 2000. 'The Case for Formalism in Relational Contract,' *Northwestern University Law Review* 94: 847–76.

Searle, J. 1969. *Speech Acts*. Cambridge: Cambridge University Press.

Shiffrin, S. 2008. 'Promising, Intimate Relationships, and Conventionalism,' *Philosophical Review* 117: 481–524.

Sheinman, S. 2011. 'Agreement as Joint Promise,' in *Promises and Agreements: Philosophical Essays*. New York: Oxford University Press.

Sommers, T. 2007. 'The Objective Attitude,' *Philosophical Quarterly* 57: 321–41.

Strawson, P. 2008 [1962]. 'Freedom and Resentment,' in *Freedom and Resentment and Other Essays*. London: Routledge.

Watson, G. 2009. 'Promises, Reasons and Normative Powers', in D. Sobel and S. Wall (eds.), *Reasons for Action*. Cambridge: Cambridge University Press.

Williamson, T. 2000. *Knowledge and its Limits*. Oxford: Oxford University Press.

Wolf, S. 1981. 'The Importance of Free Will,' *Mind* 90: 386–405.

Wynn, L. 2008. 'Marriage Contract and Women's Rights in Saudi Arabia,' in A. Quraishi and F. Vogel (eds.), *The Islamic Marriage Contract*. Cambridge, MA: Harvard University Press.

9

Legal Sex*

LUÍS DUARTE D'ALMEIDA

I

1

Most legal provisions apply to classes of individuals not coincident with the class of all persons. The classification used may follow any criterion whatsoever; a common taxonomy divides persons, according to their 'sex', into 'women' and 'men'. Laws assigning different statuses to men and women are by now fewer in number, and less in import, than in other periods in modern history. The general pattern of denying women a set of rights and benefits typically granted to men, though not yet expunged from contemporary legal systems, is nonetheless mitigated. But the law continues to distinguish between women and men. I shall here be concerned with one instance of this differentiation—an instance that remains in play in the law of marriage in the majority of legal systems.

Many jurisdictions still prevent women from marrying women, and men from marrying men. Whether provisions of this kind amount to wrongful discrimination is a disputed issue. Even among those who find that policy to be discriminatory (as I do), it has been debated what the grounds of such discrimination are. I do not purport here to address these questions. My interest is in the *meaning* of those terms—'man' and 'woman'—as they figure in the kind of provisions by which, in different systems, 'same-sex' marriage is proscribed.

* For helpful comments and discussion I am grateful to Andrea Dolcetti, Barbara Havelk-ová, Benjamin Spagnolo, James Edwards, Jenny Saul, John Gardner, Leslie Green, Matthew Kramer, Pedro Múrias, and audiences in Barcelona, Buenos Aires, Cambridge, Edinburgh, and Oxford.

This chapter is thus occupied, in a way, with a matter of legal interpretation. No particular allusion will however be made to the materials of any given legal system. The discussion will instead be held at a higher level of generality, so as to range over any jurisdiction whose laws on marriage include provisions stipulating that

(1) No woman may marry another woman; a woman may only marry a man;

(2) No man may marry another man; a man may only marry a woman;

and which accordingly determine that

(3) A couple is allowed to marry only if it is a couple of a woman and a man.

Marriage in such jurisdictions is often defined as being a relationship only between persons of 'opposite sexes', or of persons of 'different sexes', or as a union between 'a man and a woman'. The precise words are irrelevant for my purposes. Provided that the content of the corresponding provisions can be stated (or restated) in the conjunction of (1), (2), and (3)—and provided, moreover, that no-one is by law prevented on the grounds of 'sex' from marrying *someone*—then such a jurisdiction falls within the scope of my discussion. For expository convenience I will sometimes refer to (1), (2), and (3) as 'provisions', as if those formulations were themselves the very provisions they mean to restate.

In any particular case, of course, the application of these provisions requires that we be able to ascertain a person's membership of one of the two classes—that we have a criterion by which to determine when an individual counts as a woman or a man. This is the question I mean to address.

Most legal systems adopt the practice of officially registering a person's 'sex' in documents of a special kind—for example, on birth certificates, issued shortly after the moment of birth, and subsequently in various other documents. Moreover, the law often instructs judges and other legal officials to rely on such documents whenever for some reason the need arises to establish whether someone is a woman or a man. If and when such rules exist, there is a sense in which we may say that someone registered as a 'woman' (or a 'man') would *count as* a woman (or a man) for the purposes of provisions (1) to (3). One would count as such in virtue of the rule prescribing officials to rely on the content of the documentary inscription to determine whether the conditions of those provisions are satisfied.

This is not, however, the sense of 'counting as' in which I am interested. The point may be made clear if we think of another element which, like sex, is usually officially certified: a person's birth date. That one was born on a given date is a fact that exists independently of registration, a fact that law purports faithfully to document. The inscription in a birth certificate of a person's birth date is thus, in a sense, descriptive; it is the type of inscription which we may intelligibly say to be true or false. Suppose, then, that some legal provision defines a specific legal status for individuals of a certain age: take, for example, a provision stipulating that everyone aged 65 or older is entitled to some health-related benefits. Suppose, additionally, that when it comes to determining whether some person falls under that age-class the officials in charge of applying this provision are legally required to take into account only the inscription in a birth certificate of a person's birth date—assume, in other words, that the inscription has the force of what is normally called an irrebuttable (or *iuris et de iure*) presumption. In this example, a person will be *deemed* by legal officials *as* falling under the legally relevant age-class if and only if the age calculated from the registered birth date is, at the moment of applying the provision, 65 years or more. We remain nonetheless perfectly capable of distinguishing between the fact described in the provision as a condition of the benefit—which is the fact that someone 'really' is 65 years or older—and the fact that someone is *registered as* being 65 years or older. These facts ideally coincide. But the registered information may for any number of reasons (including false beliefs on the part of the acting officer) not match the reality that it purports to describe. Some of those documents upon which legal officials are instructed to rely may in fact happen to be false. Whether or not an individual 'really' is 65 years old becomes in practice irrelevant if these documents are given this kind of conclusive force. But it seems clear that if we wonder what the relevant age-related terms in our imaginary provision may mean—if we wonder what it means for someone to *be* 65 years or older—the answer to this question will have nothing to do with whether some system is actually in place for registering people's ages, nor with whether such documents, should they exist, happen to be given the force conclusively to determine when someone will, in practice, be deemed as falling under one of those terms. The question about the terms' meaning is independent of these facts about registration and its force.

To be sure, this distinction cannot be drawn with regard to all register inscriptions. It holds only for those inscriptions that purport to document some fact or event that exists independently of the registration system itself. Contrast birthdates with another type of element also commonly registered in birth certificates and similar documents: names. We may in different contexts have different names. We may be 'Ernest in town and Jack in the country'. And we all normally have a name in the legal context, a name for legal purposes—a legal name. Now, names, whatever the context, are always the result of an act of name-attribution. Names are given to us. Procedures may of course vary; some names in some contexts may have been intentionally chosen by someone; some are self-given; others may have been the result of collective, non-intentional dubbing processes. In the legal context the attribution of a legal name is often performed by the inscription of a name in a birth certificate or a similar document. The act of validly and successfully inscribing a name in such a document, then, is in this case the act by which the name is given, as a legal name, to an individual. Such an inscription is neither true nor false: it is attributive, rather than descriptive.[1]

---

[1] Some further remarks may help ensure that this point is sufficiently clear. In any context, town or country, and whatever the process by which a name has been given to you, it will, once validly assigned, *become* your name in that context. The *fact* that that is your name, in other words, will thenceforth have come into existence, and the proposition will from then on be true that your name in that context *is* such-and-such. The same holds with regard to your legal name. If and when the attribution is validly performed, you thereby acquire a legal name. Your legal name is the product, rather than the object, of the inscription in the certificate; if the inscription is successful—if it is validly performed—the relevant person will then have been given a legal name. The point, thus, is not that there is no fact of the matter about what a person's legal name is. Of course there is. The point is that there is (and there can be) no fact of the matter about a person's legal name that a certificate purports to match. For the legal name itself is a product of the inscriptive act, and has no prior and independent existence. Nor is the non-descriptive, attributive character of legal name-registering in any way impugned by the fact that, usually, legal name-formulations are chosen by persons acting in a non-official capacity—by one's parents, for example—and stated by them before the registry officer, who is then under the duty to inscribe, in the certificate, precisely the name so stated. Rules to this effect, when they exist, will form part of the legally determined procedure on whose observance the valid assignment of legal names depends—a procedure that ordinarily also incorporates several other positive and negative requisites (e.g. ruling out some names as ineligible, or determining what surnames may or must be registered, and in what order). But that the name inscribed needs, as a matter of valid procedure, to match the name-formulation chosen by the parents does not mean that the legal register of one's name is descriptive in purpose. The

The law, it is true, does not often associate particular legal conse-quences to classes of individuals defined according to their names. This is hardly surprising, given that a person's name, being as it is the product of an arbitrary ascription, does not signal any relevant distinction that might justifiably ground the imposition of differential treatment. When the law does distinguish persons according to their names, it normally does so for purely organizational purposes (as when it makes use of alphabetical ordering to determine in which electoral section a person should vote). When or if it does, however, it will be clear that the ques-tion whether someone 'really' is a member of the legally defined class cannot be dissociated of the question of *as what* (i.e. under what name) that person is registered. The fact described in the provision—the fact that someone is named such-and-such—is in this case a fact created by the register. It will therefore be impossible to determine whether someone is a member of the relevant class without taking the register into account. In contrast to what happens with one's birth date and age, there is no room here for false positives or negatives nor for any distinction in con-tent between what 'is' the case and what, on the basis of some document or certificate, 'counts as' being the case. One's 'real' name just is one's registered name.

One may thus wonder: when asking what it means for someone to *be* a man or a woman for the purposes of provisions (1) to (3), is it the case that—as with provisions that attach legal consequences to a person's age—'man' and 'woman' refer to facts about persons that exist inde-pendently of the law and of any system of registration? Or is it instead that—as with provisions associating legal effects to one's name—these terms refer to facts about persons that are produced by the legally adopted system of registration? Is our sex more like our age, or more like our name? The answer may be thought to be evident: you *are* of course a man or a woman irrespective of what your certificate says. This seems indeed to be widely assumed. I will suggest otherwise.

inscription itself is meant neither as a register of what the name-formulation stated by the parents was, nor as a register of the fact that the parents have made such a statement. If the inscribed name happens not to coincide with the formulation stated by the parents, the inscrip-tion may or may not be invalid, but it is certainly not false; and coincidence will make it valid rather than true. It is likewise commonly the case that the acting officer is under the duty to register as one's date of birth the date stated before him by the parents, but it does not follow that the purpose of the inscription is to register either the statement made or its content: the purpose is in any case to register the actual birth date.

2

Let me reiterate that my concern is solely with the terms 'woman' and 'man' as they are employed in the typical provisions on the validity of marriage that the conjunction of formulations (1) to (3) is meant to apprehend. And we have established that, *if*, in such provisions, 'man' and 'woman' are descriptive of facts that exist independently of the law and of our documenting practices, we should be able (as we are with a person's age) to pursue the question of what those terms may mean while leaving aside all issues pertaining to the register of a person's 'sex' or to the force of such documents. In order to explore this hypothesis, then, let us now directly concentrate on the provisions themselves.

What law-independent facts about an individual might make it true that someone is a woman or a man? In searching for an answer one will naturally turn to the biological factors of sexual differentiation in the human species. There are several such factors. In a common way of presenting them, we may distinguish among genetic factors (or chromosomal: XX for females, XY for males); gonadal factors (reproductive sex glands: ovaries or testes); internal morphological factors (vagina, uterus, fallopian tubes for females; seminal vesicles and prostate for males); external morphological factors (genitals: clitoris and labia for females, penis and scrotum for males); hormonal patterns (predominance of estrogens or androgens); and phenotypical factors (breasts for females; facial and chest hair for males).[2]

The exact values exhibited for each of these factors by any individual are undoubtedly a matter of fact, independent of any law or register. But before we ponder whether we can appropriately rely on any one—or any combination—of these factors to determine what it means for someone to be a 'man' or a 'woman' for the purposes of our provisions on marriage, let me underline a point that, trivial as it may sound, should be kept in mind. The facts for which we are looking have to be such that the following is true:

(4) Any person is either a man or a woman.

---

[2] There are many summaries available, addressed at lay audiences, of the relevant medical information. A particularly detailed and useful digest is given by Julie A. Greenberg, 'Defining Male and Female: Intersexuality and the Collision between Law and Biology', *Arizona Law Review* 41 (1999) 265–328.

The disjunction in (4) is exclusive: no one person may be both a man and a woman. For the purposes of our provisions, moreover, the man/woman distinction also has to be exhaustive of the domain of persons: there is no room for the possibility that someone is neither a woman nor a man. These two requirements may be derived from provisions (1) to (3) themselves. On the one hand, these provisions clearly determine that only a union of a man and a woman may count as a marriage. If the terms 'man' and 'woman' were not here jointly exhaustive of the universe of persons, some individuals would count as neither men nor women. Those persons would then not be allowed to marry anyone at all. But, as noted, this possibility is clearly ruled out, as a matter of law, in the legal systems that I am considering. In these systems, while the fact that a couple is composed of a man and a woman is only a necessary condition for such union to be recognized as a marriage, and not a sufficient one (a father and a daughter, for example, are generally not allowed to marry), the hetero-sexuality requirement is clearly not *itself* intended to exclude anyone from the very possibility of entering a marriage. Provided all other conditions and impediments are observed, the type of unions defined by the hetero-sexuality requirement is such that anybody may be a member of one.

This assumption that the 'woman'/'man' distinction, as employed in the law of marriage, is exhaustive of the universe of individuals is, by the way, extremely common. It is clearly behind, for example, the formulation in article 16 of the Universal Declaration of Human Rights, which reads (with my italics): '*Men* and *women* of full age, without any limitation due to race, nationality or religion, have the right to marry and to found a family'. If marriage is recognized as a human right—as it is here, and also at the constitutional level of many legal systems that allow only woman/man marriages—then it is necessarily assumed that the combination of the classes of 'men' and 'women' exhausts the class of persons.[3]

The exclusivity of the distinction also stems from the provisions on marriage. This requisite can be grounded on the combination of the exhaustiveness requirement and the fact (just underlined) that no-one will be prevented, just on the grounds of sex, from marrying someone.

---

[3] Article 2 moreover determines that '*everyone* is entitled to all the rights and freedoms set forth in this Declaration, without distinction of any kind, such as race, colour, *sex*, language, religion, political or other opinion, national or social origin, property, birth, or other status' (italics added); precisely to the same effect, cf. articles 12 and 14 of the European Convention on Human Rights.

For if it were possible for someone to count both as a 'man' and a 'woman', the result would again be that this person would not be able to marry anyone: this person, counting as a man, would be precluded from marrying a man; and for converse reasons would also be prevented from marrying a woman. Given the exhaustiveness requirement, this would imply that the person would not be able to marry anyone: there would be no one left to marry. But the exclusivity requirement may likewise be derived from the seeming purpose of these provisions, which appear to mean symmetrically to constrict the right of everyone to marry a person of the same sex, while allowing everyone to marry a person of the 'opposite' sex; which again seems to assume that everyone is of one and only one sex.

The meanings of 'man' and 'woman', then, as typically employed in the provisions of legal systems relative to which (1), (2), and (3) are simultaneously true, have to be such that it is the case both that every person who is not a woman is man, and that every person who is not a man is a woman. Each class has to be definable as the complement of the other in the domain of persons.

3

As I am paying closer attention to provisions (1) to (3) themselves, I shall take the opportunity—before moving on to consider the facts of sex—to make a further remark.

Speaking somewhat broadly, we tend to treat the content of any policy or legislative provision that *is* the law at any given moment as if its adoption or enactment were, in some sense, the result of a decision made by a rational agent. If some particular policy has in fact been espoused, and implemented as law, there must have been some rationale for its adoption; there will be for every *lex*, we tend to think, a corresponding *ratio legis*.

Let me offer a general reconstruction of this idea. For any policy which has in fact been validly adopted, we may plausibly attribute to the adopting authority—and indeed, more broadly, to 'the law' itself—a commitment to the normative proposition that that policy *should* be the case. Suppose, for example, that in some legal system a provision is validly enacted which denies the right to vote to individuals younger than 18 years. The proposition will then be true, as a matter of law, and relative to that system, that

(5) Individuals younger than 18 years are not allowed to vote.

Consider, now, the proposition that

(6) Individuals younger than 18 years should not be allowed to vote.

If (6) is true, there is a sense in which we may say that the policy described in (5) is justified; for then what *is* the case (in that system) matches what *should be* the case (in the same system). And given that law stipulates that (5), we may sensibly suppose that law is committed to—that it holds a belief, as it were, in—(6).[4]

The rationale for (5), then—and this is my suggestion—will be given by a valid argument having (6) as its conclusion. As (6) is a normative proposition, any such argument will have to combine, as premises, at least one normative proposition and one descriptive, factual proposition. But not just any valid argument having (6) as its conclusion will provide a rationale for (5). Indeed, there are an infinite number of valid arguments that we might construct with (6) as a conclusion and that would not give us a rationale for (4). Here is an example:

(A1) Individuals with green eyes should not be allowed to vote;
     Every individual younger than 18 years has green eyes;
     ∴ Individuals younger than 18 years should not be allowed to vote.

(A1), although valid, does not provide us with a rationale for the provision that individuals under 18 years of age are not allowed to vote. The problem is not that the premises are false or unwarranted, as they both clearly are. The problem is that—excluding from consideration surreal legal systems extravagantly aloof from what we might actually find in our societies—we may not plausibly assume that the reason why the policy was legally adopted of denying active electoral capacity to anyone under 18 years old was because of a commitment to *those* premises. A more plausible articulation of the rationale for a provision such as (5) would perhaps look something more like this:

---

[4] This idiom is at least partly metaphorical; but it stands at the same explanatory level at which we normally, and intelligibly, speak of what 'the law' 'requires', or 'says', or even 'wants'.

(A2) Only individuals sufficiently mature to make rational choices
　　　should be allowed to vote;
　　　An individual is sufficiently mature to make rational choices if and
　　　only if that individual is 18 years or older;
　　　∴ Individuals younger than 18 years old should not be allowed to
　　　vote.

The premises might of course still be false, but that is beside the point. And you might disagree with the conclusion—in which case you might directly dispute one or both premises; or you might endorse a different set of premises that entails a conclusion incompatible with (6), which would implicitly commit you to denying at least one of the premises. Or you might refute the premises but agree with the conclusion, provided that you endorse a different set of premises that entails (6). But whether we agree or disagree with the conclusion, we can at least grasp how such a rationale might lie behind the legal adoption of a provision like (5).[5]

Thus (and I mean this simply as a general, inchoate way of explaining our notion of a legal provision's rationale) when we look for the rationale of some given legal provision or policy, we are looking for a valid argument with premises that we may plausibly attribute to the adopting authority as the premises on which it may have relied to get to that normative conclusion which, if true, justifies the adopted policy. If we can assume that the authority took those premises took to be true, we are able to explain why it also took the corresponding normative conclusion to be true. So we can take on this general reconstruction:

Rationale: the rationale of a legal provision is a set of premises such that
　　　(*a*) they jointly entail a normative proposition which, if true, justifies
　　　the provision; and (*b*) we can plausibly attribute to the enacting or
　　　adopting authority (and thus, more generally, to 'the law') a commit-
　　　ment to (or a belief in) their truth.

---

[5] Though a weaker second premise—stating simply that an individual's being 18 years or older is a necessary (not also a sufficient) condition of that individual being sufficiently mature to make rational choices—would suffice for (A2) to be logically valid, we need the stronger kind of premise if our rationale is fully to account for the *specific* adoption of the provision in question (as opposed to some other, broader provision or policy that might conceivably serve the same purpose). I return to this point in section 4.

Some qualifications need to be added. First, the articulation of a ration-ale is not meant to display the actual, historical reasons or motives of the person or organ that enacted the provision—although it may be that such historical facts need in some way to be taken into account in the operation. Second, I do not wish to suggest that the rationale of a legal provision will necessarily take the form of a single, simple argument. It may be necessary to go on enquiring what further premises accepted by law as true explain its commitment to the premises that *directly* ground the normative conclusion which, if true, would justify the provision; and in this case the rationale will be presented in the form of a complex chain of arguments. There is no logical limit to the strands of complex-ity here, though the enquiry will be pragmatically bounded by the needs of legal practitioners. Third, I also do not mean my definition to imply that for any given provision only one rationale can be plausibly articu-lated. There may well be several competing plausible reconstructions of a legal provision's rationale.

Nor do I intend to suggest that for any provision or policy which is the law at any place and time there will necessarily *be* at least one devis-able rationale. Compare, for example,

(7) Persons born on Wednesdays are not allowed to vote;

and

(8) Women are not allowed to vote.

Even if you find that no plausible rationale for it has premises that you agree to be true, the policy in (8)—which was once the law in many countries—will not come out as a policy *without* a rationale. But (7), on the other hand, will probably strike you as an arbitrary or irrational policy. You will be unable to fathom what the fact that someone is born on a Wednesday could possibly have to do with being allowed to vote.

It is not often that we find a legal provision for which *no* rationale can be formulated. Generally speaking, we expect that if some policy became the law, it became the law for some reason or other. The expectation is defeasible, but normally justified.

4

All this is true of the provisions on marriage I am discussing, which it may be useful once again to exhibit:

(1) No woman may marry another woman; a woman may only marry a man;
(2) No man may marry another man; a man may only marry a woman;
(3) A couple is allowed to marry only if it is a couple of a woman and a man.

Perhaps it is especially to be expected that a rationale underlying these provisions can be articulated. Not only is the heterosexuality requirement enforced as law in many countries; it is among the most publicly discussed of legal policies today. When arguing in favour of provisions (1) to (3), as many people do, one will be expressing a commitment to an underlying rationale; and likewise the arguments of opponents of the heterosexuality requirement are arguments that typically engage with, and question the truth of, possible premises of possible rationales.

There must moreover be a *common* rationale to these provisions. The point is worth mentioning: (1) and (2), as they stand, are logically independent. It would be possible for law to determine that men would be allowed to marry only women, but at the same time to grant women the right to marry anyone, or vice versa. But it seems sensible to assume that the reason why in our legal systems a man is not allowed to marry another man is the same reason why a woman is not allowed to marry another woman. It will be the reason for not allowing 'same-sex' marriages, permitting only woman/man couples to count as married; and so it will also be the reason for (3). The underlying rationale will take the form of a valid argument whose conclusion will be

(9) A couple should be allowed to marry only if it is a couple of a woman and a man.

So the rationale will have to refer to some property or feature whose presence is considered *necessary* for marriage to be recognized, and which all and only woman/man couples are deemed to exhibit. Here is the structure that the corresponding argument will have to display:

(A3) A couple should be allowed to marry only if it is...;
        A couple is...if and only if it is a couple of a woman and a man;
        ∴ A couple should be allowed to marry only if it is a couple of a woman and a man.

The normative premise in (A3) will state some necessary, though not sufficient, condition for a couple to be allowed to marry (a condition which is in (A3) represented by '…'). This is meant to capture the possibility that law makes other demands which a couple will also need to meet in order to be allowed to marry.[6] The descriptive premise, in turn, states a condition both necessary and sufficient for a couple to meet the *necessary condition for marriage* stated in the normative premise. Why this stronger premise? The law must hold, first, that only woman/man couples exhibit the feature identified in the normative premise as a necessary condition for marriage. The law must hold, in other words, that that feature is not displayed by either of the other two possible combinations, woman/woman or man/man. But the law must also hold all 'woman'/'man' couples to exhibit such a feature; for it cannot otherwise be the case that the rationale behind the adoption of this *particular* policy (the heterosexuality requirement), instead of any other policy focusing on some condition necessary for a couple to be…, is grounded—or grounded simply—on the law's commitment to a normative premise like the one in (A3).

Taking stock: the meaning of 'man' and 'woman' in provisions (1) to (3) has to be such that it is simultaneously the case that

(*a*) the fact that one is a man or a woman is connected in some non-arbitrary way (i.e. according to some rationale) to the consequence of allowing only woman/man couples to marry; and that

(*b*) every person is either a man or a woman, and no person is both a man and a woman.

This is no surprise. These requisites are requisites that we actually expect to be simultaneously satisfied by the terms 'man' and 'woman' as they occur in the familiar provisions that prevent same-sex couples from marrying.

What facts, then, might make it true that someone is a woman or a man in a sense that satisfies both (*a*) and (*b*)? None. There are no such facts. Or so I will now suggest.

5

(5.1) Consider what might seem like a good candidate rationale for allowing only woman/man couples to marry: a rationale somehow

---

[6] This is normally the case, as already noted; each such other demand will have its own particular rationale.

linked to the ability of the spouses jointly to produce offspring by engaging in biological reproduction. The normative premise in the corresponding justificatory argument could be formulated along the following lines:

A couple should be allowed to marry only if its members are jointly able to engage in biological reproduction.[7]

If this were our normative premise, could we find any facts about being a 'woman' or a 'man' that might, in the minor premise, do the necessary work? Yes, we could. Human biological reproduction requires the intervention of two members of the species, each of whom possessing a different set of characteristics directly connected to the distinction between female and male humans. Resorting to our stock of possibly relevant facts, we would be able to define 'man', for example, as a human individual having a male reproductive system—which would involve the cumulative possession of male gonads, male internal morphologic sex, and male external morphologic sex (no congruence as to chromosomal sex would be necessary, nor as to phenotype)—and to define 'woman' along similar lines.

Observe, however, that each of these predicates, 'man' and 'woman', either applies or does not apply to each possible individual: every person is either a man or not a man; either a woman or not a woman. And under the definitions just suggested it is not necessarily the case that for every person who is not a woman, that person is a man, nor that for every person who is not a man, that person is a woman. For, as a matter of fact, there are persons who have neither male nor female reproductive organs. While it is statistically true that most individuals, by far, are central cases of 'male' or 'female' relative to each factor of sexual differentiation, and true, also, that a majority of individuals is likewise congruent across factors, there are nonetheless not only persons who are incongruent across factors (even if they may for each factor be central cases), but also persons who are central cases of neither male nor female,

---

[7] We could think of different degrees of precision that the formulation of any such premise might take, and of various ways in which this requirement should be delimited. Ought we to say 'jointly able and willing'? Should the fertility of the spouses be required? Or should it be sufficient that the spouses be able to engage in the type of acts that would, *were* they fertile, lead to reproduction? The premise's plausibility would vary accordingly. For my purposes, however, I now need only to convey, in these broad strokes, what such a premise might more or less look like.

relatively to any one factor, or to several factors. Each factor comes, as is often said, in a continuum.[8]

To define 'man' and 'woman' in this way would therefore leave some people outside the intension (and, as a matter of statistical fact, the extension) of the combined classes. Some individuals, according to that definition, would count as neither 'men' nor 'women'. As we saw in section 2, however, these individuals would not be allowed to marry anyone at all. We thus have to conclude that that cannot be what in our provisions is meant by 'man' and 'woman'. The problem is not that there would be no plausible rationale for such a stance on marriage. The problem is that the rationale underlying *our* laws cannot be that.

This problem, it appears, will hold for any candidate interpretation of 'man' and 'woman' that tracks only central cases of maleness and femaleness in what is in fact the mentioned continuum of possibilities. The terms 'man' and 'woman' cannot behave relatively to one another in the manner that, say, the terms 'bolt' and 'nut' behave in relation to one another. Some things are neither nuts nor bolts. Of course, and incidentally, if the law allowed for more than just two sexes—if some intermediate class were defined—the terms 'man' and 'woman' could reciprocally behave like 'nut' and 'bolt'. If that were the case, however, the rationale under scrutiny would still not fit the constraints that we have identified: it would still imply that individuals in the intermediate class would not be able to marry anyone at all.

(5.2) Perhaps this problem can be overcome if instead of having two autonomous predicates to define 'woman' and 'man' only *one* predicate is employed—and used positively to define either one of the terms, the other being defined by negation. 'Woman', for example, might designate any person belonging to the class of central cases in relation to either one or a combination of factors of sexual differentiation; and 'man' could then simply be defined as 'not a woman' (or the other way around). Would this do?

Given these meanings, the 'man'/'woman' distinction *would* exhaust the domain of persons. But under these definitions the terms would still not to behave as they are supposed to behave. A first, minor, point is that there would be no apparent reason to decide which of the two terms

---

[8] Cf. Greenberg, 'Defining Male and Female' (n. 2) 281 ff.

would be the one to define in positive terms. This matters, of course, for each term would take up different extensions according to whether it is positively or negatively defined. If 'woman' is defined negatively (as 'not a man') the dividing line in the continuum of the factors of sexual differentiation will be drawn at a different point than it will if it is 'man' that is defined simply as 'not a woman'. The main objection, however, is the loss of any adequate rationale for the heterosexuality requirement. Whatever the positively defined term, the corresponding descriptive premise in the resulting rationale would be so blatantly false that we would not be able plausibly to attribute to law any sort of or commitment to it.

This, in turn, invites the suggestion that in order for any plausible rationale for provisions (1) to (3) to be unveiled, no one-predicate approach to the definition of 'man' and 'woman'—according to which one of the terms is defined only negatively by the absence of a property—will ever be adequate. Any rationale for the provisions restricting marriage to man/woman pairs will have to establish why *at least* one, but also *at most* one of the members of the couple must be a man; and also why at least *and* at most one must be a woman. And it seems that no one-predicate approach will succeed in fulfilling this desideratum. Take a one-predicate approach defining woman as 'not a man': 'man' could be defined, for example, as above, somewhere along the lines of 'individual with male reproductive organs'. Any rationale for provisions (1) to (3) would then have to establish why *that* would be necessary. It would have to establish why in every marriage there must be *a man*, in this sense of the term. But the rationale would also have to establish why there cannot be *two*—why there cannot be a superfluity of men, which is not ruled away by the mere fact that a man is necessary. In order to establish that in a marriage there can be only one man, then, the rationale would have to establish that some other property—a property such that no man is able to exhibit it—is also necessary for marriage: a property such that another person is required to satisfy it, and also such that it is incompatible with that other person's being a man; a property that only non-men would display. In other words: the only adequate basis for demanding that *at most* one of the spouses should be a man must be that some *other* property is required of the other spouse, and that such property is incompatible with that other spouse being a man. The rationale has to articulate that property.

And this takes two predicates: one positively to define 'man', another positively to define 'woman'.

(5.3) We thus need 'man' and 'woman' reciprocally to behave both as 'nut' and 'bolt' *and* as 'nut' and 'not-nut' or 'bolt' and 'not-bolt'. We need two predicates, but two predicates such that the class defined by the negation of each predicate matches the class defined by the affirmation of the other, and such, also, that they jointly exhaust the domain of human persons. If 'man' and 'woman' in our provisions (1) to (3) are indeed to behave like this, we should be able to draw a line in the continuum of sexual differentiation factors, dividing it in two, but allowing us to define two autonomous predicates for 'man' and 'woman'.

Should we thus aim at the very middle, or at some point that ensures that the continuum is divided in such a way that all the clear, central cases of maleness would fall on one side, and all the clear, central cases of femaleness on the other? No: this approach would not allow the articulation of a plausible rationale for the legal policies under scrutiny.

But why not? It is surely possible, and not at all uncommon, for a legal provision directly to apply to some expressly defined class of persons which does not coincide with the class of persons that the provision normatively targets: the class defined in the provision may be under- or over-inclusive relatively to the targeted class. Here is an example. Recall the provision previously identified as (5):

(5) Individuals younger than 18 years are not allowed to vote.

A provision like (5) might conceivably have as its rationale, not the argument above given as (A2), whose descriptive premise stated that

(A2d) An individual is sufficiently mature to make rational choices if and only if that individual is 18 years or older,

but, rather, a rationale including the following descriptive premise:

(A2d ′) An individual sufficiently mature to make rational choices is *normally* aged 18 years or older, and an individual aged 18 years or older is *normally* sufficiently mature to make rational choices.

It would be possible to articulate a rationale for (5) grounded on both (A2d ′) and the proposition featured as the normative premise in (A2),

(A2n) Only individuals sufficiently mature to make rational choices
should be allowed to vote.

In that case, the classes of individuals affected by the legal provision
(i.e. the class of all individuals younger than 18 years, who are thereby
denied the right to vote, and the class of all individuals aged 18 years
or older, who are not denied that right) would each be simultaneously
over- and under-inclusive relative to the normatively *targeted* classes
(i.e. the class of individuals who are, and the class of individuals who
are not, sufficiently mature to make rational choices). The reconstruction of such a rationale, to be sure, would yield a complex argument
that would necessarily include further premises—including, for example, premises stating reasons not to adopt a provision directly affecting
the targeted classes, and to enact instead a particular type of over- and/
or under-inclusive provision; and premises stating that the classes of
individuals over and under 18 years of age are the most adequate over-
and/or under-inclusive class to define for such purposes. It would then
be convenient to qualify the normative proposition in (A2n), which
would now indicate something more along the lines of an *ideal* state of
normative affairs which the law endeavours to maximize but chooses,
all things considered, not directly to pursue. The point, however, is
that provisions of this over- and/or under-inclusive kind are quite
common in legal systems, and that plausible rationales may normally
be found for them.

Why, then, would it not be possible for a rationale of this kind to
underlie our provisions concerning the validity of marriage? Could it
not be that the law's normatively targeted classes were only the clear,
central cases of human males and females—but that, at the same time,
and in formulating the provisions themselves, the law over-inclusively
defined both the terms 'man' and 'woman' so as not to exclude anybody
from the possibility of marrying?

As I said, I believe the answer is negative. The reason we are now
pondering the suitability of these definitions of 'man' and 'woman',
remember, is that for the purposes of our provisions on marriage the
combination of both terms has to be exhaustive of the domain of persons. And the reason *this* has to be the case is that, as we saw, those
otherwise left out would not be able to marry anyone. Now in the jurisdictions over which our discussion is meant to range, as pointed out in

section 1, this possibility is excluded. Why is it excluded? Surely not because the principle that everybody may marry someone—or rather, more precisely, the principle that no one may solely on the grounds of one's sex be prevented from marrying someone—operates as some kind of constraint imposed upon the law (externally, as it were), a constraint with which law would have to comply to the detriment of what it regards as the ideal state of normative affairs. Rather, in these jurisdictions, marriage—to someone—is recognized, sometimes even at the constitutional level, as we have seen, as a basic right of every person regardless of one's sex. Yet if (1) to (3) were over-inclusive in the way suggested in the previous paragraph, their rationale would have to include a normative premise stating that, ideally, only couples formed by one clear instance of a male human and one clear instance of a female human should be allowed to marry. This proposition is incompatible with the proposition that no one should ever be prevented from marrying solely on the grounds of one's sex. The law cannot be committed to both. Since in our case the law is clearly committed to the latter, it cannot be committed to the former. Consequently, provisions (1) to (3) cannot be over-inclusive relative to the normatively targeted classes; the targeted classes *themselves* must be defined in such a way as not to exclude anyone.

II

6

Let us recapitulate: no satisfactory interpretation can be given of the terms 'man' and 'woman', as employed in provisions (1) to (3), on the grounds of natural, biological facts about human individuals. No facts of that kind seem to exist that allow us to make sense of the distinction in a way that conforms to the constraints that, as we saw, those terms are expected simultaneously to meet.

This is not without serious consequences, as I shall shortly explain. But that so widely adopted a regime may prove so intractable is, I think, quite an extraordinary state of legal affairs. That it is the product of legislative inability is unimaginable. How, then, can we explain its ratification in a legal system? Let me suggest a hypothesis.

Imagine a world in which, as a matter of biological fact, the factors of sexual differentiation do not come in a continuum, and in which incongruence among factors is not even biologically possible: a world, thus, in which all humans are necessarily (what we would call) 'clear' cases of male or female. In such a world, provisions like our own would indeed be capable of referring to natural facts about persons in a way that would concomitantly meet the exhaustiveness and exclusivity requirements under some intelligible rationale for recognizing as married only woman/man couples.[9] Provisions (1) to (3) seem to be just the kind of clauses that would or might well be enacted in such an imaginary world. It is, in a way, as if our provisions have been designed with such a world in mind.

In an admittedly broad formulation (which in section 8 I try to refine), my hypothesis is that our provisions *do* rely on the assumption that everybody is necessarily a 'clear' woman or a 'clear' man; and that the reason why the constraints placed on the meanings of 'man' and 'woman' are impossible to satisfy is that such an assumption is falsified by the facts of our world. Even though our provisions would perfectly fit the facts thus assumed, they just cannot be made to function when contrasted, as they evidently must be, with the facts that actually obtain.

Not that the mismatch between both sets of facts will necessarily constitute an obstacle to the application in *our* world of provisions (1) to (3). This lack of fit between both worlds is indeed barely discernible, when not completely shrouded behind the legal practices of those legal functionaries called upon to decide on the validity of marriages. And this is hardly surprising. After all, we have arrived at our conclusions so far only by asking what the sex terms included in our provisions may mean—and this is a question that legal officials, including judges, seldom need to pursue in order to apply (1) to (3). But how can this be? Functionaries in charge of issuing marriage licenses, for example, will need to comply with the heterosexuality requirement defined in the provisions under scrutiny. Does it not then follow that in order to do so they need to understand what 'man' and 'woman' therein mean?

Actually, it does not. Almost everybody is 'clearly' either a male or a female. According to available estimates, individuals not clearly displaying some factor or factors and/or not congruent among factors of sexual differentiation amount to no more than 4% of the human population;

---

[9] I do not mean to imply, of course, that this policy would be justified. I do not think it would, and I have stated my arguments to this effect in *O Casamento Entre Pessoas do Mesmo Sexo*, Coimbra: Almedina (2008). But this is not my present topic.

some studies assert that the maximum value is below 2%.[10] Our world is, in fact, *almost* like my hypothesized world necessarily comprising only 'clear' males and females. Now, one does not have to know what the terms 'man' and 'woman' actually mean in provisions (1) to (3) in order to be able safely to tell that these provisions do seek to prevent two 'clear' females or two 'clear' males from marrying each other, and therefore that those terms (*whatever* their intensions may be) are meant extensionally to include 'clear' males and 'clear' females, respectively. For a legal official comfortably to conclude, then, that 'clear' males and 'clear' females necessarily belong to different classes—and so that two 'clear' specimens of the same 'sex' may not marry each other, and that a 'clear' female may marry any 'clear' male—the question of what 'woman' and 'man' *mean* does not strictly speaking need to arise. It is not likely to arise in 96% to 98% of the occasions when provisions (1) to (3) have to be applied. Officials may even falsely believe that *that* is what the terms mean—that 'man' refers to a clear male, and 'woman' to a clear female—and go through their entire careers without giving any thought to (let alone having to deal with) the problem of how to act if faced with some less-than-clear case.

Moreover, a very common legal device exists which has the effect of pre-emptively neutralizing even those relatively rare, 'unclear' cases. I made passing reference to it at the beginning of this chapter. In most jurisdictions a system of documentation is normally adopted that, providing for the record of one's 'sex', admits of only two possible inscriptions—'man' and 'woman'—so that everyone will necessarily be registered as one or the other. And it may additionally be that, as I also noted, legal officials are required by law to be heedful of the content of such documents if called upon to apply provisions (1) to (3). If this is the case, however, all individuals will have been classified beforehand. The official will be legally bound to act in accordance with the inscription—and that is also *all* the official has to do in this regard. No thought needs to be given to

---

[10] See Anne Fausto-Sterling, 'The Five Sexes', *The Sciences* (March/April 1993) 21–2; M. Blackless et al., 'How Sexually Dimorphic Are We? Review and Synthesis', *American Journal of Human Biology* 12 (2000) 151–66; or Alice Domurat Dreger, *Hermaphrodites and the Medical Invention of Sex*, Cambridge, MA: Harvard University Press (1998) 40ff. As Dreger recalls, prevalence values will evidently vary according to the way in which the relevant categories are defined: cf. '"Ambiguous Sex"—Or Ambivalent Medicine? Ethical Issues in the Treatment of Intersexuality', *The Hastings Center Report* 28:3 (1998) 26.

what our provisions' sex terms may mean, and, given that even 'unclear' males or females will have been previously registered as either 'men' or 'women',[11] no difficult cases will emerge at all.

The visibility of the asymmetry between our world and that hypothesized world of 'clear' specimens is thus greatly clouded, when not effaced, by these factors.

7

(7.1) Why does this matter? Consider, to begin, jurisdictions in which those documents (like birth certificates) that record one's 'sex' are indeed given by law the force conclusively to establish whether a person counts as 'man' or 'woman' for the purposes of some legal provision.

This solution seems at first blush unremarkable. Many kinds of documents, in law or elsewhere, are taken to provide evidence for the occurrence of certain facts. And when any such fact happens to be described, in a legal provision, as the condition of some legally prescribed effect, it seems reasonable not only that judges and other officials make use of official documents in order to verify whether that condition is satisfied, but also that a specific evidentiary force is assigned to such documents. This is indeed the point, or part of the point, of having and maintaining public records of some facts about individuals. Recall, from section 1, the example of a provision granting some benefits to subjects aged 65 years or older, and the two senses in which it may be said that an individual 'counts as' a member of the legally defined class. We were able to distinguish between, on the one hand, the fact that some individual 'really' is a member of that class and, on the other hand, the fact that some individual is *deemed* its member in virtue of some rule instructing officials to rely on the registered birth date to calculate a person's age. The general form of a rule of this type may be rendered along the following lines (where 'D' refers to some material document, and 'S' to some content therein registered):

(R) An official shall deem that condition C, to which a legal effect is attached in a legal provision P, is satisfied if D documents that S.

---

[11] The criterion according to which, in practice, the exhaustive labelling of newborns as either 'boys' or 'girls' is undertaken seems to be the presence or absence, respectively, of an 'adequate' or 'acceptable' penis; and 'adequacy' or 'acceptability' is here, it appears, to be measured in centimetres. Naturally, some divergence among the medical community subsists as to what constitutes 'adequate' penile length. Cf. Dreger, ' "Ambiguous Sex" ' (n. 10) 29, and *Hermaphrodites and the Medical Invention of Sex* (n. 10) 180ff.

Broadly speaking, the case for having rules of this kind relies, cumulatively, and for each such conceivable rule, on, first, either the identity of *C* (the fact described as a condition in the legal provision in question) and *S* (the fact documented in *D*) or some other kind of relation such that allows us to infer *C* from *S*; and, second, on *D* being—at least to a satisfactory extent—a reliable, trustworthy document as to the occurrence of *S*. Whenever these two conditions are met, *D* may be said to constitute evidence of the verification of some condition *C* included in some legal provision.

That some document *D* constitutes evidence for the verification of a condition *C* included in a provision *P* may therefore be a reason for having, in respect of *P*, a rule like (R). In the case of *descriptive* documents— such as the inscription of one's age in a birth certificate—and their relations to the fact or facts *S* that they purport to describe, the extent to which *D* may reasonably be taken as evidence for the occurrence of those facts will of course vary according to the reliability of the adopted procedures. The risk of false inscriptions can never be fully eliminated, to be sure; but this is not in itself a sufficient reason not to give these documents the specific force conferred by a rule like (R) if and when the facts to which in some legal provision certain effects are attached are the same as, or implied by, the facts that *D* reliably purports to describe.

But rules like (R) have some noteworthy features. For such a rule to be enacted and dutifully complied with, neither of the conditions above identified needs to be satisfied. It may be that the officials are instructed by law to consider that some condition *C* is satisfied if *D* documents *S*, without it being the case that *S* and *C* coincide or are related by implication: for example, a legal official may be instructed to deem a member of the class of those aged '65 years or older' any individual whose birth happened, according to register, on an odd calendar day. This would of course be an absurd instruction, but that is not the issue here. The issue is that the 'count-as' effect brought about by a rule like (R) does not *have* to be grounded on any sort of evidentiary relation between what is documented in *D* and what is described in *C*.

This 'count-as' effect, moreover, does not even presuppose that *C* contains any proper description of facts. *C* may well be meaningless: this will in no way prevent the application of an (R)-rule in determining when *C* shall 'count as' satisfied. A condition that cannot *be* satisfied can nevertheless be *deemed* satisfied. There is in this case, however, no room for any talk of 'evidence' when speaking about the relation between the document and the condition. Whatever the document, whatever its content, whatever procedures may have been followed in its elaboration, no document will ever 'prove' any facts described in *C* if *C* is meaningless, and if, therefore, no facts exist that may satisfy it.

This, it appears, may provide us with an apposite way of characterizing what happens in those jurisdictions in which officials are instructed by law to rely on the register of a person's 'sex' in order to determine when a person counts as a 'man' or a 'woman' for the purposes of our provisions (1) to (3): in jurisdictions, that is, in which there is an (R)-type rule to that effect. In such systems, as we saw in the previous section, legal officials will be able, in a way, to 'apply' those provisions without further worries. But that you are registered as 'man' or 'woman', whether or not it may constitute sound evidence of some fact or facts about you, provides no evidence of any supposed fact that you *are* a 'man' or a 'woman' in the sense in which the terms occur in provisions (1) to (3)—for, as we also have seen, no such fact-of-the-matter about human individuals exists. Albeit under the guise of a 'count-as' rule, then—under the guise, that is, of the type of rule that appears to be justified only when the document in question provides evidence for the occurrence of the conditioning facts described in a legal provision—these documental inscriptions behave in a manner that cannot be explained in evidentiary terms.

To look at it from a different perspective, suppose that you are one of the several million sexually 'not so clear' individuals, and that you live in a jurisdiction like the ones that I have been discussing in this subsection. As a subject of that legal system, you may naturally wish to know whether or not, as *a matter of general, applicable law*, you are allowed to marry a given person. You will be able to obtain a straightforward answer: 'Yes, because you are a man', for example, or 'No, because you are a woman'. In a way, this answer would, as a matter of law, be true. Such a clear and ready reply, however, can only be given if and *because* the relevant (R)-type rule exists. In other words, without such an (R)-type rule no such answer would be possible. Without such a rule, no one would be able to tell you whether or not, as a matter of law, you and some other person were allowed to marry each other.

(7.2) In jurisdictions in which no such an (R)-type rule exists, however, judges and other legal officials may (and normally will) be required nevertheless to decide every legal issue appropriately brought before them, and thus to apply provisions (1) to (3) in all relevant cases. What, then, if the official is called upon to decide on the validity, on the grounds of the spouses' 'sex', of some past or future marriage in one of those relatively rare, but possible, instances in which at least one of the parties is neither clearly male nor female?

In order strictly speaking to 'apply' those provisions the official would first have to verify, for each of the members of the couple, whether that person *is* a woman or a man in the pertinent sense of the terms. But this is an impossible task to perform. There is to this question no correct reply; not in the ordinary sense that more than one acceptable answer might be available, but in the stronger sense that the very formulation of the question is grounded on a false presupposition—the presupposition that 'man' and 'woman' in provisions (1) to (3) refer to natural facts about individuals.

Indeed, a merely cursory look at the way in which courts have attempted to tackle the point is sufficient to impress upon us the vivid picture of an inglorious, Sisyphean struggle. In the well-known, and leading, English case of *Corbett v Corbett* (1971),[12] the issue addressed was precisely our own. The court preoccupied itself, not with any general determination of one's legal sex 'at large', but with the question of determining 'what is meant by the word "woman" in the context of a marriage'. The adopted criterion was that of a congruous combination of 'chromosomal, gonadal, and genital' factors. The problem with this approach is of course that it leads to the unwarranted (and more or less inadvertent) conclusion that some people cannot marry anyone at all.[13] This problem also affects the simpler chromosomal criterion followed, for example, in the likewise notorious decisions reached in the Australian case *Marriage of C and D* (1979),[14] or in the Texas case of *Littleton v Prange* (1999).[15] Given the inalterability of chromosomal makeup, these decisions imply that sex is immutably fixed at birth. But even when chromosomal sex has not been regarded as determinant—as in the

---

[12] *Corbett v. Corbett* [1970] 2 All ER 33 (PDA).
[13] As has been noted by commentators: see, e.g., Katherine O'Donovan, *Sexual Divisions in Law*, London: Weidenfeld and Nicolson (1985) 66; Greenberg, 'Defining Male and Female' (n. 2) 305; or Loren Cannon, 'Trans-Marriage and the Unacceptability of Same-Sex Marriage Restrictions', in *Social Philosophy Today* 25 (2009) 83.
[14] *Marriage of C and D (falsely called C)* [1979] 35 FLR 340 (Fam Ct Australia).
[15] *Littleton v Prange* [1999] 9 SW 3d 223 (Tex App).

European Court of Human Rights' *Goodwin v United Kingdom* (2002)[16] and the subsequent House of Lords' decision in *Bellinger v Bellinger* (2003)[17]—courts have nonetheless persisted in their quest for the natural facts (or, at any rate, the non-institutional facts) to which 'man' and 'woman' supposedly refer.

In these instances, courts seem to have falsely believed that some interpretation of 'man' and 'woman' in terms of natural facts was possible. They were nevertheless required by law to ascertain the conformity of some candidate or putative marriage to the heterosexuality condition—a necessary condition, after all, for a marriage to count as valid. And there is in fact no way of doing this that does not depend on the official first assigning the individual to one of the two sex classes. This ad hoc assignment, hence, is not declarative of any fact about the individual's membership to such a class, but rather, and in itself (and however the judge chooses to formulate it), constitutive, in each case, of that very membership.[18] Having so decided that the person will fall under, say, the class of 'men', the official will then be able to deem that person's marriage to another 'man' invalid, or to accept or recognize or confirm the validity of a marriage to a 'woman'. It will then be possible, in other words, to ground the decision on the fact that the individual 'is' a man for the purposes of provisions (1) to (3). But what in fact *makes* that person a man is merely that the official has so decided.

(7.3) In either of these scenarios, then—whether judges and other officials are instructed by law to rely on documents that register one's 'sex', which was the situation addressed in subsection (7.1); or whether they are left to decide by themselves under which class an 'unclear' individual will fall, as discussed in subsection (7.2)—it is law, not nature, that makes those individuals 'men' or 'women'. They are 'men' and 'women' by *fiat*. And so whether or not they are allowed or prevented from marrying some other given person under provisions (1) to (3) is something that will in no instance depend on any property or feature that they are taken to possess or display. They will be granted or denied access to

---

[16] *Goodwin v United Kingdom* [2002] 35 EHRR 18 (ECHR).

[17] *Bellinger v Bellinger* [2003] UKHL 21 (HL).

[18] See the related discussions in Katherine M. Franke, 'The Central Mistake of Sex Discrimination Law', *University of Pennsylvania Law Review* 144 (1995) 1–99, at 51ff; and Matthew Gayle, 'Female by Operation of Law: Feminist Jurisprudence and the Legal Imposition of Sex', *William and Mary Journal of Women and the Law* 12 (2006) 737–59.

marriage with any given person not because they *are* men or women, but because they are *catalogued as* 'men' or 'women'. No other property exists that might determine one's membership in either class. And this is a necessary state of affairs in any legal system in which provisions (1) to (3) happen to be valid law. In any such system—in any one of the systems over which our discussion is meant to range—the law will circularly label its subjects as 'men' or 'women' and *then* assign them different statuses according to the label imposed. You may not marry someone else because, the law will tell you, you are a woman (or a man); what makes it the case that you are woman (or a man), however, is that the law says so.

Clearly, any question regarding the justification of any set of legal policies which in fact operate in this manner will be quite distinct from the question about the justification of provisions (1) to (3) in that imaginary world composed only of 'clear' male and female specimens. The contemporary debate on the legitimacy of the heterosexuality requirement seems to be mostly occupied with the latter—it seems to be held under the more or less implicit postulate that ours is indeed a world of only 'clear' males and females.[19] But in our world it is the former question fundamentally demands discussion.

8

In section 6 a hypothesis was set forth for the somewhat disconcerting fact that provisions (1) to (3) appear to impose—upon *our* world—a set of constraints that cannot be simultaneously met. The hypothesis was that our provisions rely on the false assumption that every human is necessarily either a clear female or a clear male. But this idea that law 'relies' on such an assumption—an idea that once again makes use of that idiomatic manner of speaking with which we intelligibly if metaphorically refer to (or report) types of intentional actions performed by 'the law'—may be unpacked in two different ways.

(8.1) Let me first entertain what might perhaps be called the 'good faith' version of the hypothesis, by accepting that something along the lines of

---

[19] As I noted already in passing, this debate, in which 'man' and 'woman' are normally held to refer to natural facts about people, may easily be recast as a debate between endorsers and opponents of possible premises of possible rationales for the heterosexuality condition. In our world, however, as we have seen, no intelligible rationale may even be *articulated* for provisions (1) to (3) that preserves a natural reading of 'man' and 'woman'.

a *sincere* belief in the proposition that there exist (and can exist) only 'clear' males and females can be said to underlie provisions (1) to (3).

The good faith version seems to have considerable explanatory power while imposing minimal theoretical costs. It allows for the articulation of a plausible rationale, for we will be able to include therein (as a proposition to which the law can be said to be committed) a premise stating that the sex of any human individual is always, and by necessity, clearly differentiated as male or female. That the law is sincerely committed to that false proposition also seems satisfactorily to explain that our common official practices of dichotomously registering everyone's sex may be descriptive in purpose; and that the corresponding (R)-rules, when they exist, may accordingly have been enacted for proper evidentiary reasons.

Under this version, the very fact that that descriptive premise is falsified by reality will ground the case against the heterosexuality requirement. Once the assumption has conclusively been shown to be false, it becomes clear that law's purpose of tracking natural facts about individuals with the terms 'woman' and 'man' is unattainable; it becomes clear that these terms, as they stand in provisions (1) to (3), cannot behave as they were meant to behave. Rational pursuit of that descriptive purpose, in other words, necessarily assumes that there are only clear cases, and must therefore be abandoned once the assumption is negated.

Our common system of registration will likewise be shown to fail in its descriptive endeavour. For even if most inscriptions may in our world in fact be true—as most individuals registered as 'men' will be clear males, and most registered as 'women' clear females—our system not only incorporates the possibility of false positives, but cannot avoid yielding inscriptions that are *necessarily* false. A system which purports descriptively to document everyone's 'real' sex and is at the same time grounded on the false assumption that everyone is unambiguously male or female will always falsely register those individuals who are, in fact, neither.

Moreover—with or without registration—no rationale for provisions (1) to (3) that includes that false premise would be capable of justifying the constraints (depicted in the previous section) imposed by these very provisions on the right to marry of persons who are not unambiguously male or female. *Ex hypothesi* unaccounted for in the rationale, these individuals are subject to restrictions which are in any case arbitrarily imposed.

So according to this version of the explanatory hypothesis—the version which maintains that the law's *intended* policy is to allow marriages only between 'clear' males and 'clear' females—the falsehood of the said premise establishes that it cannot simultaneously be that *that* is what 'man' and 'woman' respectively mean in provisions (1) to (3) *and* that the man/woman distinction exhausts the domain of individuals. This means that the law will necessarily have to abandon at least one of the two incompatible desiderata which only that false assumption was capable of holding together. If, on the one hand, one wishes to preserve law's originally intended policy of allowing only 'clear' male/female couples to marry, then one will have to relinquish the idea that no one may simply on the grounds of sex be prevented from marrying anyone at all. If, on the other hand, and conversely, one chooses to remain committed to this latter stance, the heterosexuality requirement must be abandoned.

The choice is up to each legal system. But given that, as was already noticed, the former desideratum seems to be quite firmly placed among the commonly recognized 'fundamental' or 'constitutional' rights, most systems will have in fact no option. The policy that allows only woman/man couples to marry has to be repealed.

(8.2) The good faith version derives its explanatory power from the supposition that in provisions (1) to (3) the terms 'man' and 'woman' do purport to refer to natural facts about individuals. More precisely, if this is indeed the law's purpose, it has to be the case that the law is convinced, as it were, that there exist only clear men or women.

The possibility of attributing to the law, or to some legal authority, a commitment to some proposition does not hinge, as we saw in section 4, on the truth of that proposition. But it does have to satisfy one test: plausibility. And how plausible is it, really, to attribute such a commitment to the law? How plausible is it to suppose that authorities in modern legal systems simply ignore the well-known biological facts of (so-called) intersexuality? Not very, I would argue. But if the good faith version is implausible a problem emerges. For, *modo tollente*, if the law is not unaware of those biological facts, then it cannot be the case that 'man' and 'woman' purport to refer to natural features of individuals. And is there any way of making sense of our regime without relying on the contrary supposition?

A different version of our explanatory hypothesis is actually possible that does not rely on such a supposition. According to this second version—the 'deliberateness' approach, if you wish—our marriage law is intentionally designed *as if* there were in our world only clear males and females, and therefore the law remains perfectly aware that that is not really the case. What the law then knowingly does, as it were, with provisions (1) to (3) is to force our world to conform to a counterfactually dichotomous model whose categories are shaped after a world of clear specimens. The law, in short, wants everyone to be able to marry, but stipulates that marriage is possible only in conformity to that dichotomous model, imposed upon everyone.

This version's explanatory power is not less than that of the good faith approach: on the contrary. The terms 'man' and 'woman' are shown not to be *meant* to refer to natural facts about individuals at all. Everybody will be classified as either 'man' or 'woman', certainly, either by registration or judicial decision. The classification may even be such that it purports to include all clear males in the class of 'men', and all clear females under 'women'. But *that* will not be what the terms mean. 'Man' will rather mean, quite simply, 'classified as "man"', and 'woman' 'classified as "woman"'. Differently put: under the deliberateness approach, the fact that our systems first label everyone as 'man' or 'woman', and only then define a regime for marriage according to those labels, will not be a mere consequence of the way in which provisions (1) to (3) necessarily operate (which was the point made in section 7). It will rather be the very state of affairs that the law intends to promote. Along these lines, it will no longer be necessary to devise for provisions (1) to (3) any sort of rationale grounded on natural, non-institutional differences between 'men' and 'women'. The rationale for the heterosexuality requirement, instead, assumes a completely distinct configuration. It will have to be a rationale for making the world conform to laws counterfactually designed with the model of 'clear' cases in mind.

Under this version of the explanatory hypothesis, lastly, our systems for the registration of sex emerge as attributive in purpose, and not merely in fact. They are meant to assign you to one of the two legal sexes, rather than to describe whatever 'real' sex you may have. And

(R)-rules, when they exist, might accordingly retain a proper evidentiary role, given that (in exactly the same manner in which the valid registration by which your name is attributed will from then on provide evidence of the fact that *that* is now your name) any document in which your 'sex' is constitutively and validly inscribed will provide infallible evidence for the very fact which it constitutes—the fact that you are *labelled as* 'man' or 'woman'—and which is the very fact that 'man' and 'woman', as employed in provisions (1) to (3), are meant to describe.

Under this version, indeed, the fact that you are a man or a woman in the relevant senses of the terms is rather like the fact that your legal name is such-and-such—a fact wholly created by the law—and our provisions operate just like those in which some legal effect may be associated to your name. 'Man' and 'woman' are thus meant as descriptive terms, albeit not of law-independent facts. They are descriptive of facts created by the law itself; descriptive of your *legal sex*.

(8.3) Is this second version too cynical to be propounded? Its degree of plausibility will vary from legal system to legal system. But how plausible would the alternative version (the good faith approach) be, for example, in a jurisdiction that—while enforcing the policy apprehended in the conjunction of (1), (2), and (3), and remaining committed to the exhaustiveness and the exclusivity of the man/woman divide—is willing officially to recognize for all legal purposes a person's so-called 'gender reassignment' *only if* that person is not married at the time such recognition is sought?[20]

In addition, even if the deliberateness approach is here put forward as the reconstructive explanation that makes the best sense of our provisions and of the consequences to which they necessarily give rise—and not as a historical point about what the lawmakers' 'real' purpose or set of beliefs actually are—it would not be utterly unusual for a system in fact to be designed in such a manner. For some periods until the early 18th century, historians tell us, the law in England and elsewhere appears to have admitted of two legal sexes, as it does today:

---

[20] This is the current state of legal affairs in the United Kingdom: cf. sections 4(2), 5, and 9 of the *Gender Recognition Act* 2004. For discussion, see Lisa Fishbayn, ' "Not Quite One Gender or the Other": Marriage Law and the Containment of Gender Trouble in the United Kingdom', *Journal of Gender, Social Policy & the Law* 15 (2007) 413–14.

man and woman. It mandated that males were labelled as 'men', and females as 'women'. But it moreover gave hermaphrodites the right to *choose* one of those two legal sexes (by whose regime they would subsequently be compelled to abide).[21] So while explicitly acknowledging that there may well be individuals that, in the continuum of sexual differentiation, do not fall under either of the two possible clear cases, in the legal realm the law admitted of only two sexes, which it openly imposed—as *legal sexes*—upon its subjects. (The *choice* regime, by the way, was fairer than the common contemporary one that either prevents or renders very difficult any further modification of inscriptions made, at birth, without the subject's acquiescence.) 'Man' and 'woman' were merely the names of those legal sexes, and in no way intended as descriptive of biological facts, nor intended to match any natural division.

CONCLUSION

With the argument set forth in Part I of this chapter I have attempted to show that, contrary to what is generally accepted, the terms 'woman' and 'man', as employed in the typical provisions with which in many legal systems same-sex marriage is proscribed, cannot refer to natural features of persons. Rather, I argued in Part II, in any such legal order it is necessarily the case that the facts that make it true that anyone is a 'man' or a 'woman' in the relevant sense are facts created by the law itself—either by legislators or judicial decision-makers. To explain this state of legal affairs I proposed the general hypothesis that those provisions rely on a false empirical assumption about the sexual make-up of human individuals. Two alternative versions of the hypothesis were sketched; one allows, and the other does not, that the law is sincerely committed to that false assumption. But whichever

---

[21] Cf. Randolph Trumbach, 'London's Sapphists: From Three Sexes to Four Genders in the Making of Modern Culture', in *Body Guards. The Cultural Politics of Gender Ambiguity* (J. Epstein, K. Straub eds.), New York: Routledge (1991) 113–14, 120; and see also Alice Domurat Dreger, *Hermaphrodites and the Medical Invention of Sex* (n. 10) 33; Michel Foucault, *Les Anormaux. Cours au Collège de France* (F. Ewald et al. eds.), Paris: Seuil/Gallimard (1999) 62ff; Foucault's 'Introduction' to *Herculine Barbin. Being the Recently Discovered Memories of a Nineteenth-Century French Hermaphrodite*, New York: Pantheon (1980) viii; and Saru Matambanadzo, 'Engendering Sex: Birth Certificates, Biology and the Body in Anglo-American Law', *Cardozo Journal of Law and Gender* (2005) 237ff.

version happens to be the more plausible, a fundamental issue emerges concerning the justification of a legal policy—the heterosexuality requirement—which can only be made operative in a legal system if at least some of the legal subjects are first, and arbitrarily, labelled as 'men' or 'women'.